Dedication

Dedicated to my mother, Wong Chui Yim Eng, who has always supported me in whatever I wanted to do, even when she didn't understand it.

&

From Adriene...to Lisa and David, with all my love.

About the Authors

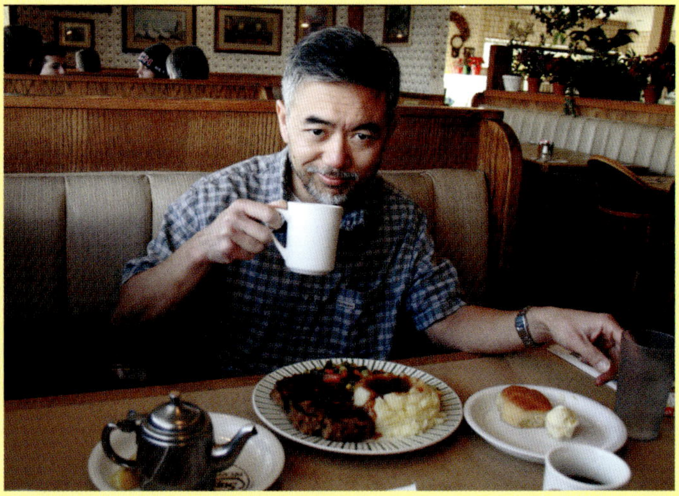

John Eng was bitten by the *film bug* while still in high school. When a friend showed up with an 8mm movie camera, they were off making kung-fu movies on the rooftops of New York the very next day. While attending the School of Visual Arts, John answered an ad by a Hungarian puppet animator looking for a model builder. This began John's professional life with film, special effects and animation.

John relocated to Los Angeles in 1981 where he produced, production designed, and supervised special effects on a number of independent feature films before he was offered a steady design position on the sci-fi series, *The Max Headroom Show*. He then produced 20 half-hour episodes of *The Real Adventures of Jonny Quest* at Hanna-Barbera. At Nickelodeon, John created three pilots and directed a DVD feature. In 2001, he co-directed *Rugrats Go Wild.* John also worked in the story department on a number of CGI features including *Barnyard, Hoodwinked 2, Heroes of Color City, Alpha and Omega,* and *Lionelville*. In 2009, John worked in Chongqing, China supervising animation layout on *Lionelville*.

Paralleling this, John shared his love for travel, local history, and photography with Adriene Biondo by driving to every corner of California and beyond. John's photography has appeared in *LA Magazine, Dwell, CA Modern* magazine, *Stern* magazine, and his own website, astroluxe.org

For Adriene Biondo, there's never been anything cozier than sharing a hot cup o' joe. Even cozier if it's in a mom and pop coffee shop off an abandoned highway warmed by an old flickering neon sign. Luckily, she grew up in 1960s and 1970s Los Angeles. Back then, amazing coffee shops and drive-ins were everywhere! Her family spent many happy weekends traveling in "Ol' Yeller," their trusty 1952 Ford station wagon. As these places began to disappear, Adriene realized she was witnessing the end of an era, both culturally and architecturally. Eventually she found her way into historic preservation and began working with the Los Angeles Conservancy, the nation's largest non-profit historic preservation organization. An award-winning preservationist, Adriene has directed significant projects that have been honored by the State Office of Historic Preservation and California Preservation Foundation. In 2008, she accepted the President's Award for leading the effort to rebuild the landmark 1958 Harvey's Broiler. By day, she's a freelance photographer and public relations liaison for CA Modern, an architectural/lifestyle magazine based in San Francisco. By night, you might catch her playing cocktail piano in one of the restaurants featured in this book. Adriene and John live with their doggies Poky and Cody, and Betty the Turtle.

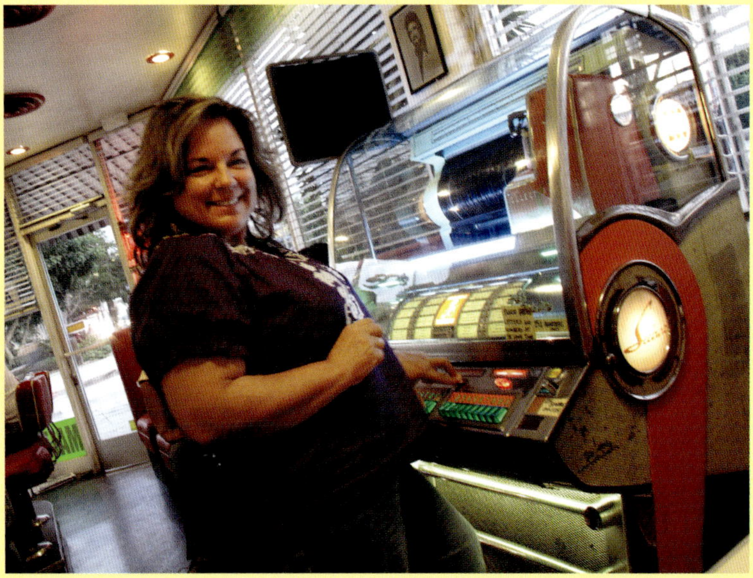

Southern California Eats 2

John Eng

Adriene Biondo

Schiffer Publishing Ltd

4880 Lower Valley Road Atglen, PA 19310

Acknowledgments

We appreciate the many individuals and restaurant owners who generously gave their time to make this book possible: Stan Abrams, Mario Abrego, John Avetyan, John Biondo Sr., Fred Conwell, Eldon Davis, John Droutsas, Albert and Chui Yim Eng, Dr. Frankenstein Body Shop, Jim Ferraro, Juan Idlla and Alma Felix, Jim Ferraro, Chris Foerstel, Alan Hess, Kim Koga, Jim Louder, Leo at the Pizza Show, Marie at Frank's, Anita Mussell, Syd Nagoshi, Carolyn Neldberg, Victor Newlove, Domenic Priore, Andrea Pruett, Loren Smith, Owen and Dale Stenzel, Marcello Vavala, and Arlene Vidor. And last, but certainly not least, our friends at the Glendale Historical Society, Jalopy Journal/H.A.M.B., Los Angeles Conservancy's Modern Committee, and Museum of Neon Art.

All photos by John Eng unless otherwise noted.

Disclaimer

Other Schiffer Books By The Author:
Southern California Eats, 978-0-7643-3332-3, $24.99

Other Schiffer Books on Related Subjects:
Hollywood Homes: Postcard Views of Early Stars' Estates, 978-0-7643-2202-8, $12.95
Final Resting Places: Orange County's Dead & Famous, 978-0-7643-3421-4, $16.99

On the cover:
Bob's Big Boy Broiler, 1958, demolished 2007, rebuilt 2009. Custom 1940 Ford DeLuxe Coupe owned by Terry Lee Minks. *Photo by John Eng*

Library of Congress Control Number: 2009925129

Designed by John Eng
Layout by John P. Cheek

ISBN: 978-0-7643-3639-3
Printed in China

Schiffer Books are available at special discounts for bulk purchases for sales promotions or premiums. Special editions, including personalized covers, corporate imprints, and excerpts can be created in large quantities for special needs. For more information contact the publisher:

Published by Schiffer Publishing Ltd.
4880 Lower Valley Road
Atglen, PA 19310
Phone: (610) 593-1777; Fax: (610) 593-2002
E-mail: Info@schifferbooks.com

For the largest selection of fine reference books on this and related subjects, please visit our web site at **www.schifferbooks.com**
We are always looking for people to write books on new and related subjects. If you have an idea for a book please contact us at the above address.

This book may be purchased from the publisher.
Include $5.00 for shipping.
Please try your bookstore first.
You may write for a free catalog.

In Europe, Schiffer books are distributed by
Bushwood Books
6 Marksbury Ave.
Kew Gardens
Surrey TW9 4JF England
Phone: 44 (0) 20 8392 8585; Fax: 44 (0) 20 8392 9876
E-mail: info@bushwoodbooks.co.uk
Website: www.bushwoodbooks.co.uk

Contents

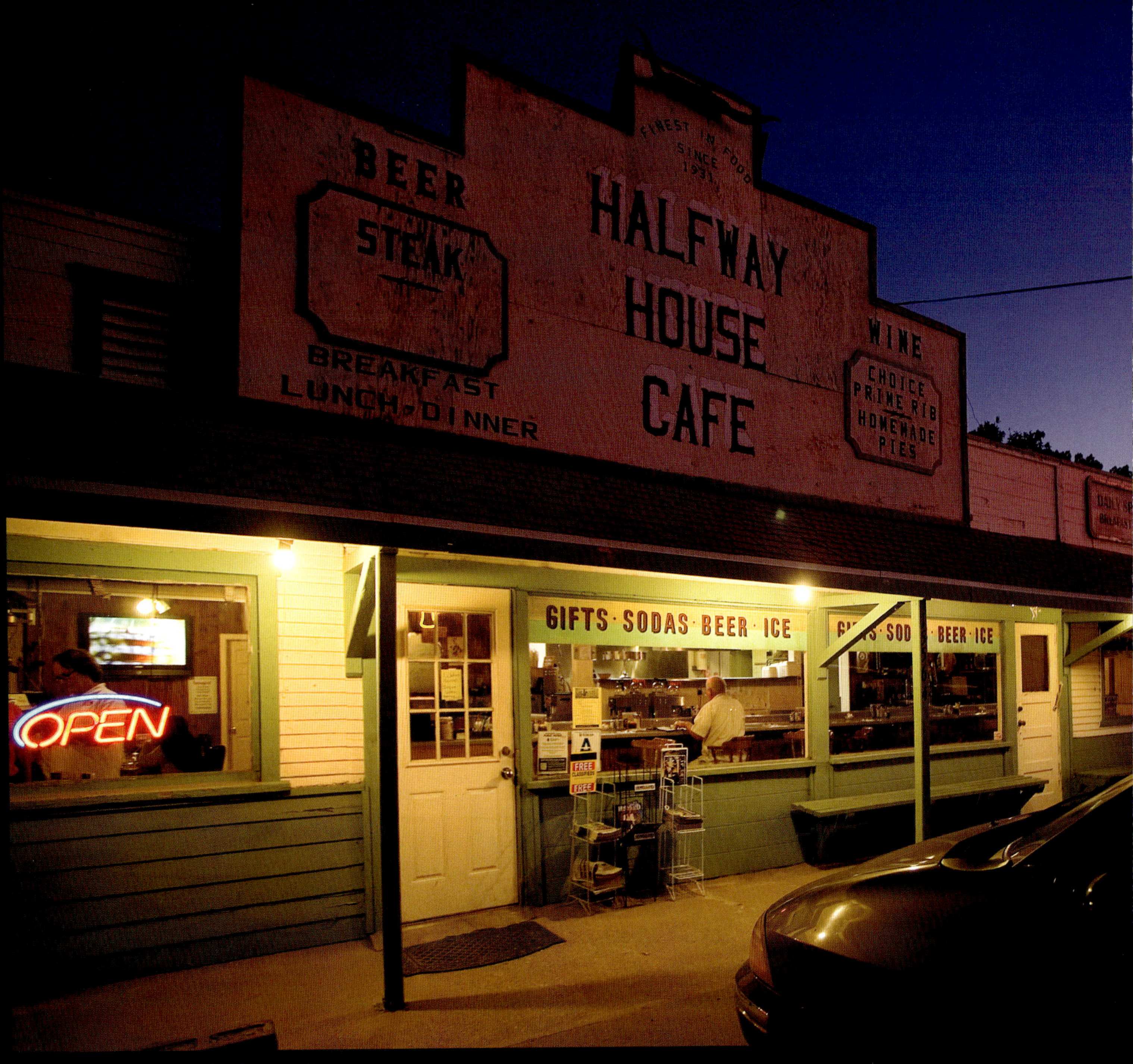

Halfway House Café, Canyon Country.

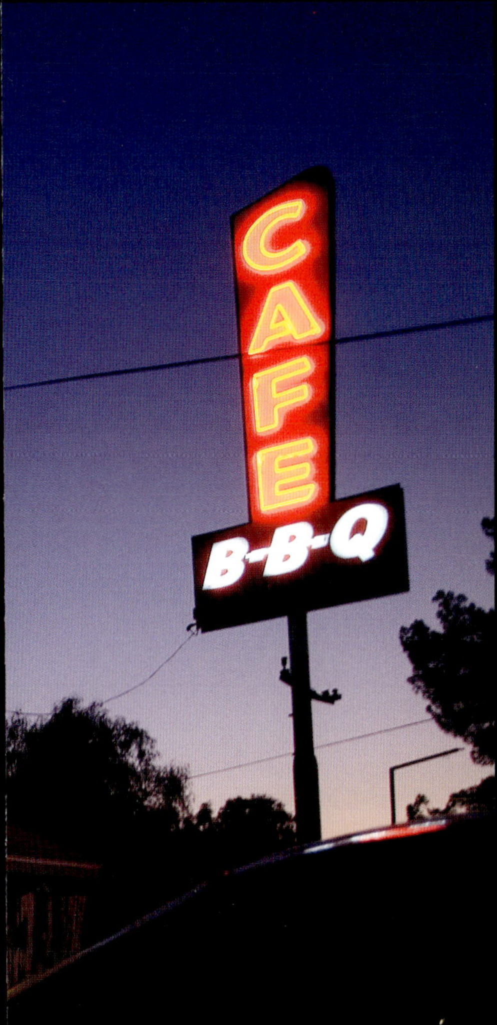

Foreword

By Alan Hess

"The past is not dead," William Faulkner assures us. "In fact, it's not even past," and thank goodness for that.

The restaurants, drive-ins, dives, milk stands, lounges, cafes, and bars of Southern California Eats 2 confirm Faulkner's words. These are the places where a hundred years of life and architecture still thrive. They are still serving food, still providing a rest for the weary traveler, a night of fun for the weary worker, and a visual treasure trove for anyone driving our highways.

Every style, and every permutation and combination of each style, can be traced in Adriene and John's superbly studied catalog. We are in excellent hands with two of the most dedicated, cutting edge, and successful historic preservationists in the nation.

This is no small achievement. Hours, days, weeks, years of driving, parking, photographing, and tasting are represented here. Our gratitude goes out to them for taking on the task, and doing it so thoroughly. Cloistered academics who believe architecture is only for the rich and fashionably tasteful rarely venture out to document such buildings as these; over the decades that restrictive approach has robbed us of the knowledge of hundreds of great buildings: Simon's drive-ins, Clifton's South Seas, Nickodell's, Yum Yums, and more. So, we need Adriene and John.

These roadside buildings turn out to be true classics. They have transcended history more successfully than mainstream modernism. But in the unpretentious designs of these vernacular restaurants, in the playfully boastful boosterism of giant donuts, in the native genius of hand-painted signs superbly scaled to their car customers, in the subtle art of classic neon signage, in the stark functionalism of the Halfway House Cafe or the distinctive high Googie of the Driftwood Dairy-Port, or the solidly unpretentious streamline moderne of the Desert Center Cafe, we see real architecture that has stood the test of time.

The reader will be able to pick out the subtleties of these designs, but let's highlight one example: Andre's Giant Burgers in Bakersfield with its magnificent spider leg supports. Many architects used this modern motif to articulate structure from enclosure. Russell Forester's original Jack in the Box prototype featured graphically strong, repetitive spider legs, but Andre's are more sinewy and muscular. They narrow down to a chisel point to touch the ground, and thicken as they rise to a muscular joint, just like the plywood bents of John Lautner's Mauer house. The flat roof is suspended from these cross beams, a concept similar to Mies van der Rohe's Crown Hall at the Illinois Institute of Technology, but with much more exuberance and delight. The wide, wide eave thoughtfully conveys its desire to shelter customers from the hot sun. The marvelous garden-dining patio uses shapely organic forms like those of Brazilian landscape architect Robert Burle Marx, and the contrasting, light-weight benches of Thomas Church. This is total design at its best.

It is to the discredit of today's architects, developers, and planning departments if they do not see what Adriene and John see. But with this book's publication, no one can ever plead ignorance.

Now, go eat!

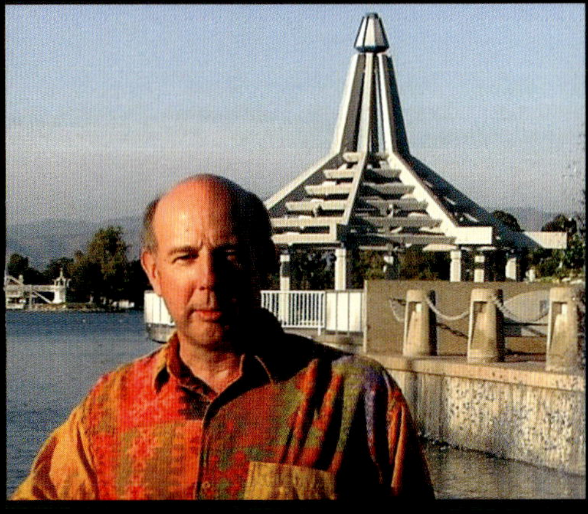

lan Hess, architect and author, on North

Unisphere, Flushing Meadows Park, New York.

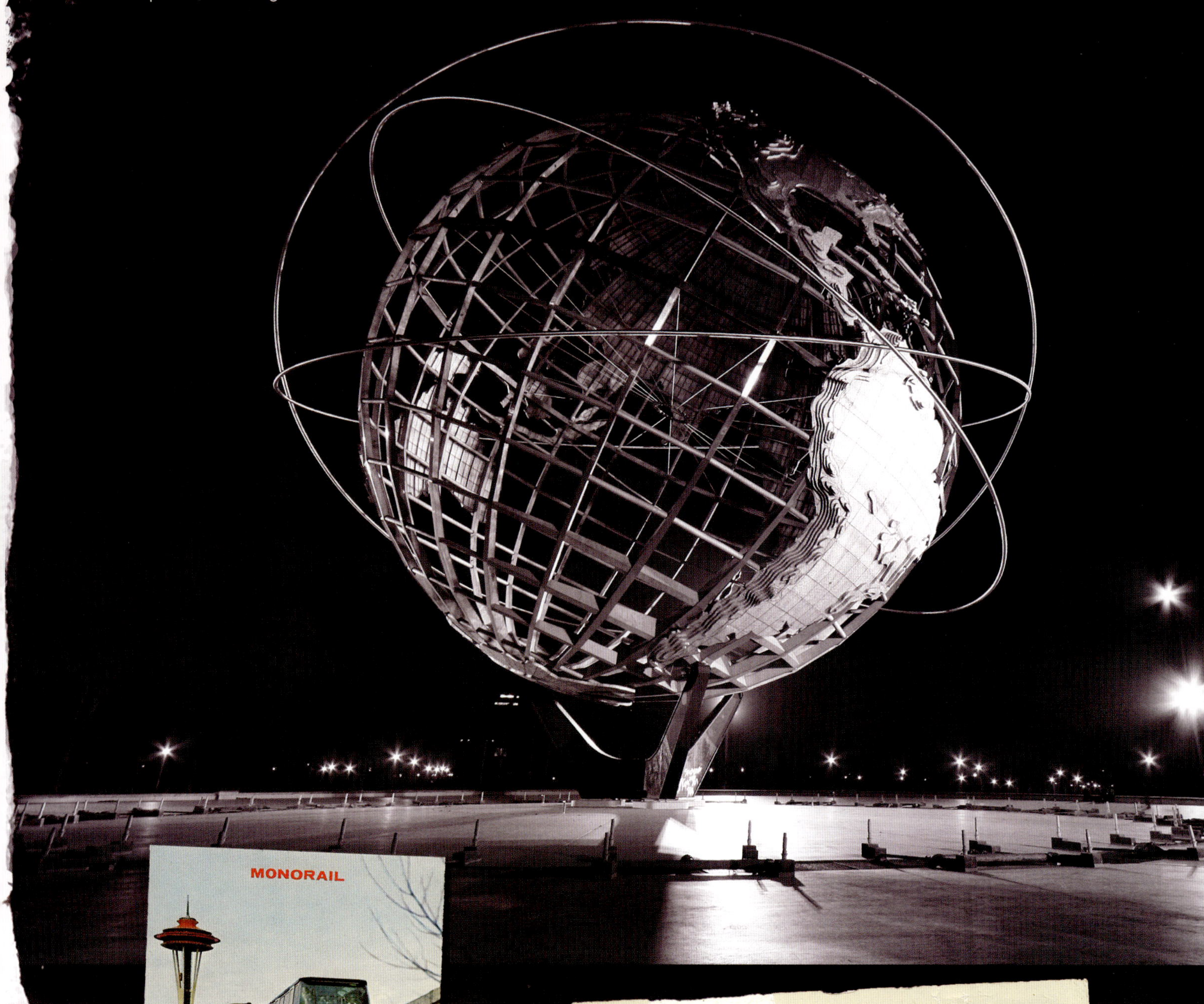

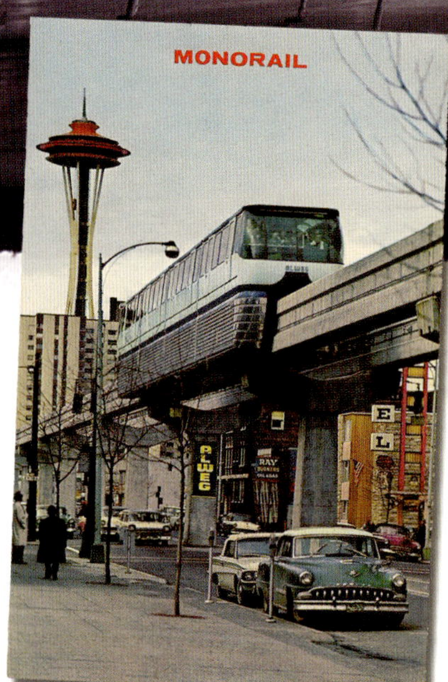

Postcard of the Seattle World's Fair, 1962.

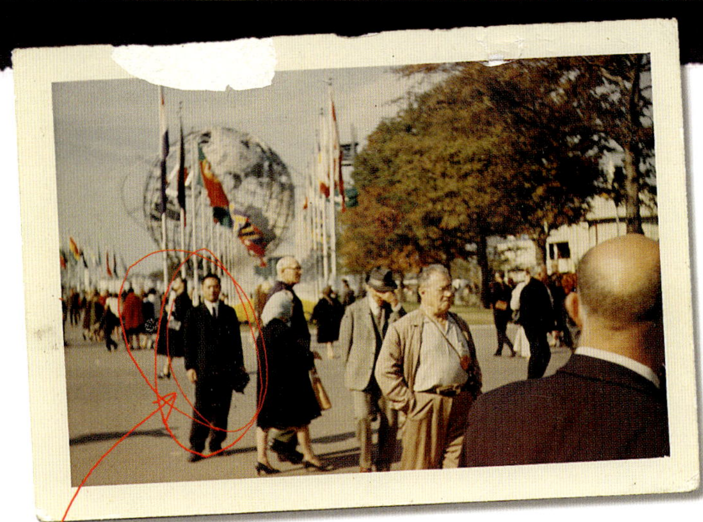

Albert Eng at the 1964-65 New York World's Fair. *Courtesy of Albert Eng.*

INTRODUCTION

Southern California Eats 2 explores more than 80 eateries, adding bold prototypes to the mix of vernacular cafes, unconventional donut shops, ice cream parlors, hot dog stands, bowling alley coffee shops, and drive-in movie theater snack bars.

One of the most frequently asked questions we received about our first book has been, "Why *these* places? What is your fascination with them?" And while the question appears simple enough, we found that coming up with the answer was anything but.

After WWII, the enormous US industrial machine returned to the private sector. The technologies and innovative materials created for the war effort were promoted to improve the lives of everyday citizens. During the 1960s, there was such a sense of optimism in the air it was infectious. Together with the good old American "can do" attitude that started years before the war, it seemed that nothing was impossible. President Kennedy boldly announced in 1961 that we were going to the Moon by decade's end, and by 1969 Neil Armstrong, Buzz Aldrin, and Michael Collins did just that. Science was at our disposal; it was our tool to conquer space, disease, and anything life had to throw our way. Anything was possible.

One of John's earliest memories is an image of his Dad, Albert Eng, at the 1964 World's Fair in New York, standing in front of the gigantic Unisphere presented by US Steel. This stainless steel sculpture of the Earth was the centerpiece of the Fair. Standing 140 feet high with orbital rings circling the planet, it was the quintessential mid-century modern atomic design—unforgettable to a five-year-old boy living in Hong Kong. Since John's aunt lived in Seattle, his dad also toured what remained after the 1962 Seattle World's Fair. Albert brought home pictures and stories of his adventures into the future, and the excitement never left John.

Years later, when the Eng family moved from Hong Kong to Queens, New York, they lived only 1 1/2 miles from Flushing Meadows—the site of both the 1939 and 1964 World's Fairs. In John's early movie-making days, he used the park and its buildings as his personal backlot. The United States Building became his sound stage, where vampires would stalk unsuspecting victims. The towers of the New York State Pavilion, designed by Philip Johnson with Norman Foster, became a futuristic city on a distant planet, while the Garden of Meditation was transformed into the forest surrounding the secret Shaolin Temple in China. After all, "Anything is possible."

Meanwhile, on the West Coast, Adriene and her family watched as US steel was transformed into an eight-story rocket ship welcoming them to Disney's

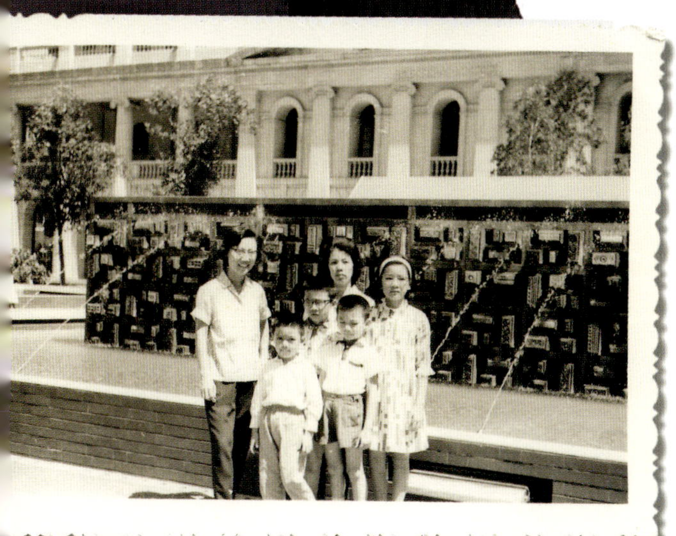

n Eng with his family while still in Hong Kong. Back row, left ight: Aunt Rita, John's mother, and John's sister Theresa. Middle , left to right: Brothers Tom (with glasses), and Joe. Front row: n Eng. Circa 1964.

Tomorrowland and space age monuments like the LAX Theme Building, with its soaring parabolic arches. Simple pleasures like enjoying a meal together were elevated via a new and imaginative world where everyone celebrated a futuristic tomorrow. Peering in through walls of glass at glittering ceilings dotted with gravity-defying sputniks, Adriene received the message loud and clear: "Anything is possible."

Fast-forwarding to 2010, we continue to find these places relevant and feel we are connected in a visceral way that's difficult to explain. Perhaps, in the same way an old song or familiar fragrance has the power to transport us to another place and time, vintage restaurants possess the ability to conjure up timeless feelings that are both personal and inherently universal. Even during Depressions, people still go out to restaurants and movies. Why? Because they need to reconnect with others, commiserate, and take a moment to escape from their routines and everyday realities. A well known film director once said that all movies are Westerns. What he was saying is that Westerns strip the complexity of life down into simple universal truths—something innately understood in all of us. Disney understood this; just look at Disneyland, with its fabled Frontierland, Adventureland, Tomorrowland, and Fantasyland. There are certain themes that resonate with people, themes that transcend culture and country.

Most of the restaurants included in this volume have withstood the test of time. And though a bit frayed and worn, they fit us like a pair of old jeans we can't bear to part with. We realize the past should not be lived in the present, but our knowledge of the past can only bring a deeper understanding and context to the present. Knowing where we've been helps us determine where we want to go. It has been said that within the stories of places we can find the stories of ourselves. It is our hope that you will recognize the parallels and discover your own personal stories as you read and view ***Southern California Eats 2.***

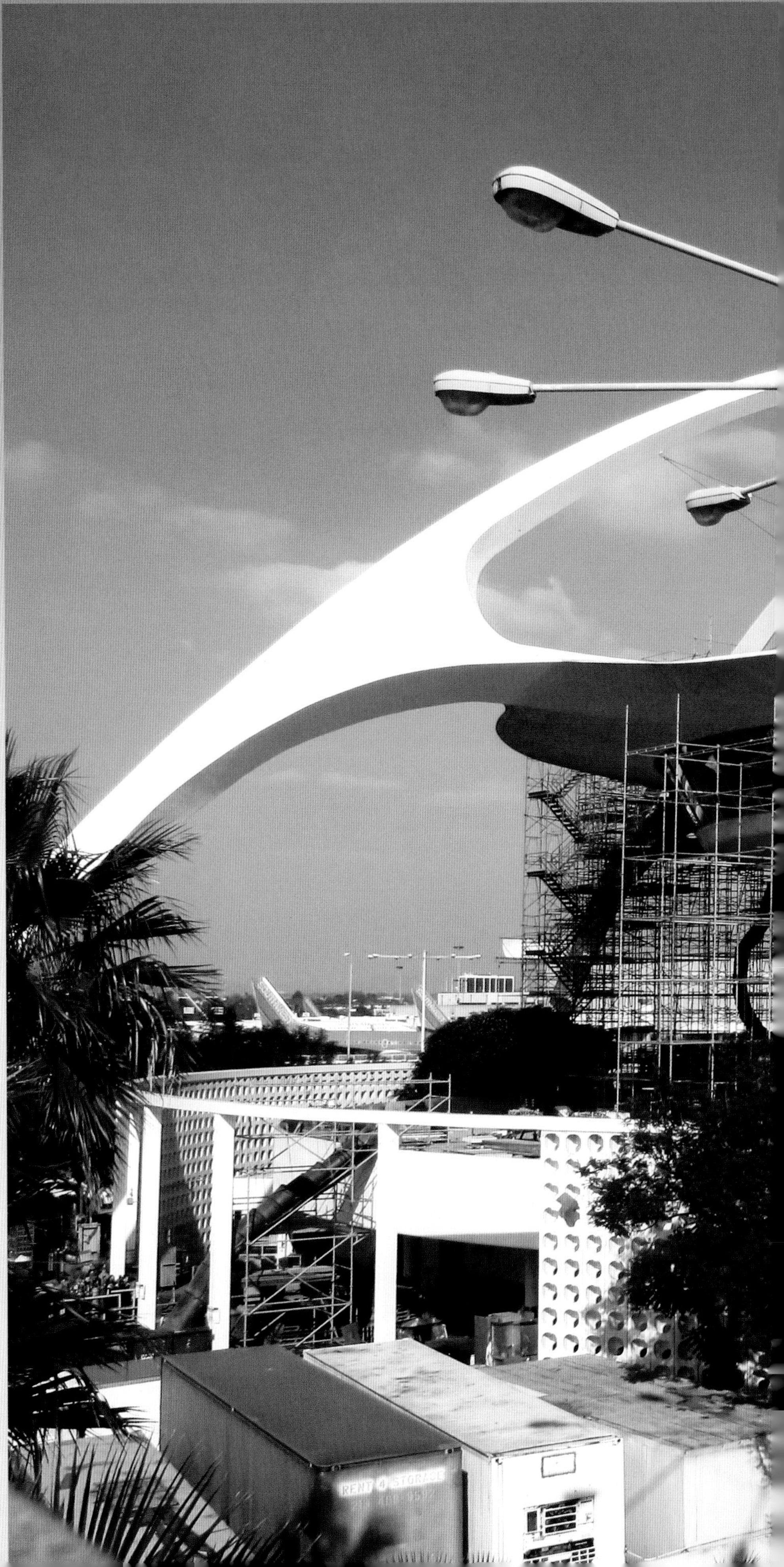

LAX Theme Building during restoration in 2009.

the **Eateries**

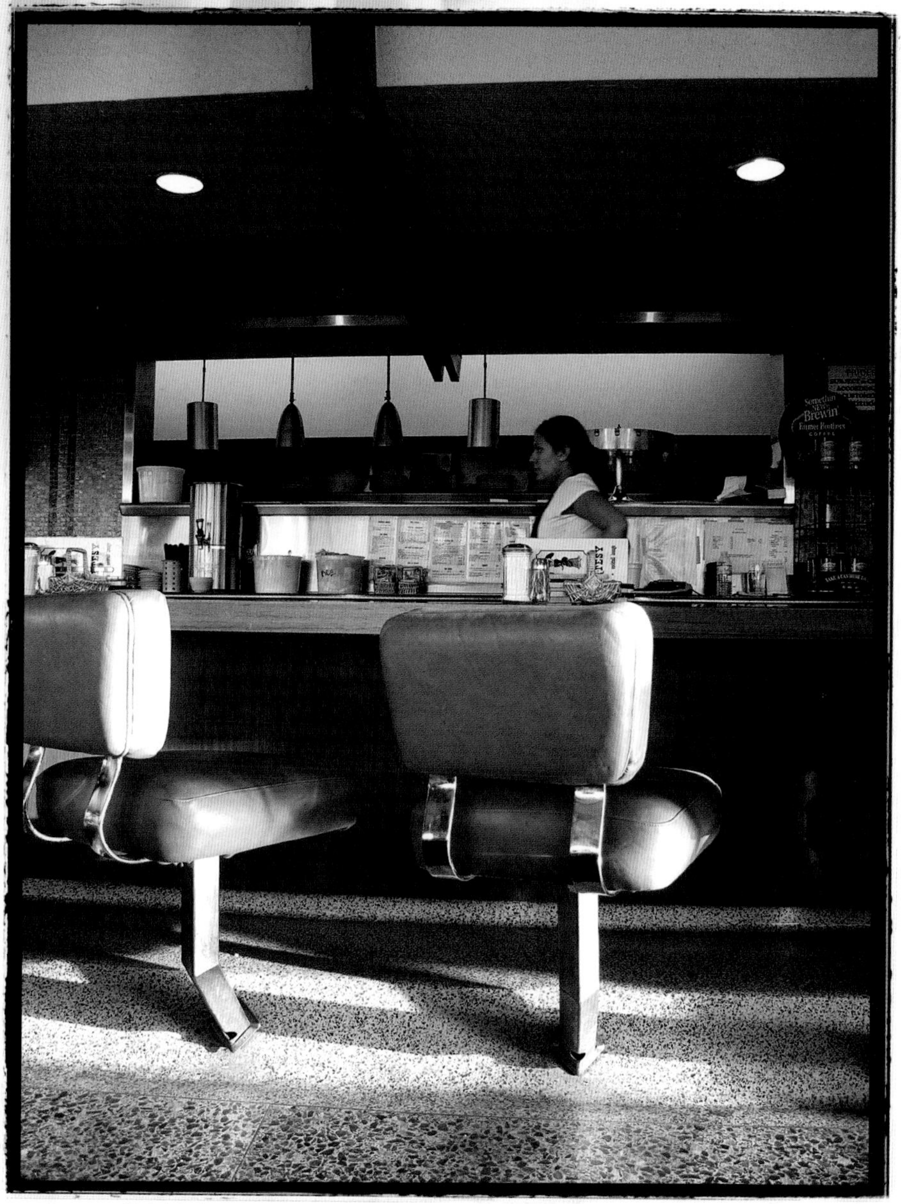

Courtesy Coffee Shop, Blythe. *Photo by Adriene Biondo.*

algemac's

Algemac's

3673 San Fernando Road, State Hwy. 99, Glendale

"Al-Gee-Mac's" dated back to 1937, a friendly stop for comfort food that made it into the 21st century before being cut down for development in 2004. Along State Highway 99 on the old Southern Pacific Railway Route, Algemac's advertised itself as being conveniently located across the street from Forest Lawn Cemetery, perhaps not the most appealing way to draw in living customers. At 300 acres, Forest Lawn is massive, and world renowned as the final resting place of Hollywood's Golden Age movie stars, among them Humphrey Bogart, Jean Harlow, and Clark Gable. Even beloved cartoon master Walt Disney is buried there. Surely

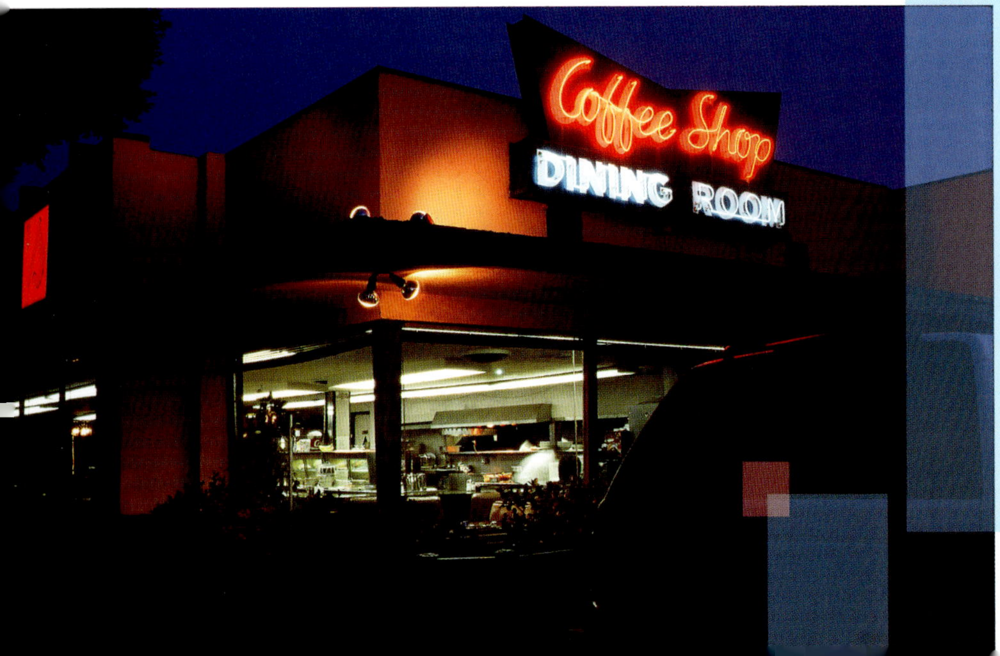

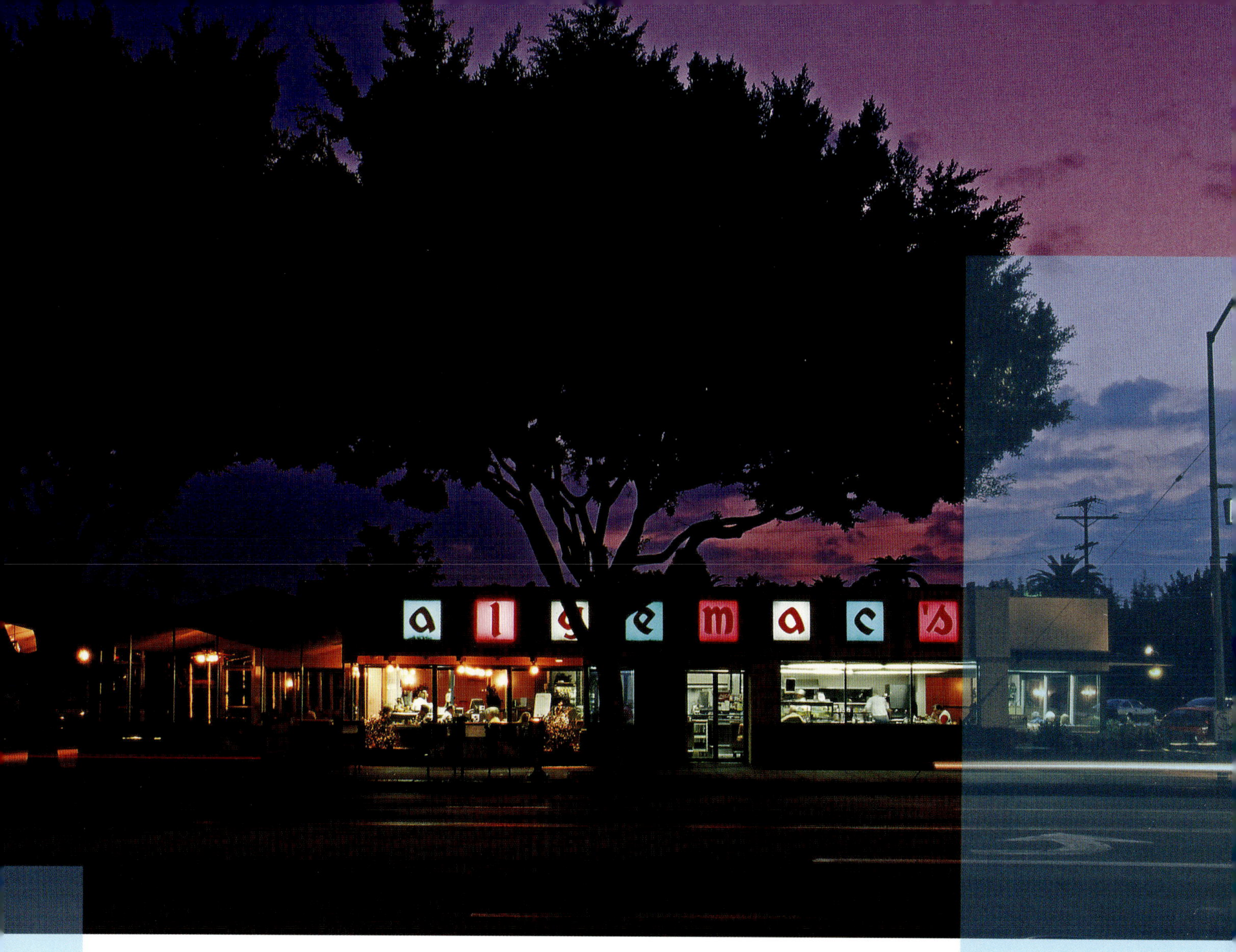

some of these movie icons made a stop at Algemac's back in the day. By the 1950s, Algemac's was updated with swanky signage and a new addition designed by African-American architect Ralph Vaughn. Vaughn was also the principal architect for Lincoln Place, a postwar garden style community in Venice that became the focus of an intensive preservation battle. Algemac's folded plate roof was incorporated into the new development, but sadly not much else.

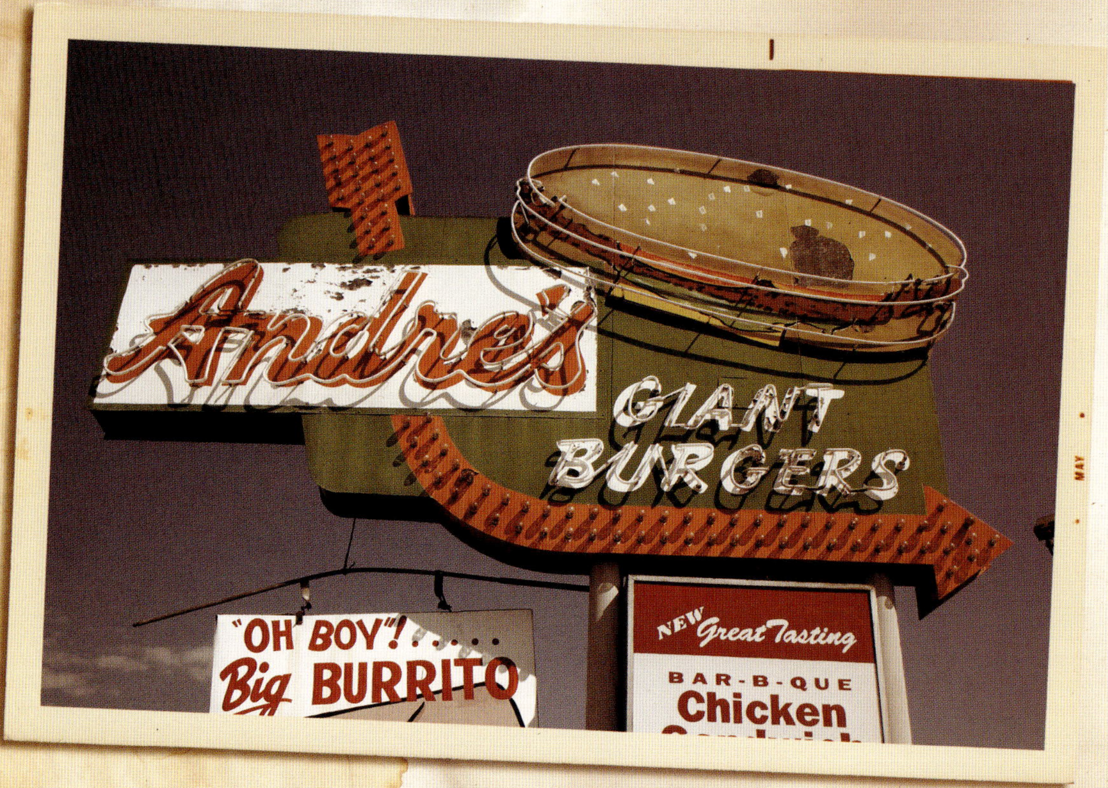
Andre's
GIANT
BURGERS
"OH BOY"!
Big BURRITO
NEW Great Tasting
BAR-B-QUE
Chicken

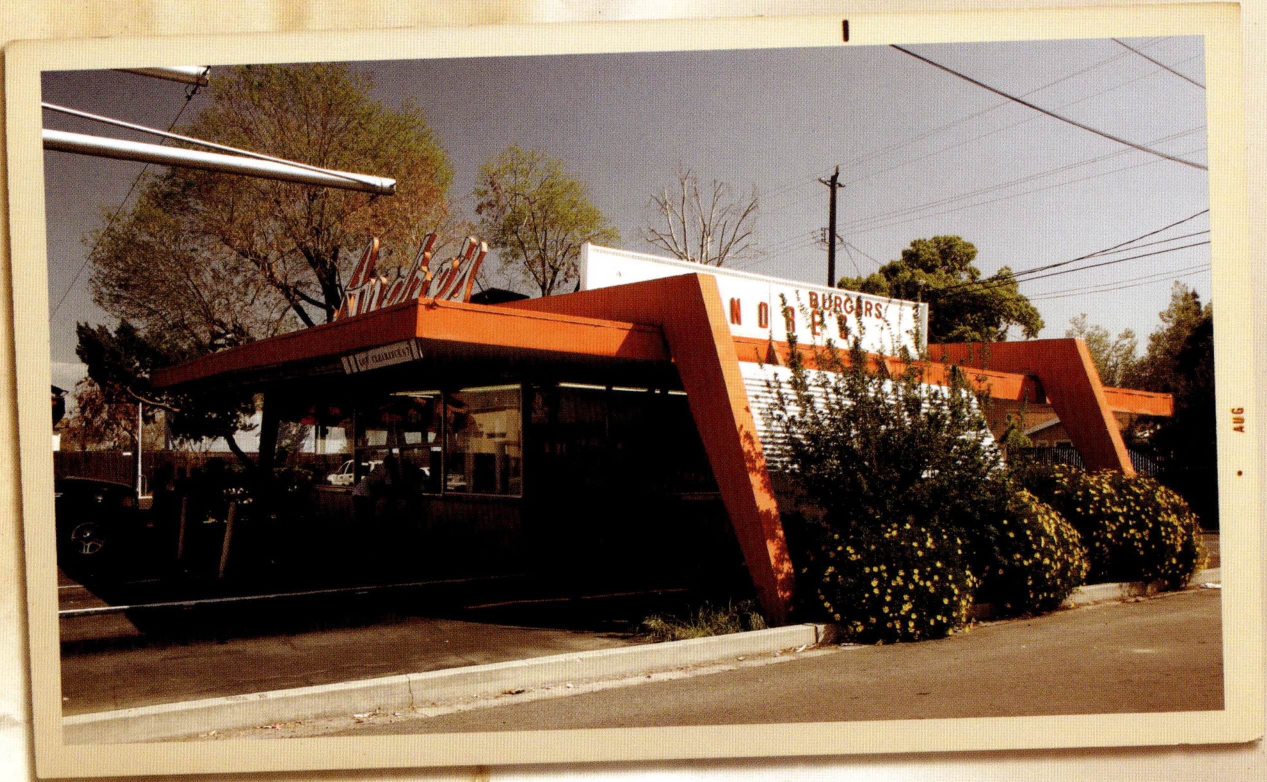
BURGERS

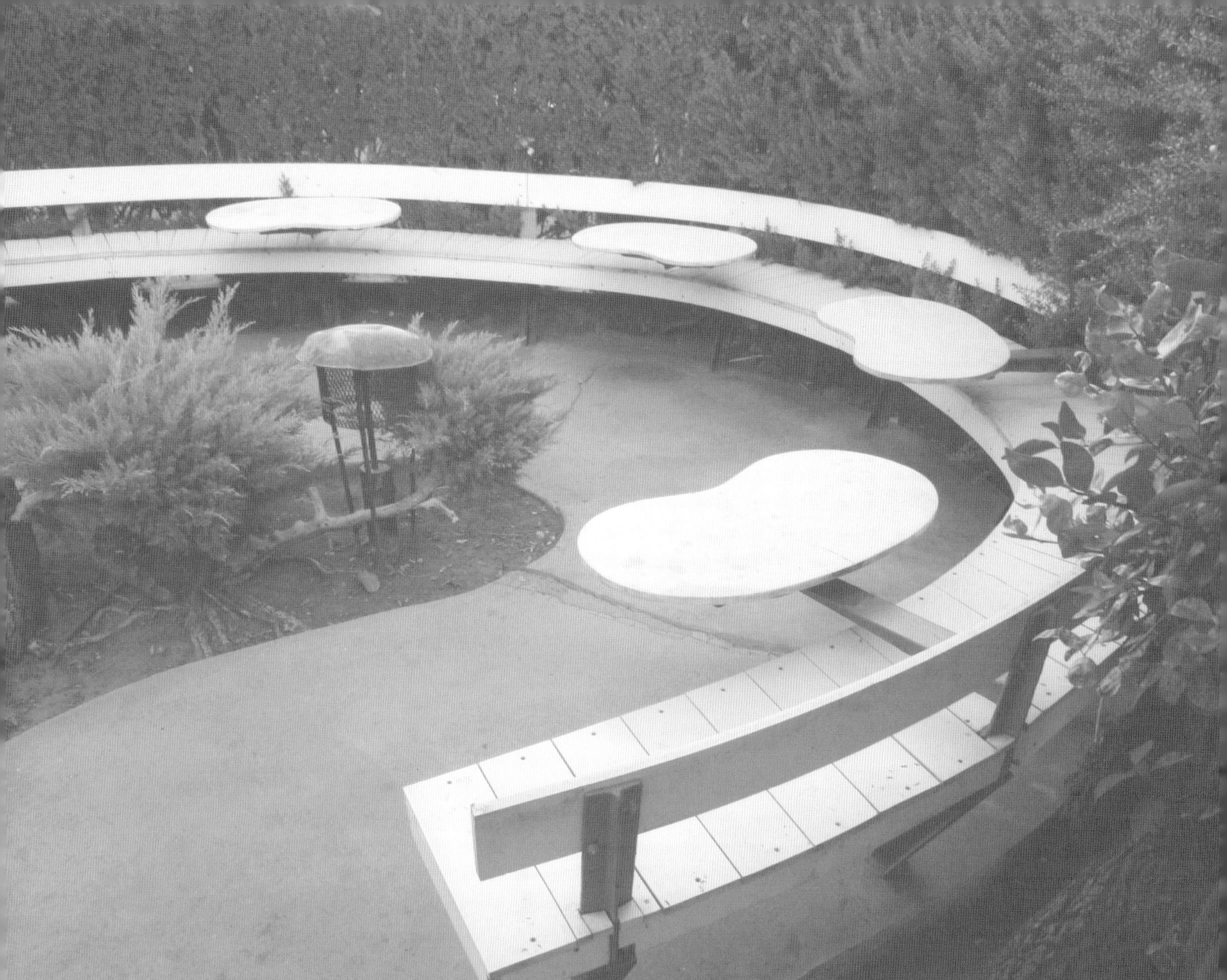

Andre's Drive In

1419 Brundage Lane, Bakersfield

The present owner, John Andre, is the son of the man who opened this classic drive-in in 1953. Even though there's a newly renovated McDonald's right across Chester Avenue, business was brisk here during our visit. The Big Burrito and Andre's fried berry pies are favorites. Locals consider it a landmark and although technically it's not, it definitely should be. A strikingly authentic neon sign advertises Andre's "French Burger Biggest in Town," while bright orange "spider legs" arch over the building like an enormous insect. The outdoor patio is comprised of semi-circular bench seating with kidney-shaped palette tables made of marbleized plastic. A central planter is also amoeba-shaped. Everything is completely original, right down to a porcelain drinking fountain that reminded us of grade school. Authentic places like this are getting so rare that we almost caused an accident when we caught this drive-in out of the corner of our eyes.

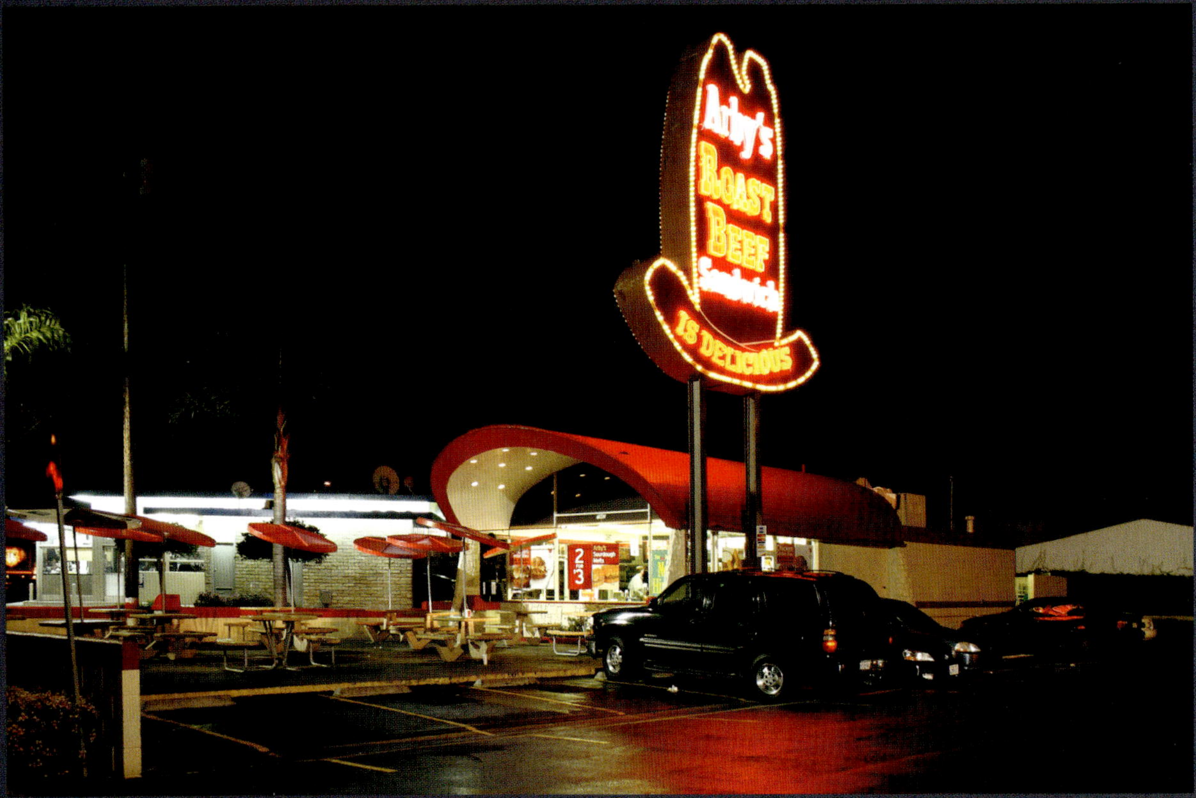

An original Arby's in Orange County which shows the chuck wagon teamed up with the cowboy hat.

Arby's

Multiple Locations

In 1964, Leroy and Forest Raffel opened the very first Arby's restaurant in Boardman, Ohio. Their first menu was a simple offering of roast beef sandwiches, potato chips, and iced tea. Though many assume that "Arby's" stands for "roast beef," the Raffel Brothers named their restaurant after their initials "R" and "B." Arby's famous ten gallon hat neon sign was originally designed to complement their Conestoga, chuckwagon-shaped restaurant. Here's a Texas-size beauty we spotted in Mission Hills. For us, the 60s vision of the modern frontier will never be out of style.

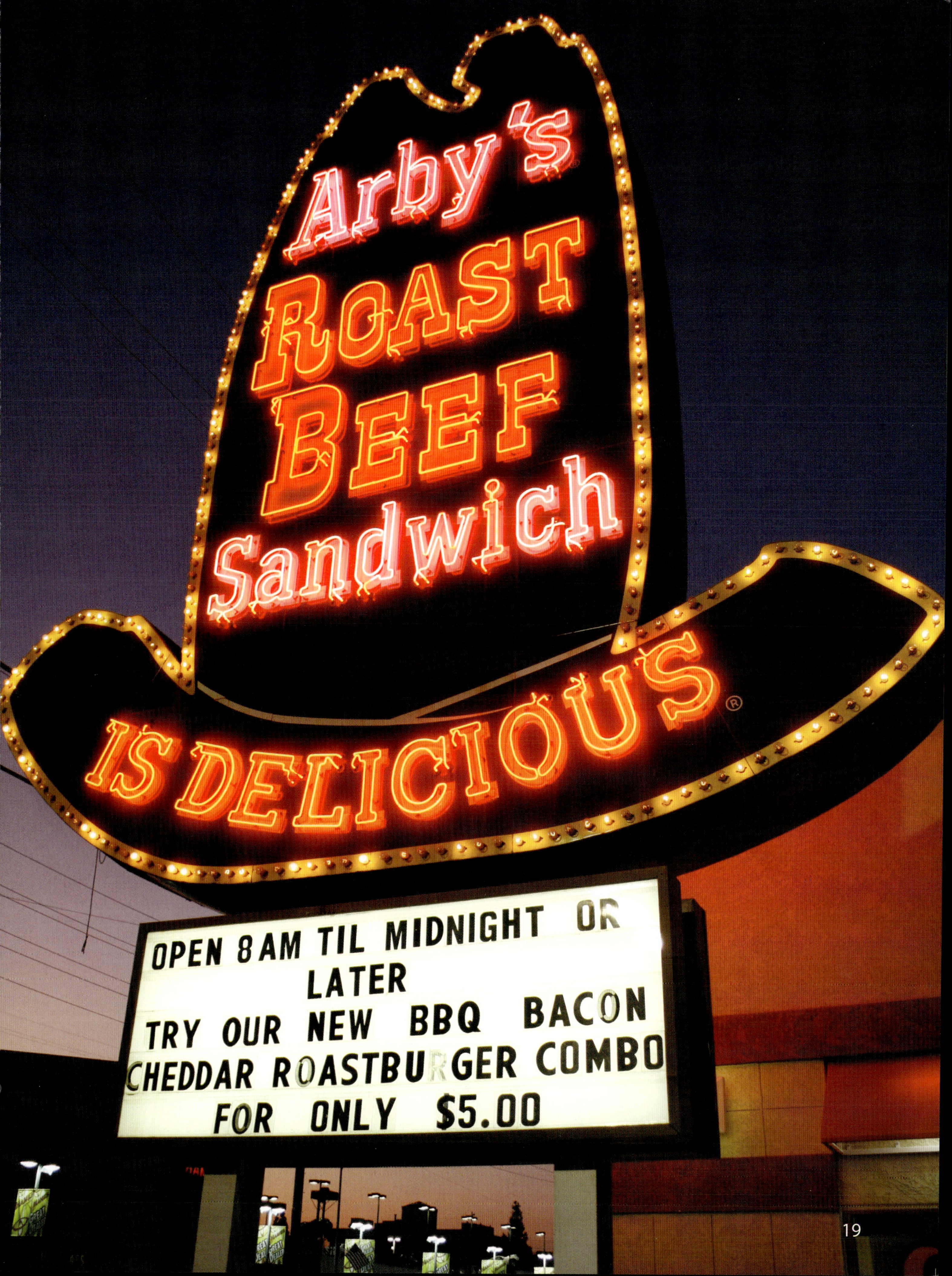
Arby's
ROAST
BEEF
Sandwich
IS DELICIOUS®
OPEN 8AM TIL MIDNIGHT OR
LATER
TRY OUR NEW BBQ BACON
CHEDDAR ROASTBURGER COMBO
FOR ONLY $5.00

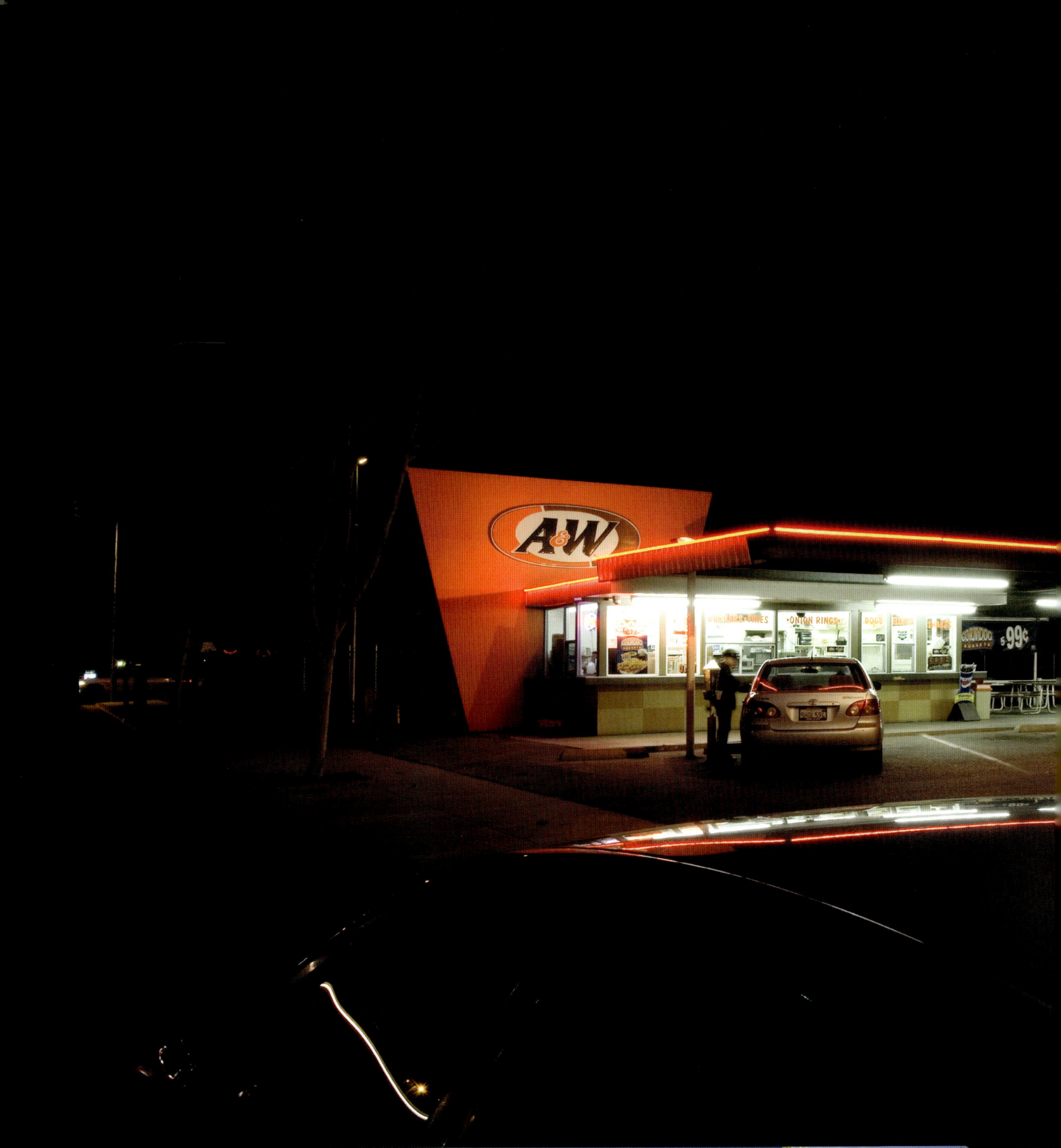
A&W
ONION RINGS
99¢

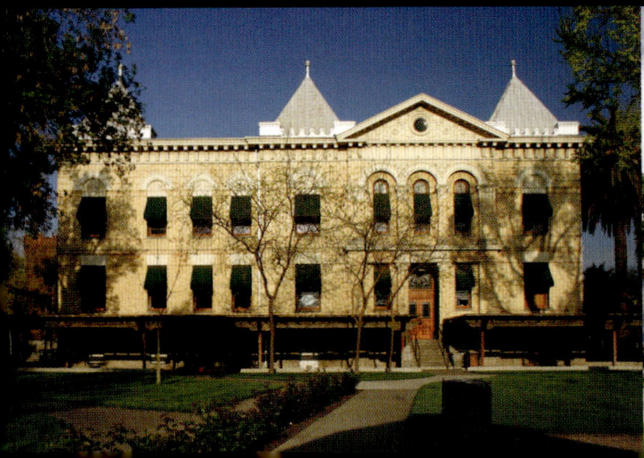

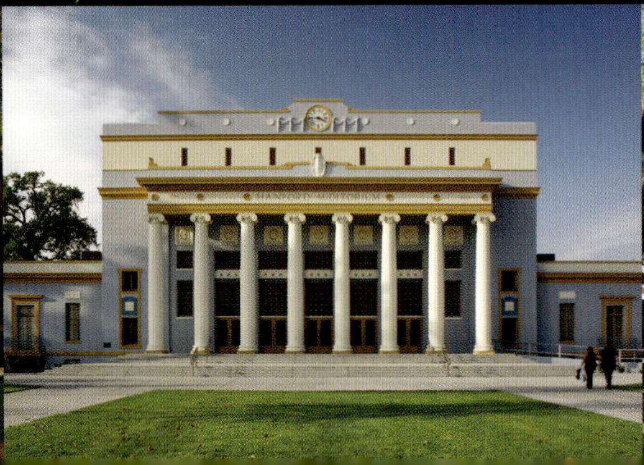
HANFORD AUDITORIUM

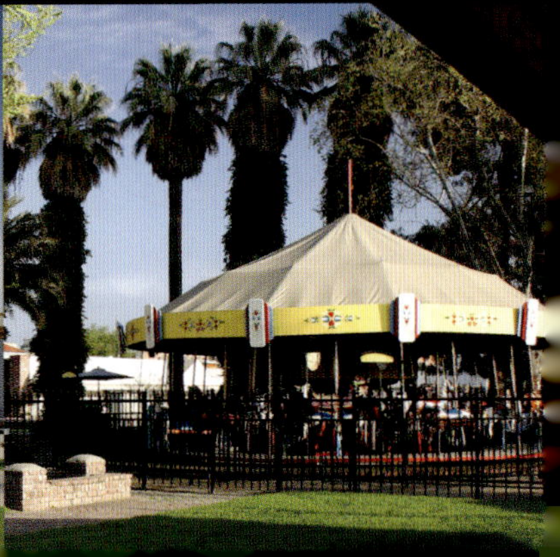

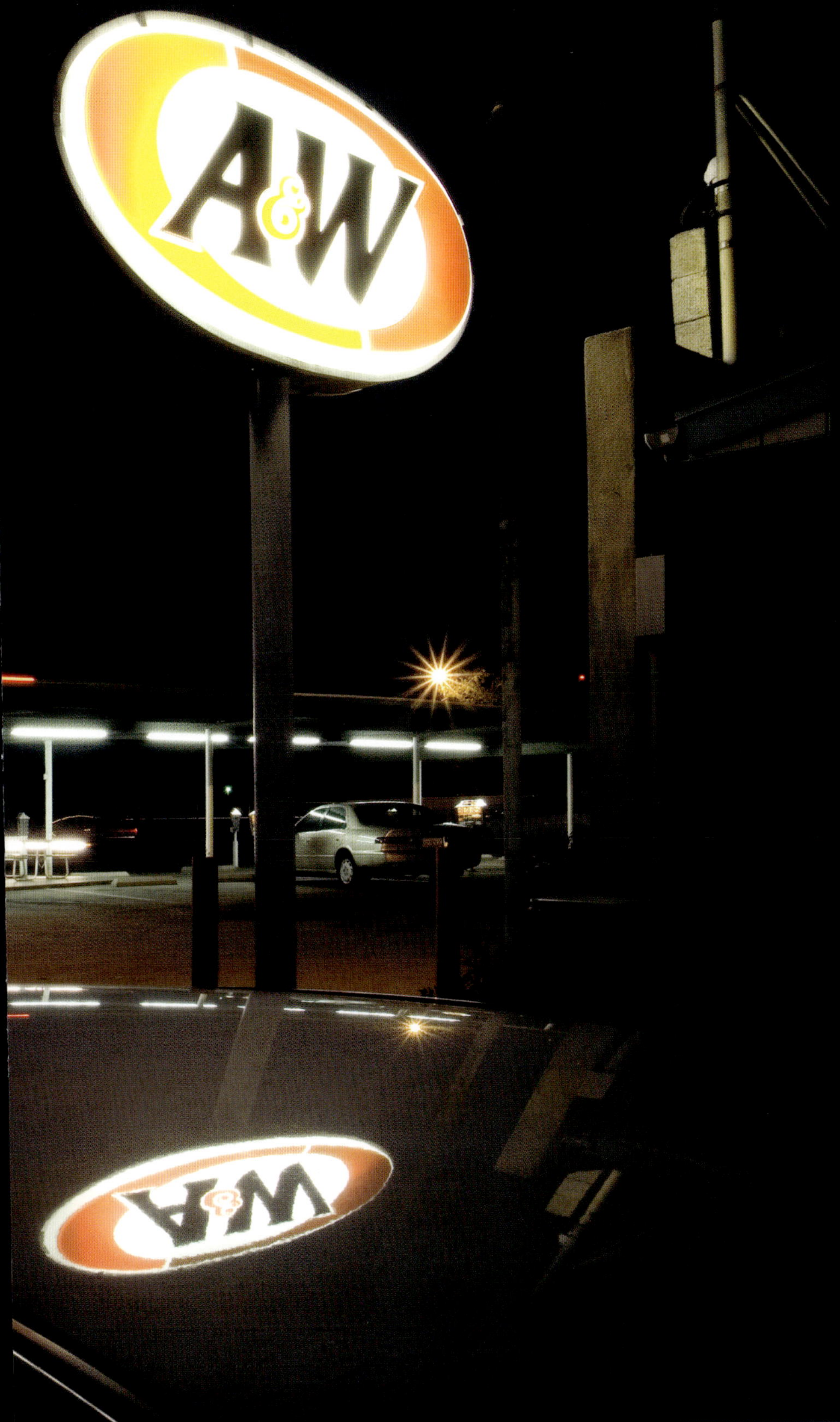

A&W Root Beer

Multiple locations

How many of us survived scorching hot summers thanks to ice cold mugs of A&W root beer? Celebrating their 91st year, A&W is known the world over. The secret root beer formula was purchased from an Arizona pharmacist by Roy Allen. Roy deemed the thirst-quenching elixir an immediate success the moment he served it from his first stand in Lodi, California. Back then it was only five cents. Soon Roy opened a second outlet in Sacramento, hiring "car-boys" to hop up on the running boards of cars and serve thirsty travelers frosty glass mugs of root beer right in their parked cars. Roy's concept is said to be the first drive-in in the nation. In 1922, Roy partnered with Lodi employee Frank Wright and "A&W Root Beer" was officially born.

This A&W in the Norman Rockwell town of Hanford is frozen in a time capsule. Hanford's town square boasts of an 1897 courthouse, 1924 civic auditorium, 1929 Fox Theater, 1930 Superior Dairy, and historic China Alley with a Taoist Temple built in 1893.

Below, left to right:
Courthouse, Hanford, CA
Civic Auditorium
Town Square, complete with carousel
Hanford Fox Theater
Superior Dairy

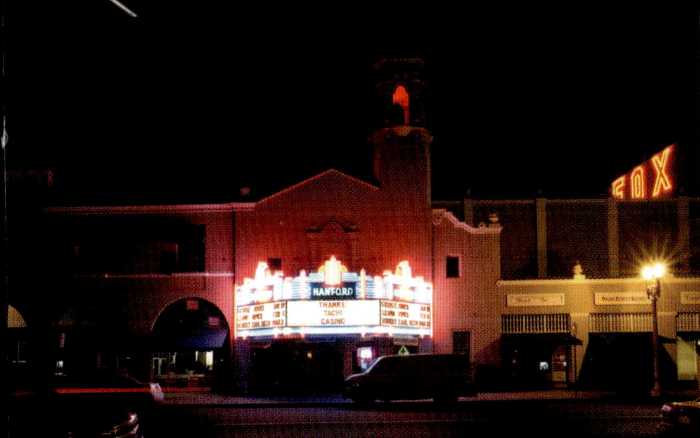

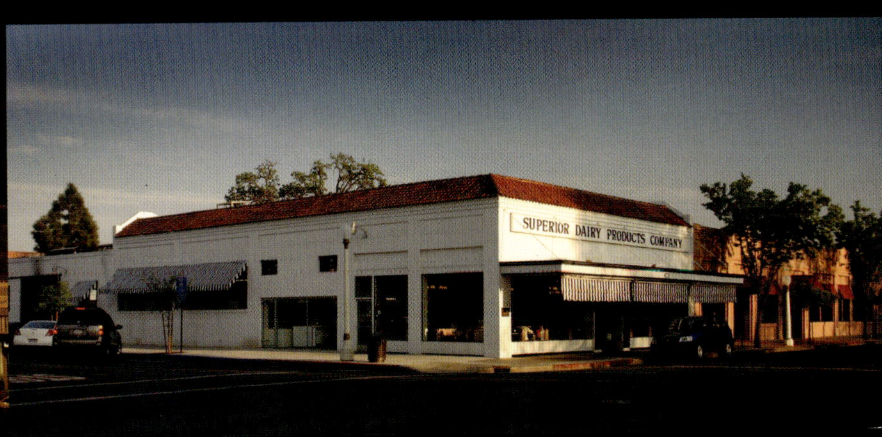

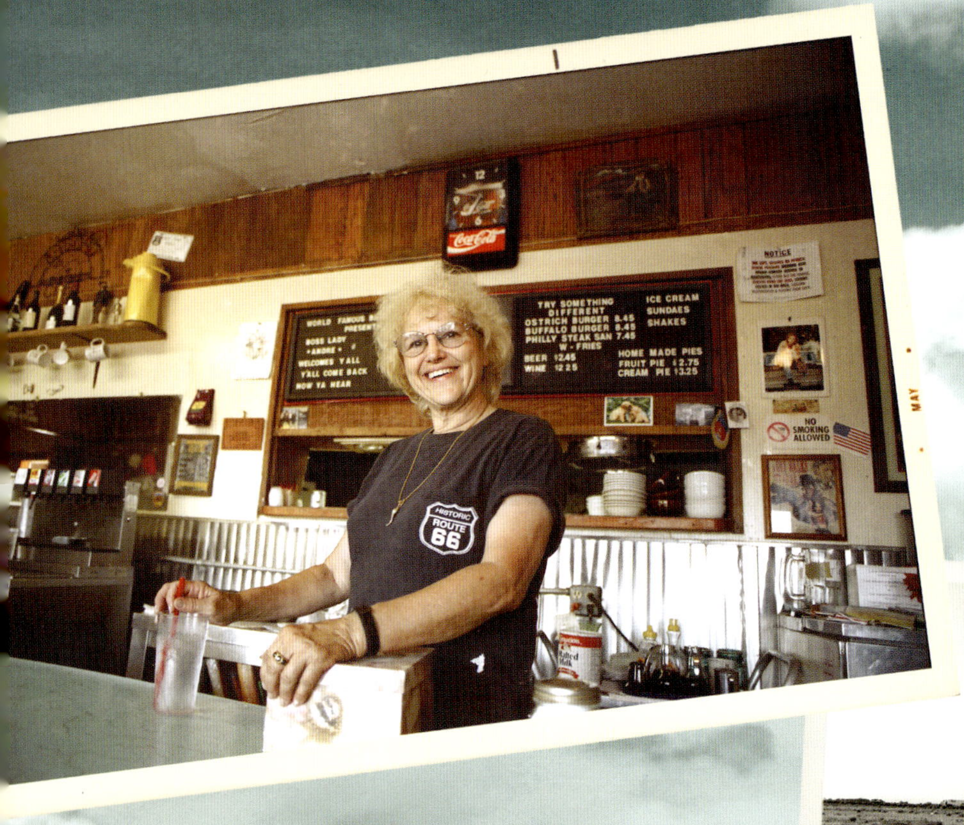

In 2004, proprietor Andrea Pruett greeted us with a friendly smile and apple pies.

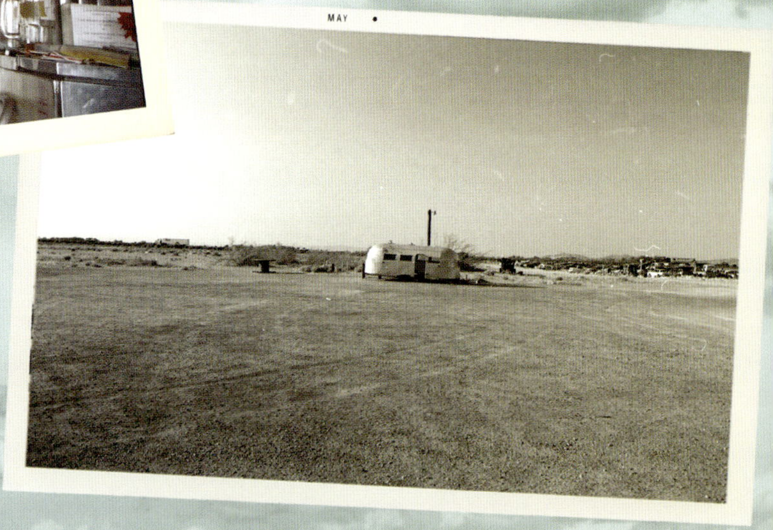

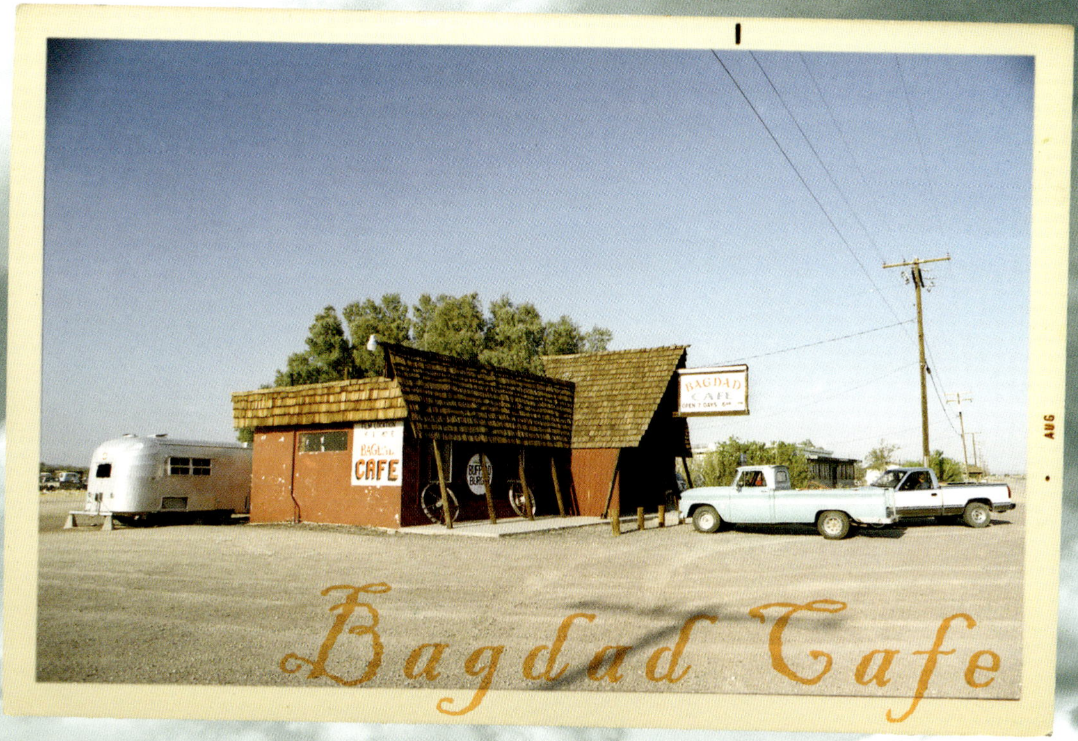

Bagdad Cafe

46548 National Trails Hwy., Route 66, Newberry Springs

Originally the Sidewinder Cafe, this restaurant was built in the 1940s on the Mother Road, aka Historic Route 66. Brought to notoriety and romanticized by Allison Ander's quirky 1988 film *Bagdad Cafe* starring Jack Palance, it became an international phenomenon and remained known as the Bagdad Cafe. Owner Andrea Pruett told us that tourists come from all over the world, making the trek to see and experience what this place is really like: hot, dry, and desolate. During a trip to Death Valley at the height of summer (something we would not recommend), we encountered a bus-full of enthusiastic Germans. When we asked them why they were so happy to be there, they told us that they don't have deserts in Germany. One said he found it so completely different than what he was used to that he felt like he had gone to another planet.

BARNEY'S BEANERY

8447 Santa Monica Boulevard, West Hollywood

Route 66 Diner. Juke Joint/Pool Hall. '50s Beatnik hangout. A drag 'n' eat pad. A place where movie people go to let their hair down. Home base of screenwriters, authors and Pop Artists. Watering hole for rock 'n' roll legends…a timeless, last bastion of the free-wheelin' American West and constant spirit of the open frontier that remains, historically, L.A.

–Domenic Priore

This 1920 eating establishment is located on the very last leg of Route 66, just before hitting the final stop, the Santa Monica Pier and the Pacific Ocean. Travelers heading west used to trade in their license plates from their home state for a pint of beer. There's food, pool, a jukebox, karaoke, and lots of liquor. Hollywood personalities frequented this place in the '30s. In the '40s, Clark Gable, Errol Flynn, Bette Davis, Hoot Gibson, and other celebrities were regulars. In the '50s, the Beatniks and Pop Artists from the Ferus Gallery on La Cienega hung out here. Barney's became the counterculture hub of L.A. In the '60s, Janis Joplin and Jimi Hendrix were regulars, while Jim Morrison was thrown out after pissing on the bar. The history of this place is so tightly interwoven with that of Los Angeles that to study one without the other would be incomplete at best, and futile at worst. For more history, check out the historical section of Barney's Beanery website by Domenic Priore (barneysbeanery.com).

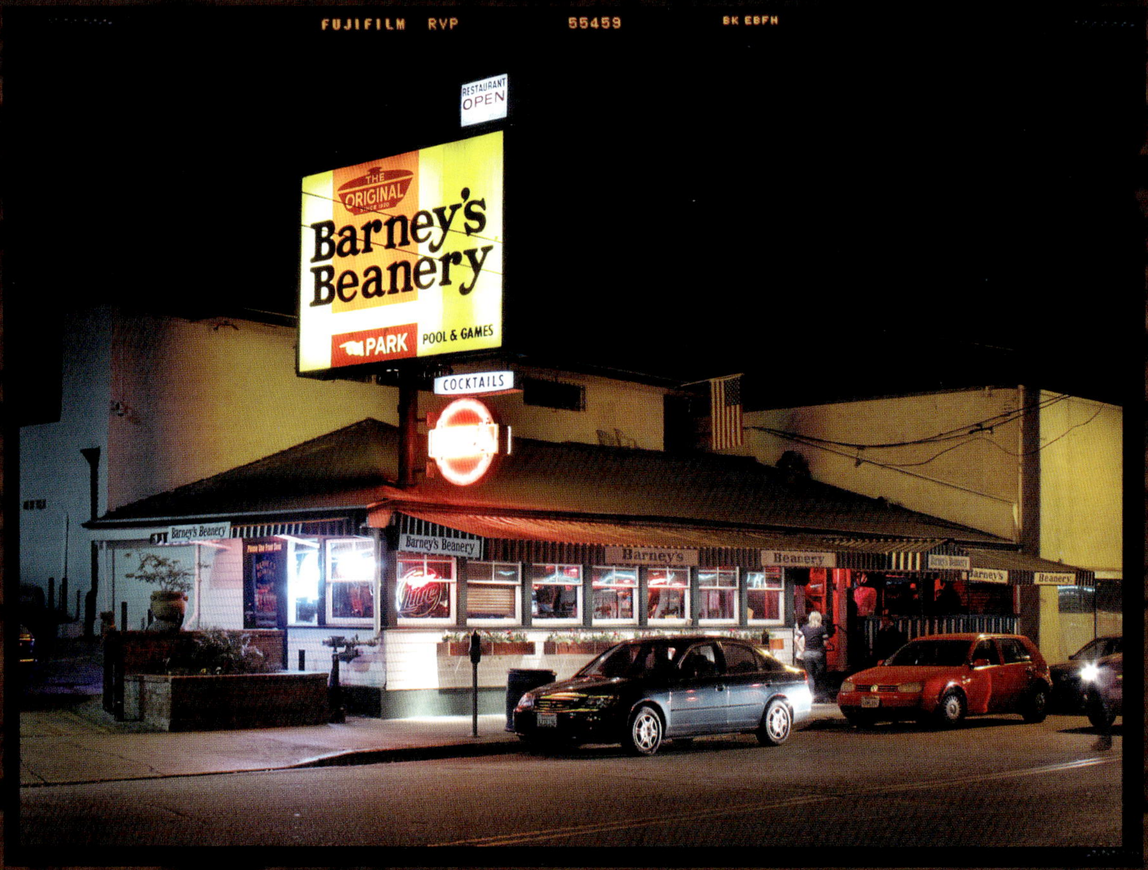

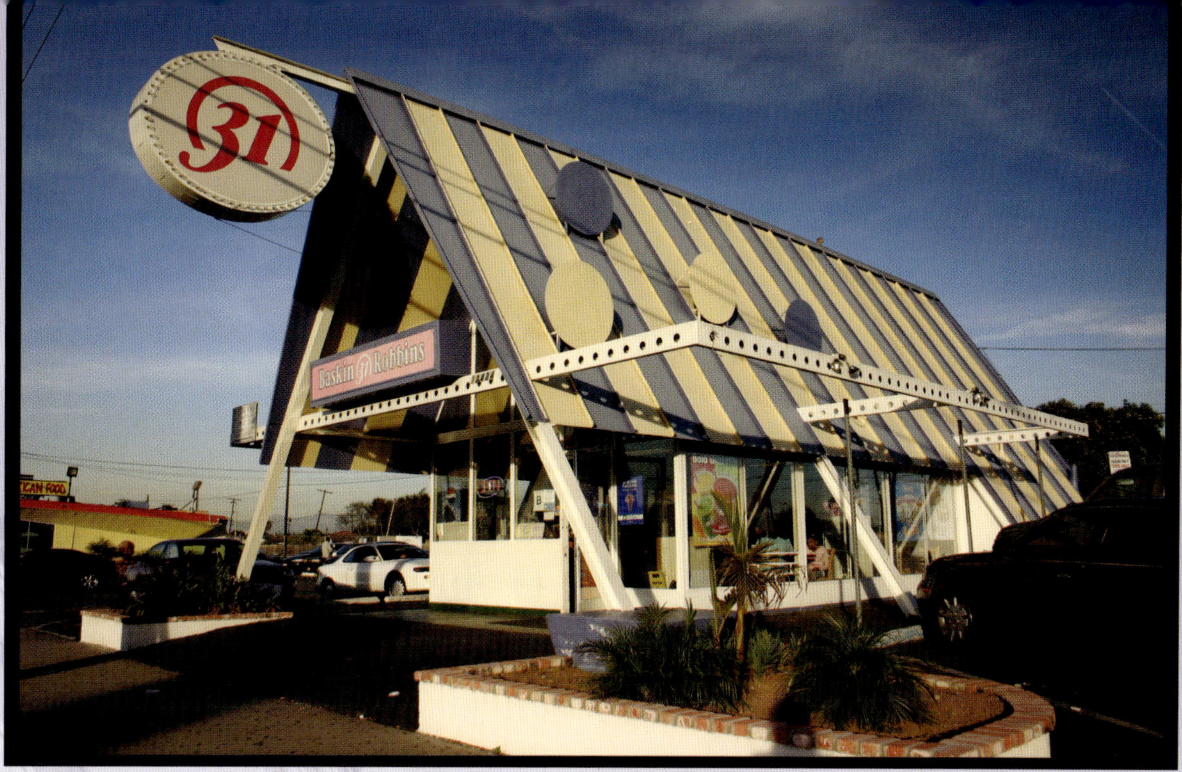

Early constructivist style A-frame in the Crenshaw district of L.A.

BASKIN + ROBBINS 31 FLAVORS

6,000 stores in 35 countries

Before Ben & Jerry there was Irv and Burt. The world renowned team of brothers-in-law, Burton Baskin and Irvine Robbins, changed the world of ice cream by realizing their own ice cream dreams. After returning to the States following their service during World War II, Irv opened his first shop in Glendale called SnowBird. He offered a variety of 21 flavors instead of the traditional trio of chocolate, vanilla, and strawberry. Meanwhile, in nearby Pasadena, Burt had started up Burton's Ice Cream, refining his early experiments of concocting exotic fruit delights while he was serving in the South Pacific. By 1947 each knew they had a good thing going and partnered up with the single-minded philosophy of selling unique flavors of ice cream. They even purchased their own dairy in Burbank so they could closely supervise the development of new flavors.

By 1953 Irv and Burt hit upon the idea of introducing a different flavor for each day of the month and Baskin-Robbins 31 Flavors was born. With original flavors like Mint Chocolate Chip, Tanganilla, Jamoca Almond Fudge, and Pralines n' Cream, who hasn't tasted one of their best-sellers? When America landed on the Moon in July 1969, Adriene remembers her mom taking the family out for Baskin-Robbins' commemorative Green Lunar Cheesecake ice cream!

By 1967, over 500 stores strong, Irv and Burt decided to sell their phenomenal enterprise to United Fruit Company. Today, with 6,000 stores, America's Favorite Neighborhood Ice Cream Shop is also the largest ice cream chain in the world.

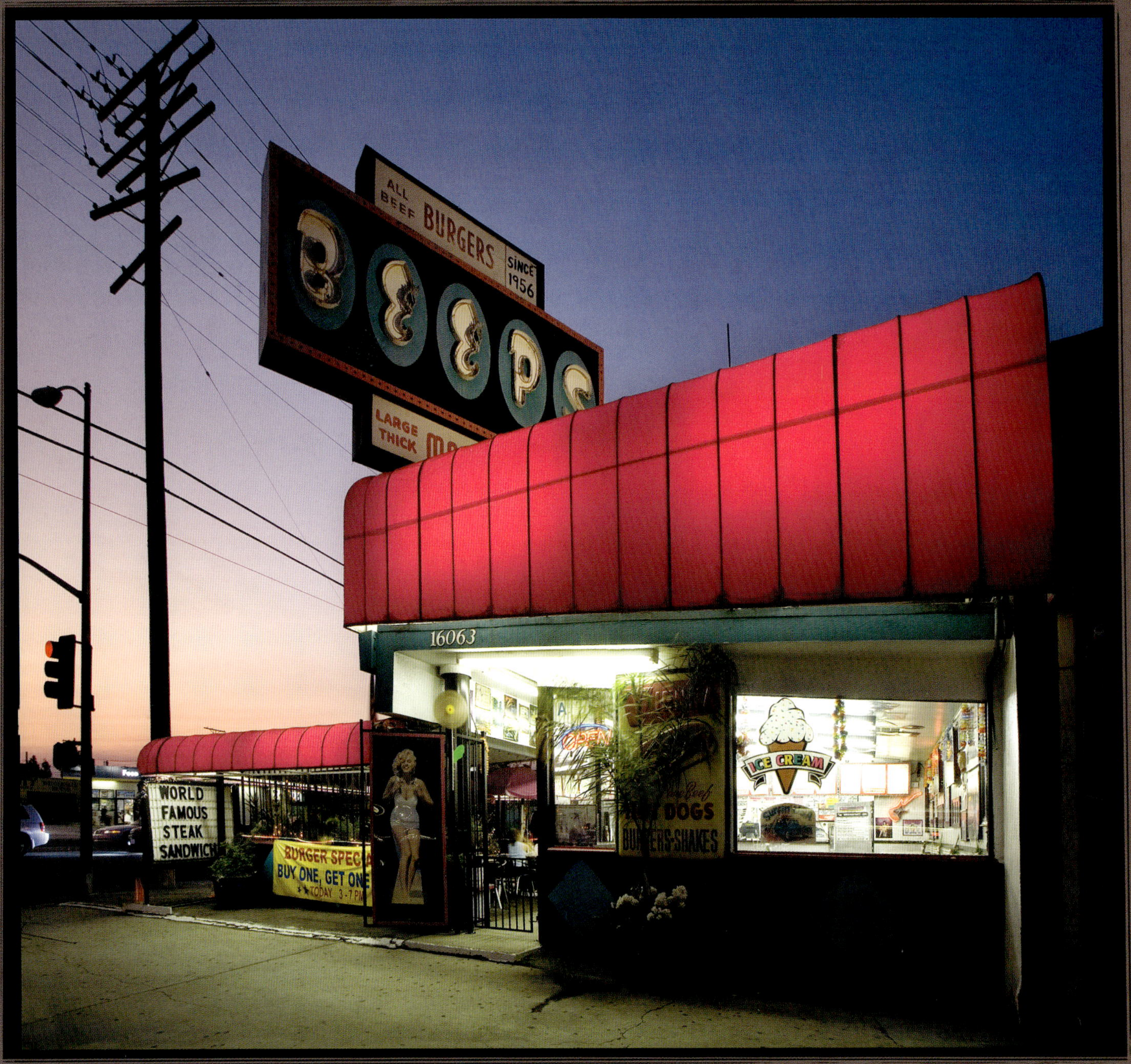

BEEPS Drive-In

16063 Sherman Way, Van Nuys

Beep's is proud to be "A Valley Favorite Since 1956." A friendly staff serves up old-fashioned handmade fountain treats like peanut butter cup shakes and root beer floats. They serve the Big Beeper (two ¼ lb patties), a three bun cheeseburger, a ¼ lb cheese burger, ¼ lb chili burger, bacon burger, pastrami burger, french fries, onion rings,…and the menu goes on and on and does not stop! Cruise over with a date and listen to some classic Rock n' Roll while sharing one of Beep's own Rocket 88 sundaes! Look for the baby blue neon eyes spelling out "B-E-E-P-S"!

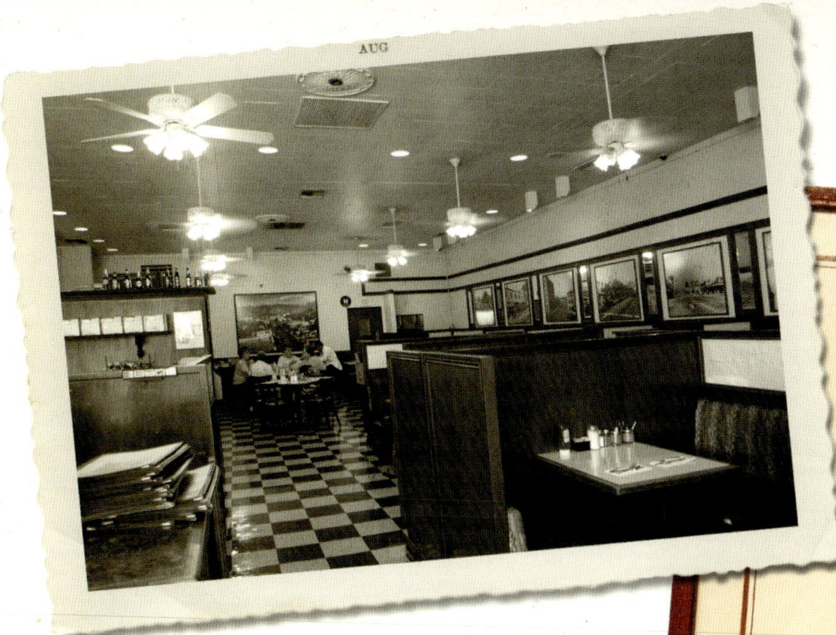

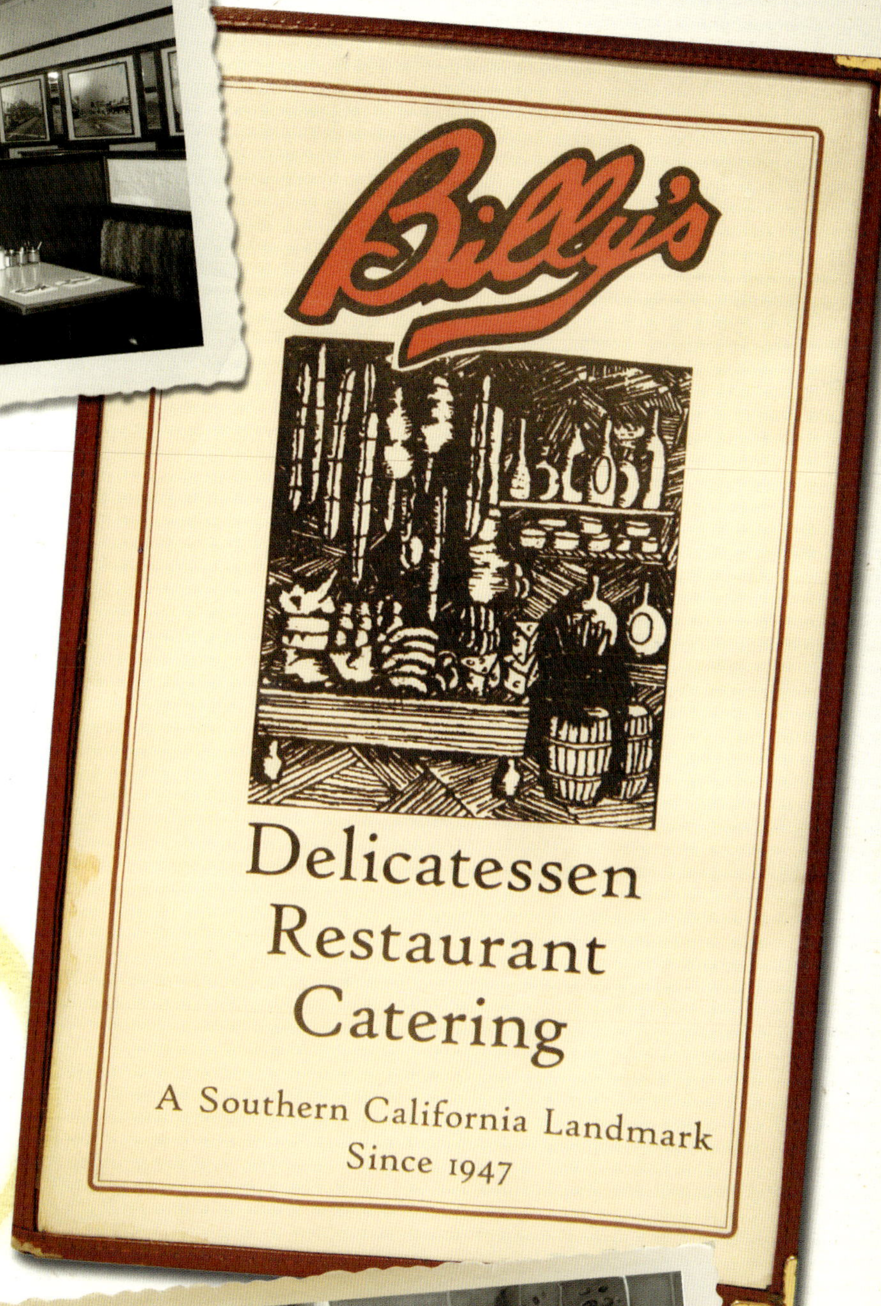

Billy's Deli & Cafe

216 N. Orange Street, Glendale

This is one of the most overlooked deli's in L.A. Even when we lived in Glendale, we rarely ate here, for some unknown reason. Billy's is not far from Damon's and has been around since 1947. It's a classic deli restaurant with their own bakery and catering service. The food is excellent and the relaxed setting contrasts with the hectic pace of Canter's on the other side of the hill. Billy was the nickname of the original owner Frank Whitten. His son created the intriguing ceramic wall of food that decorates the front of the restaurant by casting an assortment of real deli foods, everything from linked sausages to wheels of cheese.

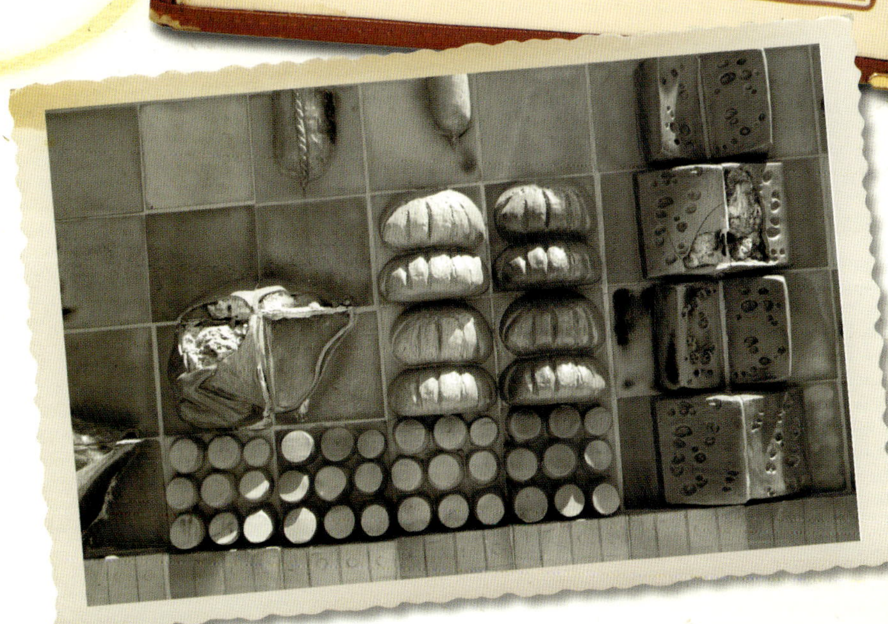

The newly rebuilt Broiler one month after opening,

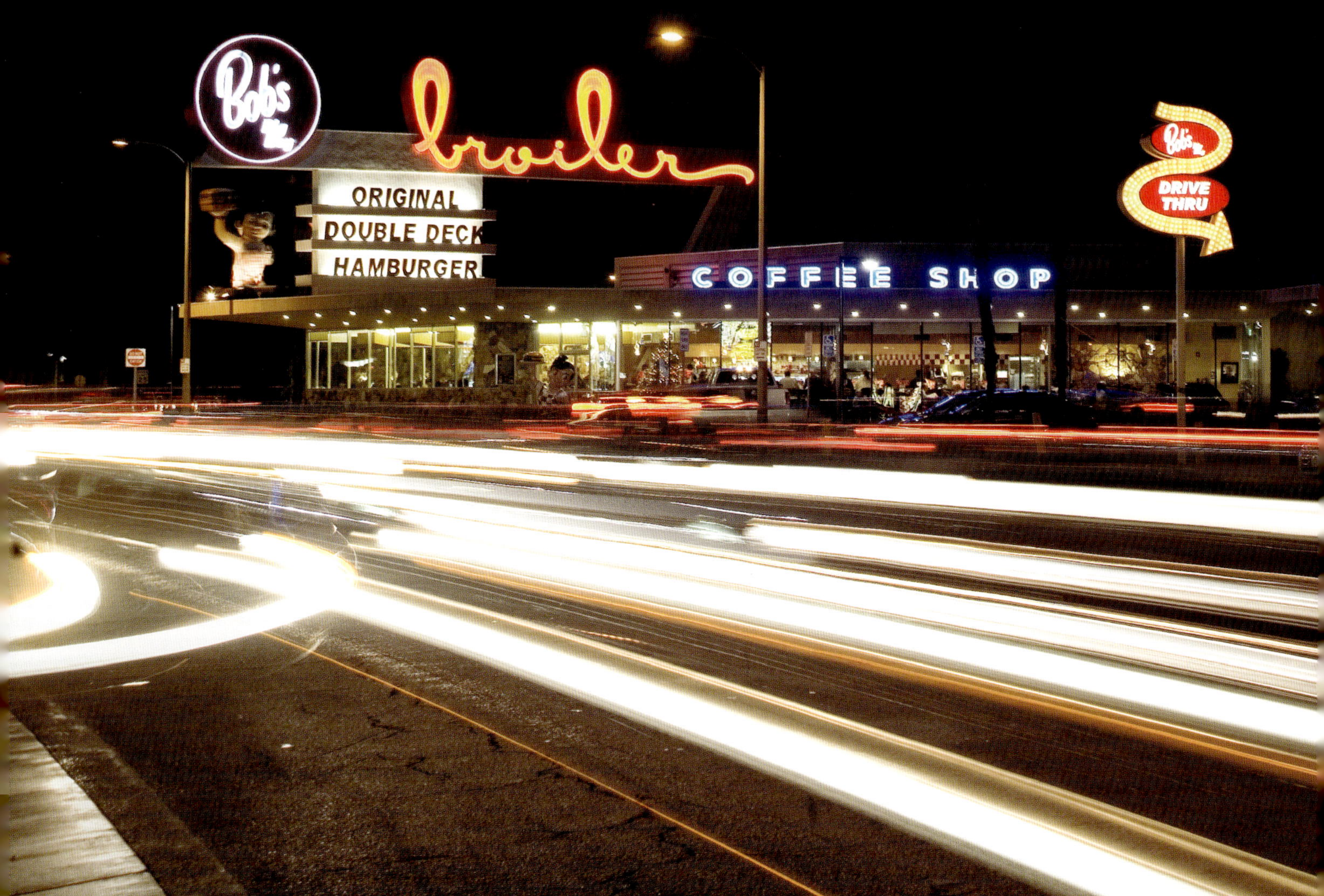

BOB'S BIG BOY *broiler*

7447 Firestone Boulevard, Downey

This Googie style BOB'S BIG BOY is a stand-out on the boulevard with over 60 feet of fabulous '50s signage and a 12-foot tall, rotating Big Boy statue! Rooftop neon "DRIVE-IN" signs invite you to cruise in and meet the cutest carhops around. With a combination drive-in and drive-thru, along with a deluxe eat-in restaurant, The Broiler is what retro-tourism is all about.

Bob's Big Boy Broiler comes with a unique pedigree. Beyond being a stunning Bob's Big Boy restaurant, the back story of the fight to Save The Broiler is now legendary. Today's travelers would never know that not long ago this 1958 drive-in, originally built as Harvey's Broiler, was reduced to a pile of rubble. Illegally demolished on January 7, 2007, news of its destruction re-launched a grass roots movement that began six years earlier when the restaurant closed its doors. Due to the dogged persistence of the

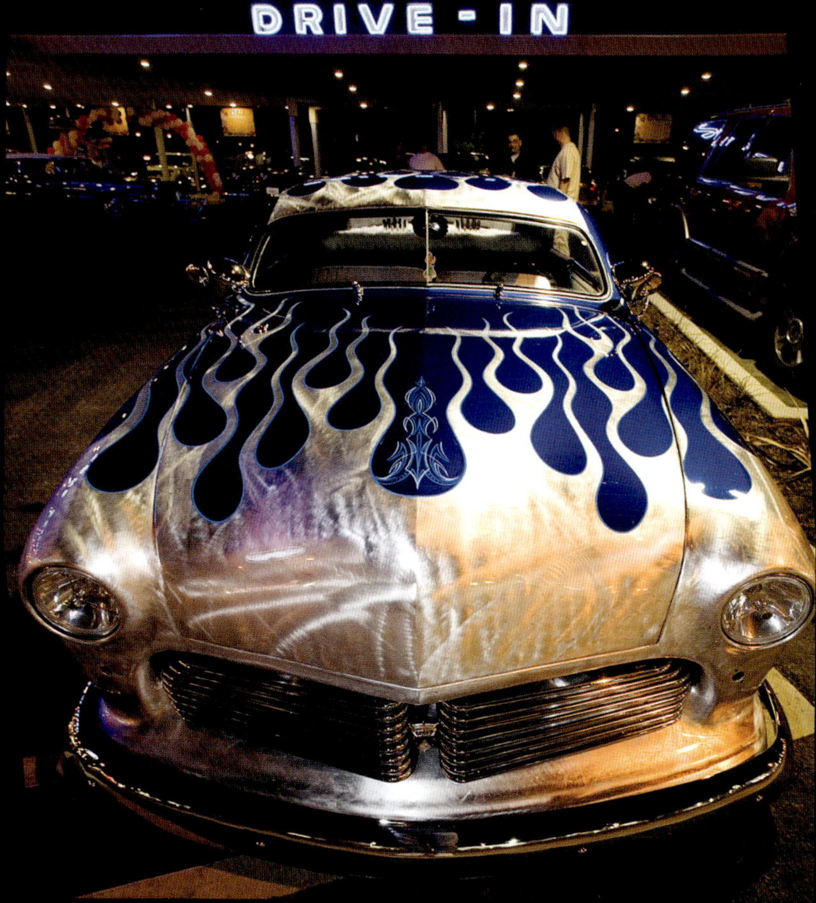

Just like back in '58, cruise nights are bringing in gorgeous customs like this one.

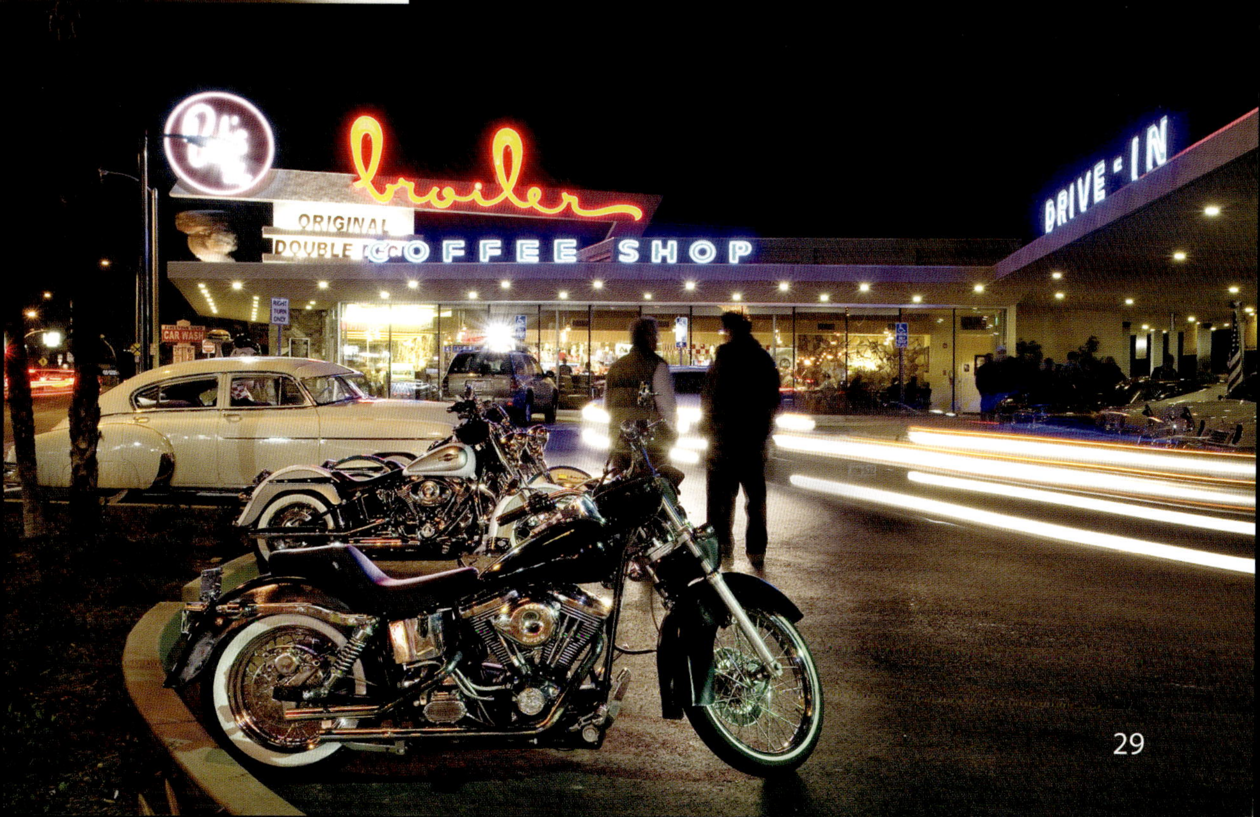

People arrive in all types of vehicles, from lead sleds to motorcycles.

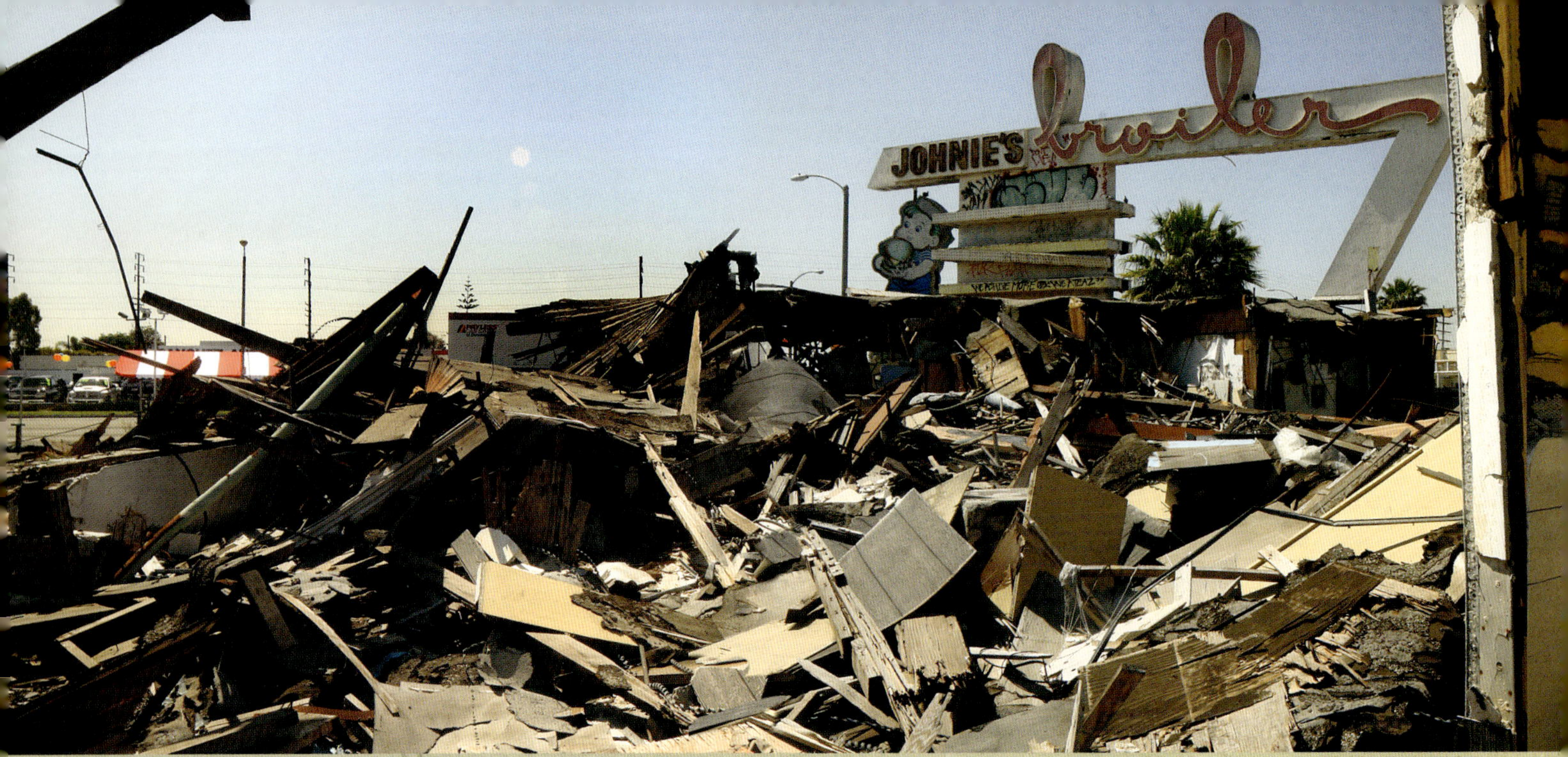

Above: The Broiler sat in wreckage for almost two years after its illegal 2007 demolition.

Below: Instead of mourning their loss, the community, preservationists, and car clubs fought to bring back the legendary drive-in.

Center right: When a new restaurant operator was found, the Coalition to Save the Broiler sponsored a cruise to show their support.

Bottom right: During reconstruction in July 2009.

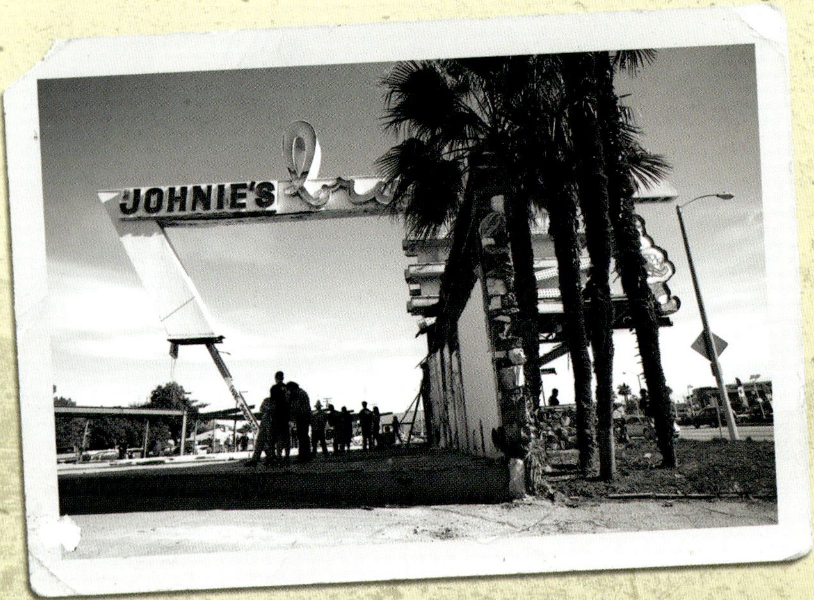

Friends of Johnie's and Coalition to Rebuild the Broiler, the City of Downey issued a moratorium to protect the site until an appropriate operator could be found. Thanks to the Louder family, this mecca of California car culture was painstakingly rebuilt, with great care taken to preserve the character and spirit of the original restaurant, right down to restoration of the neon signage and terrazzo floors. With great food and such attention to detail and authenticity, it's no wonder the Broiler is packing them in again. The story of Harvey's/Johnie's/Bob's is a real life fairytale that proves good things can still happen. "Rebuild it and they will come."

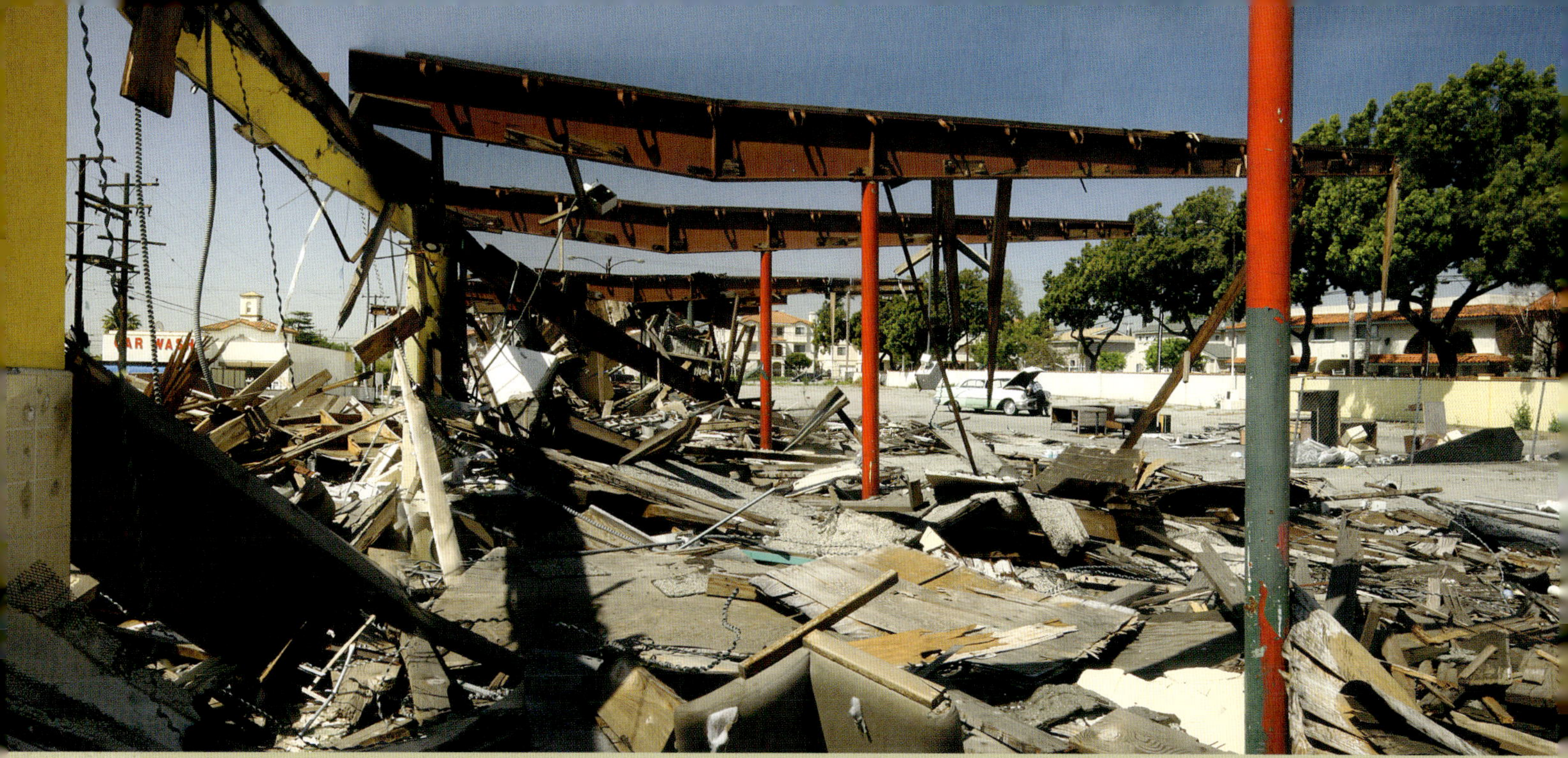

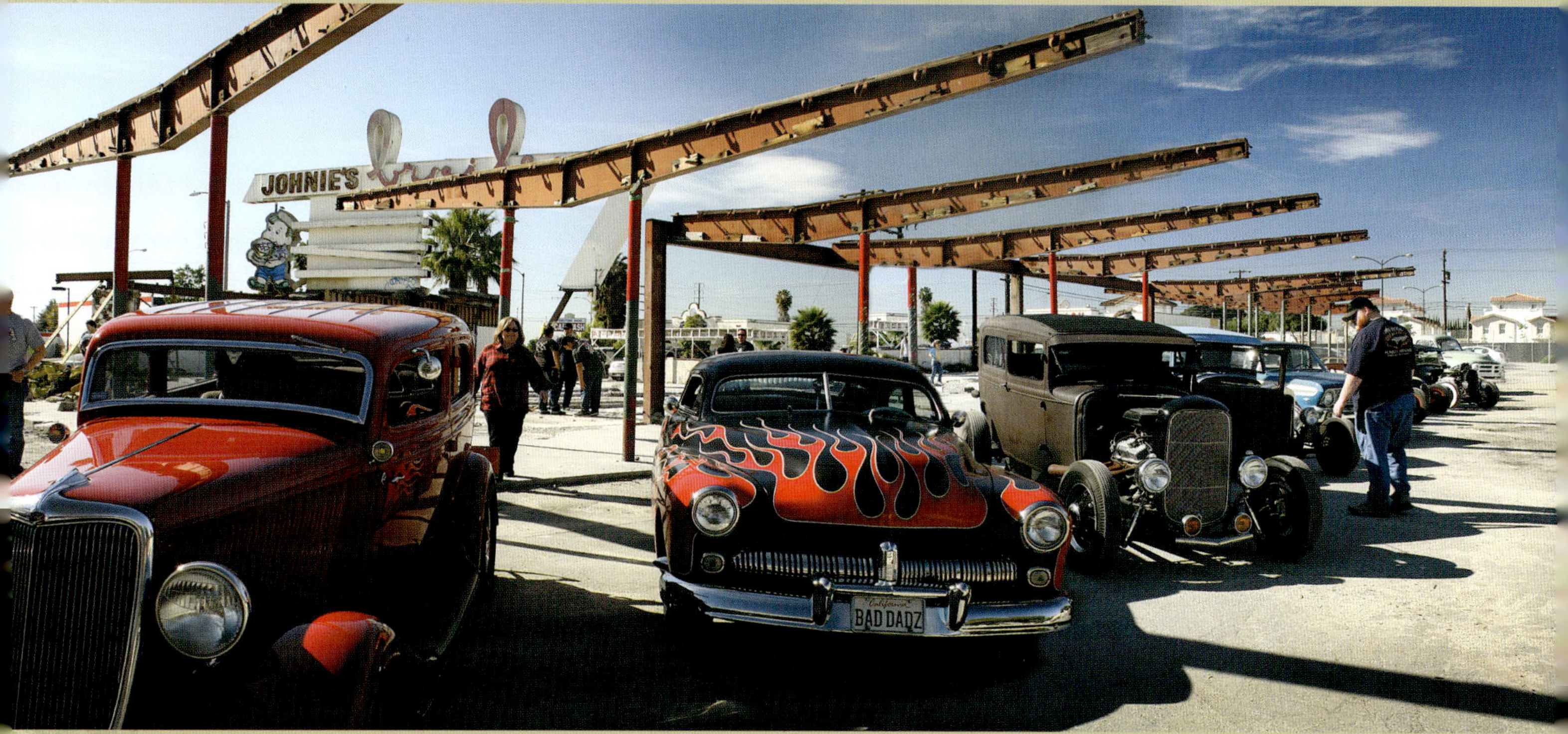
JOHNIE'S
BAD DADZ

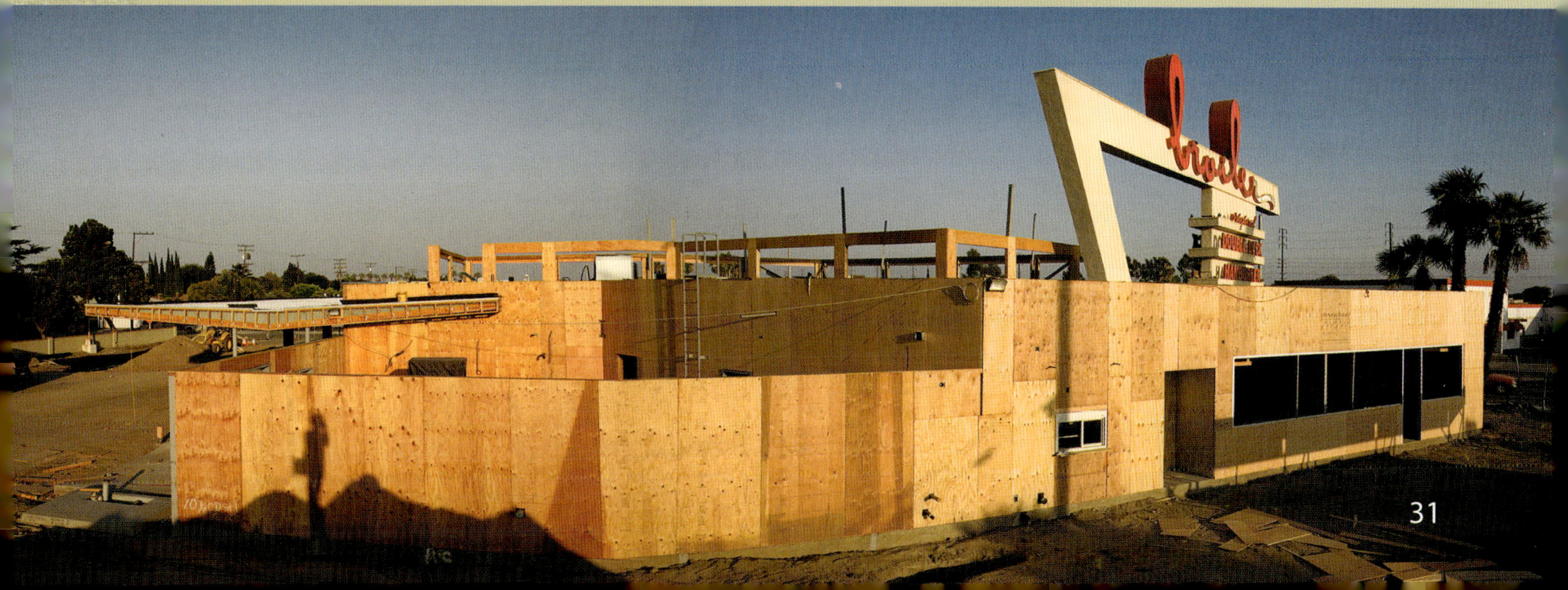

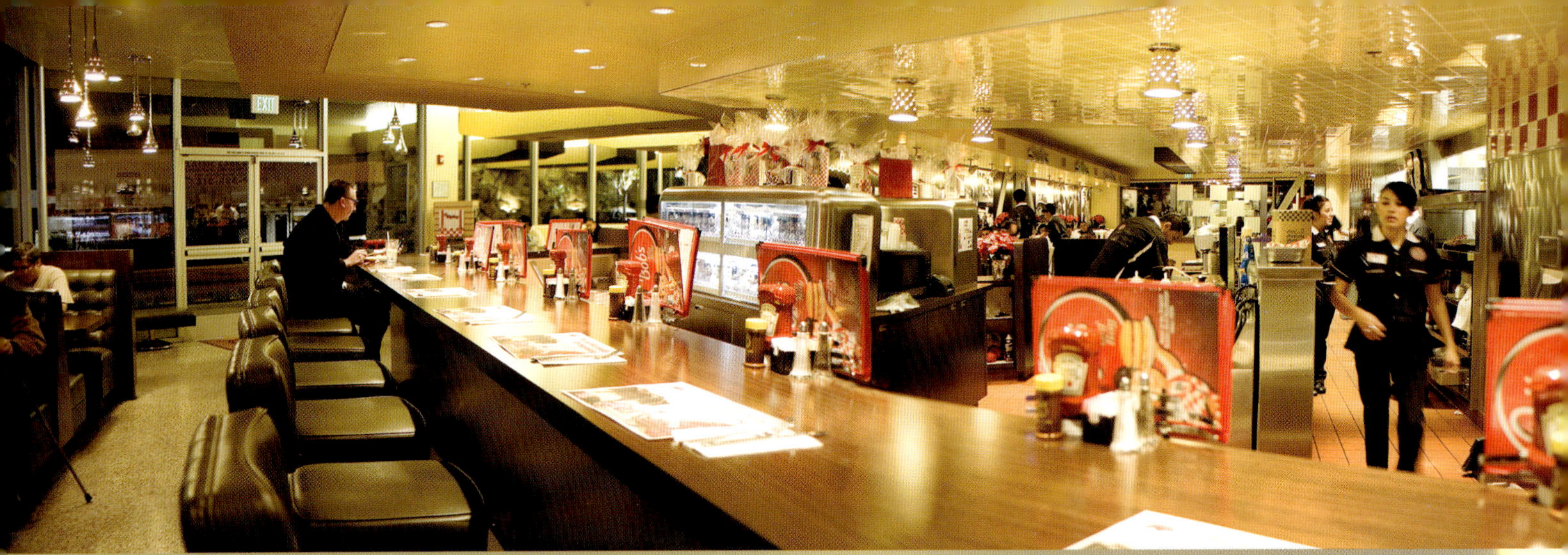

Above: Inside the new Bob's, the counter, windows, and terrazzo floor follows the spirit of the original Broiler. **Below:** Beautifully restored vintage cars, customs, and hot rods line up under the lighted car canopy on cruise nights. **Top right:** Along the 60-foot wall is a photo mural that highlights historic photos of Harvey's and Bob's Big Boy. **Bottom right:** Back when it was Harvey's, this area was part of the original kitchen. Now it is an open dining area dubbed the "Starlite Polar Lounge."

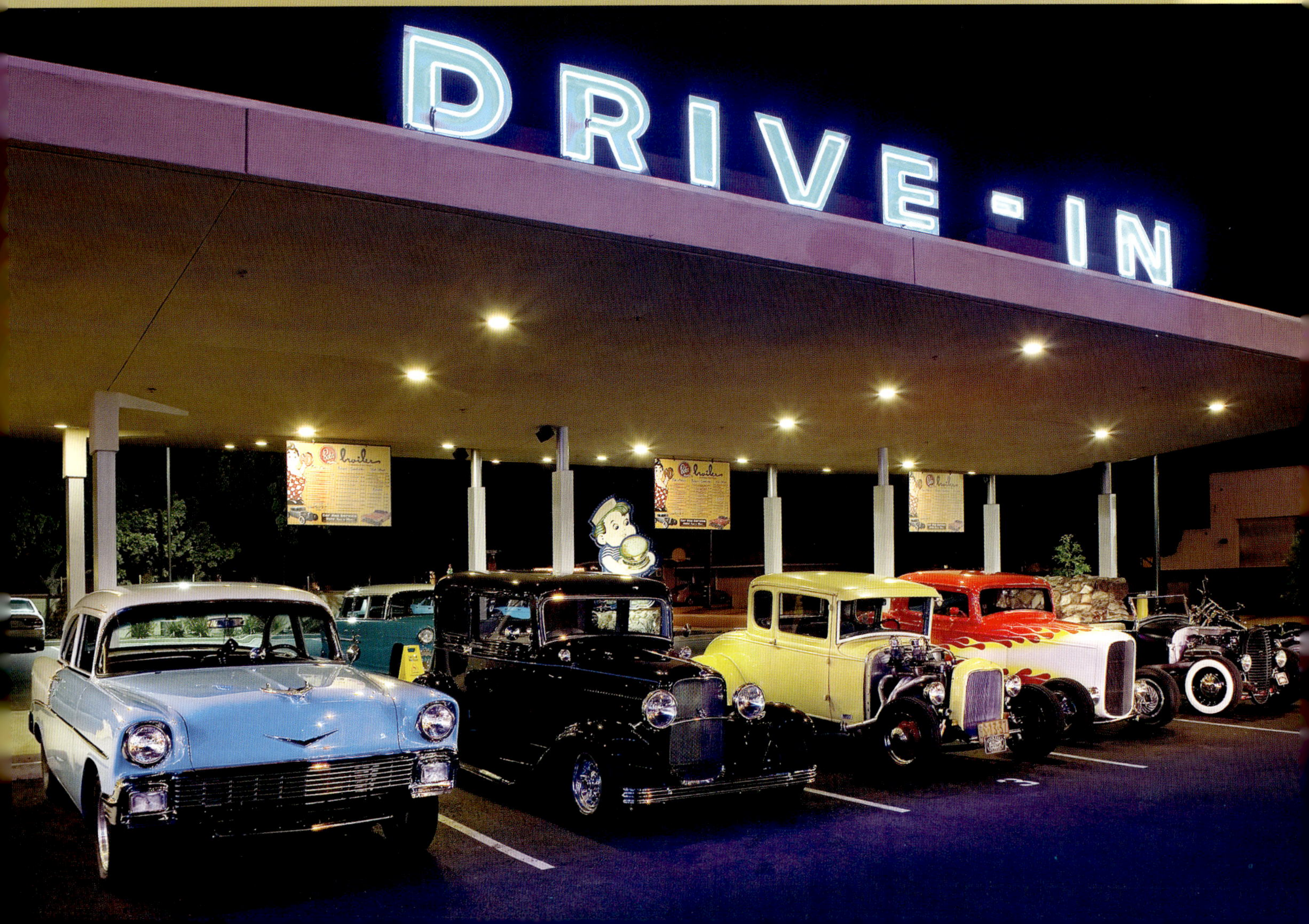

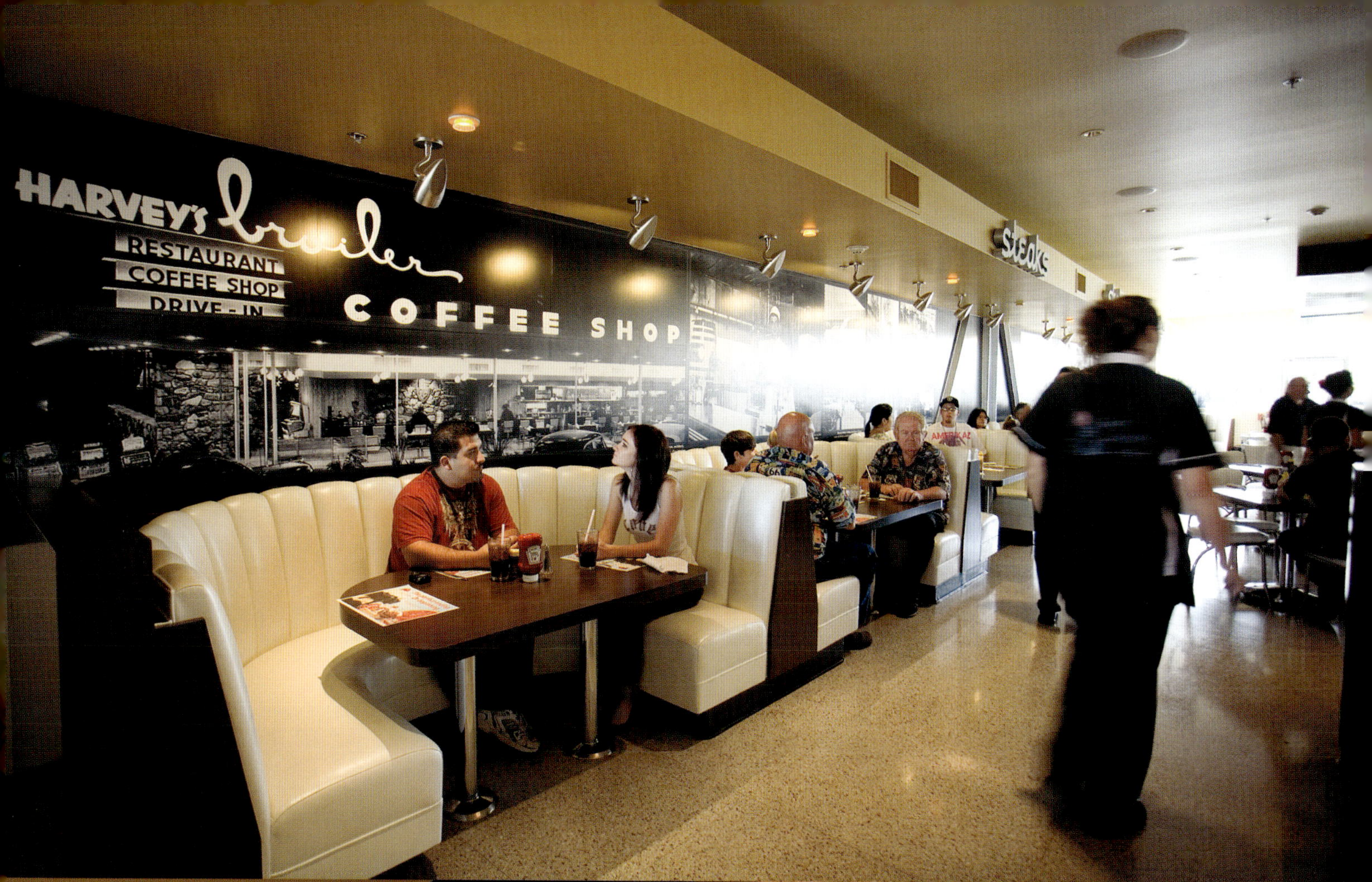
HARVEY'S broiler
RESTAURANT
COFFEE SHOP
DRIVE-IN
COFFEE SHOP
steaks

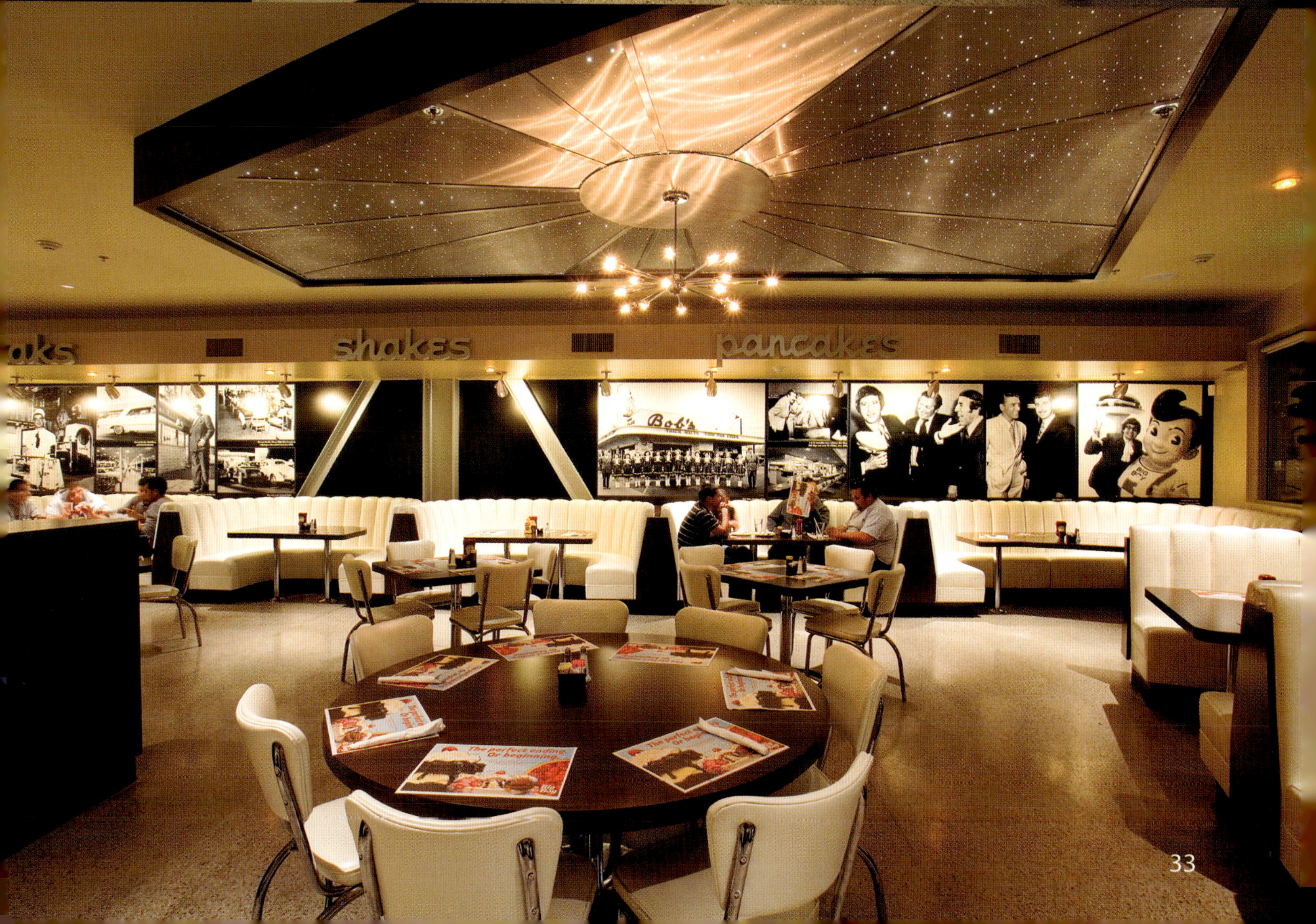
shakes
pancakes
Bob's

BONO'S ORANGE

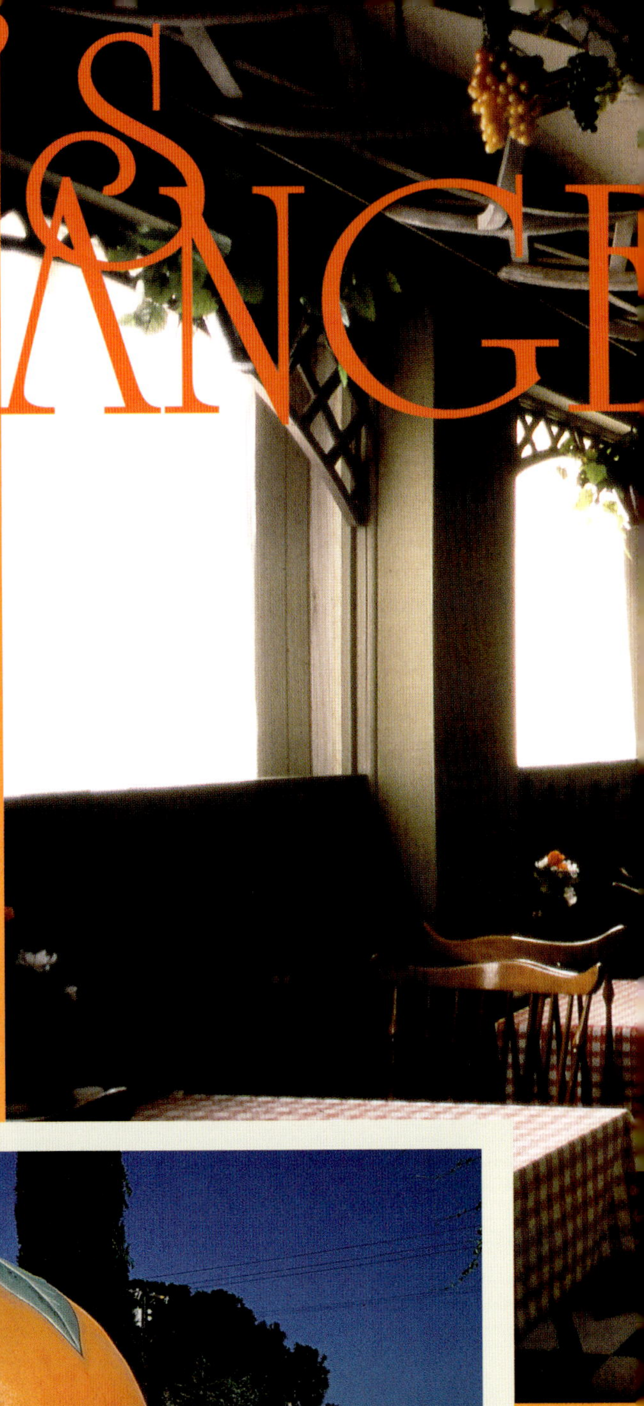

Bono's Orange Stand
15395 Foothill Boulevard, Fontana

The railroad reached Los Angeles in 1885. Many Easterners bought their tickets along with land options. A railroad advertisement read: "California, the Cornucopia of the World. 43,795,000 acres of government land untaken. Railroad & private land for a million farmers. A climate for health & wealth without Cyclones or Blizzards." More settlers came to California for land than the Gold Rush and soon orange groves spread throughout the state. Frank E. Pohl started a chain of orange juice stands in a giant programmatic orange structure in 1926. Along Route 66, the Bono's had an orange stand in addition to Bono's original 66 Restaurant. The first owner's son is a cousin to Sonny Bono, the songsmith genius behind Sonny & Cher. Years ago, when we were taking pictures by the orange stand, Mr. Bono showed us his restaurant. Even though it had already closed, it appeared to be completely intact and ready to serve their next meal. This orange stand and restaurant is just west of the Wigwam Motel, another famous milestone on the Mother Road.

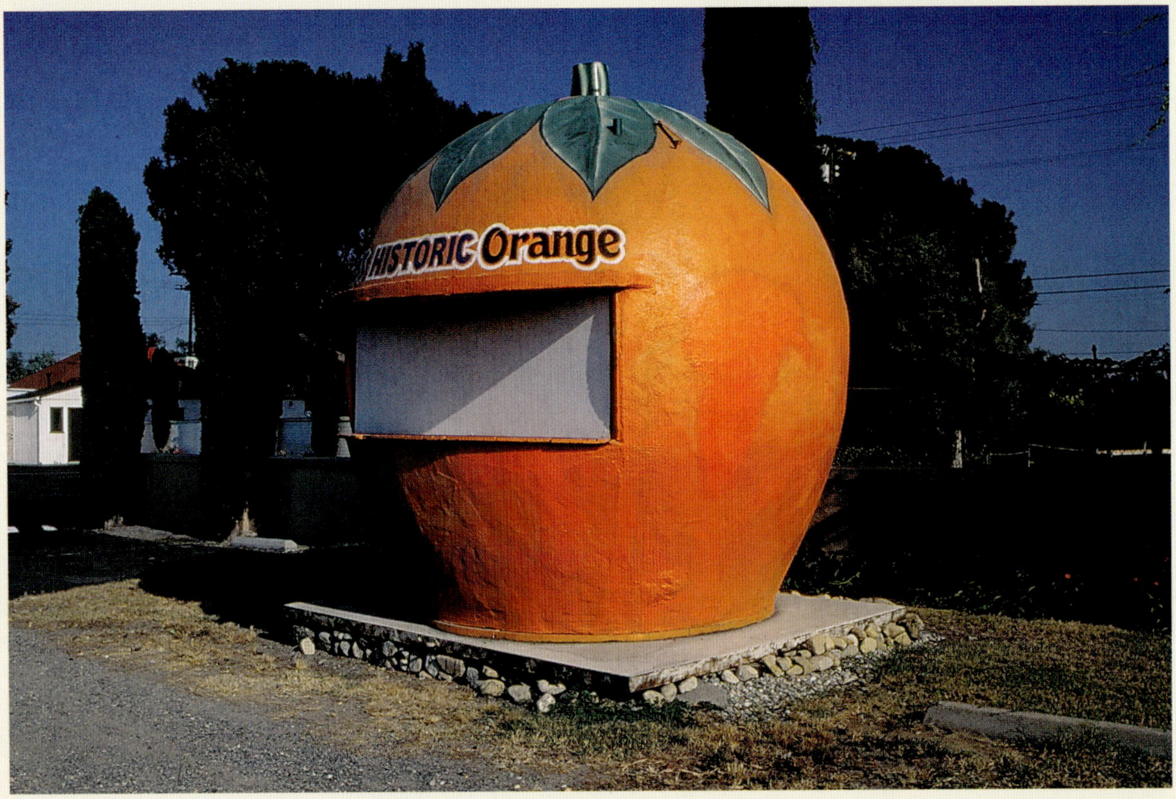

One of the original Bono Juice Stands still sits along Historic Route 66.

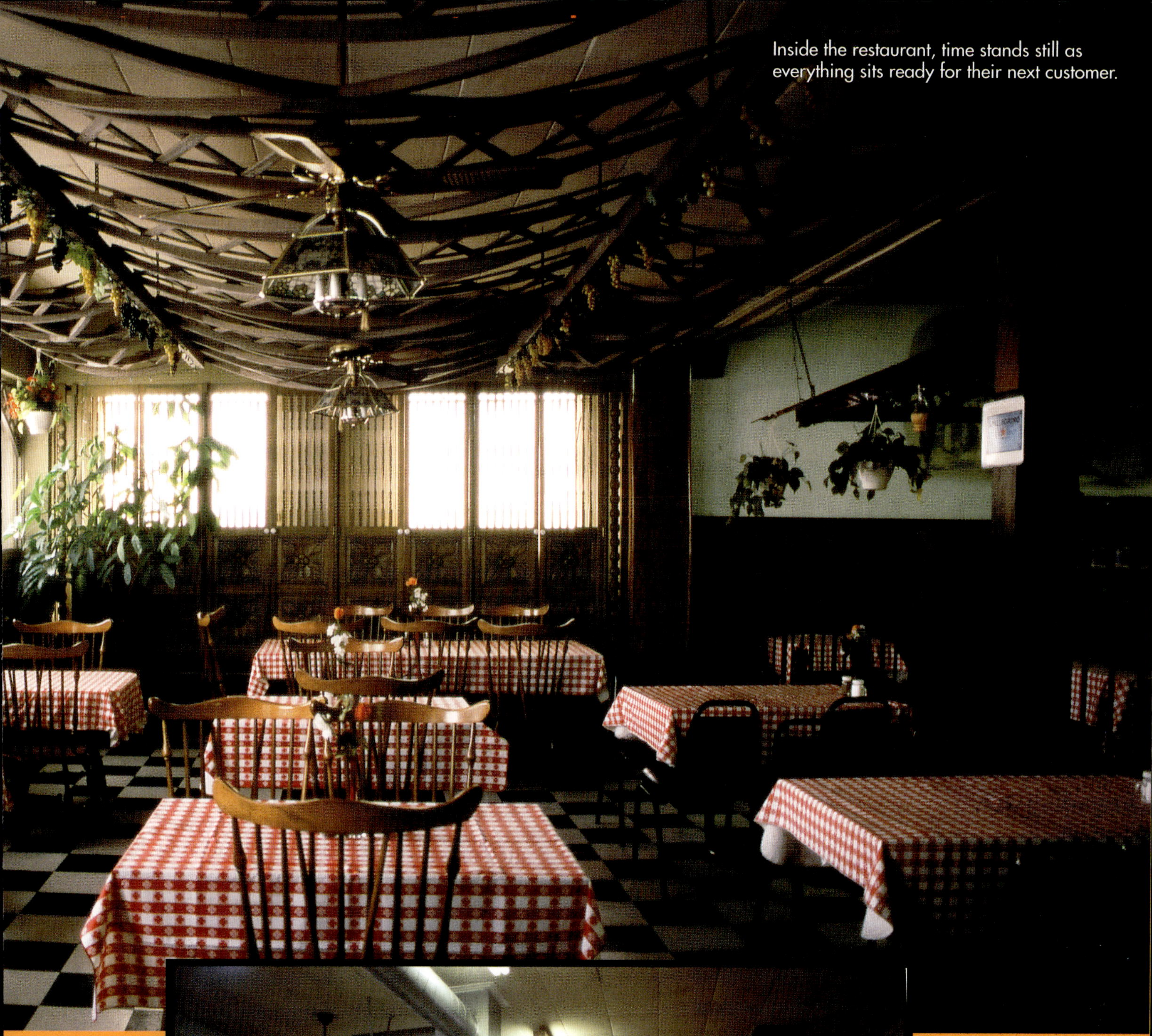

Inside the restaurant, time stands still as everything sits ready for their next customer.

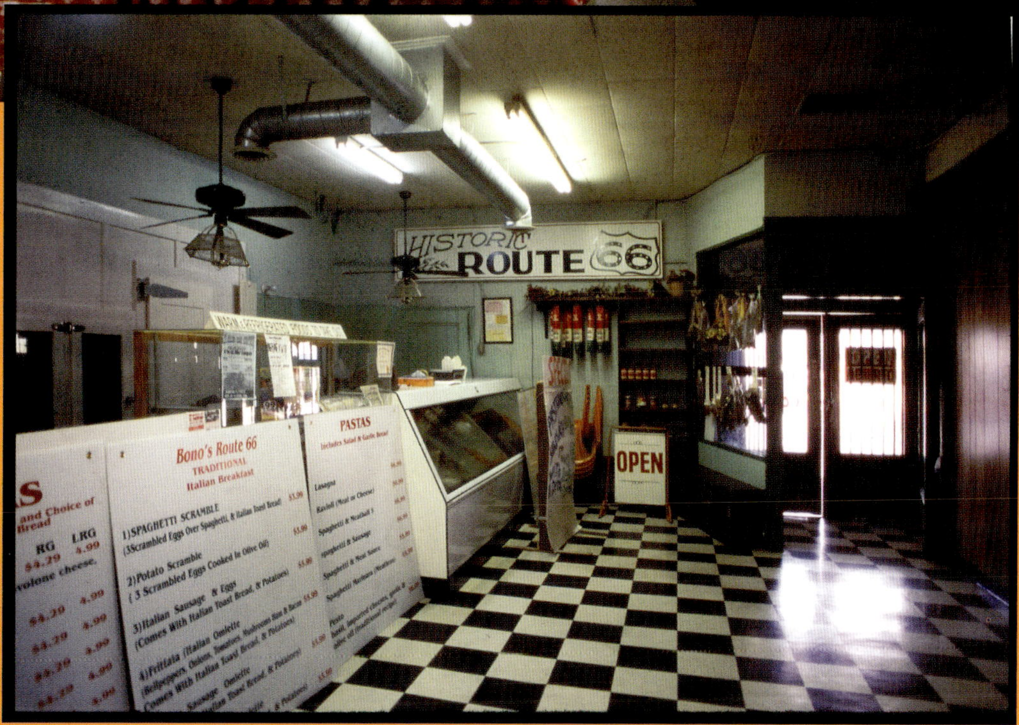

The lobby to the restaurant used to serve as their delicatessen. We felt both excited and sad when Mr. Bono gave us a personal tour of his restaurant and spotless kitchen.

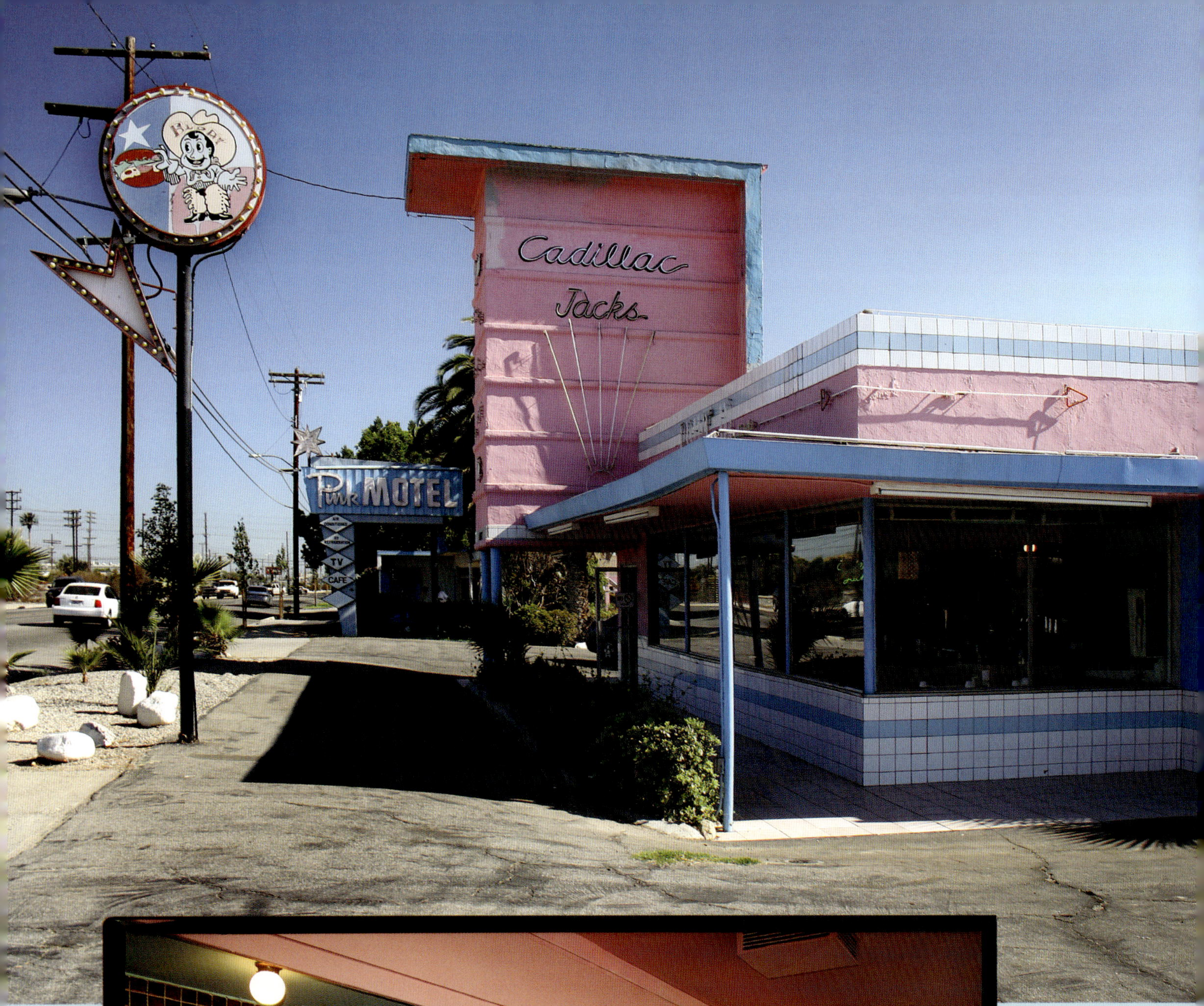
Cadillac
Jacks
Pink MOTEL
TV
CAFE

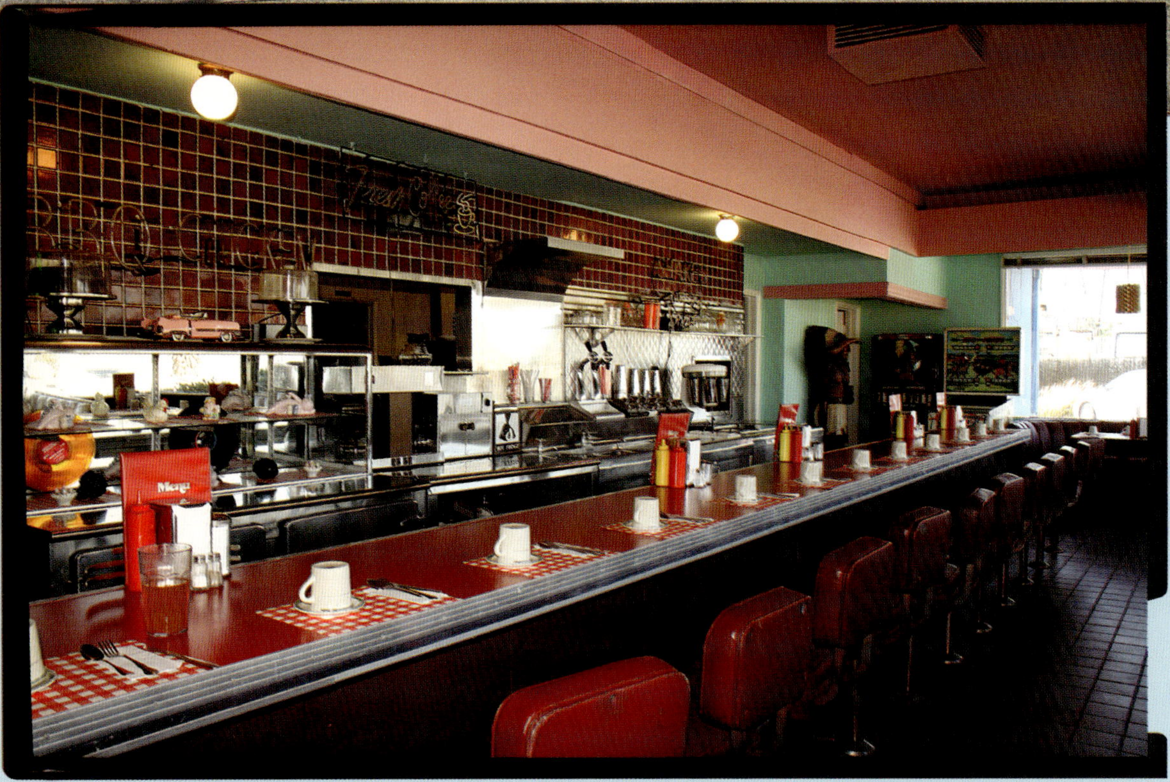
Menu

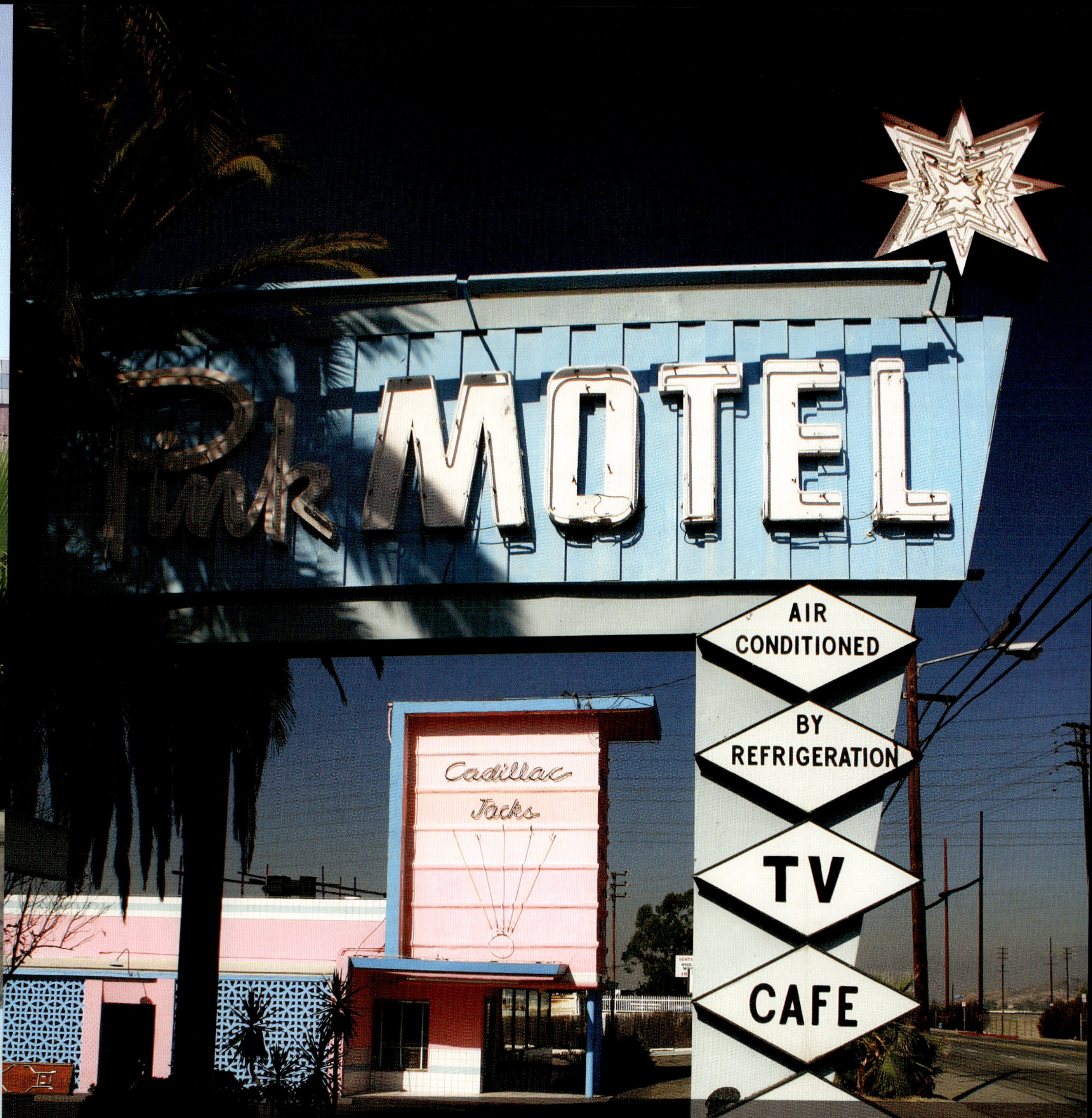

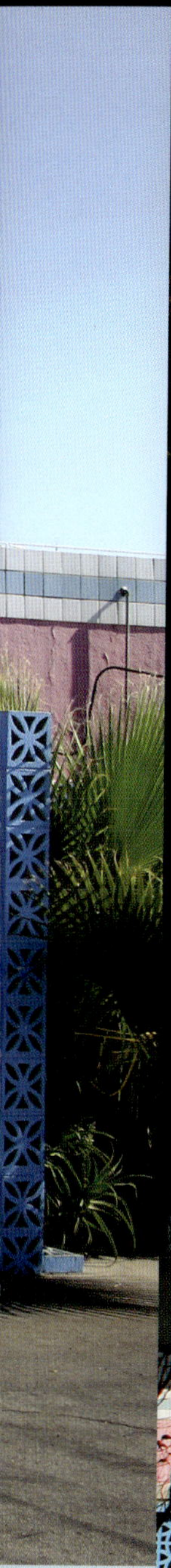

CADILLAC JACK'S PINK CAFE & PINK MOTEL

9475 San Fernando Road, Sun Valley

Before the Interstate 5 freeway, one of the main arteries connecting L.A. and Northern California through the Grapevine Pass was San Fernando Road. For weary-eyed travelers who made it over the pass but were too tired to drive another 22 miles to Downtown L.A., there was a strip of motels and cafes that offered a place to eat and rest. One of these was the Pink Motel and Pink Cafe.

Joe Thomulka built the Pink Motel and the Pink Cafe back in 1945. He painted everything bright pink so that they would stand out from all the other roadside rest stops. The Pink Motel and Pink Cafe opened in 1946 and Joe's son Monty started washing dishes there in 1950. Nineteen short years later he was running the joint. Today, the motel still functions as a motel but Monty closed the cafe in 1989 because it was "too much work for one person." And since the cafe hosted anywhere from 50 to 60 film shoots a year, it made sense to use it exclusively as a film location. It has appeared in *Highway to Heaven*; *Murder She Wrote*; *Columbo*; *Unsolved Mysteries*; *Amazing Stories*; *Grease 2*; *House of Sand and Fog*; *The O.C.*; and *The Whole Ten Yards*, starring Bruce Willis and Matthew Perry. They also have a fleet of 55 to 60 vintage cars that they rent to the studios.

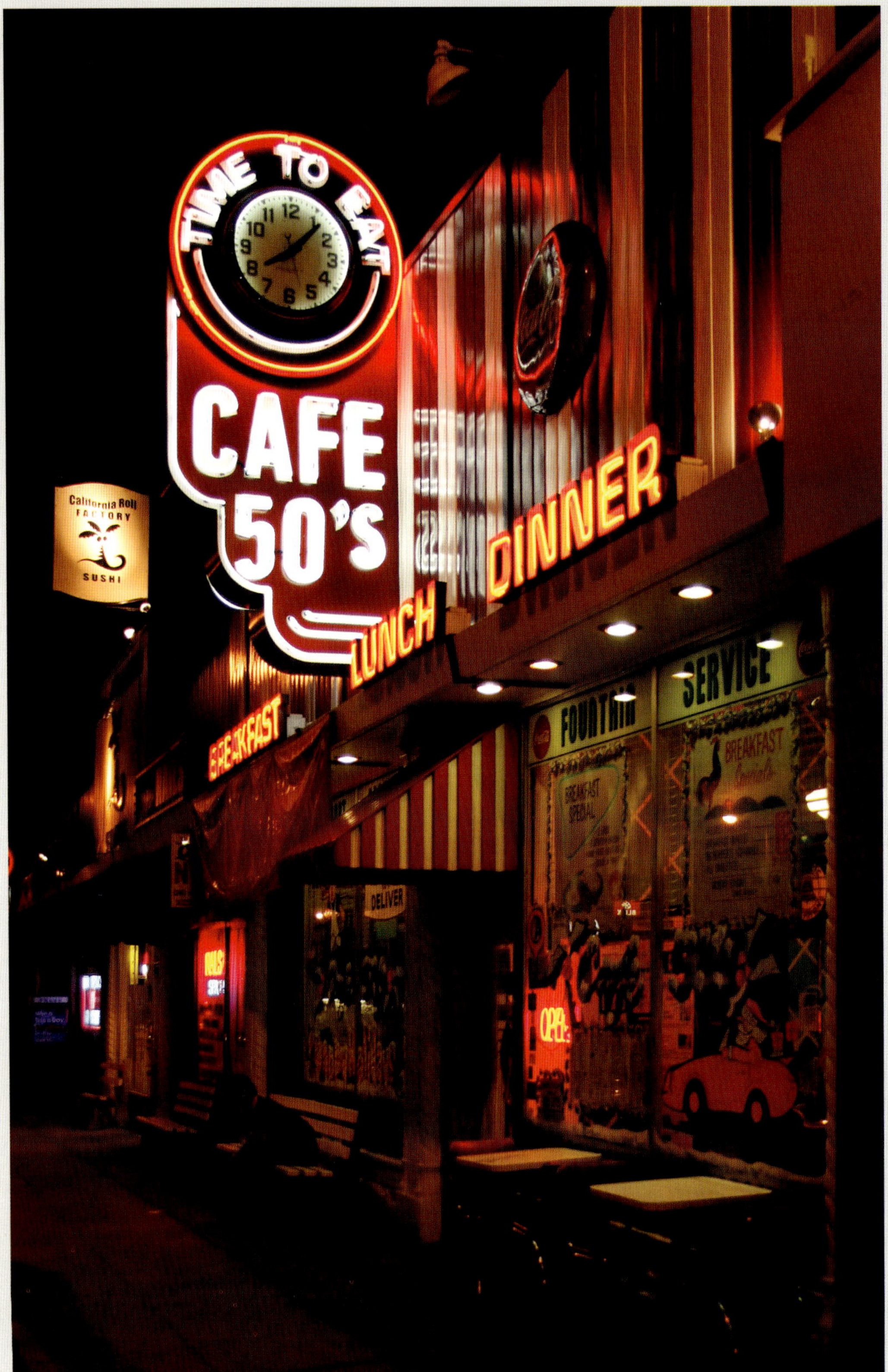
TIME TO EAT
CAFE
50's
LUNCH
DINNER
BREAKFAST
California Roll
FACTORY
SUSHI
FOUNTAIN
SERVICE
DELIVER

CAFE 50's

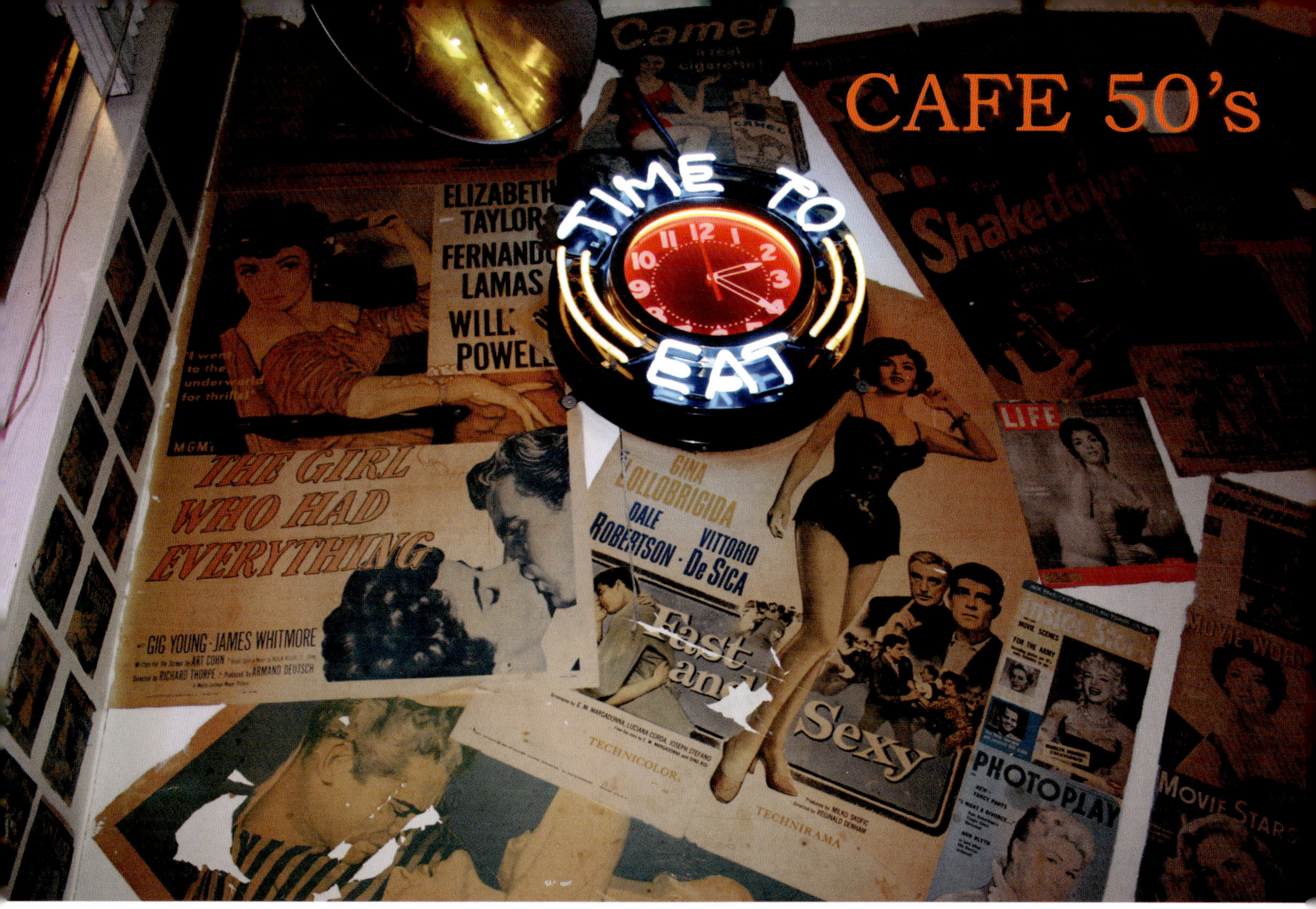

Cafe 50's

Multiple Locations

Craig Martin runs one of the most happening diners in Southern California, Cafe 50's. Inspired by movies like *American Graffiti* and *Diner*, Craig dreamed of opening an informal, '50s style cafe where folks could hang out and experience classic Americana along with a hamburger, fries, a malt...and, of course, a healthy dose of rock-and-roll. The first Cafe 50's was such a hit that he and his partners opened several more throughout the Southland. Our favorite is the one on Santa Monica Boulevard. Decked out with a jukebox, soda fountain, and lunch counter, you can order everything from a burger to freshly baked apple pie. B-movie movie posters cover every inch of wall space, from *Creature From the Black Lagoon* to Marilyn Monroe and Elvis. The visual assault continues with metal signs, vending machines, toys, cereal boxes, and baseball pennants. An authentic 1955 Muntz TV mounted near the ceiling runs *I Love Lucy* episodes 'round the clock. Ask for a vintage board game and soak in the postwar vibe while enjoying the Blue Plate Special or your own favorite comfort food. If you bring your family by on the last Wednesday of the month for Pajama Night...and you show up in traditional PJs, you eat for FREE!

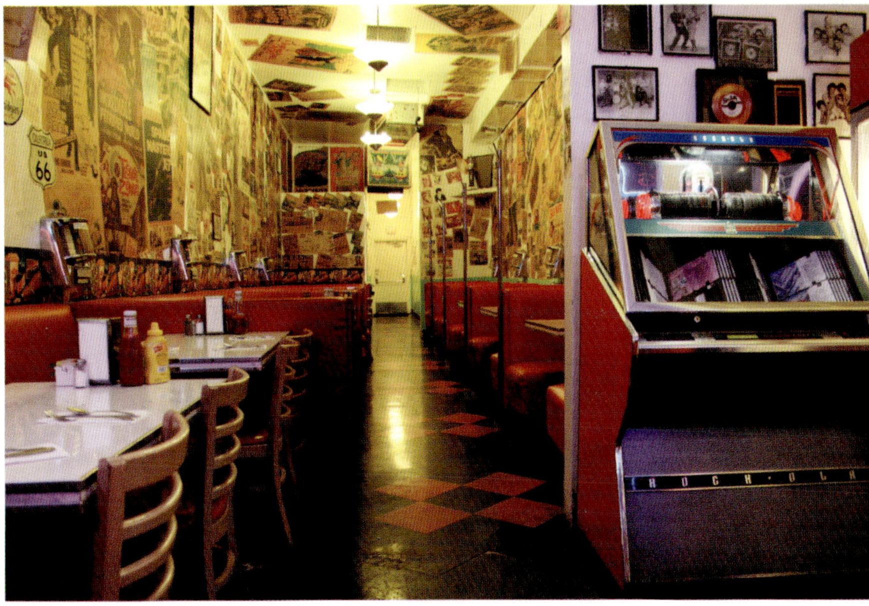

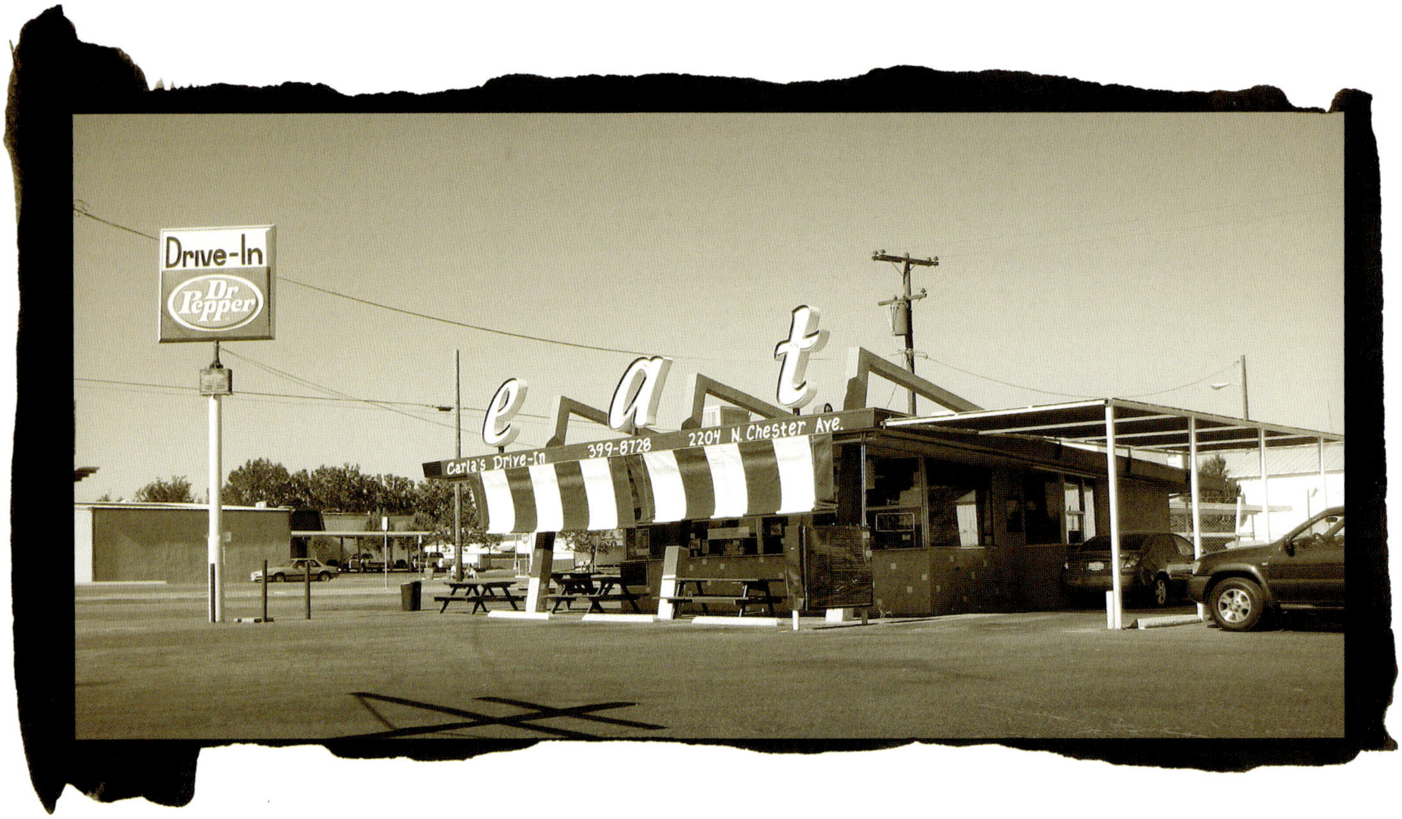

Carla's Drive-In

2204 N. Chester Avenue, Bakersfield

Carla's is a stylish and appealing '50s drive-in with a drive-thru and picnic tables. Over the years it has remained pretty much unmodified, except for much needed and tasteful sunshades. Carla's original neon sign is made of wood, not metal, and though it's starting to separate and some of the neon tubes are broken, it still spells out "e-a-t." Looks to be the same '50s vintage as Andre's Drive-In at the other end of town. We spoke to the nice Asian owner who told us that there is a picture of his drive-in on eBay. When we looked it up, we found a mediocre picture of Carla's with *no bids*...yet.

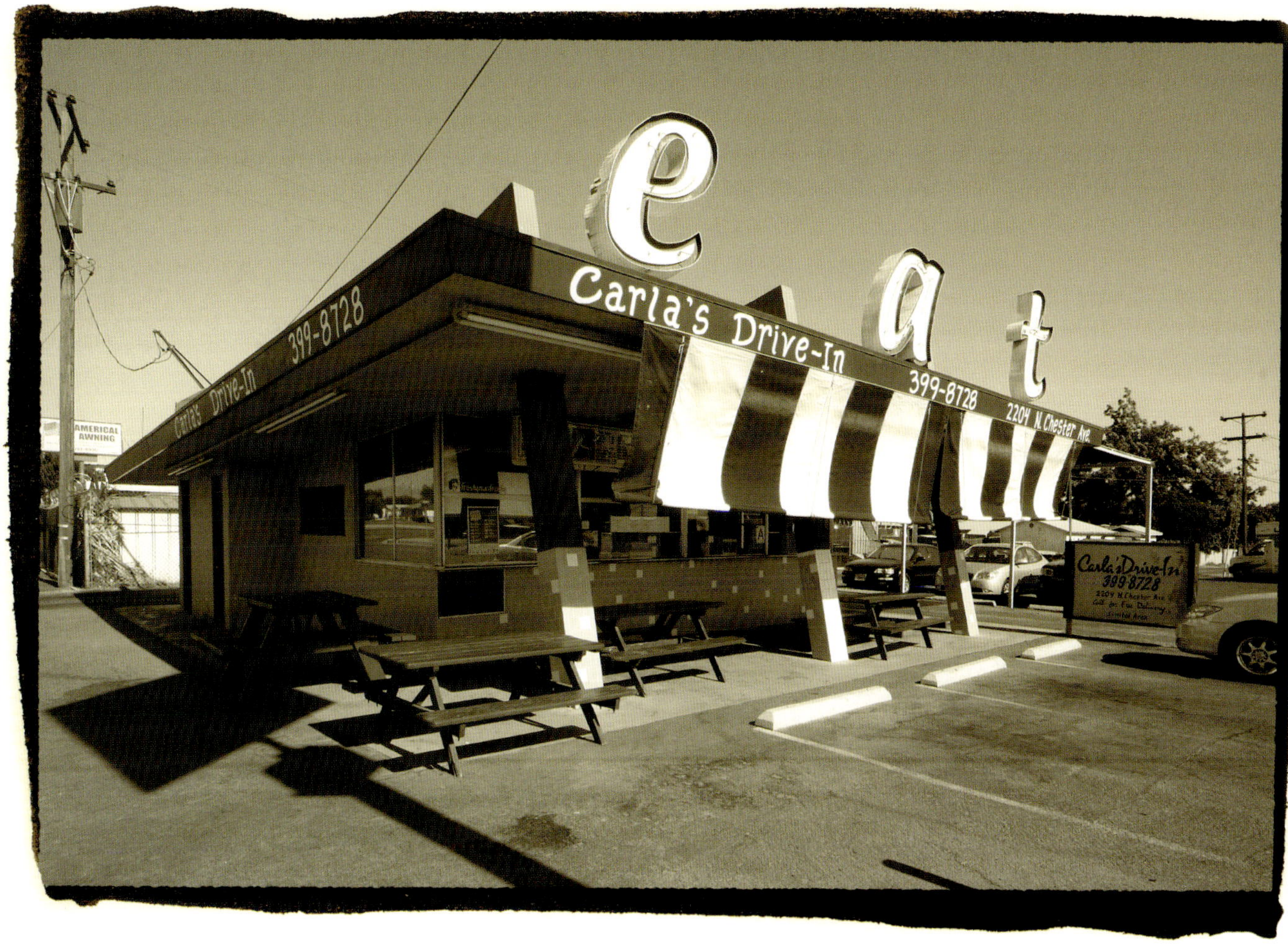
eat
Carla's Drive-In
399-8728
2204 N. Chester Ave.
Carla's Drive-In
399-8728
Carla's Drive-In
399-8728
2204 N. Chester Ave.

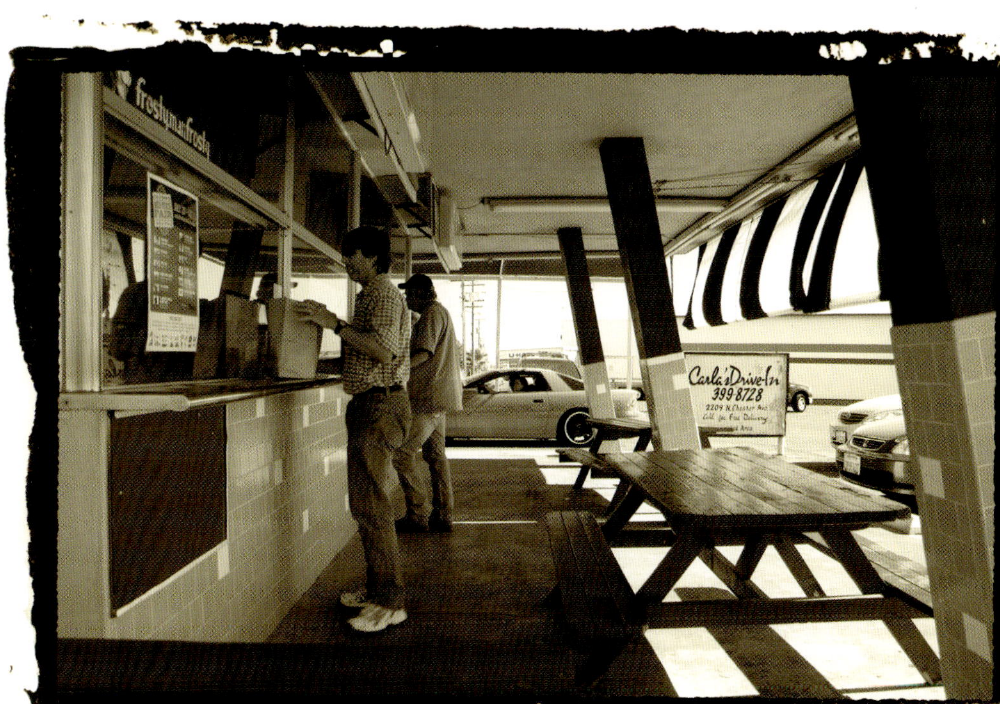
Carla's Drive-In
399-8728
2204 N. Chester Ave.

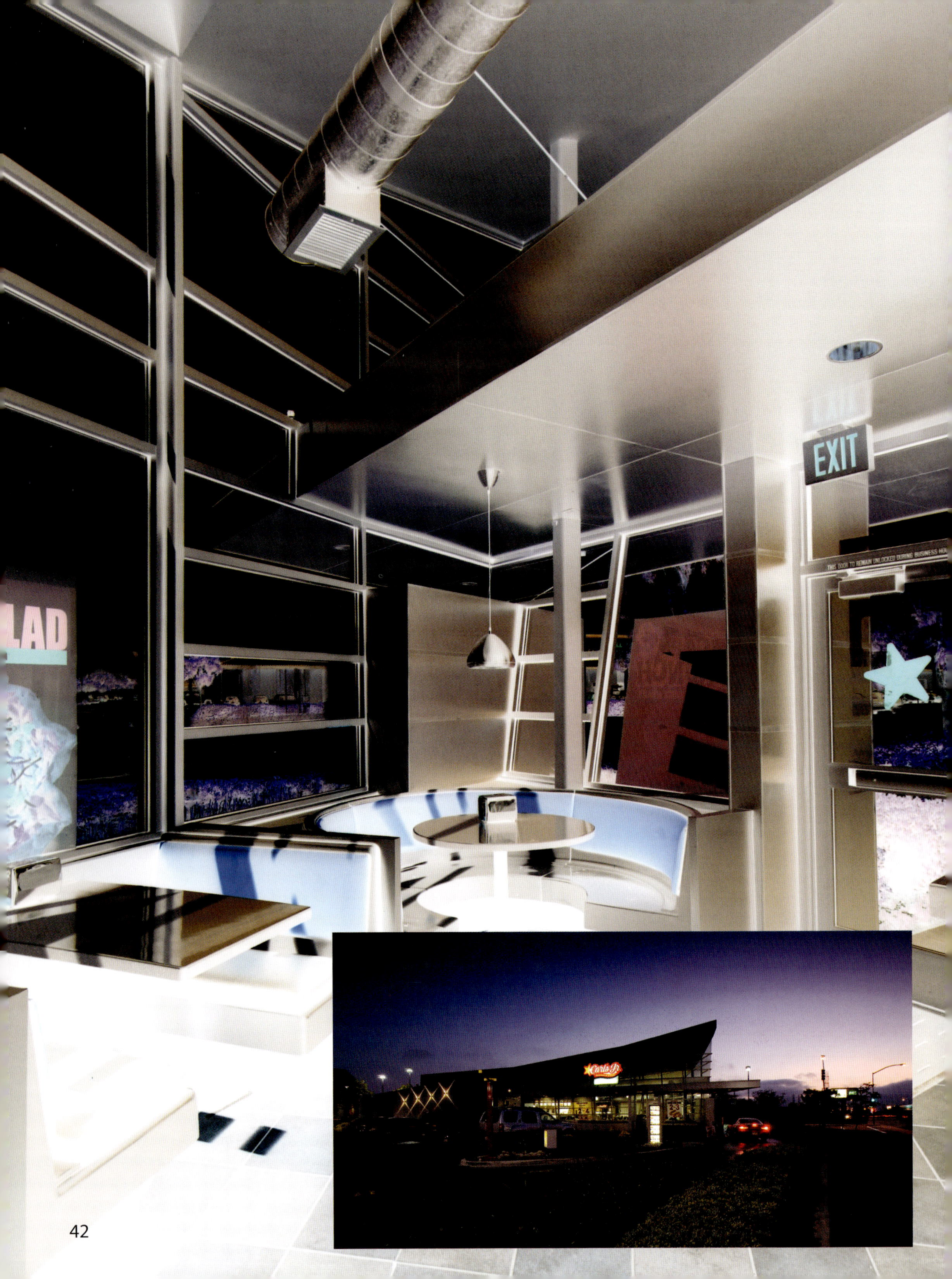
LAD
EXIT
Carl's Jr.

Carl's Jr.

Multiple Locations
7200 Firestone Boulevard, Downey

This bold and unapologetic structure surprised us when we first passed it on one of our many treks to Johnie's Broiler. Its Googie inspirations were immediately obvious. We couldn't wait for the grand opening of this "Milennium Carl's Jr." dubbed "Prototype M." This award-winning test unit designed by Rothenberg Sawasy Architects met a number of creative challenges. The environmentally friendly building incorporates curving elements, semi-circular booths, and industrial finishes, all lit by an overhead skylight. Since drive-in service makes up nearly half of Carl's restaurant business, the drive-in was located at the front. The same great service and menu is packaged in a triangular glass box. Quite a style shift, thinking back to vintage 1970s Carl's brown and orange color schemes and mansard roofs! Carl's is now the 11th largest sandwich chain in the US, a testament to Ohio founder Carl Karcher.

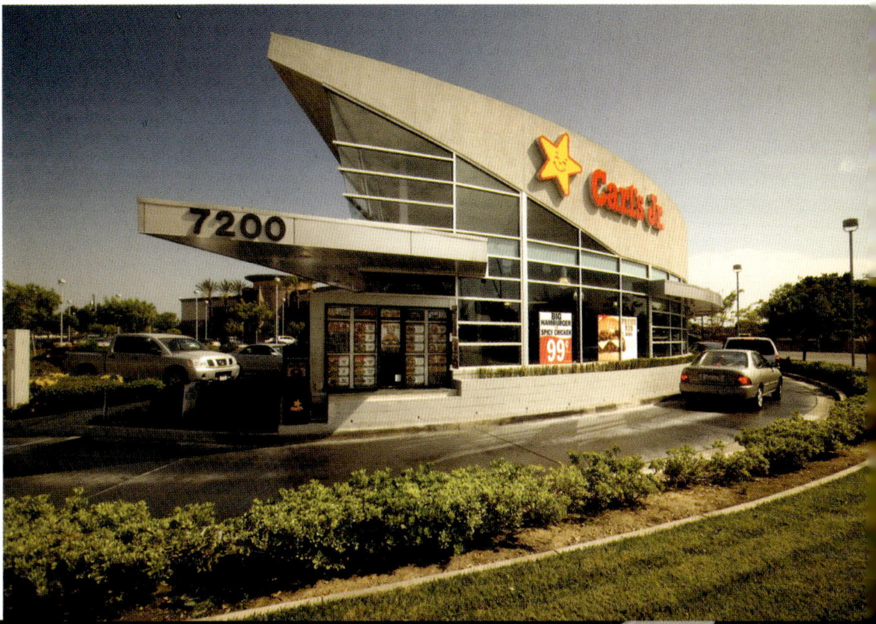

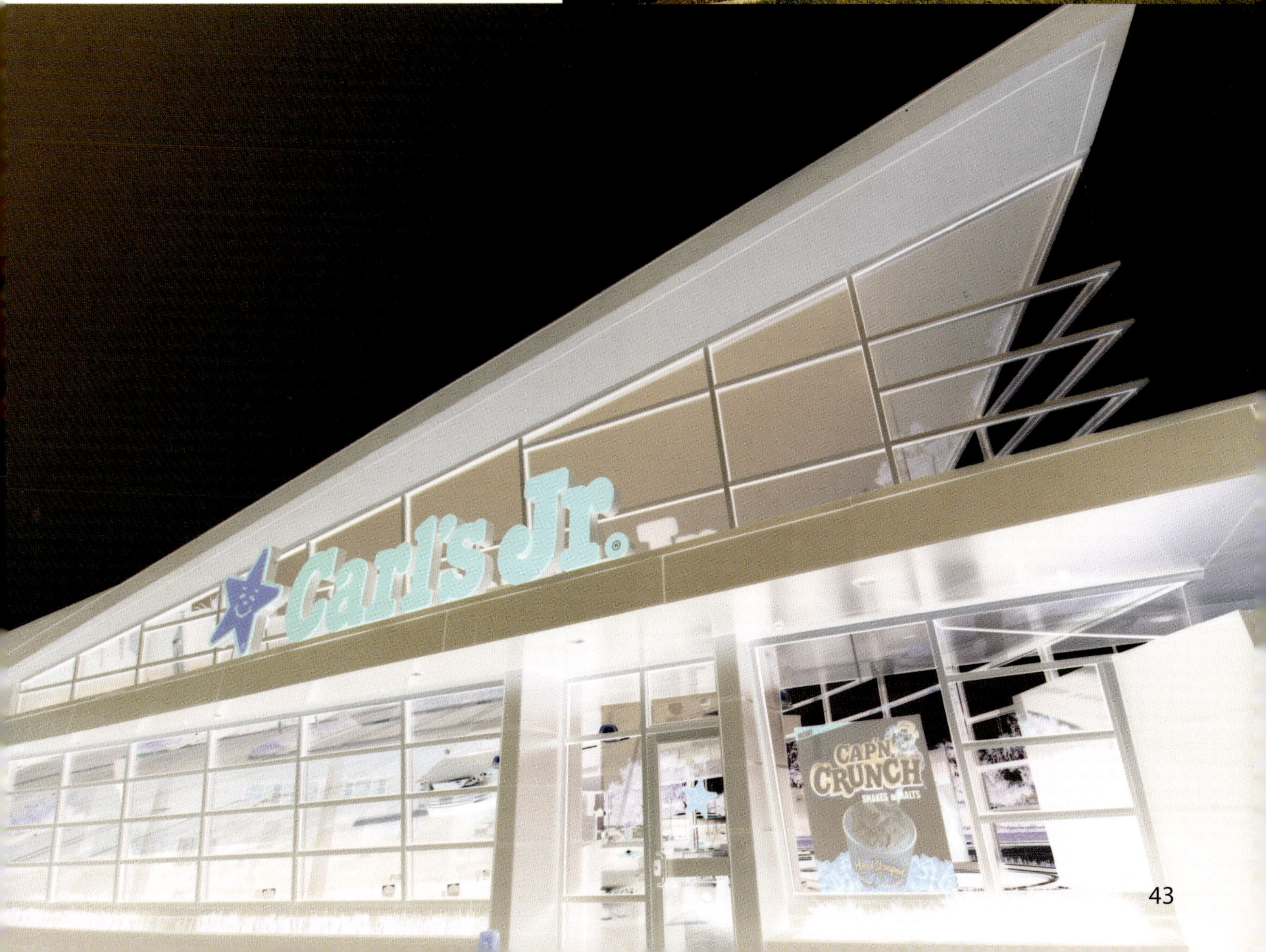

CASA CALDERON

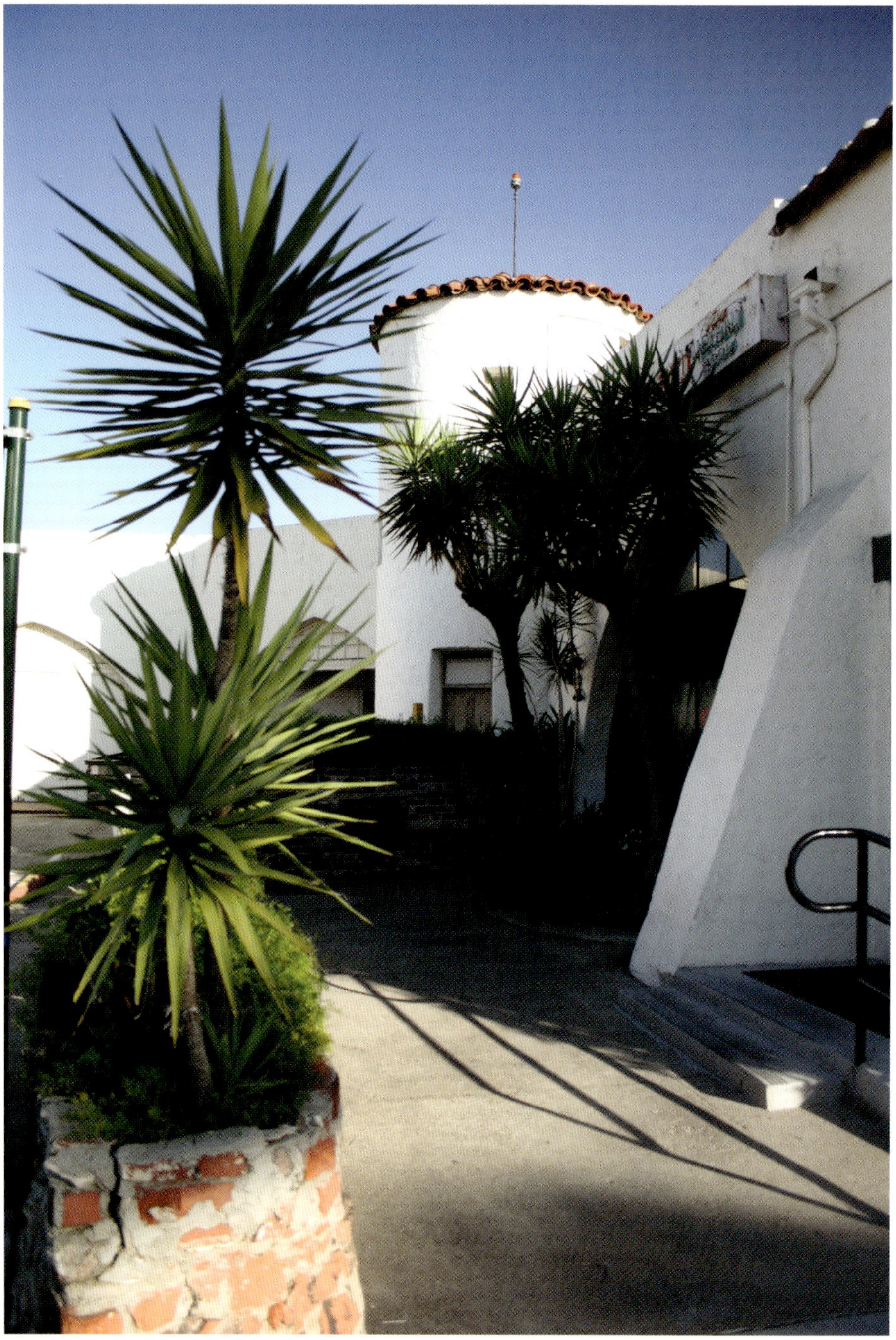

622 W. Las Tunas Drive, San Gabriel

This Mexican restaurant operating out of a quaint Spanish building (circa 1920s) fits Old San Gabriel like a glove. Nothing fancy, just a warm and inviting atmosphere where everyone is made to feel at home. Hot, homemade chips and salsa are delivered to your table by owner Linda whose albondigas soup and carne asada or "wet burrito" are to die for. After lunch, we headed over to the San Gabriel Mission District for an afternoon stroll through historic Early California. Founded in 1771, the Mission compound includes a museum, gardens, church, and cemetery. Along with shops and a fine arts gallery, you can also visit the Ramona Museum and the legendary San Gabriel Mission Playhouse, San Gabriel's own performing arts center, which was established in 1927.

CASA ESCOBAR

Casa Escobar

2500 Wilshire Boulevard,
Santa Monica

A '50s modern building distinguished by an enormous boomerang that looks like it touched down on Wilshire Boulevard, Casa Escobar is one of those dark, hideaway restaurants we love. If you consume one of their powerful margaritas, you'll completely forget whether it's day or night. The Casa's lighting is so minimal we have never actually seen our food, but whatever we order is always tasty and satisfying. Great old school cocktail lounge and piano bar lit by brightly colored chili pepper lights. Just minutes away from the Pacific Ocean, Palisades Park, the Camera Obscura, and the terminus of Route 66 at the archway to the Santa Monica Pier.

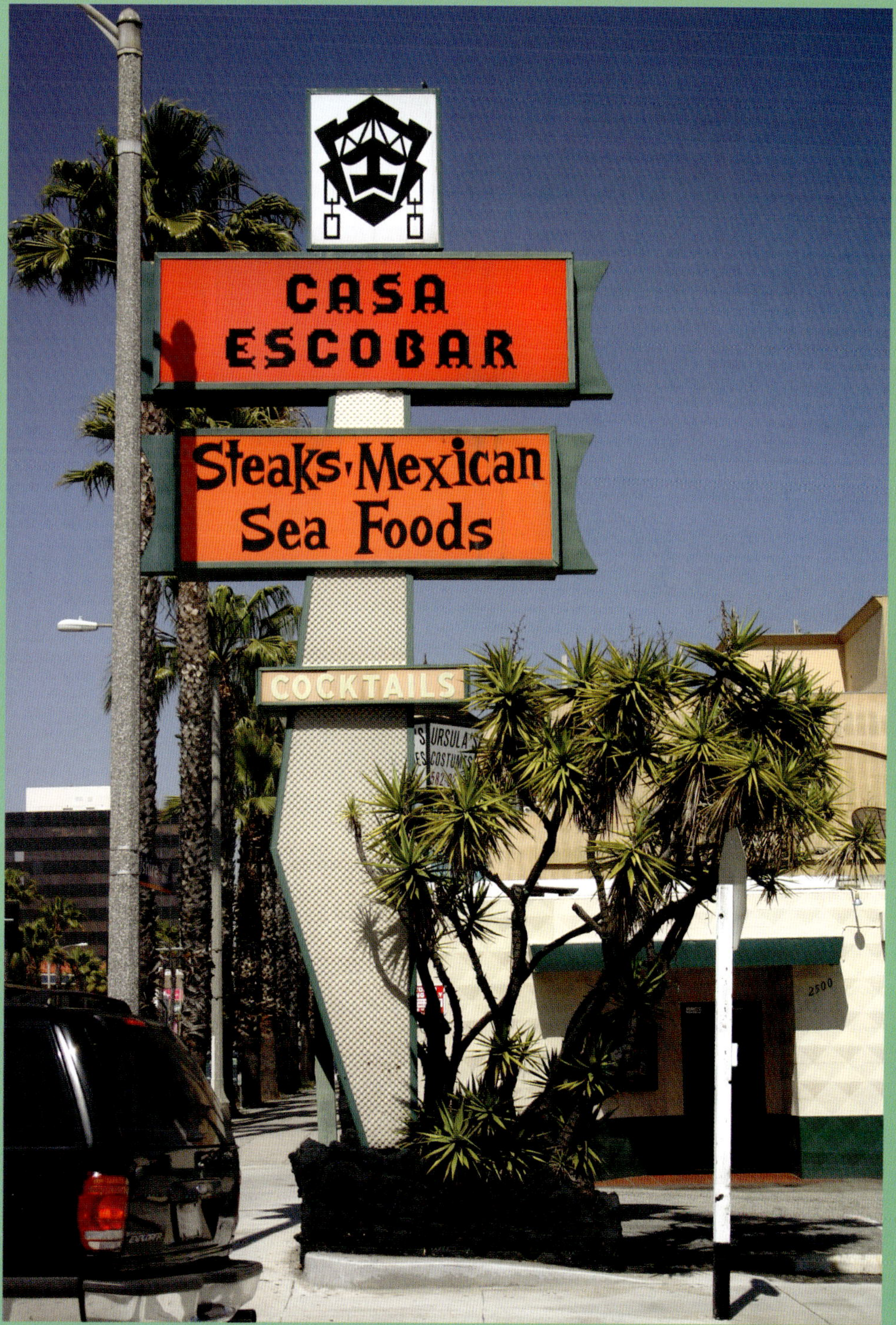

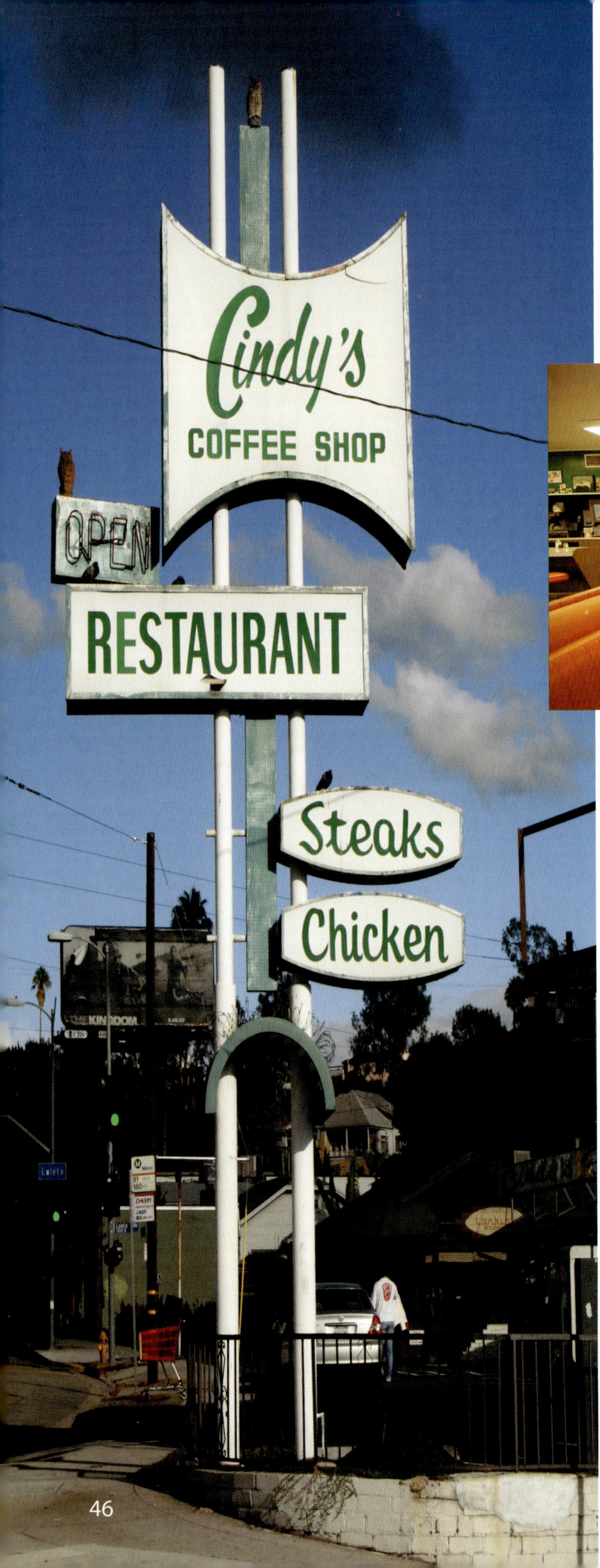

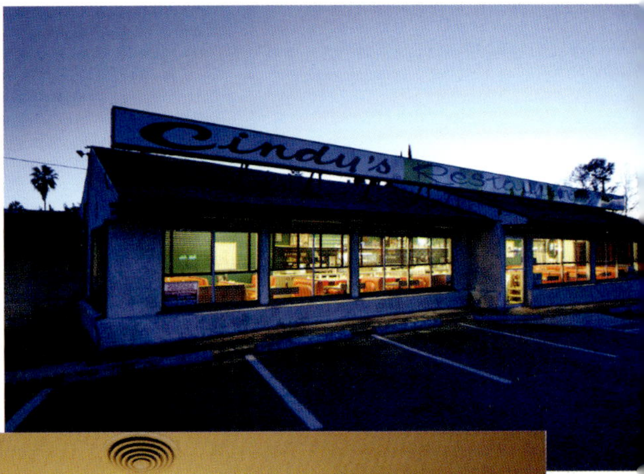

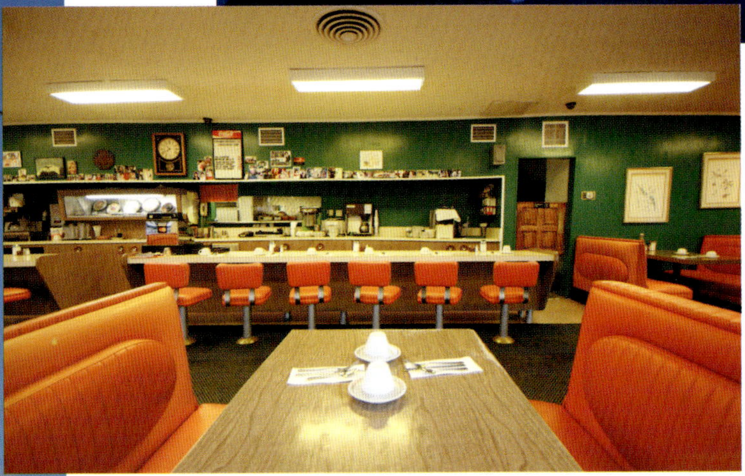

Cindy's Restaurant

1500 Colorado Boulevard, Eagle Rock

Every bit a "greasy spoon," Cindy's has a long history in Eagle Rock dating back to 1946. Back then, this lonely diner was a pleasant stop on the way to the Colorado Street Bridge and Pasadena.

In a recent brush with danger, a car went out of control in the middle of the night, plowing head first through the right side of Cindy's, demolishing dining booths and half the counter, and leaving plate glass strewn all over the front parking lot. Without skipping a beat, the wall and booths were rebuilt and within a month it was business as usual. Cindy's looks just like it did before the incident, with its bright orange vinyl booths and Formica tabletops. A convenient stopover when in the mood for a cup o' joe or a plain wrap, truck stop experience. Cindy's is frequently booked as a filming location for commercials and movie shoots.

City Hall Coffee Shop

2327 Honolulu Avenue, Montrose

The first time we stepped into City Hall, we thought we were in Kansas. The City Hall Coffee Shop thrives in Montrose, a time capsule of Americana that is now a designated historic district. The diner itself is narrow but deep and high, giving the feeling of being in a vintage Pullman dining car. Counter seats and Naugahyde booths are almost always inhabited by regulars, who seem to be sipping their coffee from mugs they brought from home. Glancing up at the walls confirms that this is true; dozens of customers" mugs are marked with their names and hung proudly from cup hooks. Everywhere else your eyes land will reveal a vintage baseball banner. This place hasn't changed in over 50 years! This is an authentic mom and pop, right down to the friendly service and rapid refill times. Don't leave Montrose without checking out Montrose Bowling Alley (circa 1936), Barru cocktail bar, and the amazing pink mosaic tile storefront of FayeRegulars ladies clothing shop.

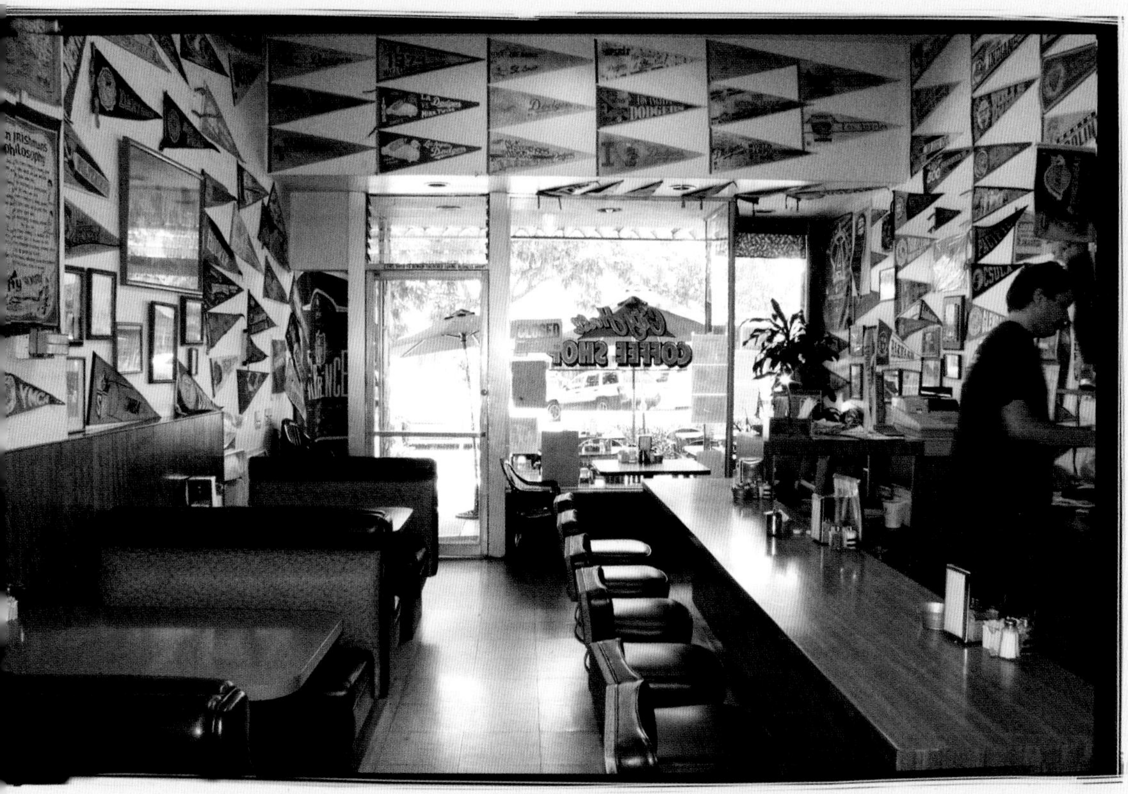

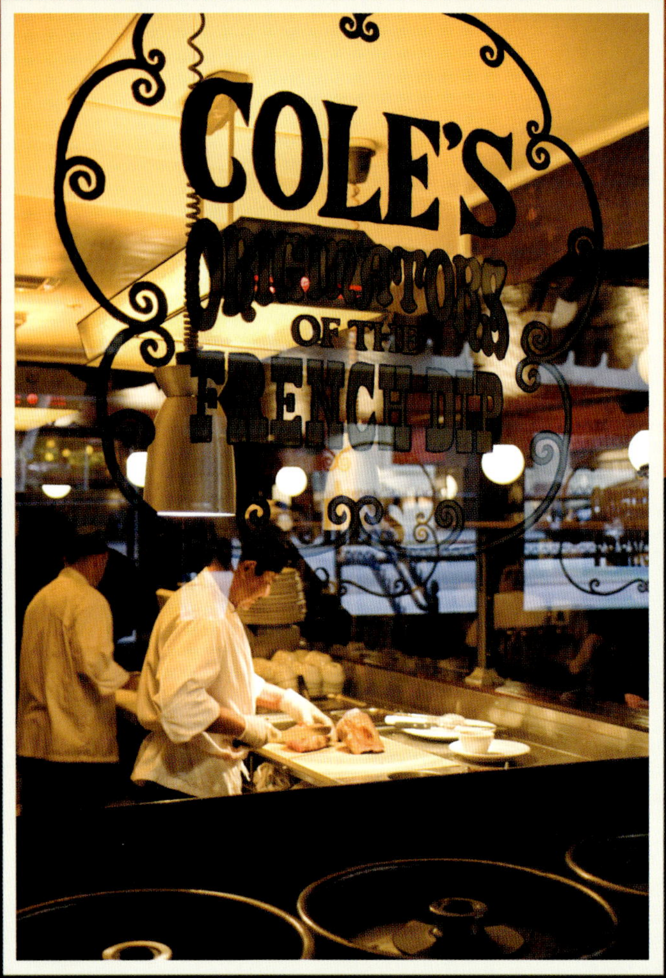

It may not seem like it here, but on a weekend evening, the wait is out the door and *shhhh, don't tell anyone, but that door in the back leads to a secret club.* After its restoration, 2009.

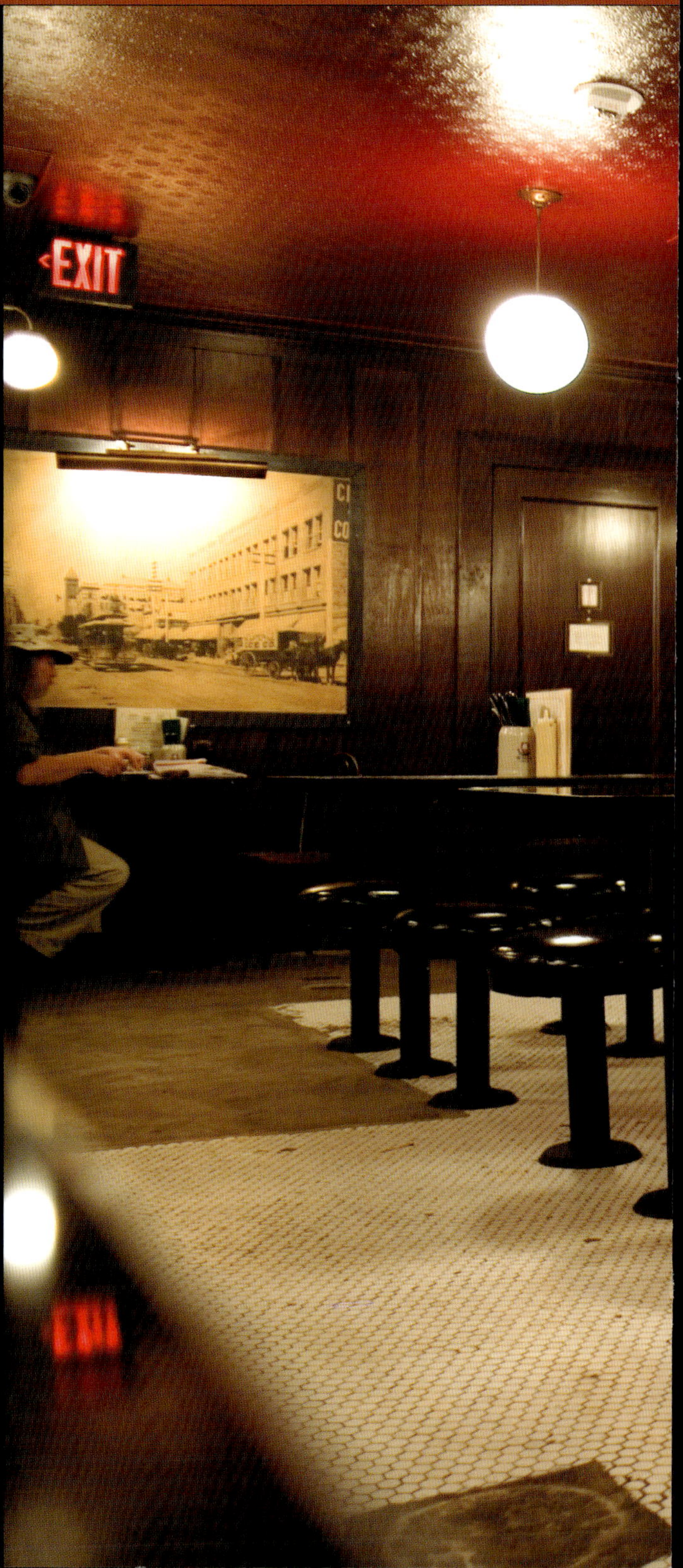

Cole's French Dip

118 E. 6th Street, Los Angeles

Because Cole's opened in 1908—the same year Philippe's opened—the debate as to which was the first French Dip restaurant in L.A. goes back a full century. Cole's is located in the Pacific Electric building, where at its peak more than 100,000 people passed through daily. This was the hub of the famous Pacific Electric Red Cars, an extensive trolley system that went from Mount Lowe all the way to the pier of Long Beach, and from Santa Monica to San Bernardino. The electric car stretched over 1,000 Los Angeles miles. The building Cole's occupies was designed by Thorton Fitzhugh in 1903 and Cole was declared Historic Cultural Monument #104 in 1972.

Cole's interior can be described as a cross between a bordello and a speakeasy. It includes a penny-tiled floor, Tiffany glass lamp shades, a 40-foot mahogany bar, historic photos (including strippers!), dark wood paneling, and blood red wallpaper. Apparently this was another favorite watering hole of gangster Mickey Cohen (the others being The Formosa and The Far East). This area of Downtown took a downward spin during the 80s and 90s but in the last half decade, the spin has slowed down and some would argue that it has reversed. In either case, new owner Cedd Moses has invested over a mil to renovate and preserve the essence of Cole's. Go see for yourself.

COLE'S *french dip*

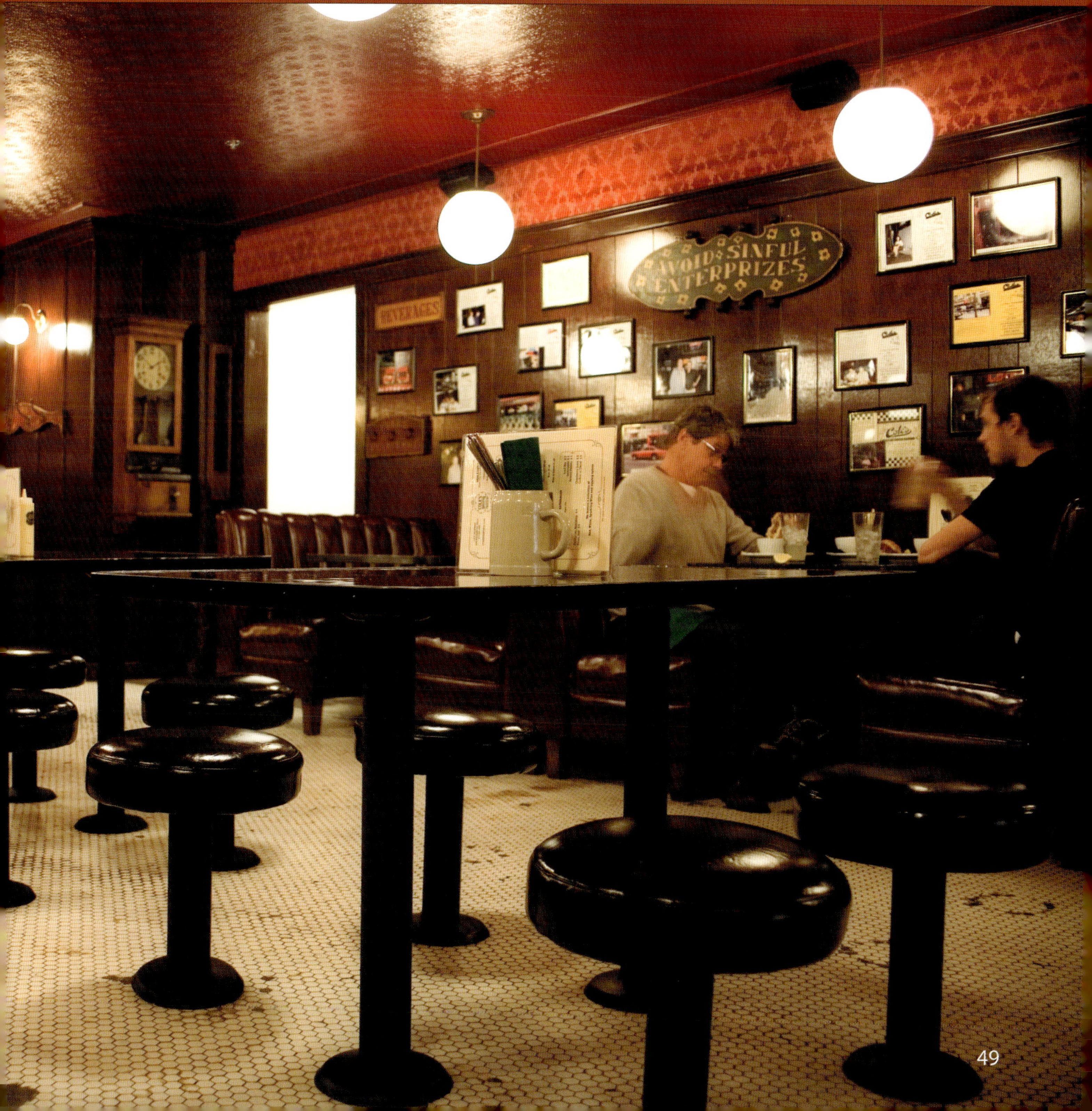

COURTESY COFFEE SHOP

800 W. Hobsonway, Blythe

You open the door to the lounge and bam! You instantly think Rat Pack, Frankie, Dino and all that…There just aren't many places left like that.

– Bruce Nellans, Palo Verde Valley Times

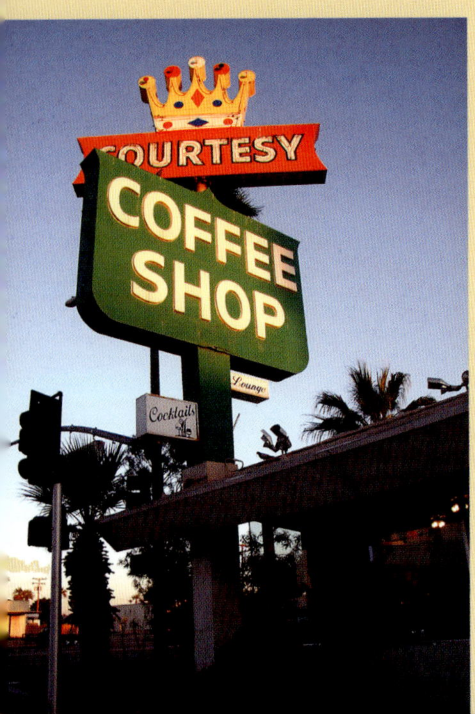

We arrived late on a hot afternoon and entered from the southwest entrance. The cocktail lounge was cool and dark but already packed. After our eyes adjusted, we were shocked at what we saw. It was 1964, sans the cigarette smoke. Walls clad in diagonal wood pattern and lava rock, red Naugahyde booths with a kazillion buttons everywhere, custom resin room dividers, and a modern bar too cool for school…we knew we had stumbled through a time warp. We picked up our jaws so we could talk to Anita Mussell, the bartender for over 20 years. She was amused at our interest and told us stories of the good old days. Later, we checked out the gift shop where we found two immense palm trees poking through the roof, bringing the outdoors in, Googie style. In the coffee shop, it quickly became clear how they earned their nickname "the fishbowl," the entire north side of the restaurant is glass. Handles on the restaurant and rest room doors were unlike anything we've ever seen. Inside

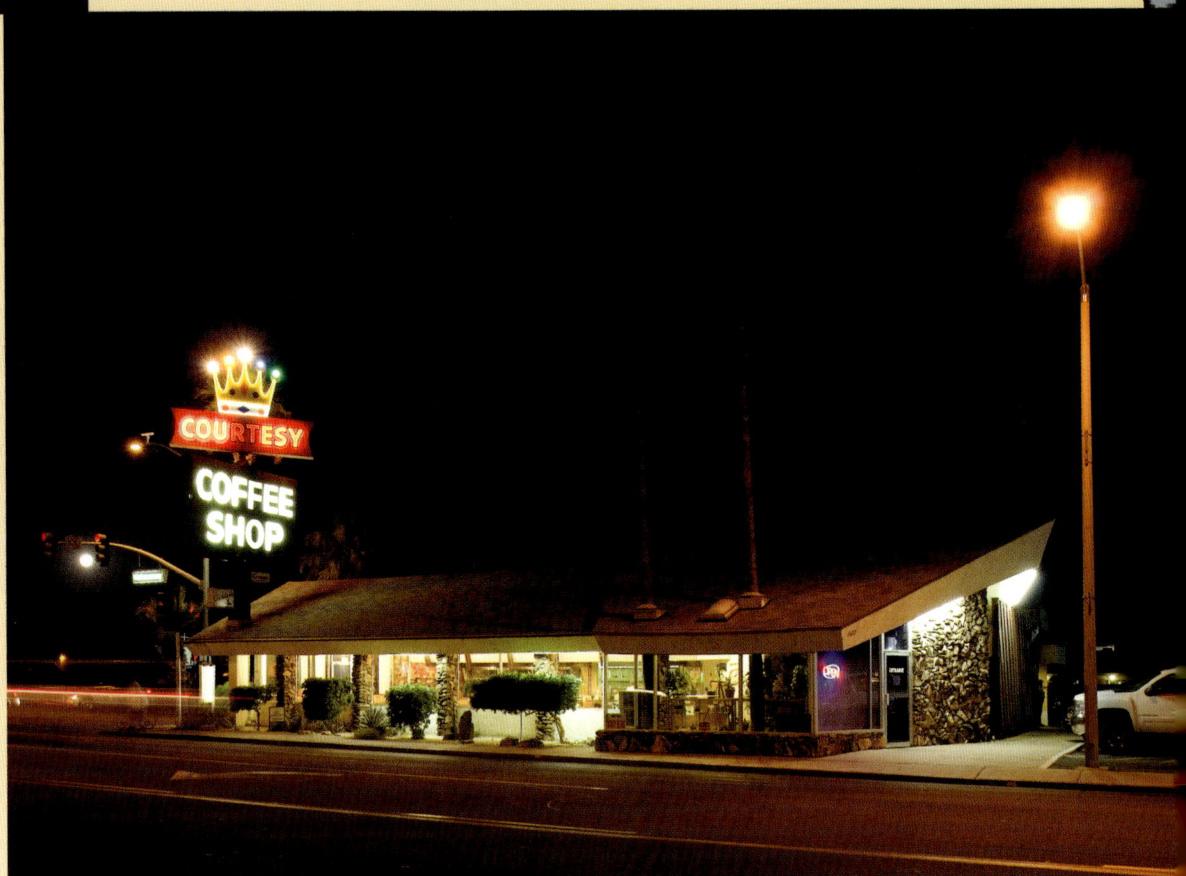

Opposite: Front door handles to this coffee shop are also unique.

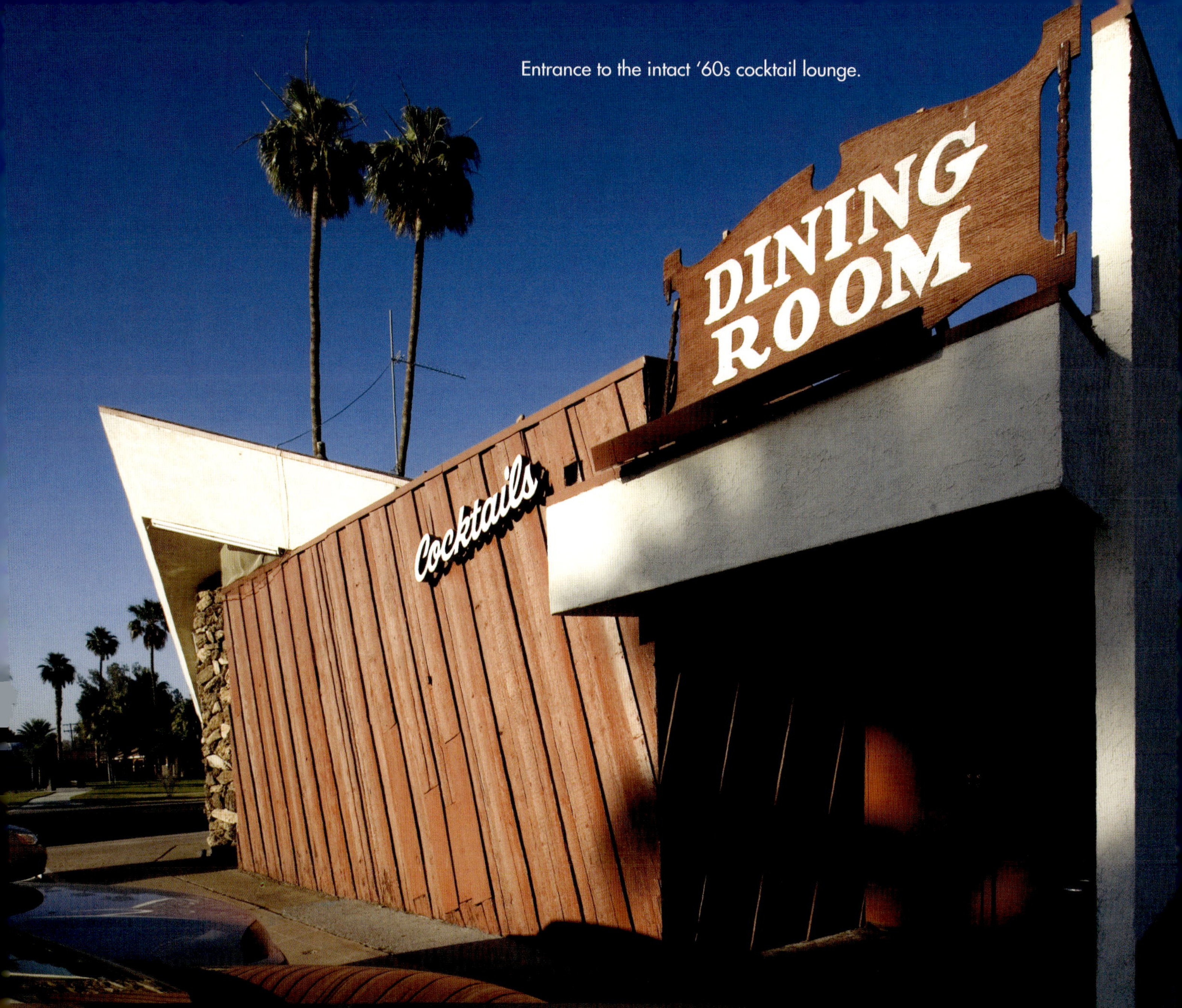

Entrance to the intact '60s cocktail lounge.

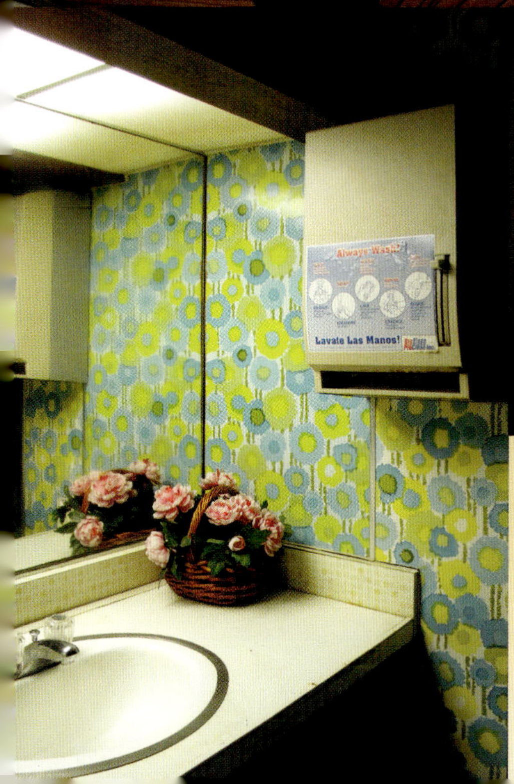

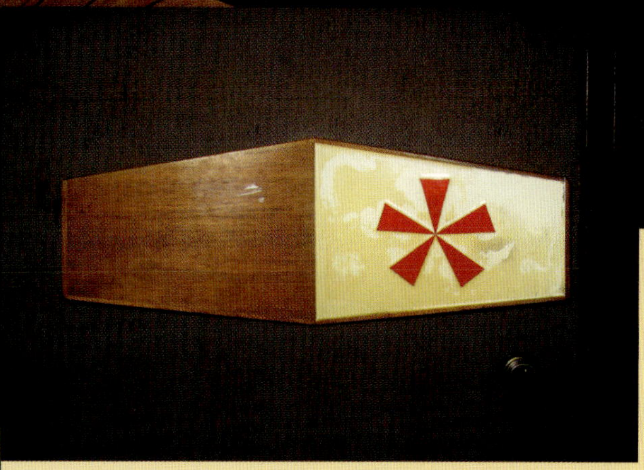

Note the groovy wall design—it's actually printed sheet metal, not wallpaper.

the rest room, the walls were covered in a bright green and blue groovy flower design printed on sheet metal. We left with a warm feeling in our hearts and a ridiculous grin on our faces knowing that somehow such a spectacular specimen of Googie architecture has survived in this rural, farming town of Blythe.

DAL RAE

9023 E. Washington Boulevard, Pico Rivera

Finally, a reason to fall in love with Pico Rivera. You'll be treated like a king here, "where everyone knows your name." The Dal Rae is hip and elegant. Imagine pulling up to the valet with your date in a '59 Cadillac convertible on a hot summer night. It's total glitz and glamour, accented with classical fleur-de-lis emblems. To the side of the parking lot is a marquee style sign, a rarity these days.

Conceived by Ben and Bill Smith, this fine dining restaurant opened in 1958. Today, the tradition of courtesy and excellence continues with second generation owners Lorin and Kevin Smith, who grew up in the restaurant business and are always on hand to say hello. In 1999, the Dal Rae was updated and now the younger crowd is discovering its "Rat Pack" ambience and piano bar. Famous for culinary delights like Steak Diane, Châteaubriand, filet mignon pepper steak, and Lobster Thermidor. Their authentic Caesar salad is absolutely over the top and prepared tableside. Grand Marnier souffle, anyone?

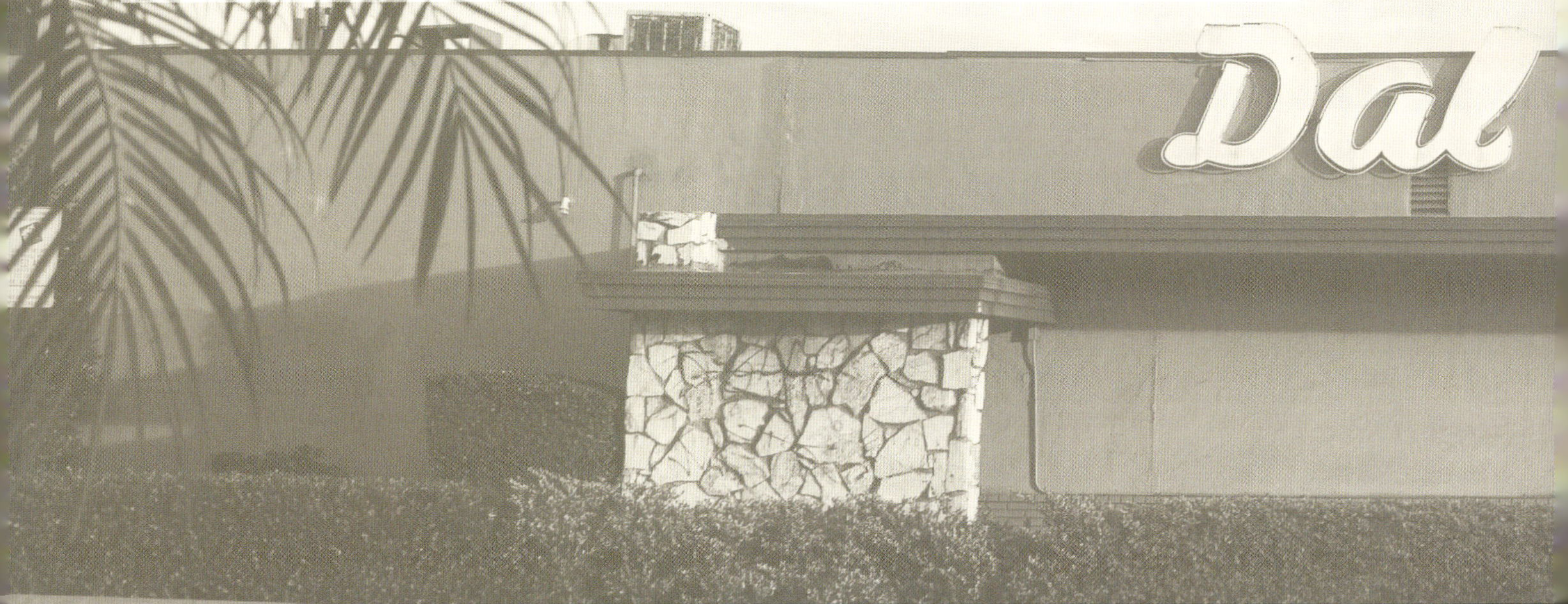

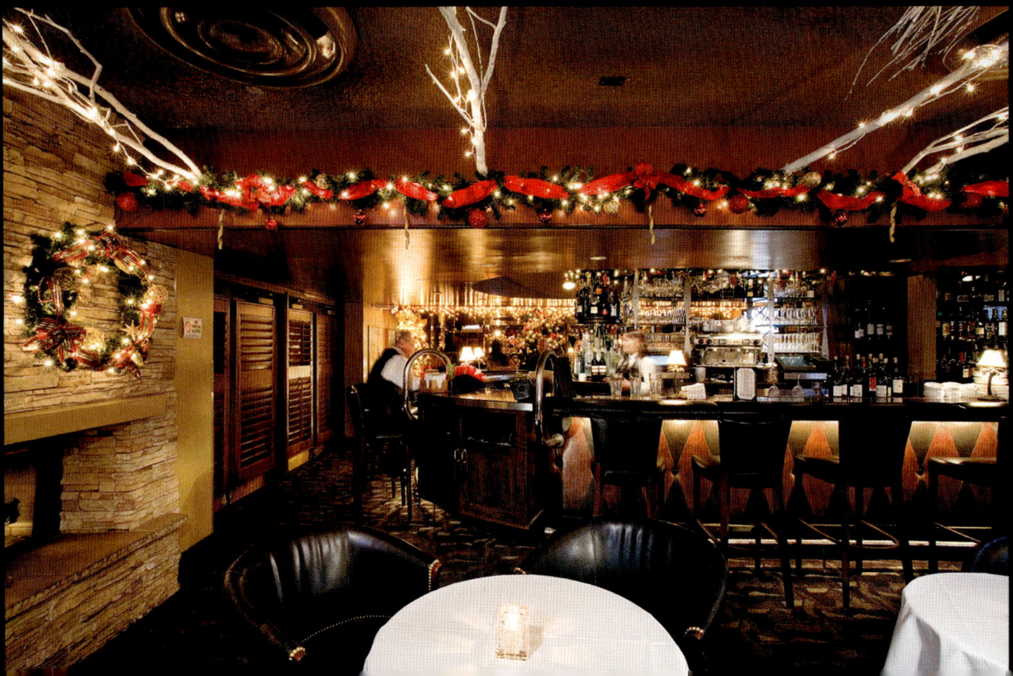

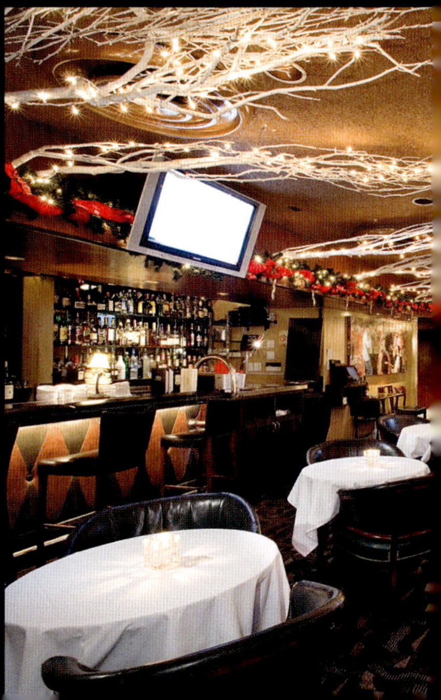

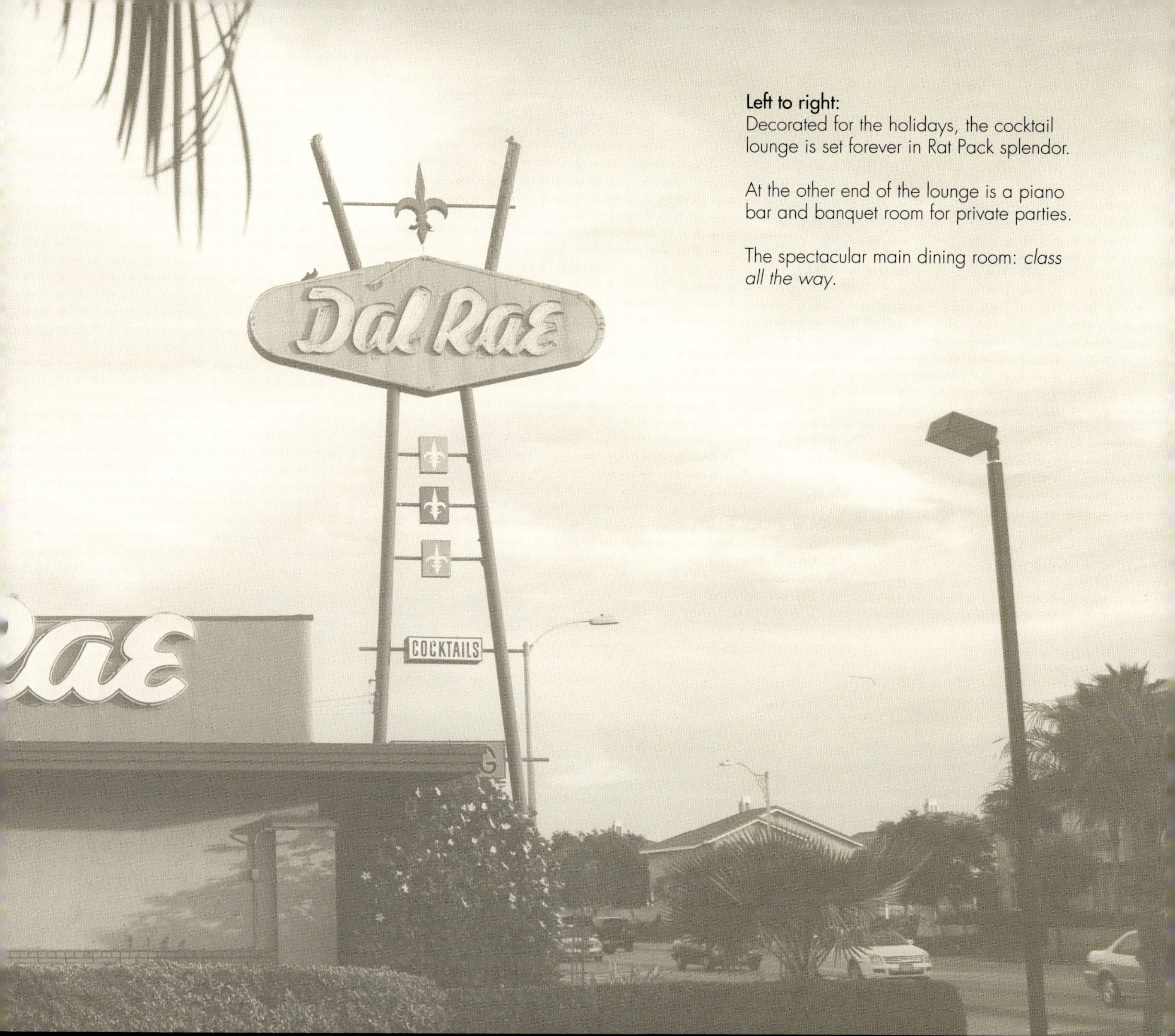

Left to right:
Decorated for the holidays, the cocktail lounge is set forever in Rat Pack splendor.

At the other end of the lounge is a piano bar and banquet room for private parties.

The spectacular main dining room: *class all the way.*

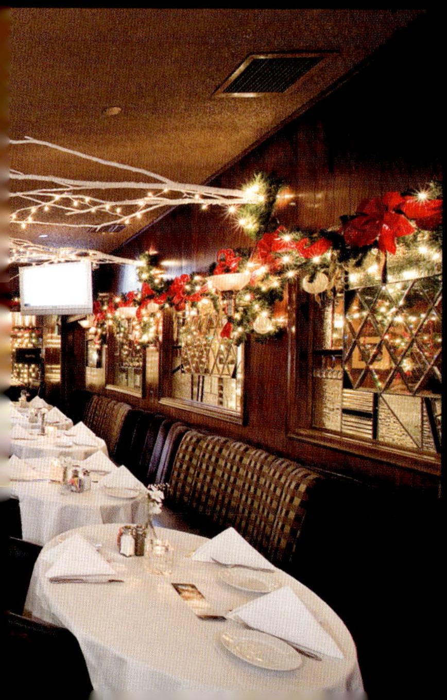

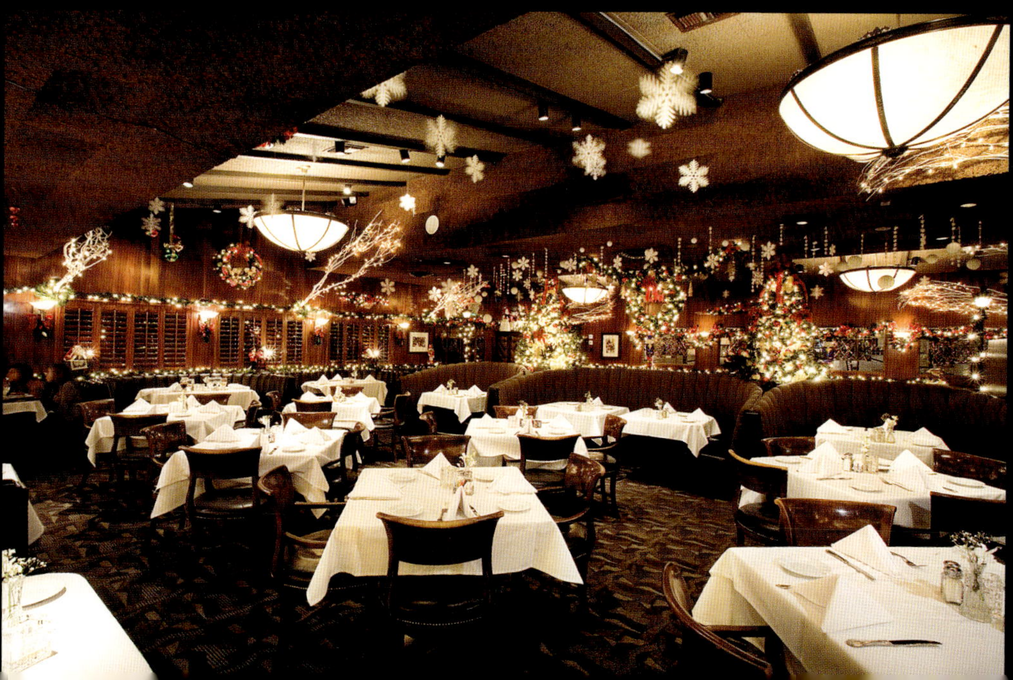

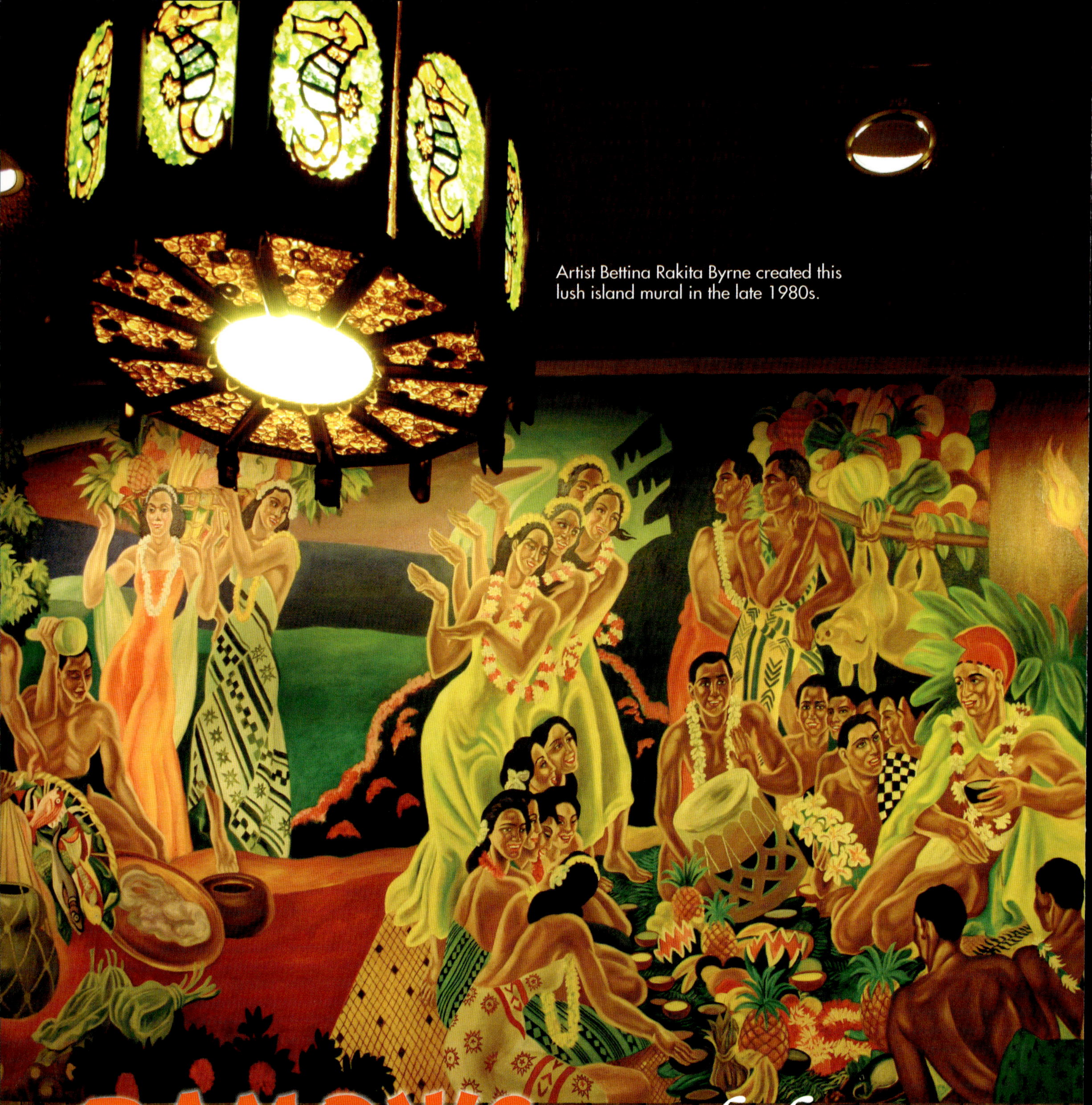

Artist Bettina Rakita Byrne created this lush island mural in the late 1980s.

DAMON'S steak house

317 N. Brand Boulevard, Glendale

Loyal Adelbert Damon was born in Medford, Oregon, in 1891. His family moved to California's Bay Area when Loyal was six years old. Twenty years later, during World War I, he served in France with the 144th field artillery. After the war, he owned two candy stores, then opened **DAMON'S STEAK HOUSE** on Central Avenue in Glendale. The South Seas theme started with a single palm tree in the middle of the restaurant. It was an immediate hit. In 1980, the restaurant moved to their present location and expanded on the tropical theme adding outriggers, exotic murals by the late Bettina Byrne, custom bamboo and resin lighting fixtures, saltwater and freshwater aquariums, and much much more. Damon's steaks, seafood and cocktails are world class. If you love Tiki, you'll love Damon's!

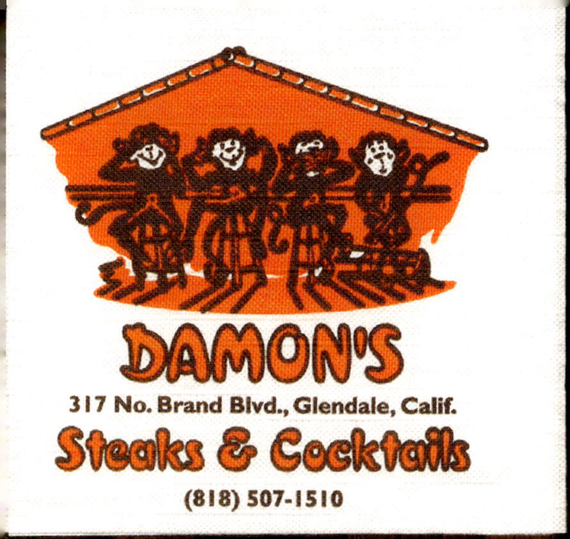

Approaching the main entrance from the rear parking lot, this Polynesian themed eatery stands out as an oasis in the urban downtown setting of Glendale.

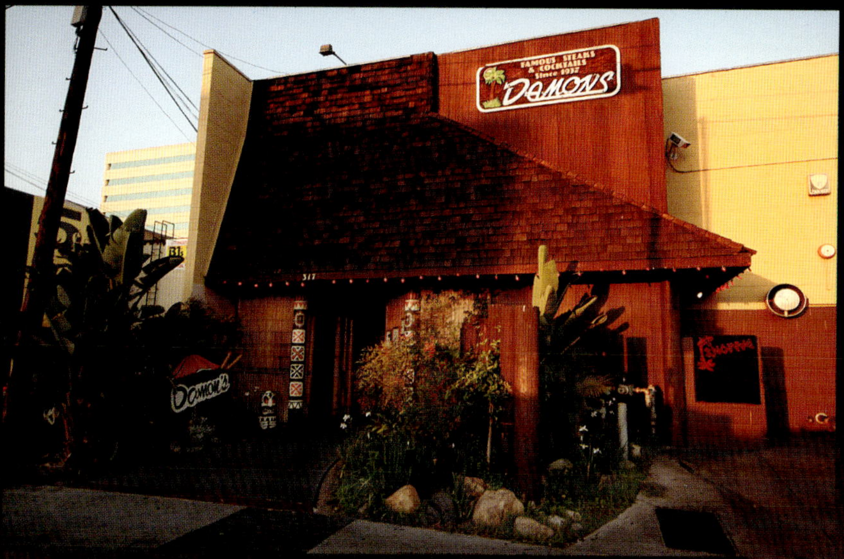

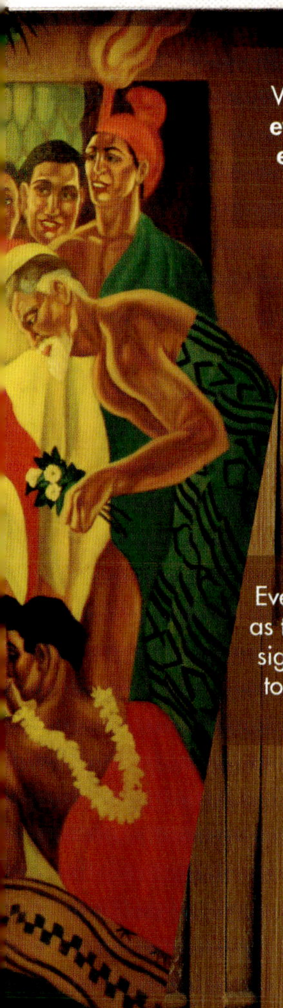

We understand the **"See no evil, hear no evil, speak no evil,"** but what is the fourth monkey trying to say?

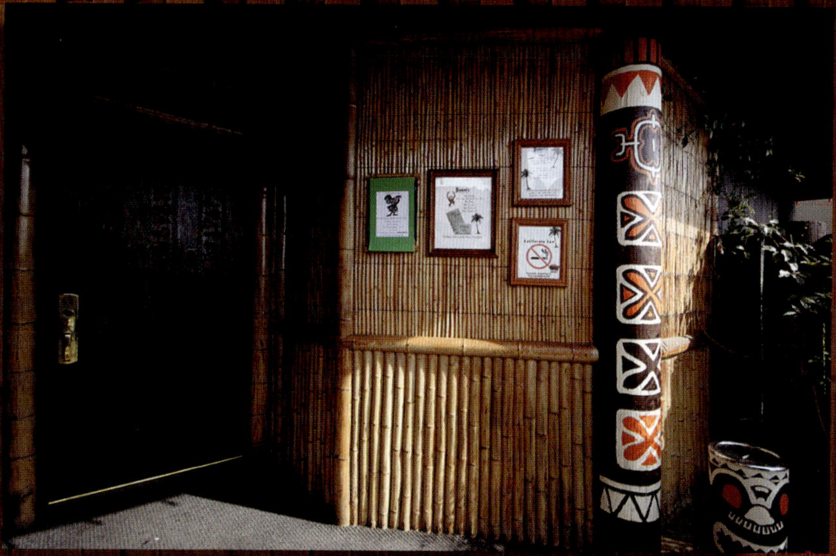

Even before entering, as soon as the city buildings are out of sight, you begin your journey to the romantic islands of the tropics.

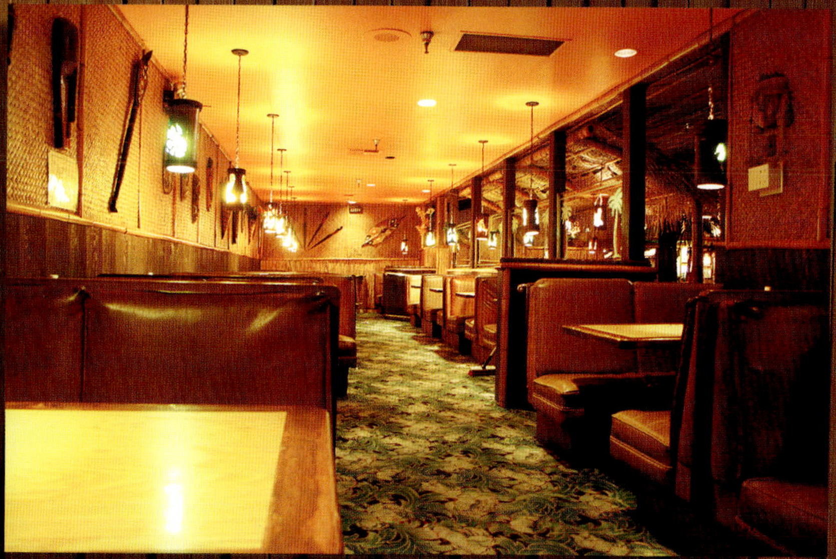

Inside, the spacious restaurant is warm and festive and decorated with fish tanks, outriggers, and blowfish. Most Tiki bars do not have windows…why spoil the illusion?

Below, left to right:
This Denny's on Wilshire is part of the historic Pellissier Building.

The classic elements of the Denny's sign were once ubiquitous to all Denny's, with familiar shapes and jaunty lettering, topped off with a lighted atomic sphere. This is the Agoura Hills Denny's, one of the last known victims to the wrecking ball in So Cal.

Except for the name, Caesar's in Gardena remains faithful to the original '60s design. It doubled as Winkie's in David Lynch's 2001 cult classic, *Mulholland Drive*.

This Googie detail from the Denny's in Lancaster still proudly surrounds and protects the main column that holds up their sign.

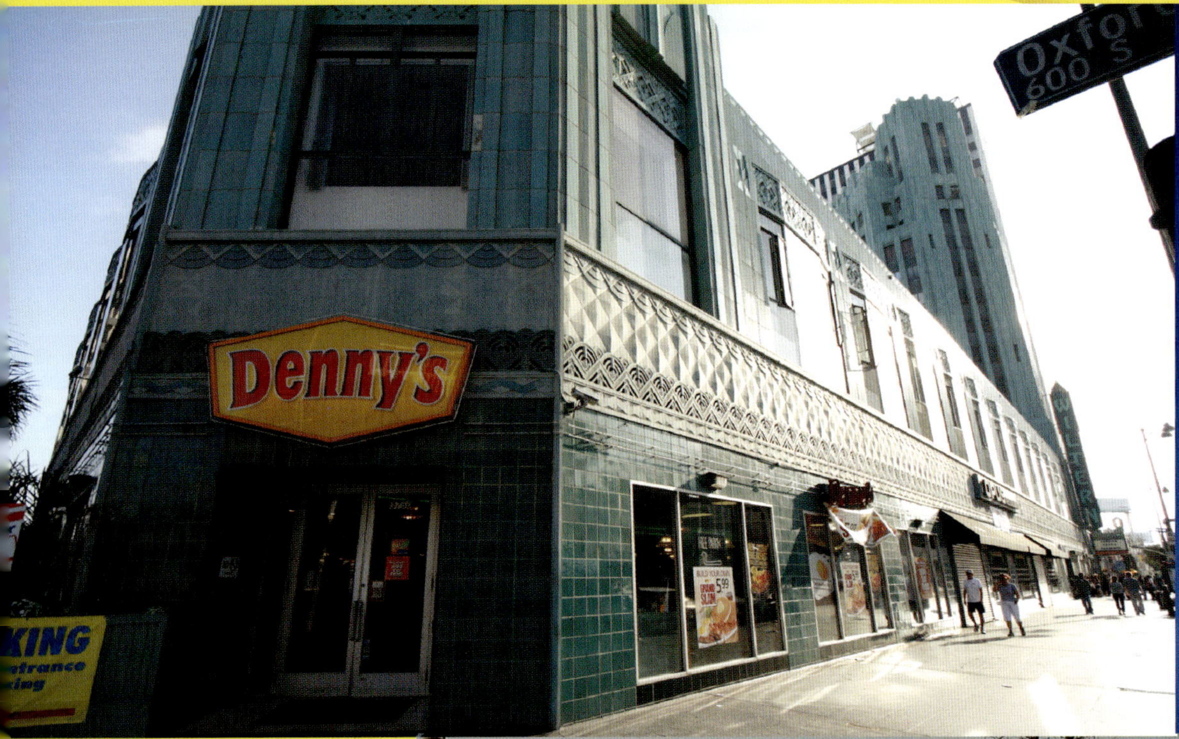

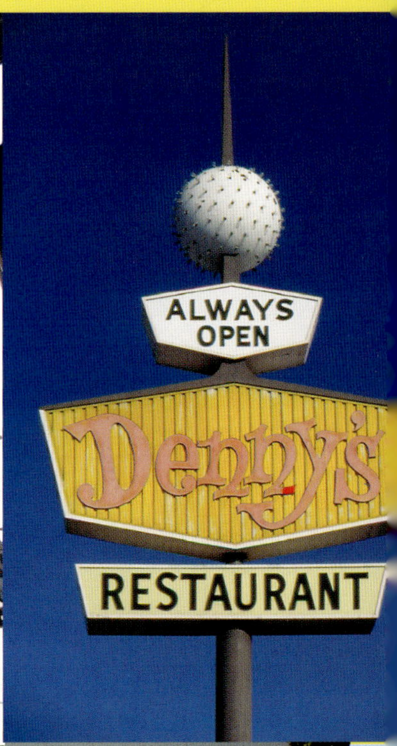

Left to right:
This Pasadena sign has been modified, but the building has survived several rounds of remodeling.

The Denny's in Fontana was constructed in early 2000 and has adopted an East Coast diner style instead of the California modern style unique to the West Coast.

Once a Van de Kamp's, this Denny's kept the Dutch windmill motif and circular layout plan.

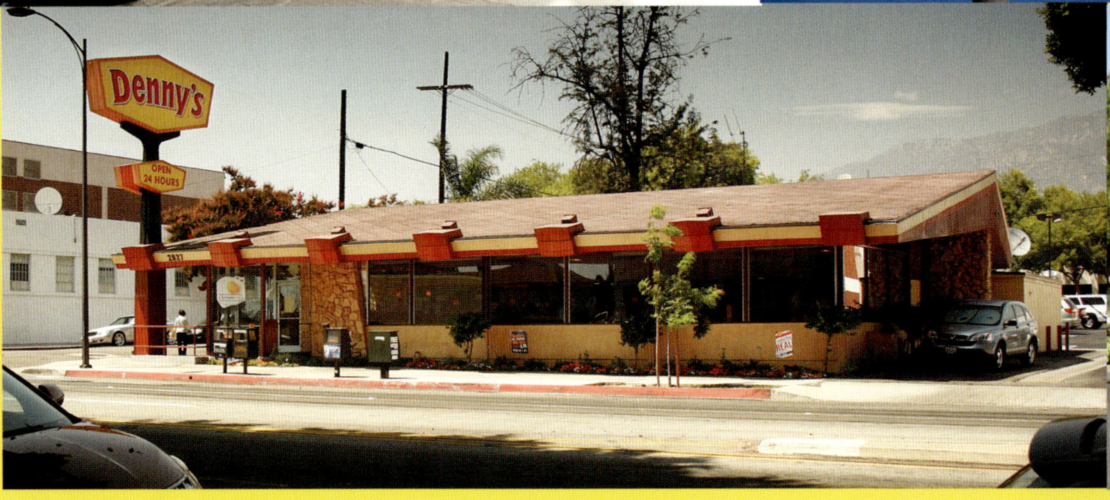

Denny's
Multiple Locations

If you're on the road late at night, Denny's is a welcome sight. Open 24 hours, the chain was founded in 1953 by Harold Butler in Lakewood, California. There are now over 1,500 Denny's restaurants across the US but each of the Denny's pictured here is distinctive thanks to their adaptive reuse and architectural history.

The Denny's on Wilshire Boulevard sits on the northeast corner of the Pellissier Building, home to the Wiltern Theatre. Declared a Historic Cultural Monument by the City of Los Angeles in 1979, this zig-zag moderne/art deco building was built in 1931 as a vaudeville theater. The entrance to the Wiltern is just spectacular. Designed by architect Stiles O. Clements with interiors by Albert Lansburgh, the 12-story building is covered in custom seafoam green terra cotta tiles.

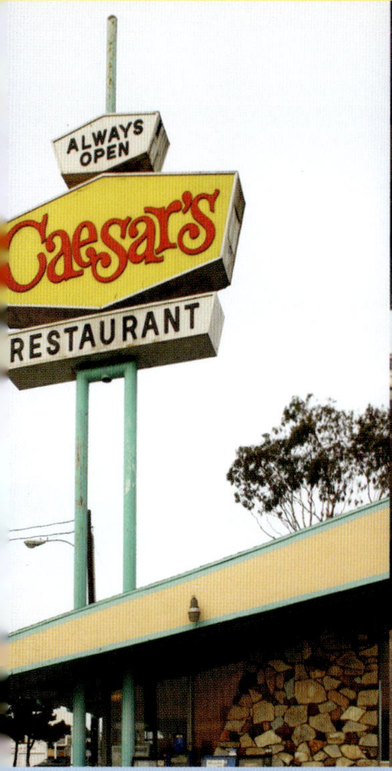

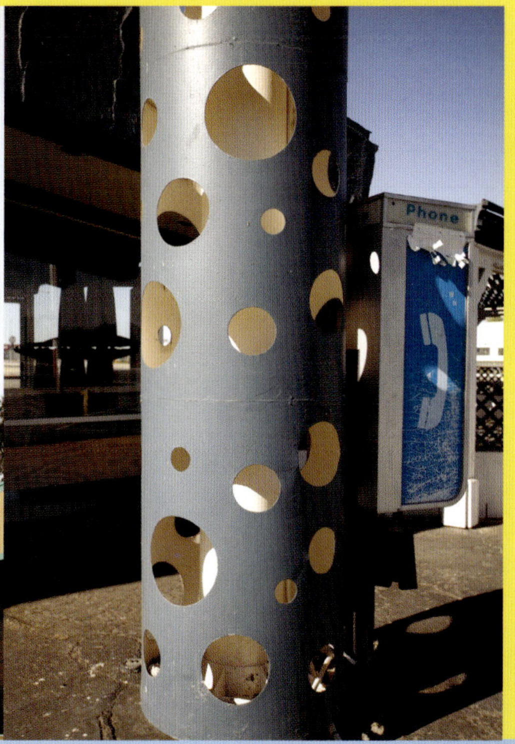

The Denny's in Arcadia was originally a Van De Kamp's restaurant constructed in the shape of a windmill and rescued by the Los Angeles Conservancy's Modern Committee. The Van De Kamp's restaurant chain started in 1921 when partners Lawrence Frank and Theodore Van de Kamp asked Hollywood art director Harry Oliver to design a Dutch windmill for their bakery outlets. These initial outlets were small windmill units just slightly larger than the Fotomats of the '70s. They were mass produced and portable. Later, a number of full scale restaurants in the shape of windmills were constructed.

When we happened upon the Denny's in Lancaster, we rejoiced to see the "swiss cheese" collar circling the base of the sign. This '60s Googie design from Armet + Davis was once ubiquitous throughout the Southwest, including Las Vegas.

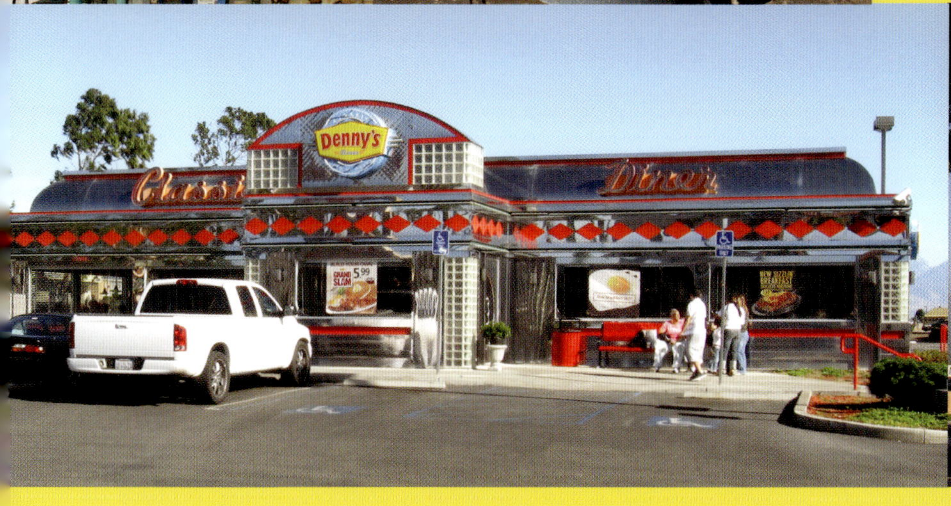

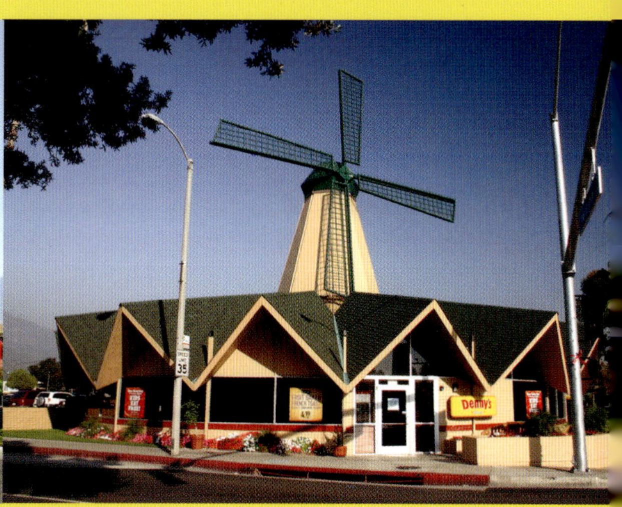

DESERT CENTER cafe

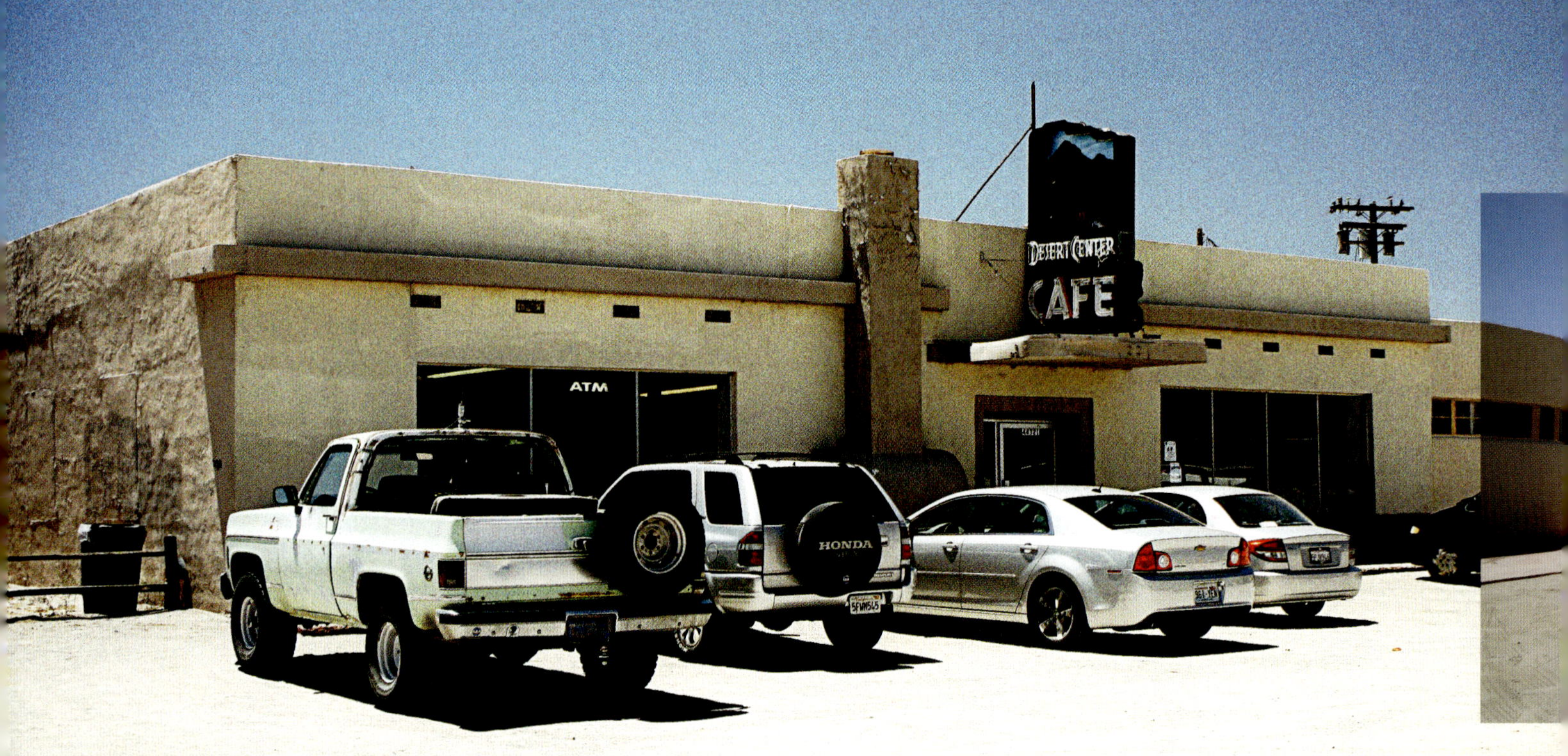

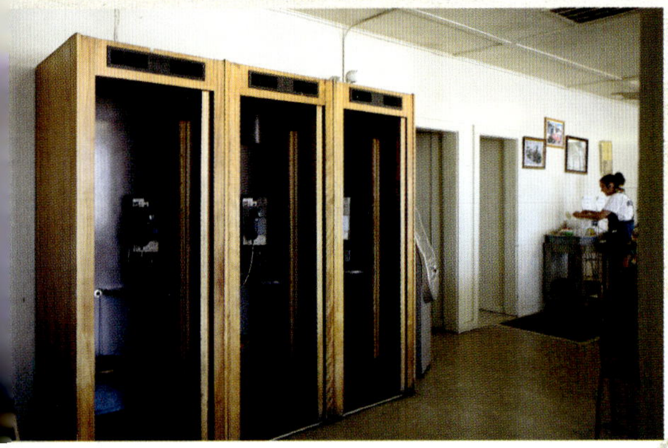

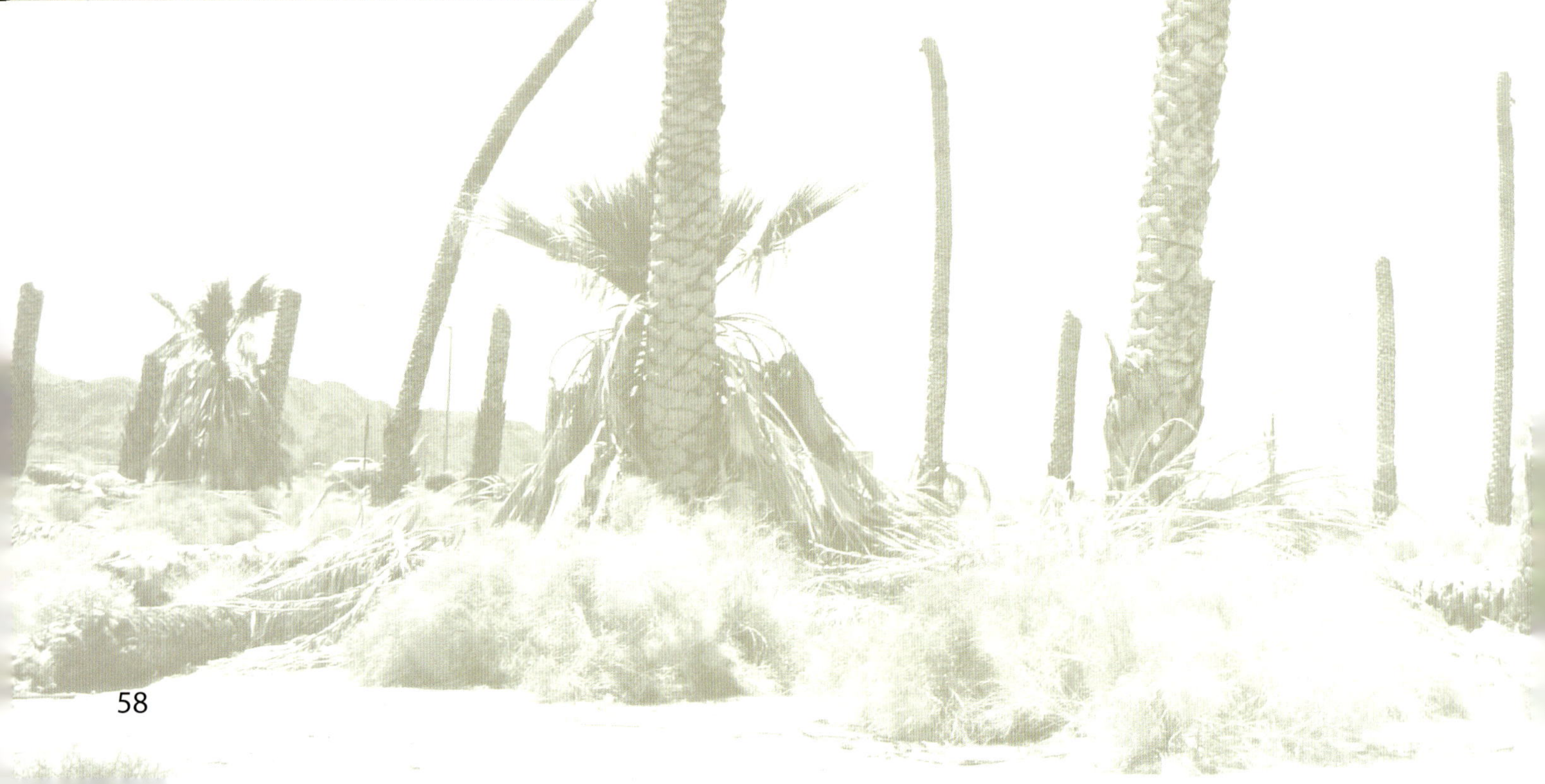

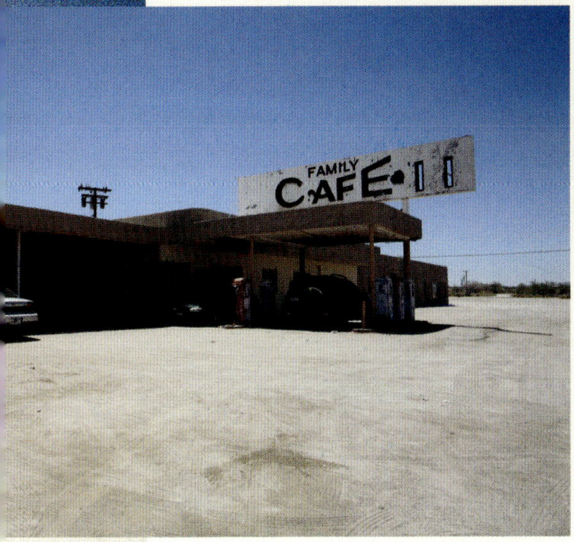

Desert Center Cafe

44321 Ragsdale Road,
Hwy. 60, Desert Center

Heading back west from Blythe via Twentynine Palms, we saw "Desert Center" on our AAA map. It was easy to spot since it was surrounded by a blank field of nothing. Just then we passed a peculiar bunch of headless palm trees in a circular pattern and knew that this was our exit. After checking out these "palm hedges" we noticed several adobe structures nearby. As we rolled in, all colors faded away and we found ourselves in a black and white film noir movie, "Detour". It was hot, flat, dusty, and desolate. This "town" was made up of a post office, a deserted gas station, and a coffee shop. Where do you think we ended up?

Stepping inside the cafe, we knew we had traveled back to 1933. We were wrong, it was founded in 1922 by Steve and Lydia Ragsdale. According to their sign, "General George S. Patton selected this area for desert training. Over one million troops trained for combat between 1942 and 1944. Open 24 hours a day, 7 days a week since 1922. WE NEVER CLOSE." After our double take, we realized it was all true. Still owned and run by the Ragsdale family, they still have wooden phone booths and counter stools that look to be the originals from 1922. (Make sure you look before you sit down though, a couple of their seats are missing.) The restrooms have not changed since they opened, hexagonal tiled floor and six-inch porcelain urinals from nearly a century earlier await you.

Anyone interested in God, hypocrisy, infidelity, and bad poetry can read more about the story of Steve Ragsdale and the founding of this town on Wikipedia under "Desert Center, CA." It's a real life California noir classic. Hmmm, do I smell a future screenplay?

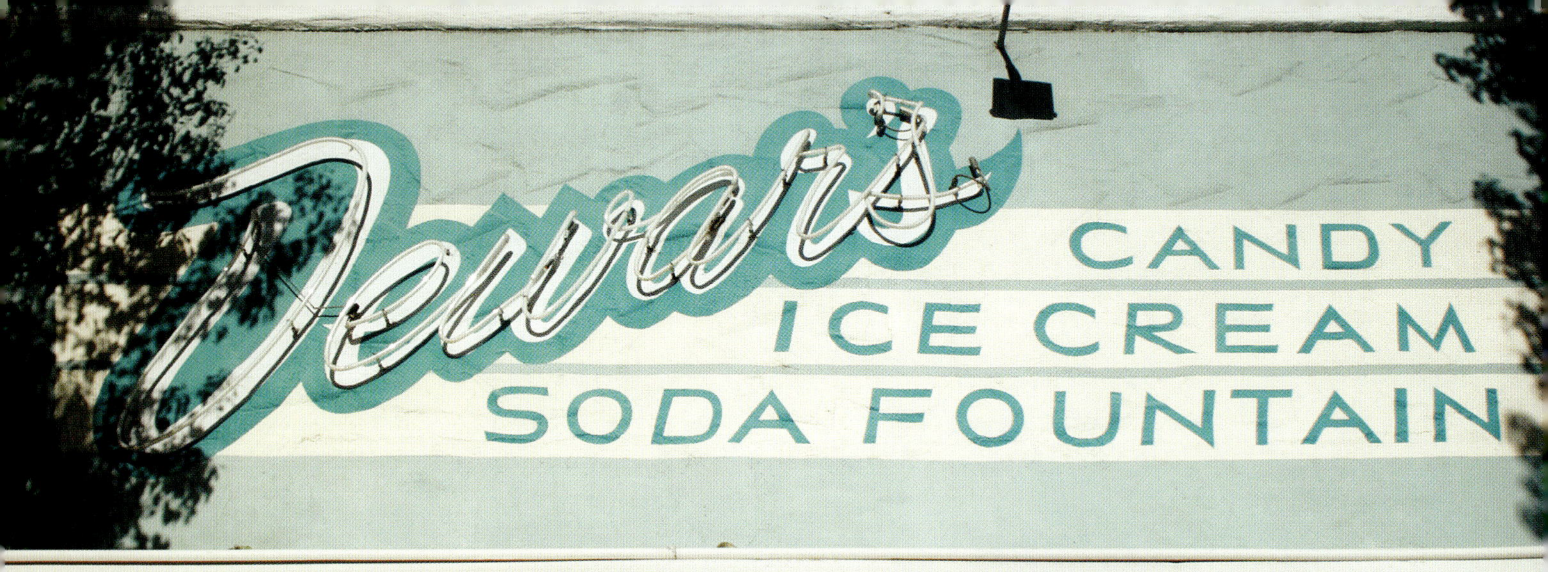

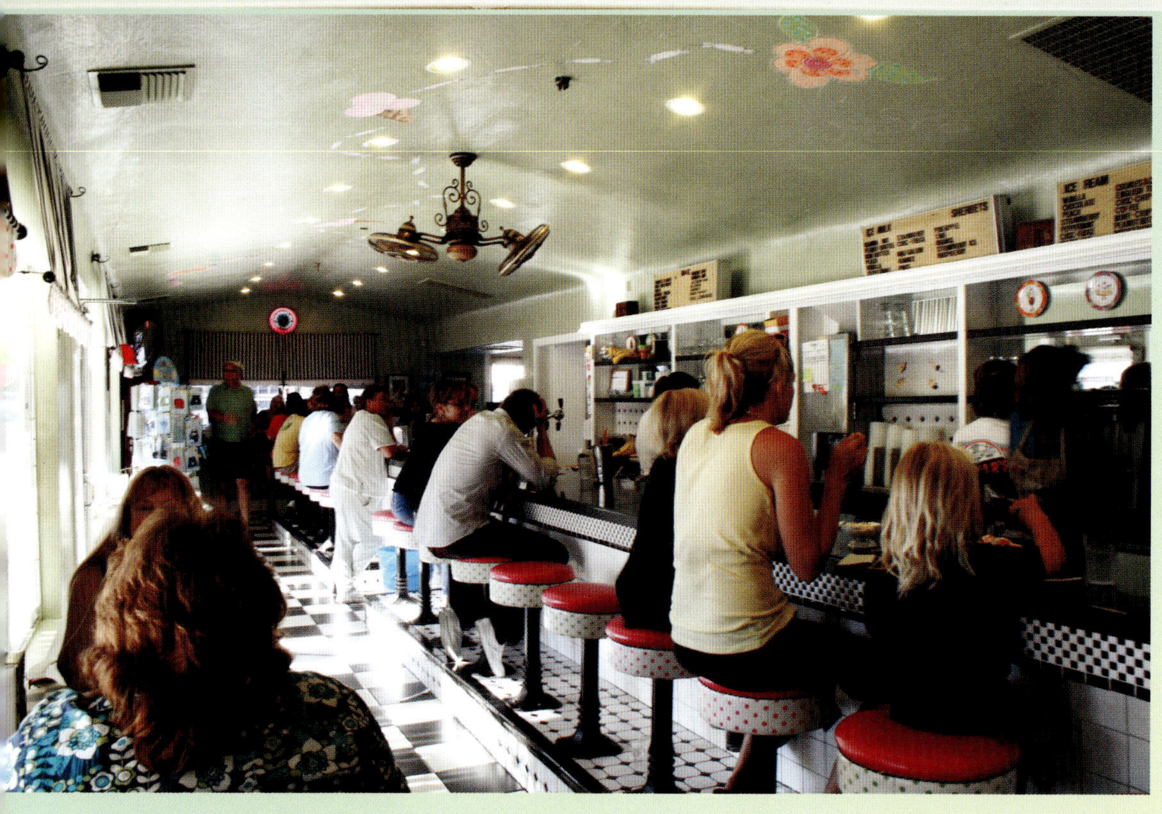

Left: On the summer day we were here, it seemed that half the town was here as well.

Below: We're not sure exactly what he is doing here but we think he came in for a banana split. *Photo by Adriene Biondo.*

Dewar's Ice Cream and Candy Shop

1120 Eye Street, Bakersfield

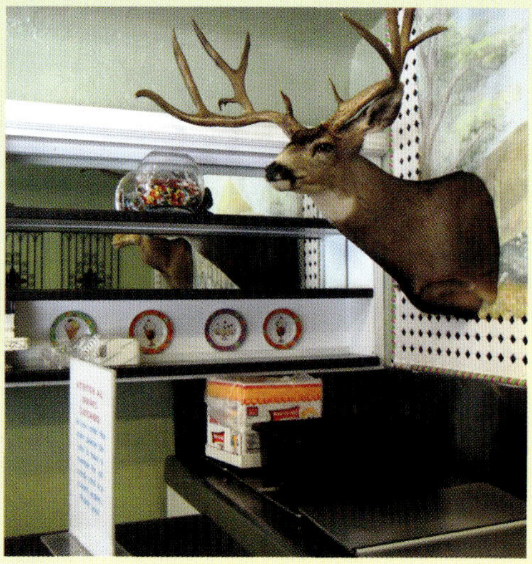

If it's a hot August night and you're craving ice cream, head to Bakersfield! We couldn't believe how many ice cream parlors we found there. After checking out Carla's and Andre's, we dropped into Dewar's. A lady ordered the Black & White Sundae which was gushing with hot fudge and homemade marshmallow cream. We sat in polka dot splendor, gazing at the rather imposing deer head mounted on the wall. A family-run institution since 1909, Dewar's just past the century mark and is still going strong. Pick up a sack of peanut butter chews for the ride home. Your sweet tooth will thank you.

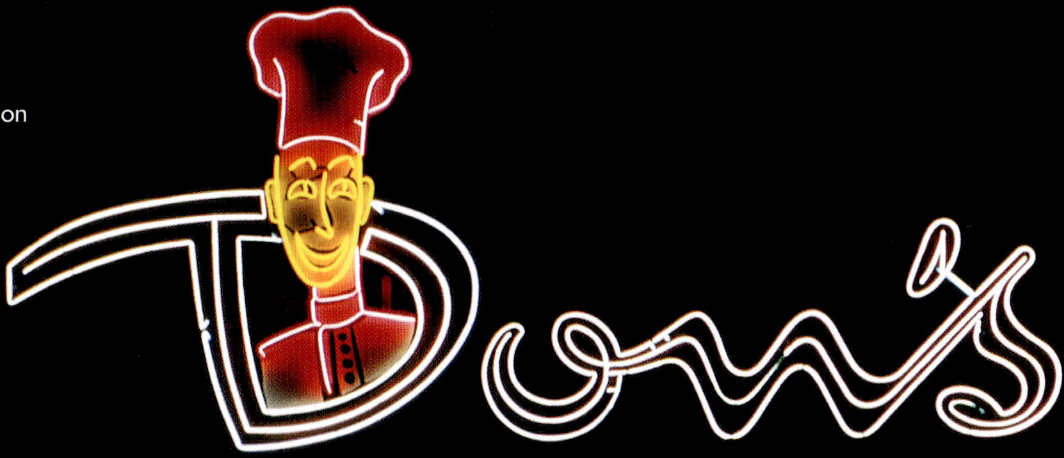

This fantastic neon sign survived the landfill and can be seen at the Gordon R. Howard Museum in Burbank.

Sunrise on the last days of Don's, 2002.

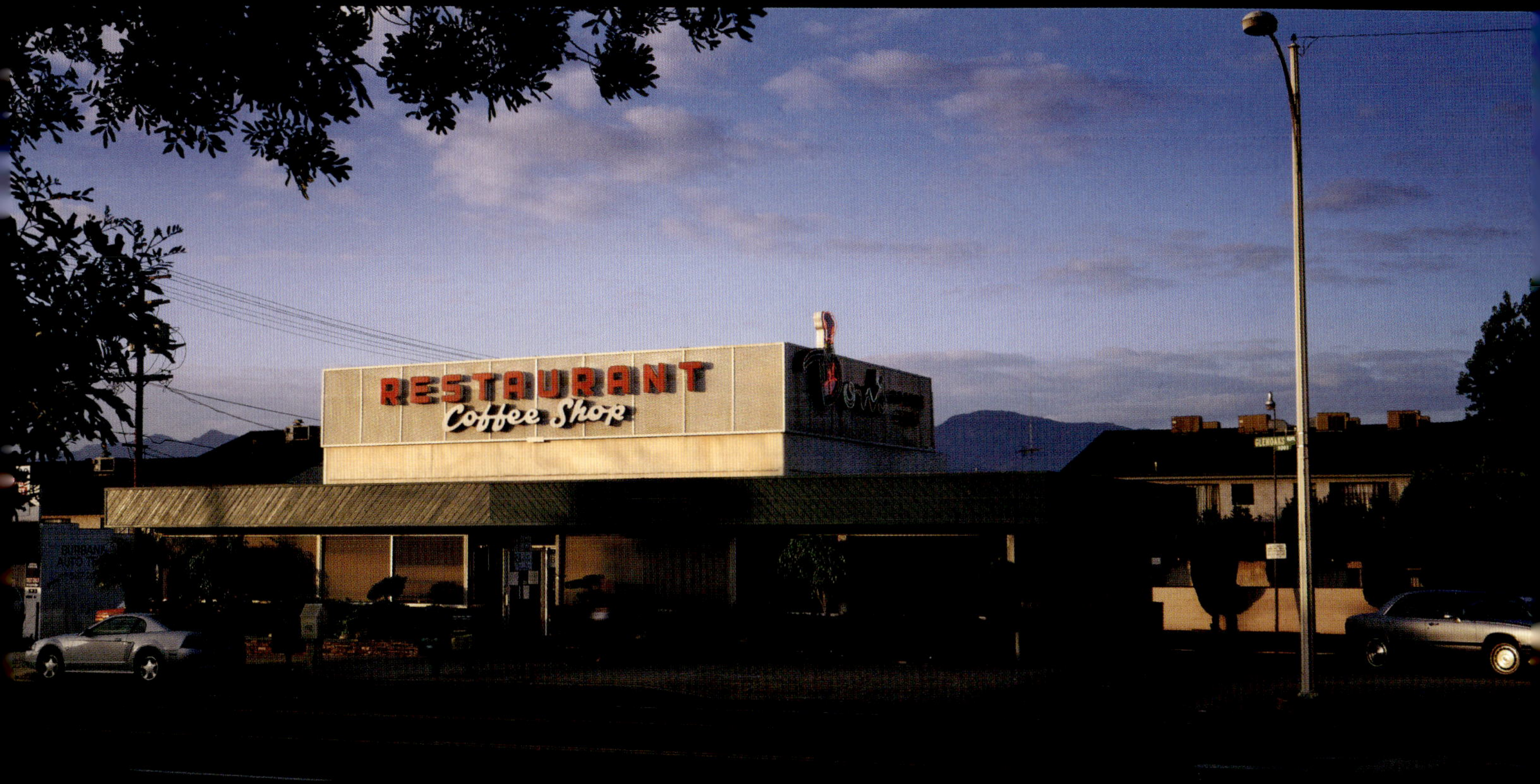

Don's Coffee Shop

509 S. Glenoaks Boulevard, Burbank

Don Draper opened Don's in 1947 as a drive-in with carhop service and outdoor rest rooms (which were still in use in 2002). Our favorite waitress was Lillie Couch, who was only sixteen when she started working at Don's as a carhop. Lillie always shared stories of Don's humble beginnings and how he fed hungry Lockheed Aircraft workers. As Don's grew, they added an indoor dining room and fancy neon signage. Fast-forward to 2002 and we found Lillie celebrating her 50th anniversary just as Don's was closing its doors to become Momotaro Japanese cuisine. The new owners generously donated Don's neon chef to the Gordon R. Howard Museum in Burbank, where it is proudly displayed today.

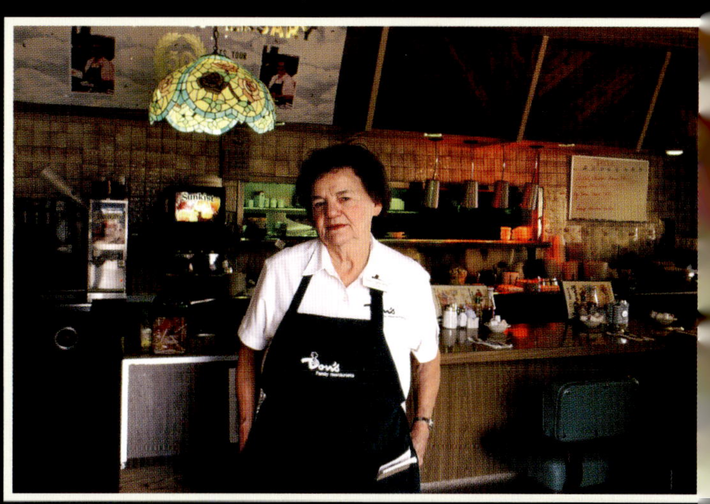

After 50 years, this was Lillie's last day, 2002.

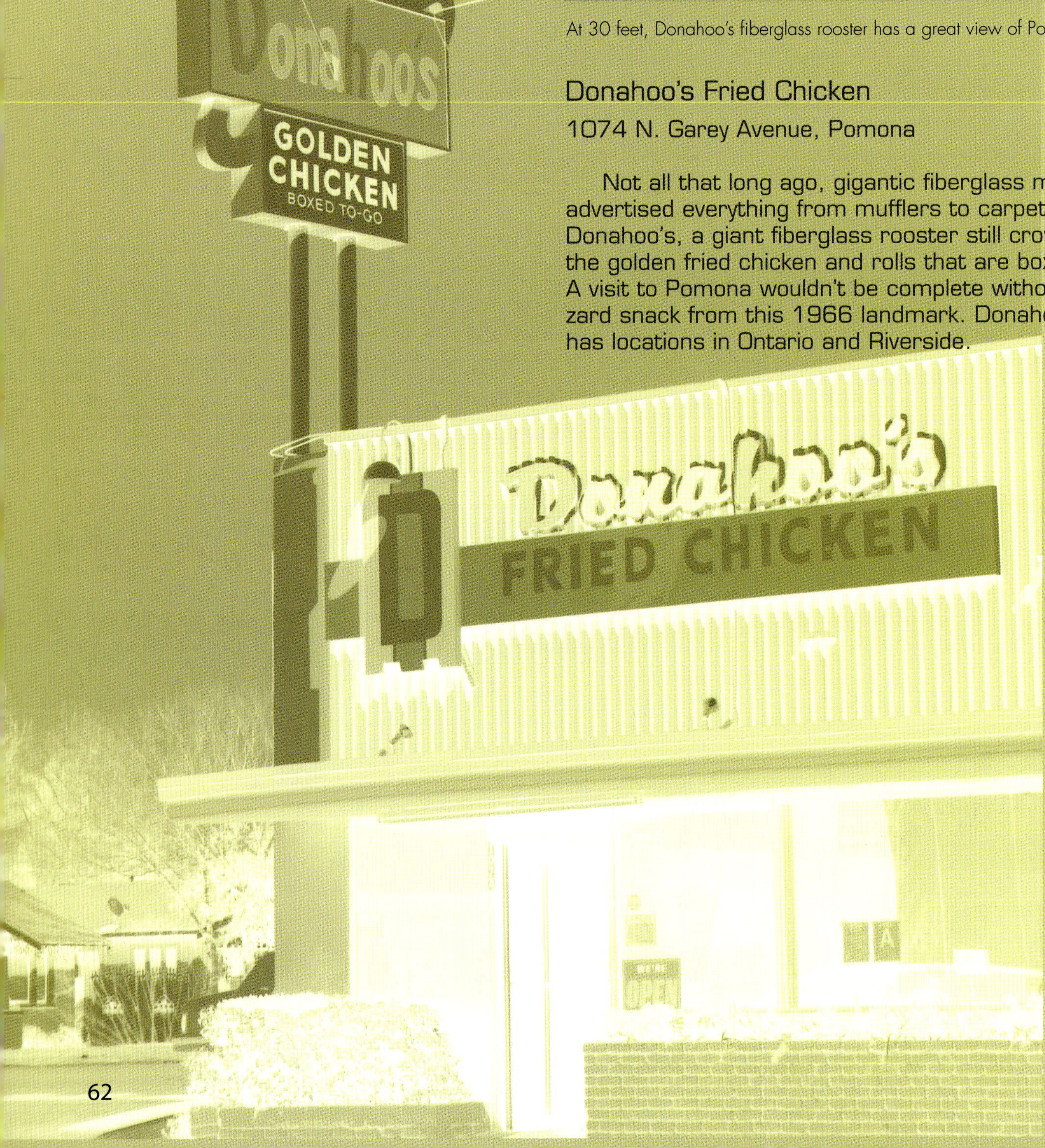

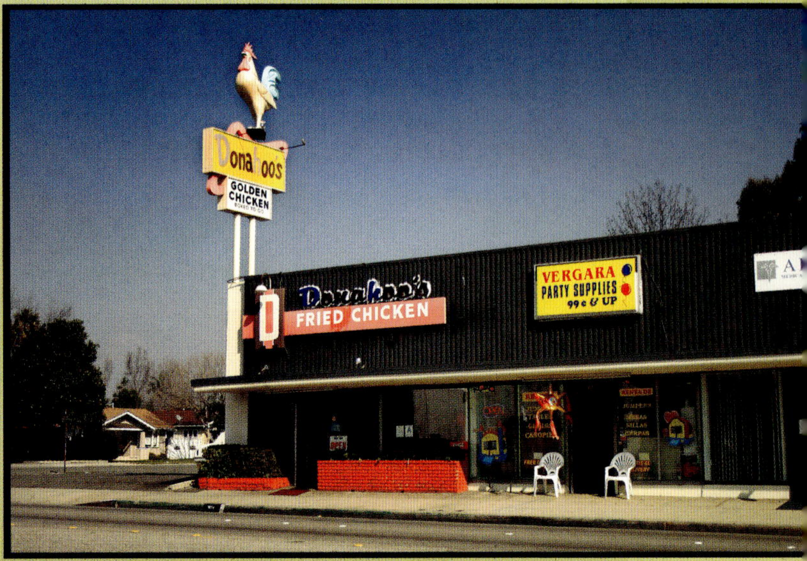

At 30 feet, Donahoo's fiberglass rooster has a great view of Pomona.

Donahoo's Fried Chicken

1074 N. Garey Avenue, Pomona

Not all that long ago, gigantic fiberglass mascots advertised everything from mufflers to carpeting. At Donahoo's, a giant fiberglass rooster still crows about the golden fried chicken and rolls that are boxed-to-go. A visit to Pomona wouldn't be complete without a gizzard snack from this 1966 landmark. Donahoo's also has locations in Ontario and Riverside.

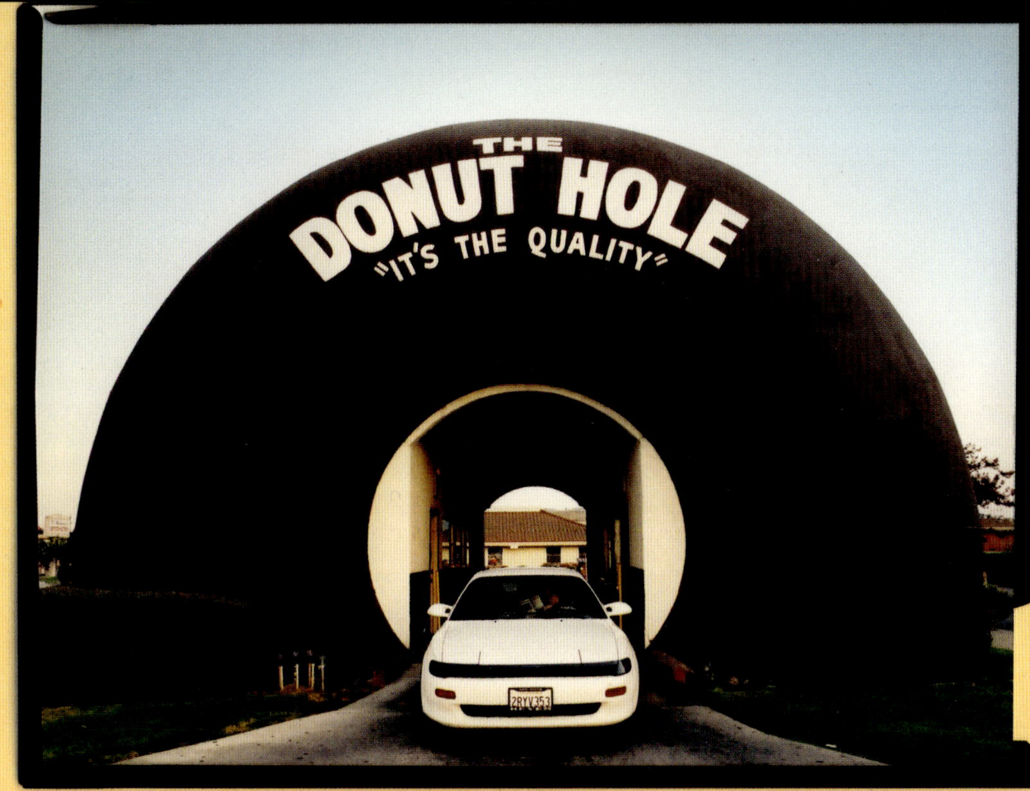

The Donut Hole

15300 E. Amar Road at Hacienda Boulevard, La Puente

This could very well be the ultimate L.A. roadside experience, driving through two immense chocolate donuts and ordering a piping hot donut baked on the premises! Built in 1968, La Puente's famous Donut Hole is a tasty programmatic treat constructed of double fiberglass donuts measuring 26 feet in diameter. A few years back a driver misjudged the distance and ended up crashing into the donut, taking a big bite out of it. At one time, there were five of these programmatic donut shops throughout the Southland. According to his son Chris Foerstel, Edmond C. Foerstel was the architect/engineer of record for the Donut Hole and the structural engineer for Harvey's Broiler, the first Taco Bell, and the first In N Out, among other local landmarks. Happily, the La Puente store is still going strong, so go see it!

DONUT HO

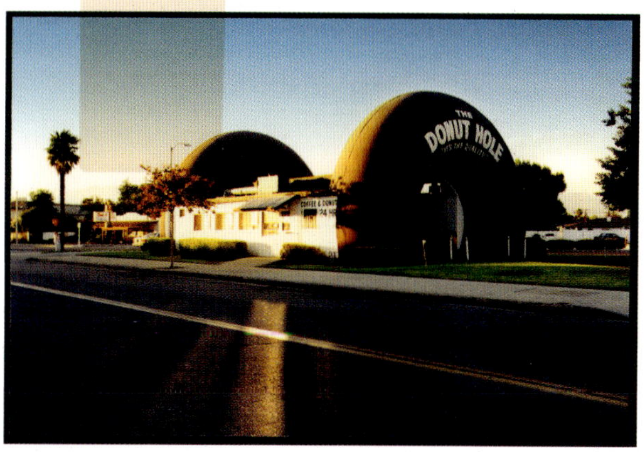

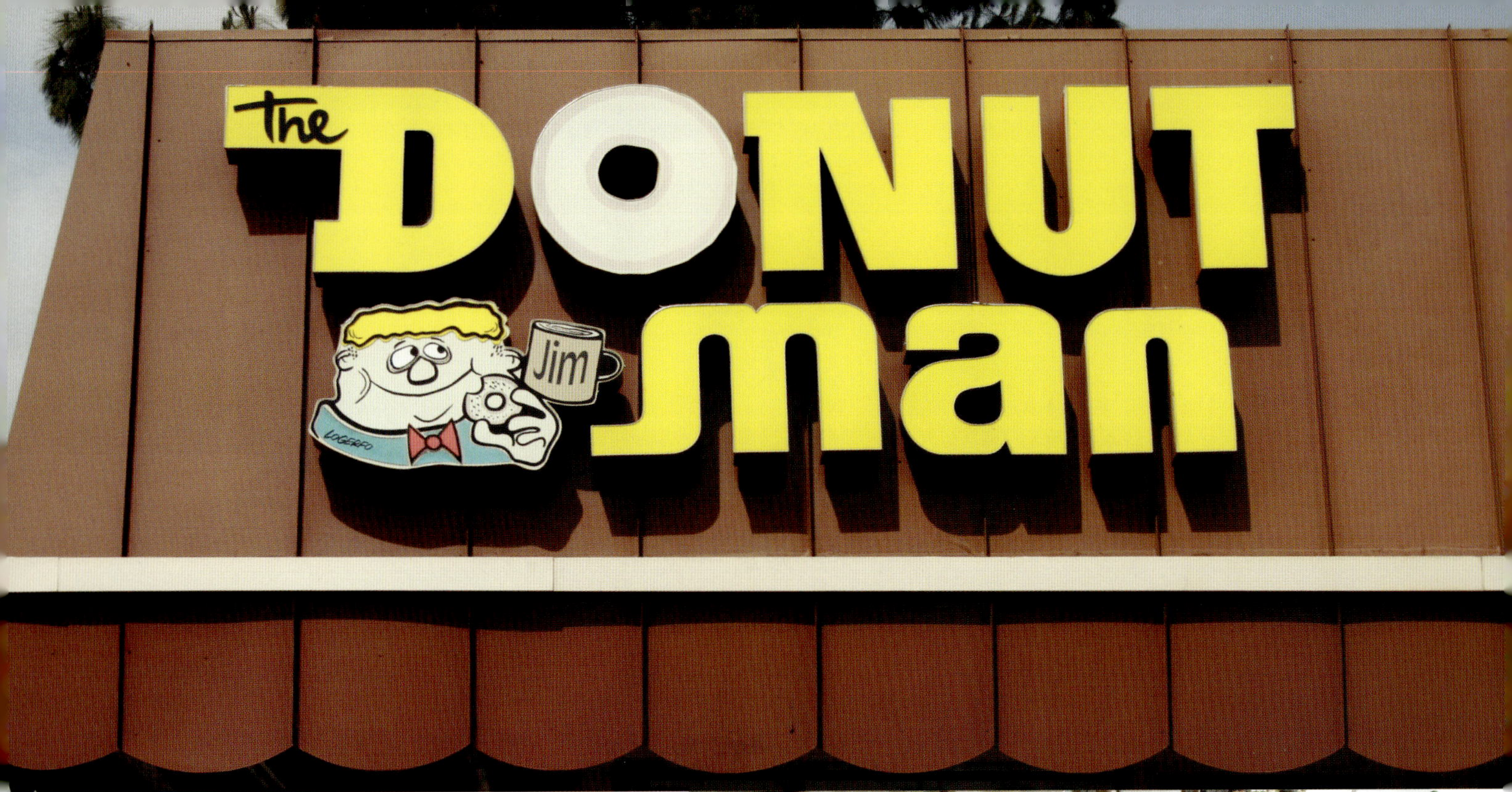

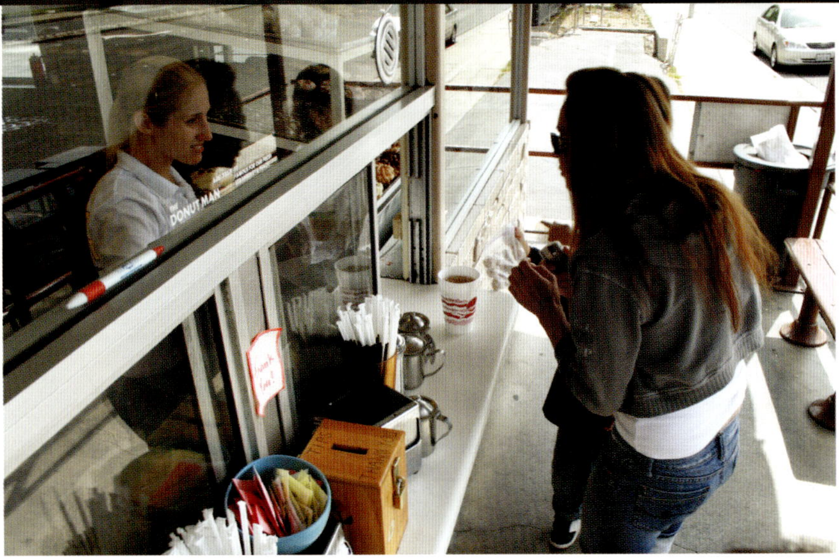

The Donut Man

915 E. Route 66, Glendora

Thank goodness The Donut Man is open 24/7 for those late night pilgrimages across Route 66 to cave in to cravings for their scrumptious strawberry donut. Jim Nakano's fresh strawberry creation is so humongous it has to be served in a box with a fork! He bakes peach too...call ahead if you want to know what's in season. Tiger Tails are also worth the drive down. Look for Jim the Donut Man, and pick up one of his classy t-shirts before you head back out onto The Mother Road. You won't need to worry about eating for the rest of the day, unless you're Homer Simpson.

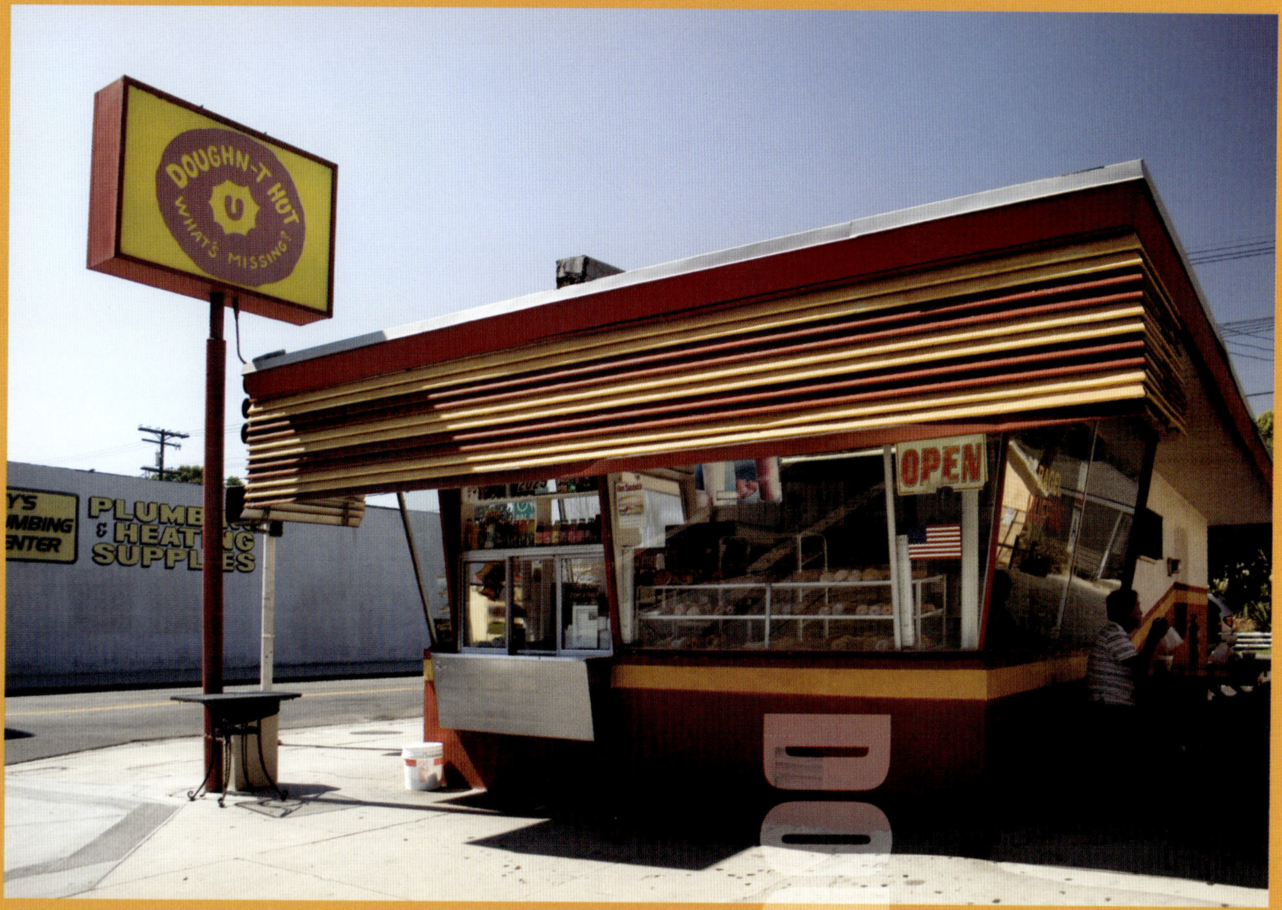

DOUGHN-T HUT

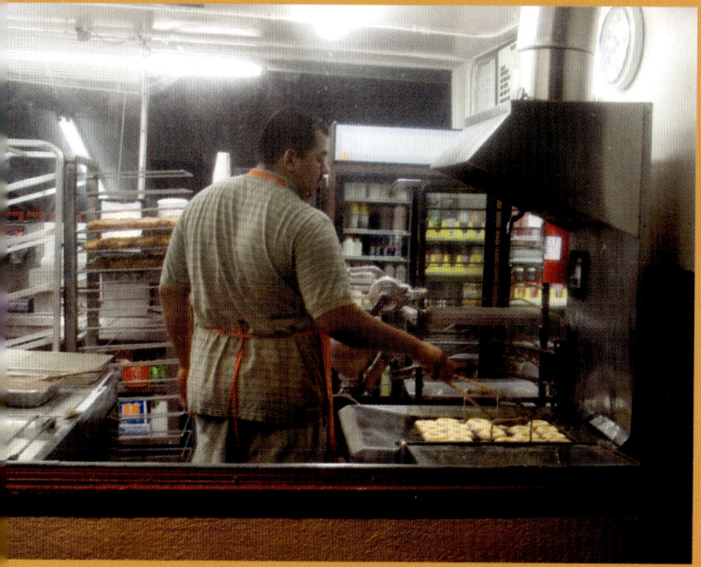

Doughn-T Hut

10544 Magnolia Boulevard, Burbank

A haven for gourmet donut lovers and those of us who can't pass up a silly sign like, "What's Missing? 'U'", Doughn-T Hut is an inverted glass box building. People adore the Doughn-T Hut's donuts; they're addictive. We enjoyed watching the baker twirl the donuts in bubbling oil with something that looked like an oversize chopstick. In no time at all, dozens upon dozens of delightfully warm, uniform donuts emerged unscathed, ready to be gobbled up. Stop in... after all, what's missing? U!

Dresden Restaurant

1760 N. Vermont Avenue, Hollywood

This is the official home of lounge lizards Marty and Elayne, forever immortalized singing "Staying Alive" in the movie Swingers. L.A.'s beloved duo was discovered by owner Carl Ferraro who instantly realized a good thing. Ferraro spotted them in 1982 playing up the street at Michael's, formerly the Brown Derby. Marty's crooning and Elayne's scatting is memorable and continues to pack them in with such hits as "Up, Up & Away" and "Misty." There's no cover charge for the privilege, and there's always a chance of spotting a celebrity. We've spent many a standing-room-only night here, sipping the Dresden's infamous Blood and Sand cocktail.

The restaurant dates back to 1934 when it operated as Pucci's. A bookman named Herman Byron who loved to collect Dresden collectibles changed the name to the Dresden in 1940. Nine years later, Carl Ferraro, a bartender working in Cleveland, Ohio, came out to visit L.A. and moved his family out west in 1951. Three years later he purchased the restaurant. Business was brisk so the Ferraro's expanded their restaurant in 1964. They hired interior yacht designer Guy Moore to transform the adjacent shoe store into the elegant fine dining space you see today. With white leatherette horseshoe booths, wheel-in tables, and 16-foot beam dividers, it's totally *Mad Men*!

Carl's son Jim Ferraro took over the restaurant in 2005 when his father passed, but not before The Dresden was rediscovered in the '90s as the hip, Hollywood place to be.

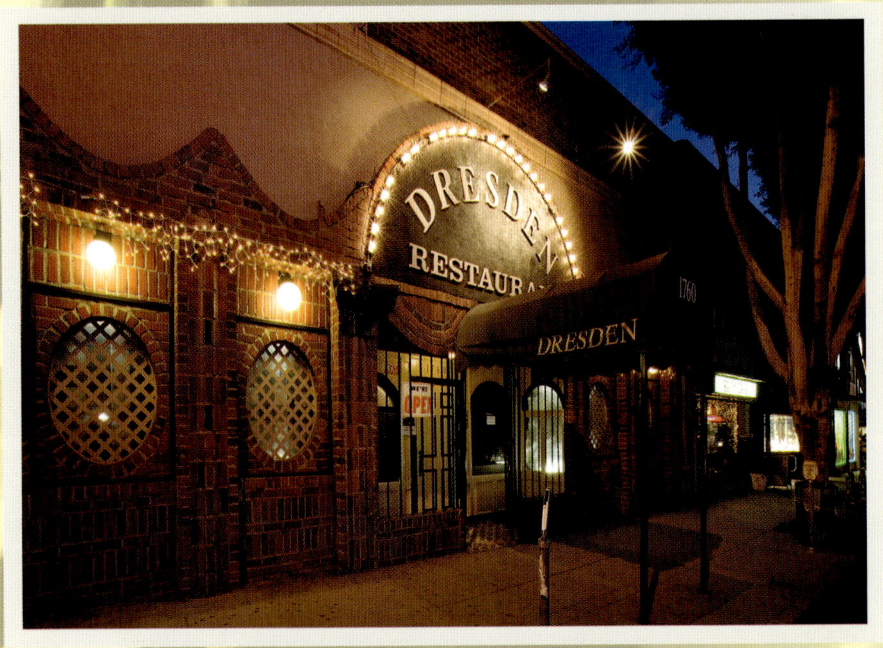

DRESDEN Restaurant

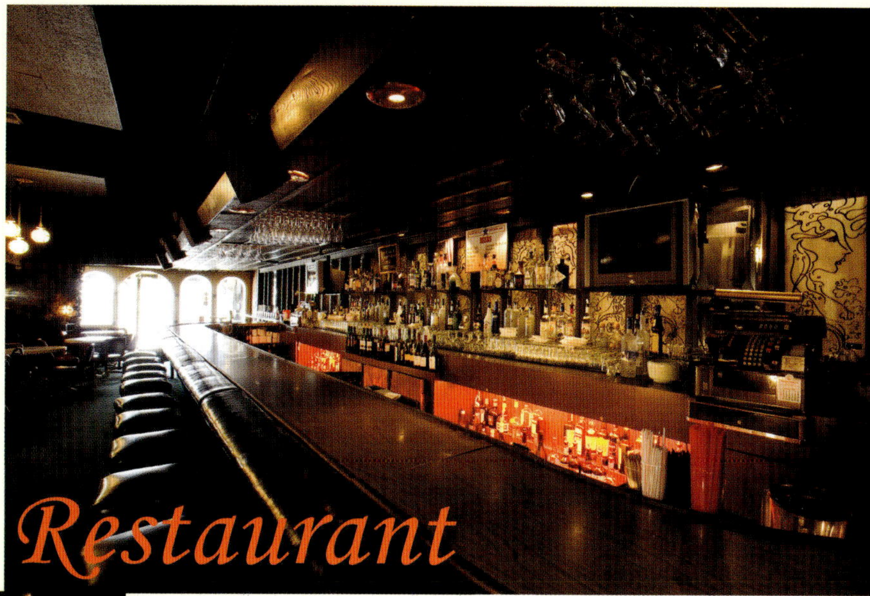

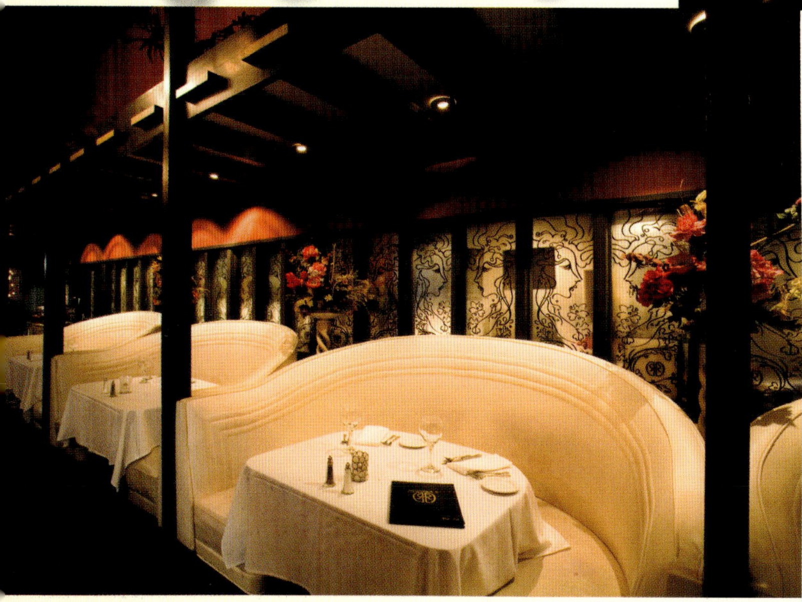

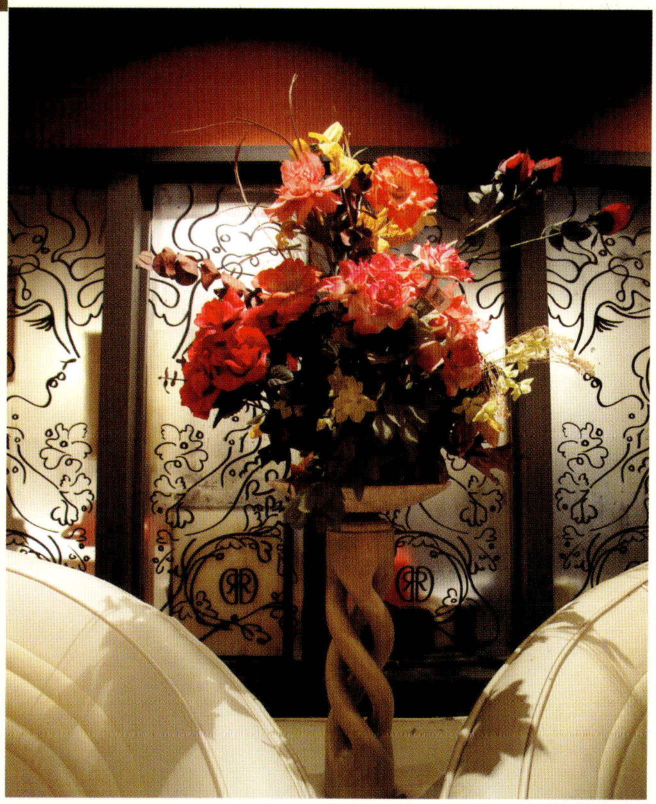

Driftyland Dairy-Port

10724 E. Lower Azusa Road, El Monte

Driftwood's history started when Pat J. Dolan, a young merchant marine from Ireland, jumped ship in Boston in search of a better life. Making his way across America, he found himself in California where he met his future wife while working in the laundry room of a L.A. hospital. Since he had worked on his father's farm in Ireland, he was eager to try something familiar, so in 1928, he bought a few cows and began his own dairy.

In the '60s, Driftwood announced their "answer to the space-age need for more speed and efficiency in the dairy drive-in field" by building a futuristic drive-thru dairy. On January 20th, 1960, the public was invited to "Blast Into Orbit With Driftyland" for three days of grand opening festivities. "Driftyland's New Space Age Dairy-Port" was celebrated as "the most modern dairy drive-in in the world."

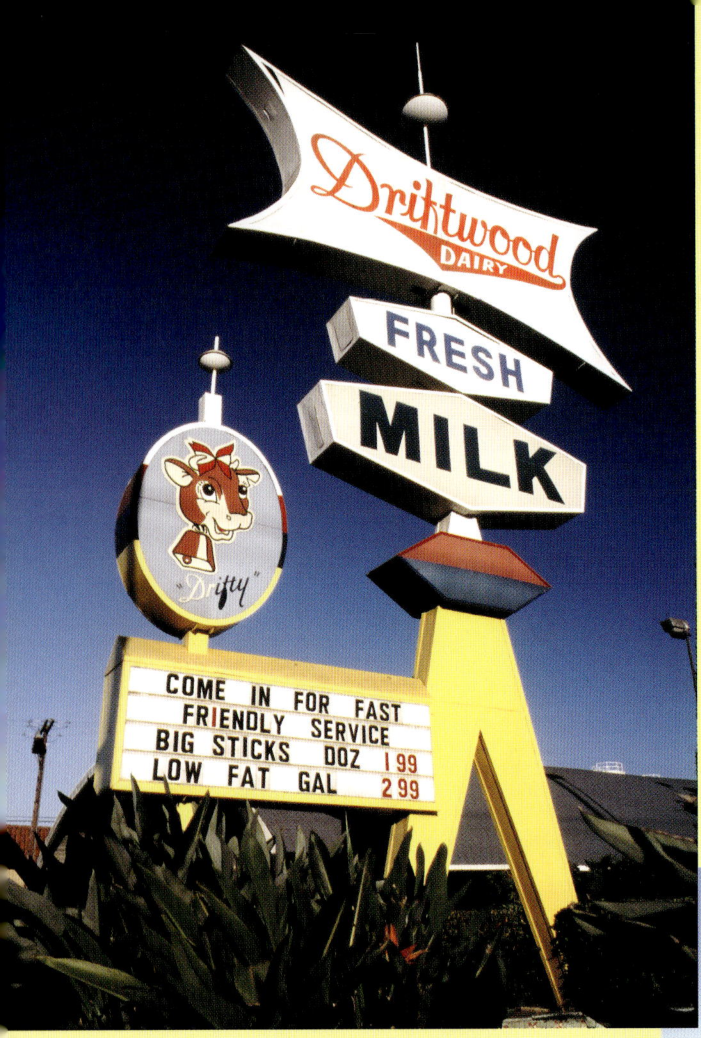

Circa 1960, this Googie sign has withstood the test of time and changing tastes. At 30 feet, Donahoo's fiberglass rooster has a great view of Pomona.

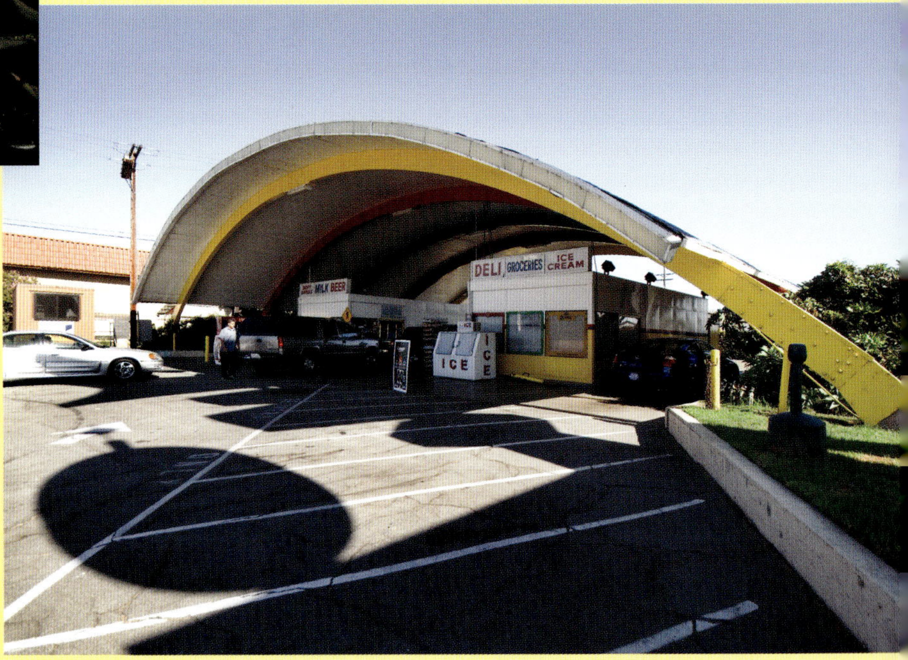

The now-historic Driftwood Dairy-Port is constructed of laminated bent wood.

Today, you can still stop in at Driftyland and enjoy an ice cream with the kids in their picnic area. Note the hand-painted tile planters featuring portraits of "Drifty the Cow" interspersed with quarts of milk. In 2008, Driftyland received the honor of qualifying as a California State Landmark.

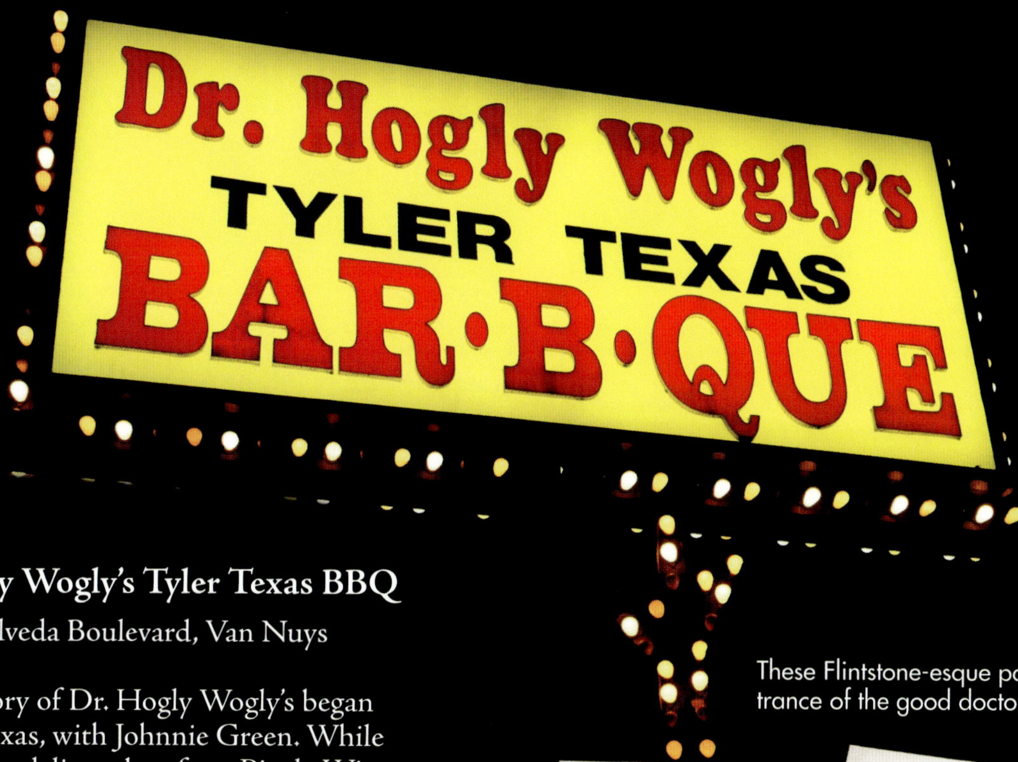

Dr. Hogly Wogly's Tyler Texas BBQ

8126 Sepulveda Boulevard, Van Nuys

The story of Dr. Hogly Wogly's began in Tyler, Texas, with Johnnie Green. While working as a delivery boy for a Piggly Wiggly grocery store, he earned the nickname "Hogly Wogly." He later became a pharmacologist but continued to receive praise for his BBQ. Legend has it that President Lyndon B. Johnson liked his food so much that he gave Johnnie some free advice, "Why not open a BBQ restaurant?" So in 1969, he did just that. He took over an old coffee shop and called his joint Dr. Hogly Wogly's Tyler Texas BBQ.

The doctor's secret recipe is still a secret, but we do know a little. Their special sauce is hand rubbed onto the meat which is cured overnight. The meats are then slow cooked in a wood burning brick pit for at least eight hours (that's why their meats are so flavorful and tender). They smoke their meats with mesquite, hickory, oak, cherry, and other woods. The sides are excellent, especially the macaroni salad and baked beans...which are to die for. Portions are so large that we usually split a two-way combo between the two of us and still have some to take home. One reviewer suggested that you "...wear your spurs" to this joint, and you know what? You wouldn't be out of place if you did.

These Flintstone-esque patio sets grace the entrance of the good doctor's restaurant.

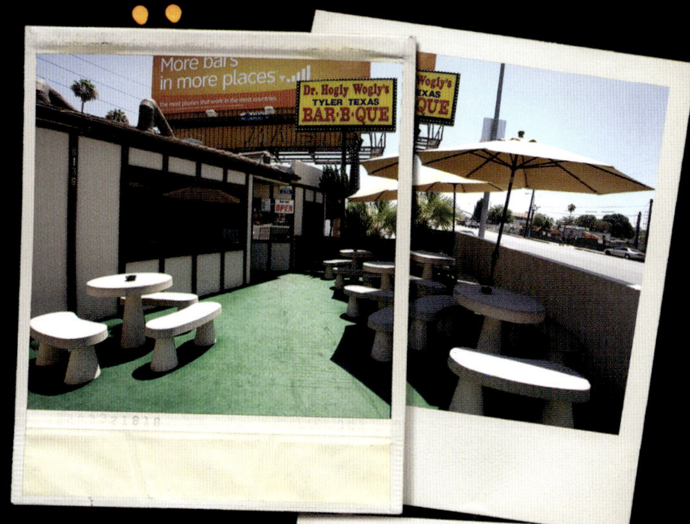

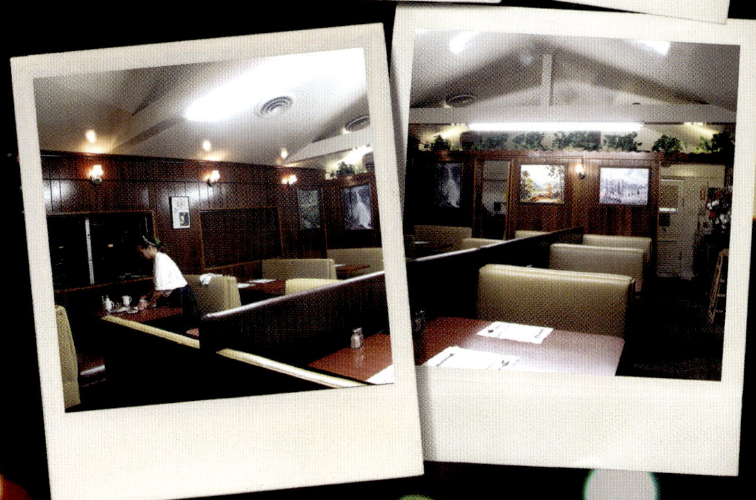

The interior of this modest eating establishment is nothing to write home about; it's all about the food here. Their outstanding BBQ melts in your mouth.

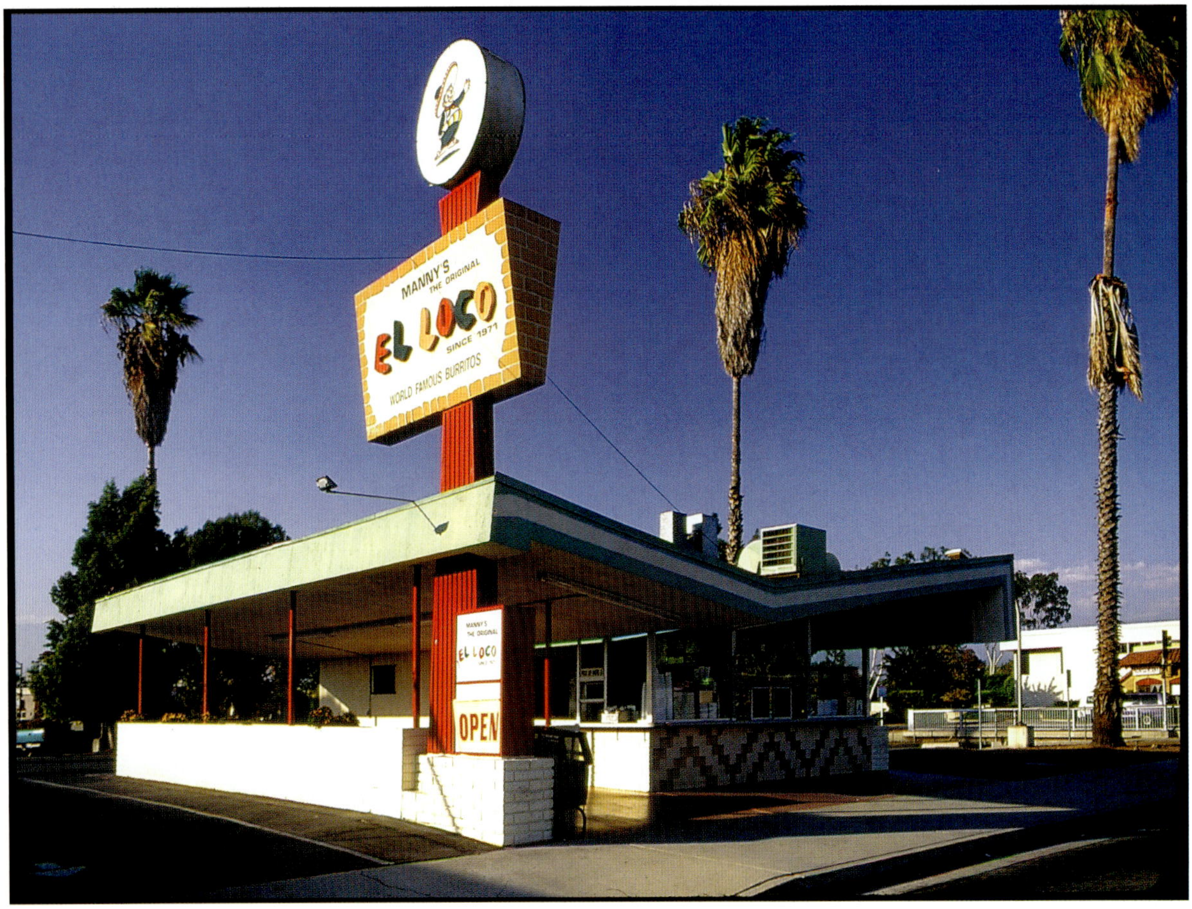

EL LOCO

437 S. Glendora, West Covina

Also known as The Original Manny's, El Loco was established in 1971. A lightweight butterfly roof adds pizazz to this otherwise ordinary food stand with an extraordinary menu. The inverted gabled roof includes folded eaves that double as sun visors. Similar in style to the Taco Paco chain, this was a successful Googie update to the standard roadside vernacular. The butterfly roof design was also favored by architects Palmer + Krisel who established the elegance of 1950s mid-century modern tract homes throughout the San Fernando Valley and Palm Springs.

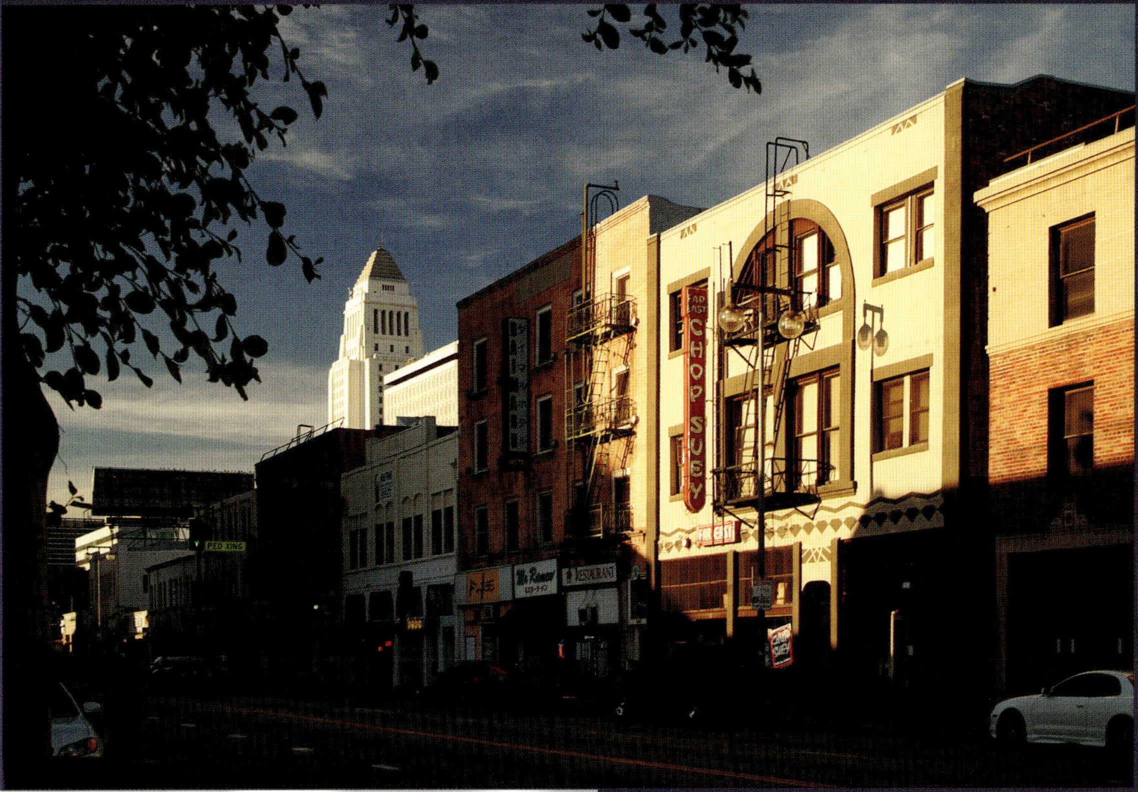

Only a couple of blocks away, Los Angeles City Hall can be seen in the background beyond the "Far East Chop Suey" sign.

FAR EAST CAFE

347 E. 1st Street, Los Angeles

Not to be confused with The Far East in Bakersfield, Sacramento, or San Francisco, this Chinese restaurant is located in the heart of Little Tokyo, Los Angeles. This historic building is one of the National Trust's "Save America's Treasures" sites and is recognized for its cultural significance. The 3-story beaux arts style building dates back to 1896. The Jung family opened The Far East restaurant in 1935, offering Cantonese specialties such as Chop Suey and Chow Mein. A double sided, two-story-tall, neon "Chop Suey" sign graces the front of the building. The main dining area is sectioned off by wood panels coated with what seem like inches of shellac. When John had a special effects studio four blocks away in the 1980s, he frequented this joint at lunchtime and marveled at how time has had zero effect on this place. It was way off the time-capsule meter. Throughout the years, The Far East has attracted celebrities, local politicians, and gangsters like Mickey Cohen. You can see it in "Chinatown", "Dragon", and "Farewell My Lovely" starring Robert Mitchum. It was damaged in the 1994 Northridge earthquake and remained closed for almost 10 years before it was renovated and re-opened as Chop Suey Cafe and Lounge.

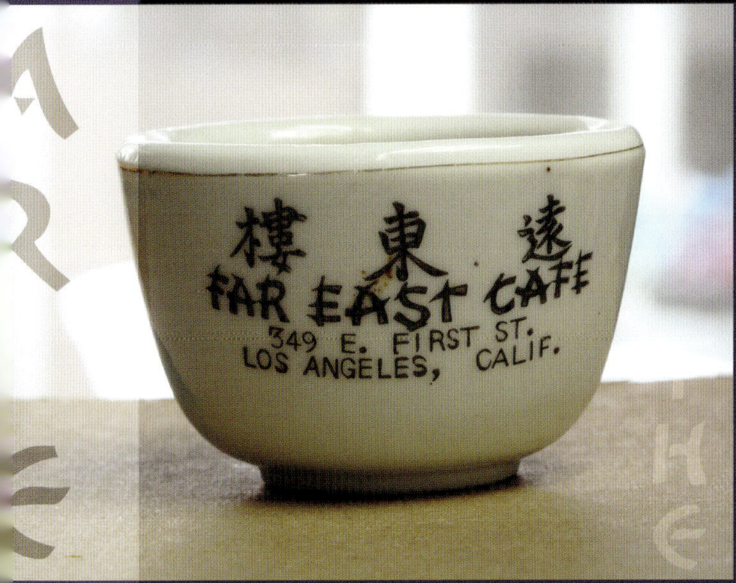

This vintage tea cup sat on their table for over 10 years before the restaurant reopened as Chop Suey Café and Lounge.

Many business buildings in Downtown L.A. have been renovated into lofts over the past 10 years. Downtown is on a comeback as the hip place to live and work. Chop Suey is one of many places that have been resurrected during this renaissance.

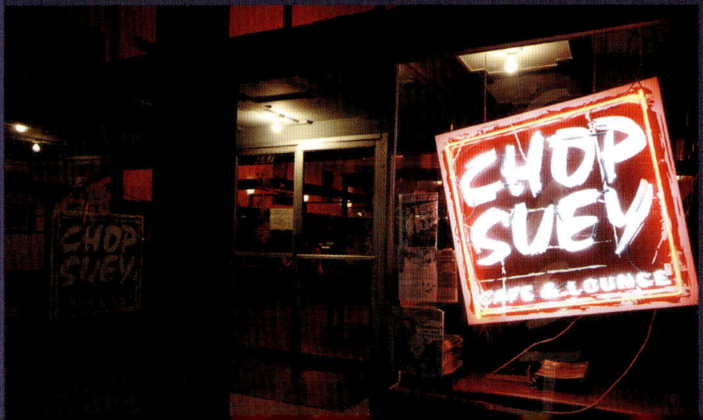

In Glassell Park, near Downtown L.A., this Fosters has changed little since the '50s.

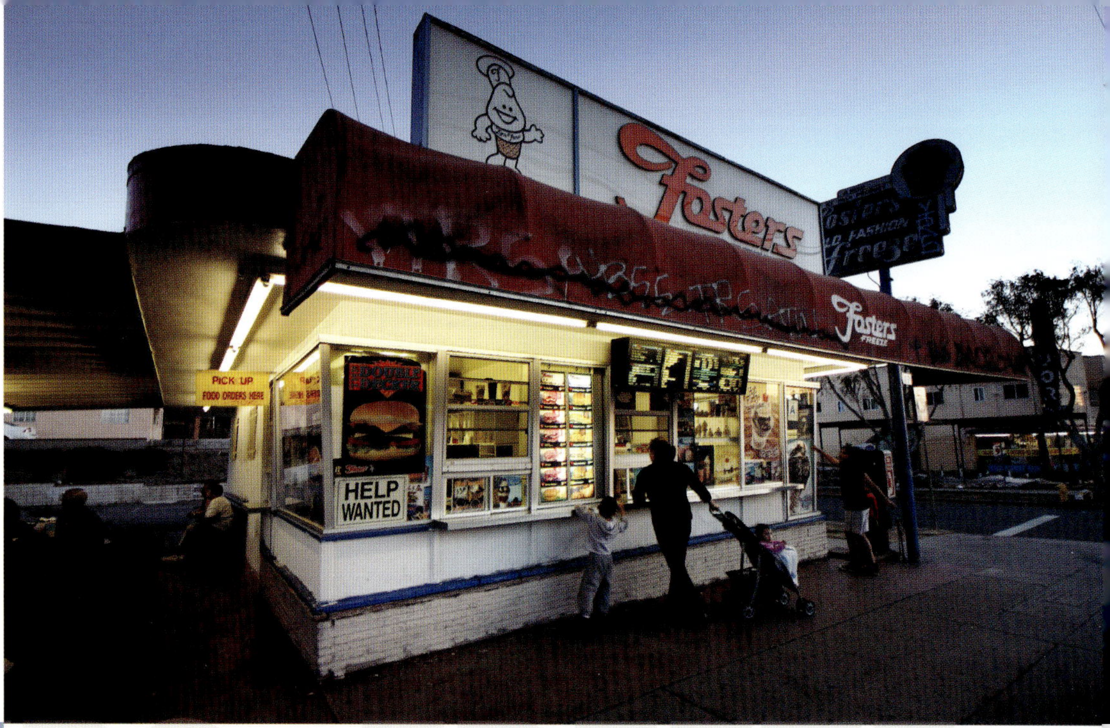

FOSTERS FREEZE

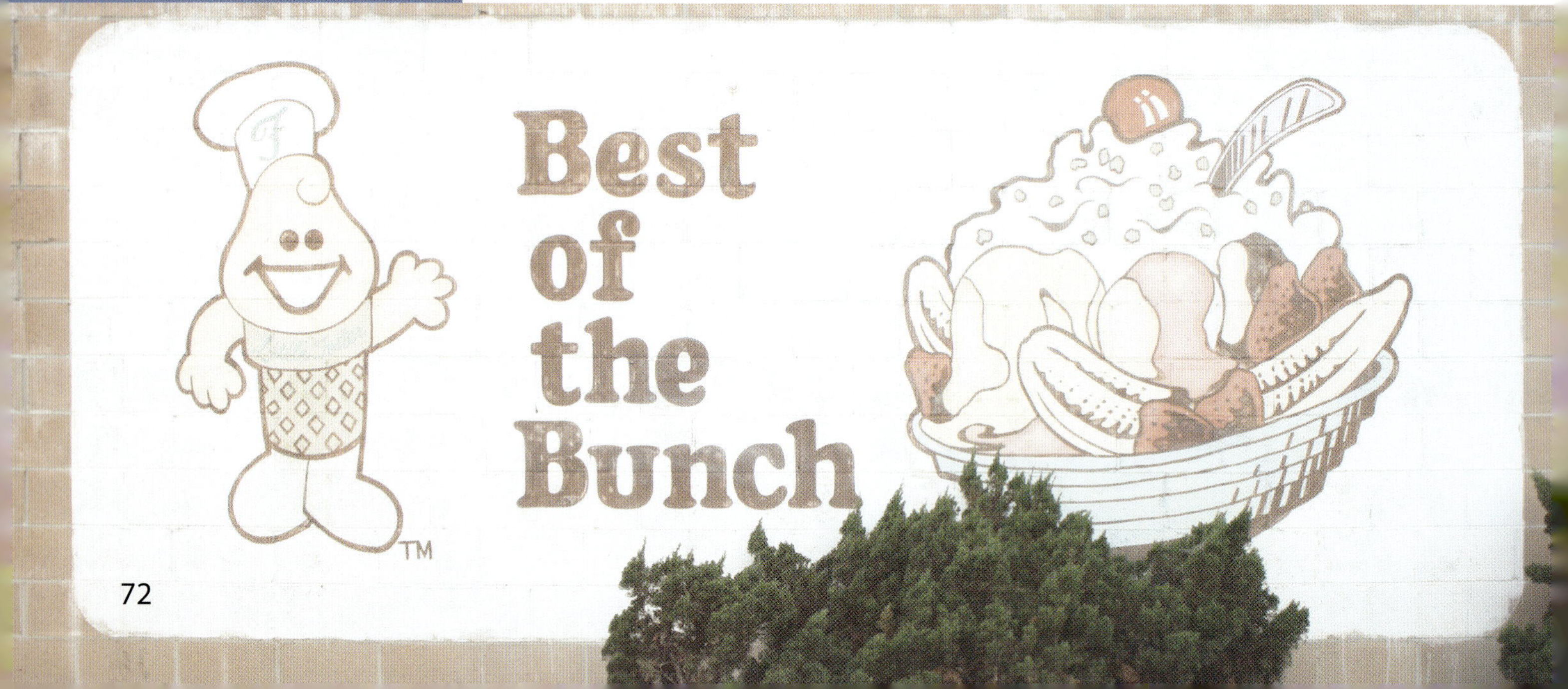

Fosters Freeze

Multiple locations

Advertised as California's first fast food chain and original soft serve, Fosters' motto is, "Everything at Fosters is wonderful to eat." In 1946, George Foster introduced the soft-serve cone here after starting up the first Fosters Freeze in Inglewood, California. Who hasn't waited in line for a chocolate dipped cone or chocolate and vanilla swirl? Fosters has always had two windows, one for ice cream orders and the other for hamburgers, fries, etc. Fosters' first franchise began in Tulare in 1955. Over the years, classic car shows became popular and soon Fosters was hosting their own cruise nights. Beach Boys' Dennis Wilson has said he was at the Hawthorne location when he was inspired to write about the girl in the T-Bird who went cruising to the hamburger stand in their song, "Fun, Fun, Fun."

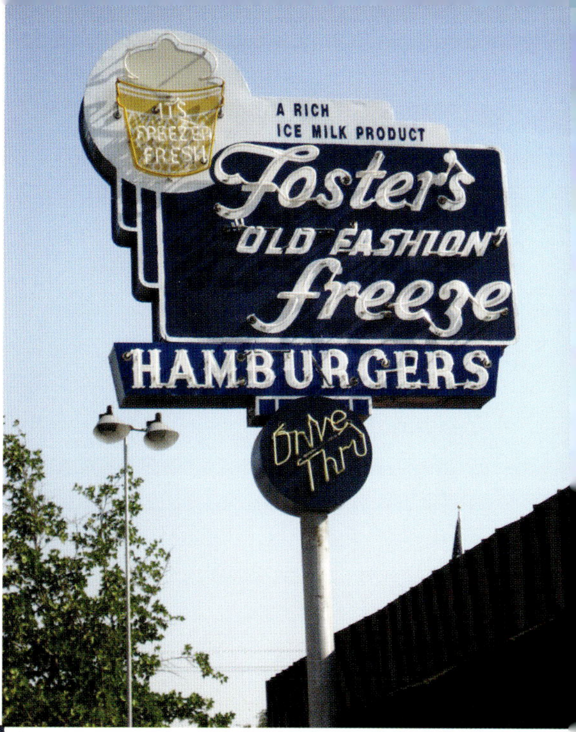

This original Fosters Freeze sign was on Glenoaks Blvd. in Glendale.

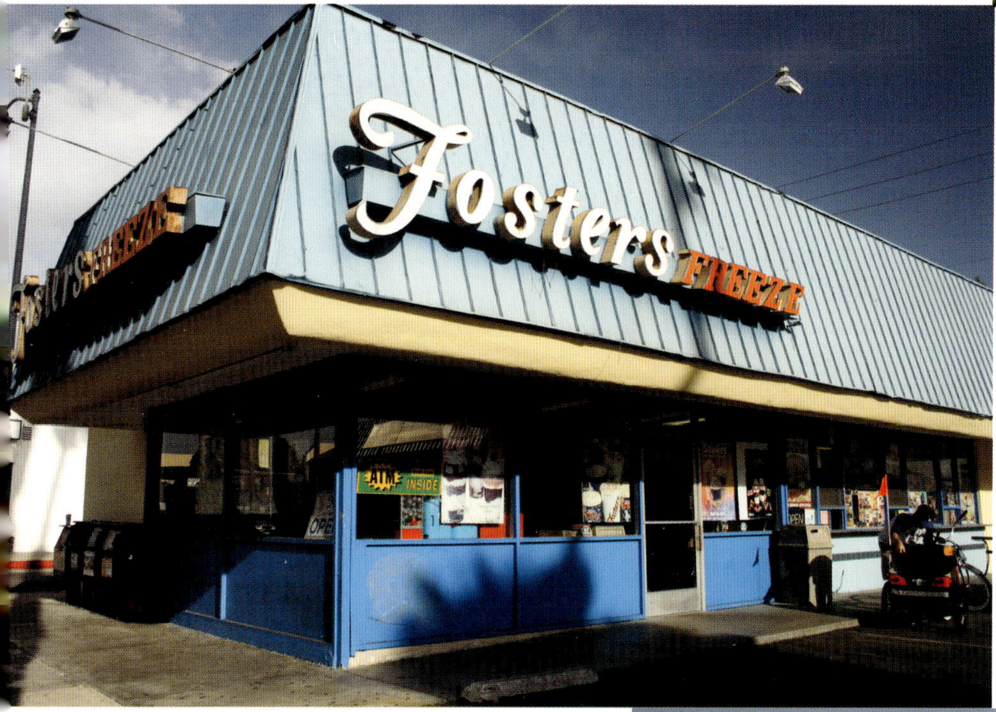

This Santa Monica Fosters Freeze shows a later design interpretation.

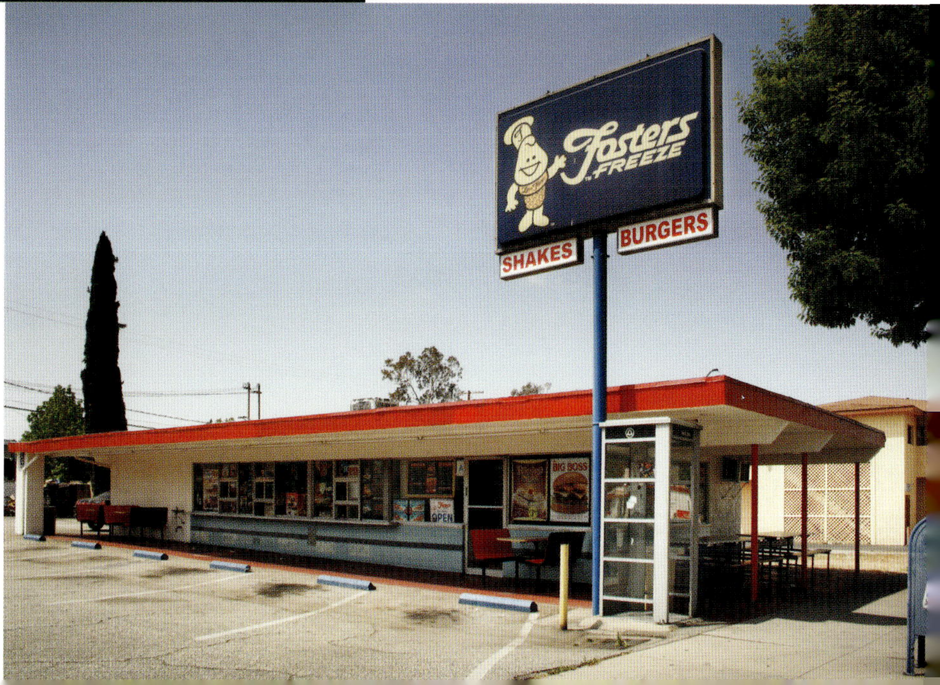

On Historic Route 66, not far from the famous Aztec Motel.

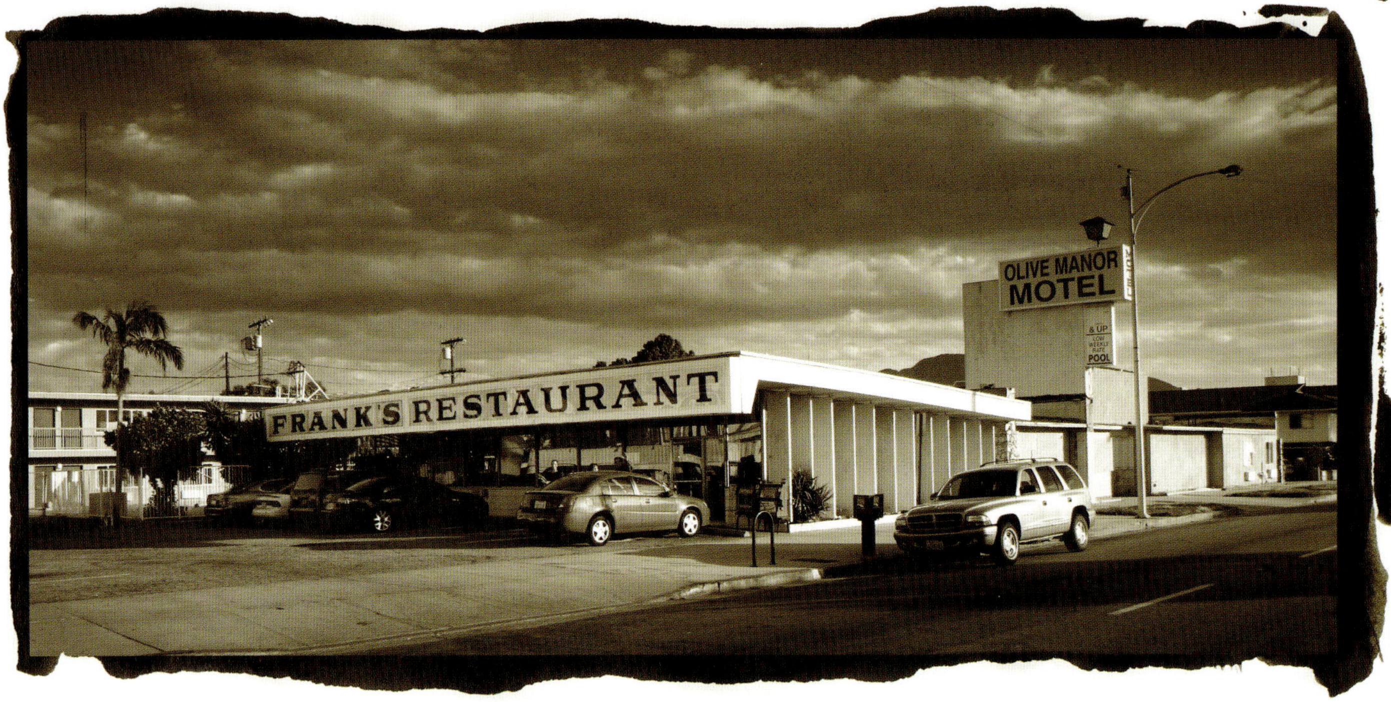

Appetizers

Shrimp Cocktail Supreme 1.25

Soups

Soup du Jour: Cup 15; Bowl 25

FRANK'S

"WHERE STEAKS ARE OUR SPECIALTY"

House Specialties

CHOICE TOP SIRLOIN STEAK SANDWICH $1.75
Baked Potato, Creamery Butter, Garlic Bread

"CHAR-CHAR" 90c
Full 1/4 Lb. Charcoal Broiled Hamburger
Crisp Mixed Green Salad, Roquefort Cheese Dressing
and Plenty of French Fries

BARBECUED BEEF OR HAM DIP 90c
With Our Own Sauce, Served on a Toasted French Roll
with Salad and French Fries

TWO CONEY ISLAND HOT DOGS 90c
With Crisp Green Salad and
French Fried Potatoes

GRILLED HAM AND AMERICAN CHEESE $1.00

From Our Char-Broile

PETITE FILET MIGNON . . . .
FRANK'S GIANT MIGNON . . . .
CHOICE GRADE "AA" TOP SIRLOIN . . . .
NEW YORK CUT SIRLOIN, "The Finest" . . . .
BROILED CENTER CUT PORK CHOPS, Apple Sauce . . . .
GROUND SIRLOIN OF BEEF (Our Own Grind) . . . . . .
BROILED VIRGINIA HAM, Fruit Sauce . . . .
GRILLED CHICKEN FRIED STEAK, Natural . . . .
ROAST OREGON TOM TURKEY, Sage Dressing . . . . . .
GRILLED CALF'S LIVER, Saute Onion Rings or Bacon . . .
ROAST SIRLOIN OF BEEF . . . .
BROCHETTE OF BEEF TENDERLOIN . . . .
PAN FRIED CHICKEN, Our Chef's Own . . . .

Above Orders Served with Soup du Jour or Crisp Mixed G
Baked Russet Potato, Sour Cream and Chives or Butter or
and Frank's Garlic Bread

CHEF'S OWN FRENCH STYLE SPAGHETTI AND MEAT SAU
Mixed Green Salad, Garlic Bread
HALF ORDER 75c

Low Calorie Specials

GROUND SIRLOIN PATTY . . . .
"Our Own Special Grind" Char-Broiled with Cottage Chee
Sliced Tomatoes, Ry-Krisp

U. S. TOP SIRLOIN STEAK . . . .
Natural, Sliced Tomatoes, Cottage Cheese, Ry-Krisp or Garlic

ROAST SIRLOIN OF BEEF . . . .
with Cottage Cheese and Peach, Sliced Tomatoes, Ry-Kris

Chili a la Mexico

Chili Straight . . . . .65 **Chili Beans** . . . .
Spaghetti and Chili, Melted Nippy Cheese . . . .
One-Quarter Pound Hamburger Size with Lots of Chili

Sea Food

Following Orders Served with Soup du Jour or Crisp Mixed
French Fries or Baked Potato

BREADED OYSTERS, Deep Fried, Tartar Sauce . . . . . .
NORTHERN HALIBUT STEA (Center Cut Boneless) To

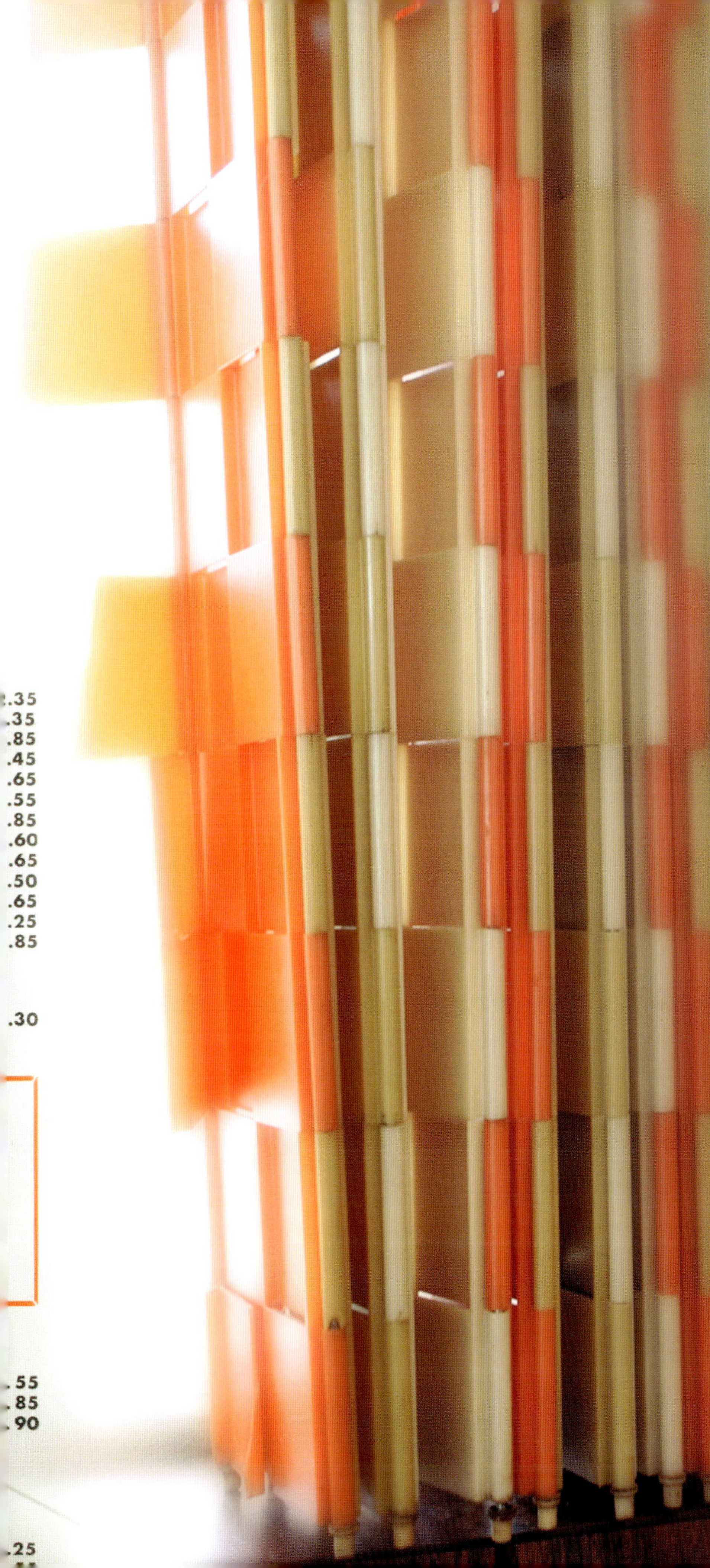

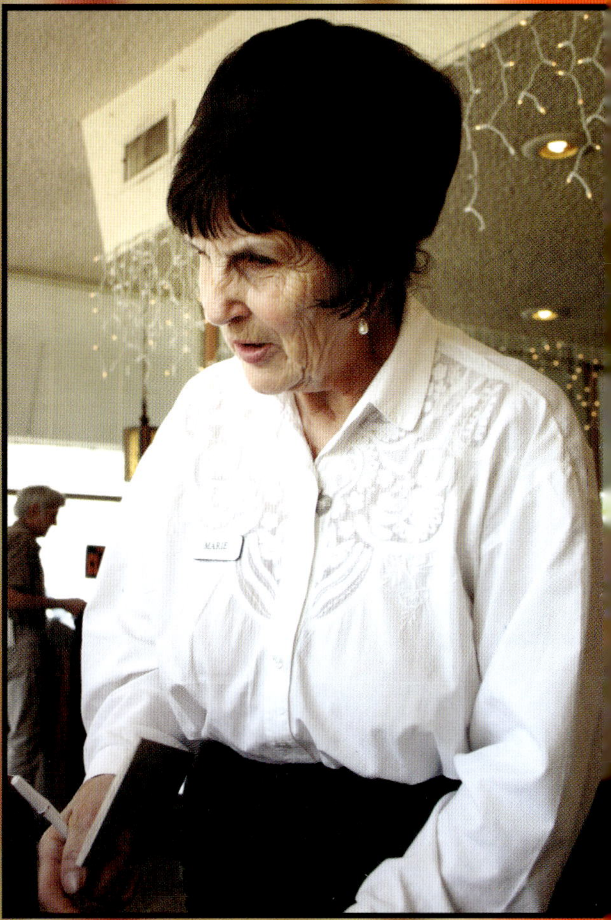

Frank's Coffee Shop

916 W. Olive Avenue, Burbank

Frank's sits next to Portofino, the old Olive Manor Motel. Steve and Athena ran the restaurant from 1960 to 2008, when they retired and sold the restaurant to Jose, the former chef of Genio's Italian restaurant.

We are always greeted with a smile by Frank's longtime waitress Marie, whom we seem to be following. The first time we met Marie was at the second Frank's Coffee Shop in North Hollywood. Marie is a rarity in this town. She's not an actress acting as a waitress, but an actual career waitress. She worked at the Rheinlander on 5th and Manchester and the Old Heidelberg in Van Nuys before it became The Matterhorn Chef. Originally from Germany, Marie told us an American GI brought her here in 1966 and she has remained in the States ever since. Seeing Marie makes our day.

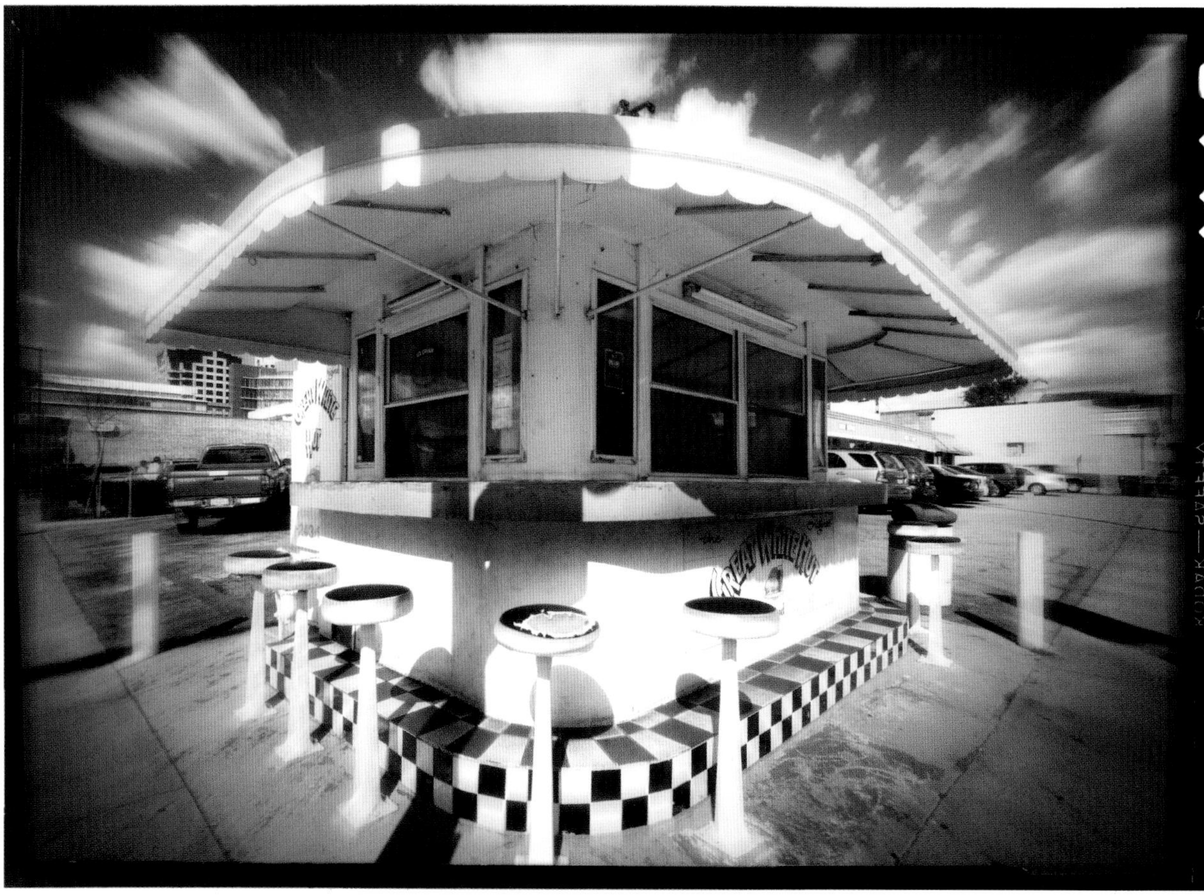

The Great White Hut

121 W. California Avenue, Glendale

This tiny lunch stand, with barely ten stools, was known as Paul's Great White Hut for many years. Their sign proclaims "The Original Great White Hut, Second to None." The architect for this diminutive streamline moderne building is listed as Karl W. Ponsy. The original building permit was pulled in 1946 by J.D. Zinke, founder of Zinke's Shoe Repair right next door, a Glendale institution since 1919. This is such a swell corner! You can read your newspaper over breakfast at The Hut while you get your favorite spats re-soled at Zinke's.

Greenblatt's

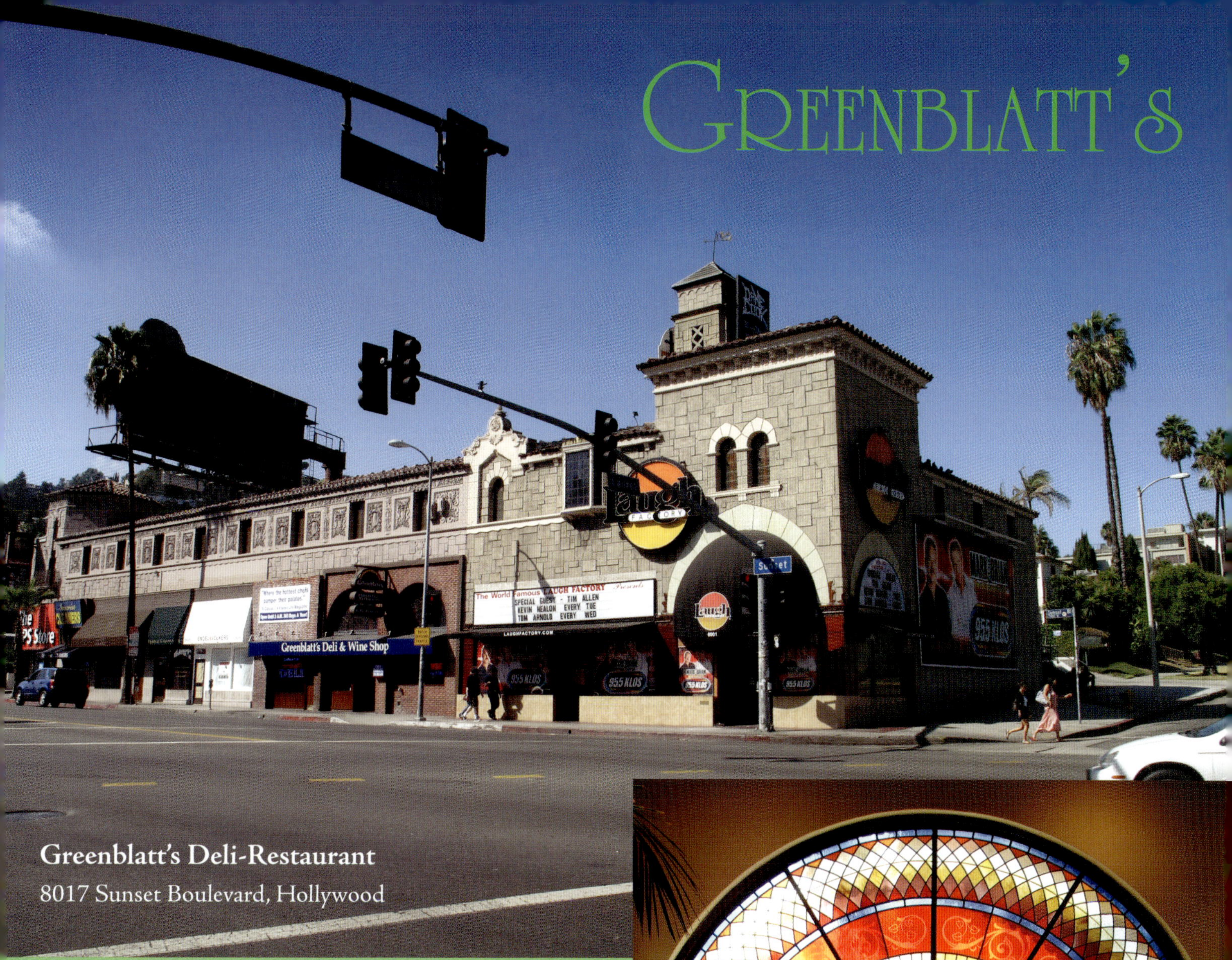

Greenblatt's Deli-Restaurant

8017 Sunset Boulevard, Hollywood

Located on the famous Sunset Strip, and founded by Herman Greenblatt in 1926, the Kavin Family bought Greenblatt's in the early '40s and still runs it today. In addition to terrific deli food, they also have an exceptional fine wine and spirits shop. The clientele for this eatery is so rich with Hollywood history that it could easily fill this book. Marilyn Monroe, Joe DiMaggio, F. Scott Fitzgerald, Billie Holiday, Bing Crosby, Bela Lugosi, Marlon Brando, Lenny Bruce, and Janis Joplin were regulars.

Within this historic building is L.A. icon The Laugh Factory. Richard Pryor was the very first comedian to appear here when they opened in '79, followed by some of the biggest names in entertainment, including Jim Carrey, Robin Williams, Rodney Dangerfield, Jerry Seinfeld, Damon Wayans, Dave Chapelle, Chris Rock, Chris Tucker, Kathy Griffin, and Roseanne Barr.

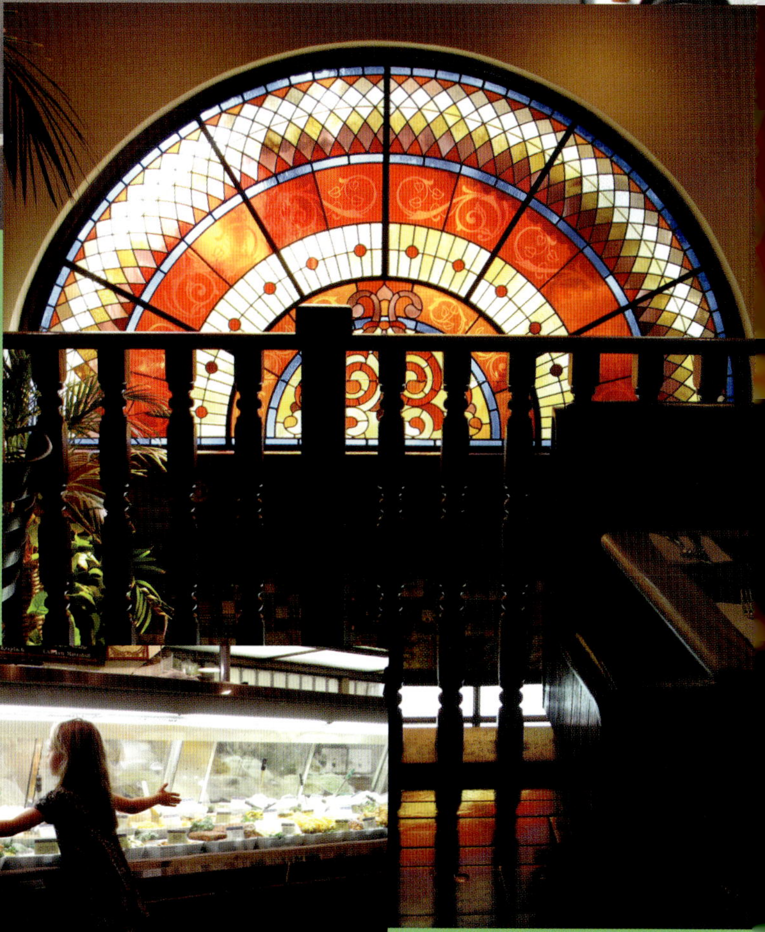

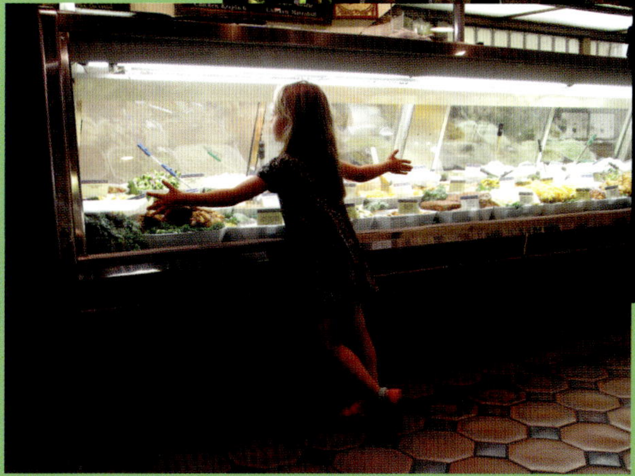

The Grinder Haven

724 W. Holt Boulevard, Route 66, Ontario

Like the force of a black hole, it was impossible to resist the pull of an enormous glowing submarine sandwich sign right there on the Mother Road. A tracer arrow directed us off of Route 66 and into their huge parking lot. There before us stood The Grinder Haven, circa 1958, with three sets of A-framed beams piercing the roof like giant knives. We felt the tinge of excitement usually reserved for discovering something that was thought to be extinct. After rushing out of our car, we spotted a customer smiling as he carted off a four-foot grinder sandwich. Adriene flashed back to the old AMC Pacer commercial from the '70s, in which The Sandwich King was able to assemble a four-foot sandwich in the roomy back seat of the new Pacer and still make his delivery on time. It was a good night.

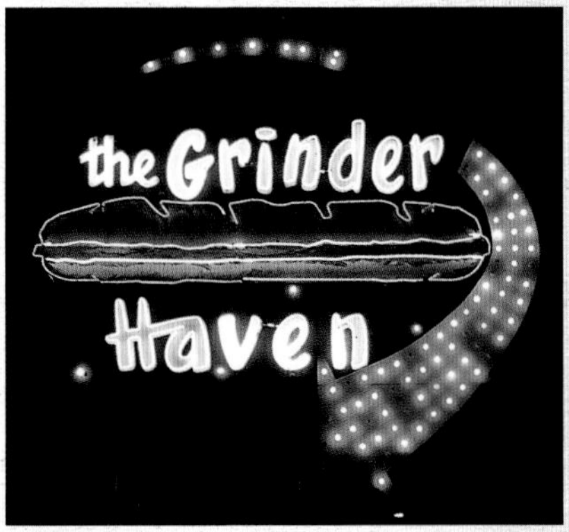

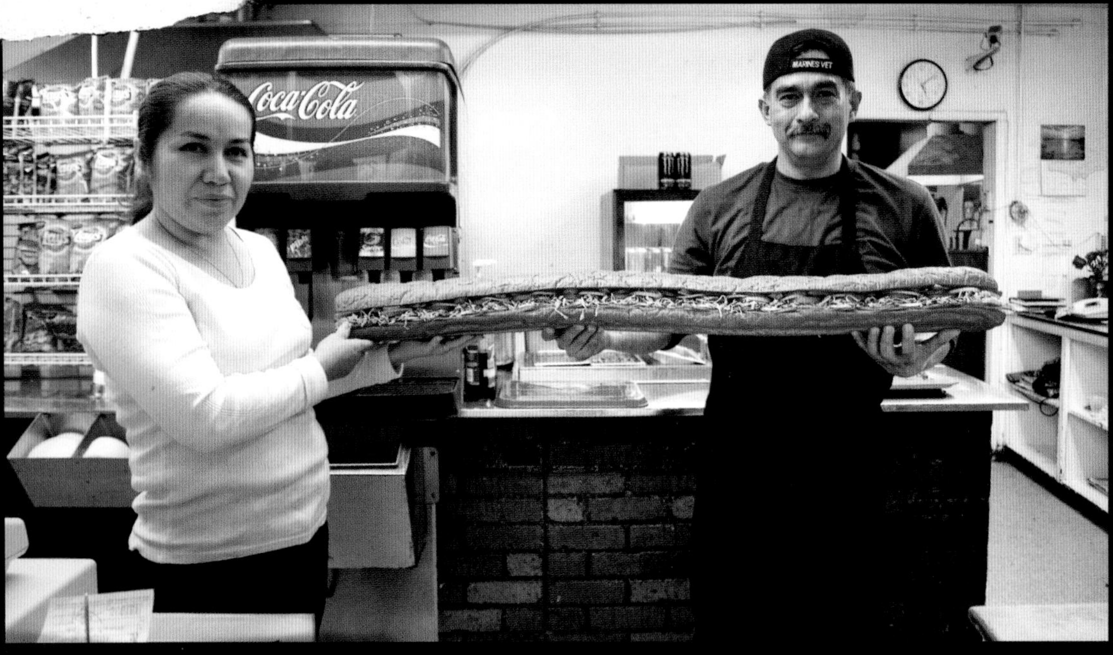

Alma and Juan Idlla showing off their special four-foot grinder sandwich.

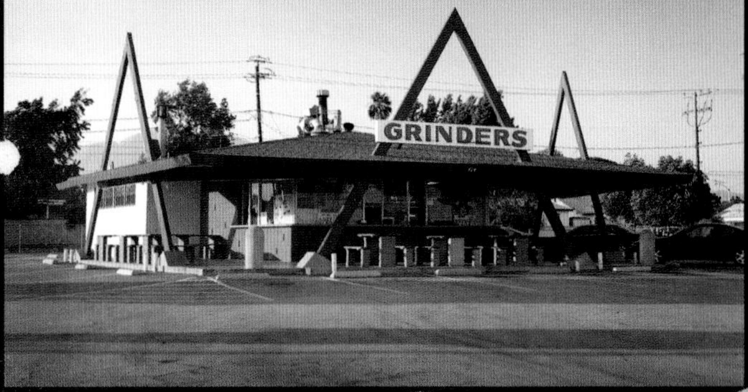

HALFWAY HOUSE CAFE 15564 Sierra Highway, Santa Clarita

Named the Halfway House because it is located halfway between Los Angeles and Palmdale, the cafe opened here in 1931 at an authentic trading post where farmers met back in the 1900s.

Marooned on Sierra Highway (old US Route 6), this quaint roadside cafe transcends time and place. It can easily stand in for Mississippi, Kansas, or even a WPA Depression-era Dust Bowl town, though it's only 40 minutes from Downtown L.A. You probably saw it in the Pepsi commercial with Cindy Crawford or "Twilight Zone: The Movie." It's been in countless movies like "Heartbreak Ridge" and "Space Cowboys", both starring Clint Eastwood; "Life" with Eddie Murphy and Martin Lawrence; and "Spartan" with Val Kilmer. Halfway House attracts some serious film work, not just a few short scenes but major movie sequences.

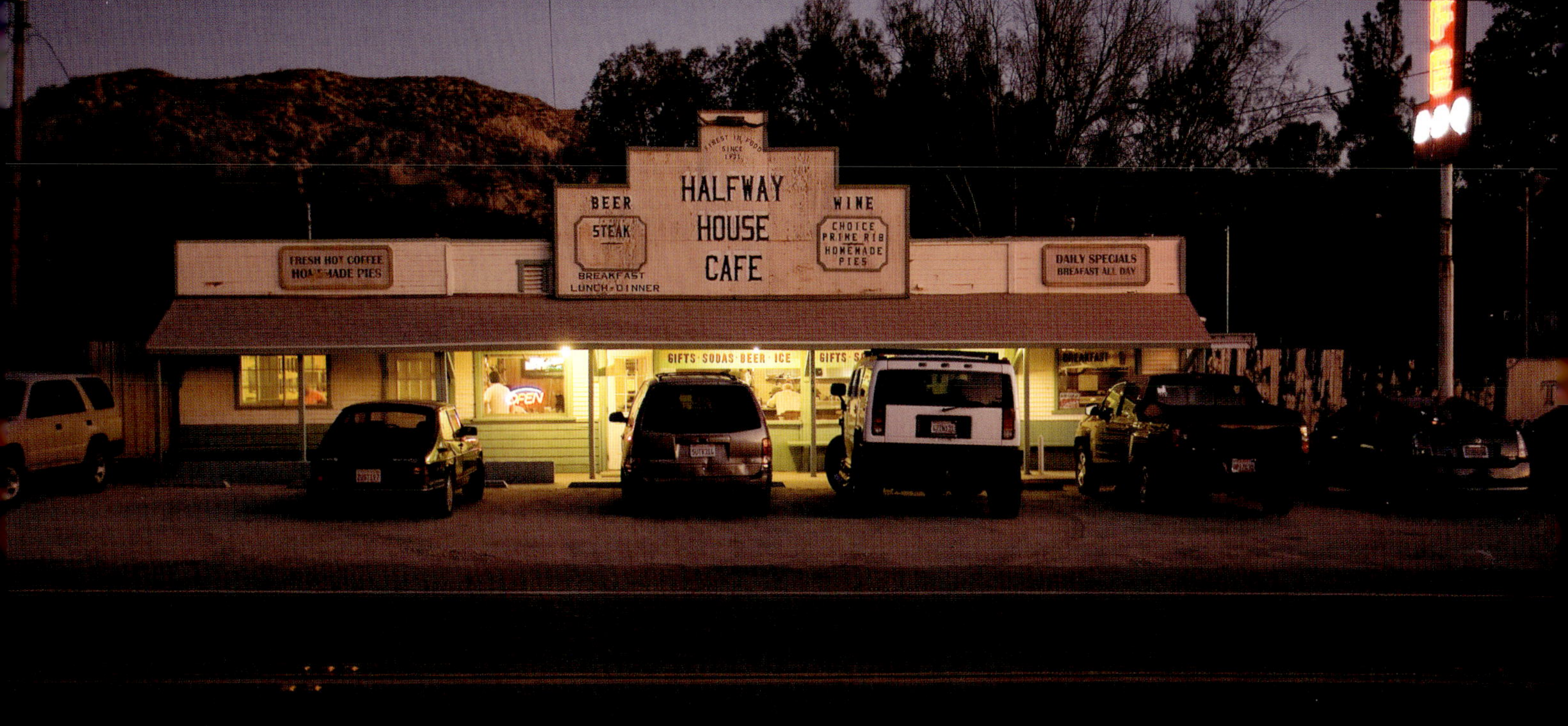

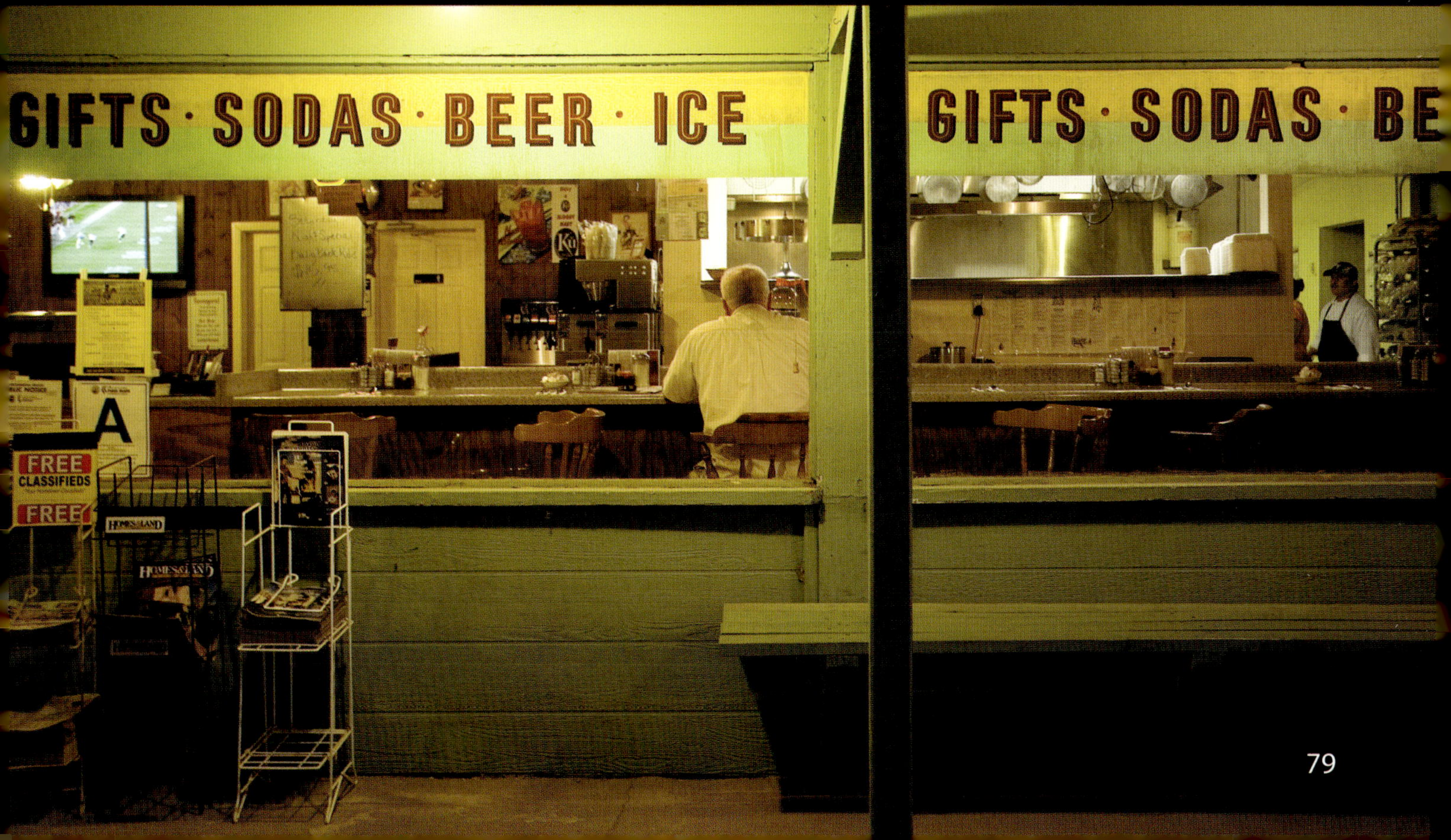

HARBOR HOUSE CAFE

Harbor House Cafe

16341 Pacific Coast Highway, Sunset Beach, CA

This is an amazing circa 1939 cafe, open day and night, 365 days a year. A stone's throw from the Pacific Ocean, we love to stop in after a day at the beach. It's also handy around 3 A.M. when you just can't sleep. Lots of people swear it's the best little cafe in the world 'cause it's as comfortable as hanging out in your own living room. The food is great and the portions are huge. There's every kind of food available, from fresh crab omelettes to Cobb salads to Alaskan halibut steaks. With cozy booths and walls plastered with vintage movie posters, you can't go wrong here.

Afterwards, shoot a few games of pool at Turc's, or cross PCH and chill out at the new Don the Beachcomber's (formerly Sam's Seafood). Check out the converted water tower, it's now someone's home. You can't miss it, it's three stories high and sticks out like the Martian space craft in *War of the Worlds*. Remember, the Harbor House never sleeps.

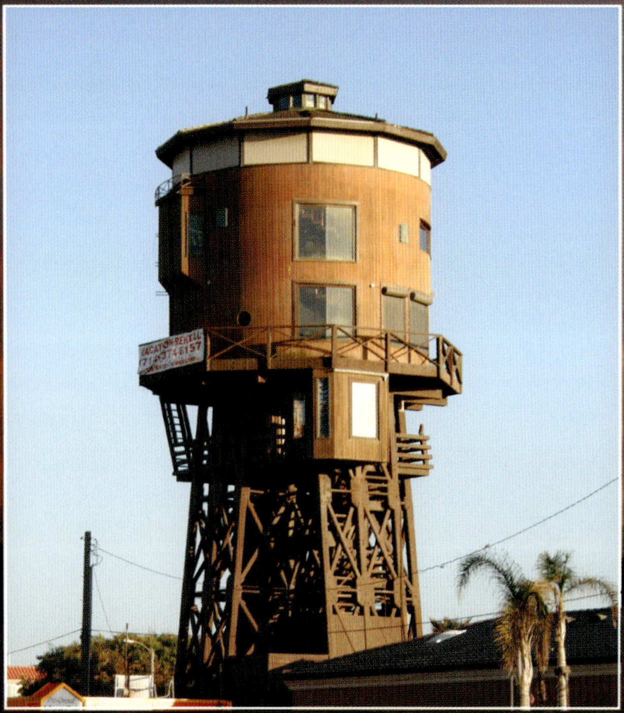

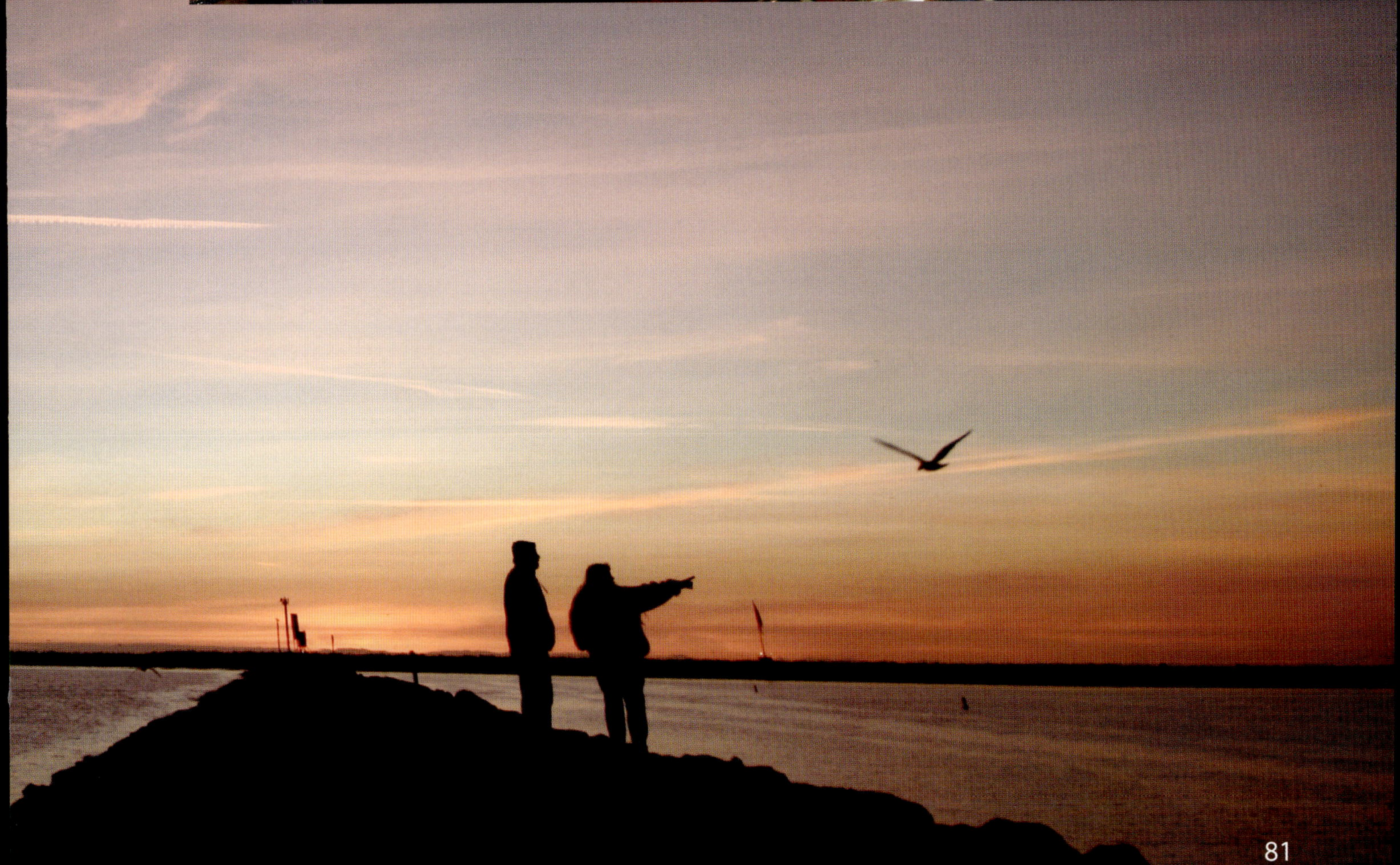

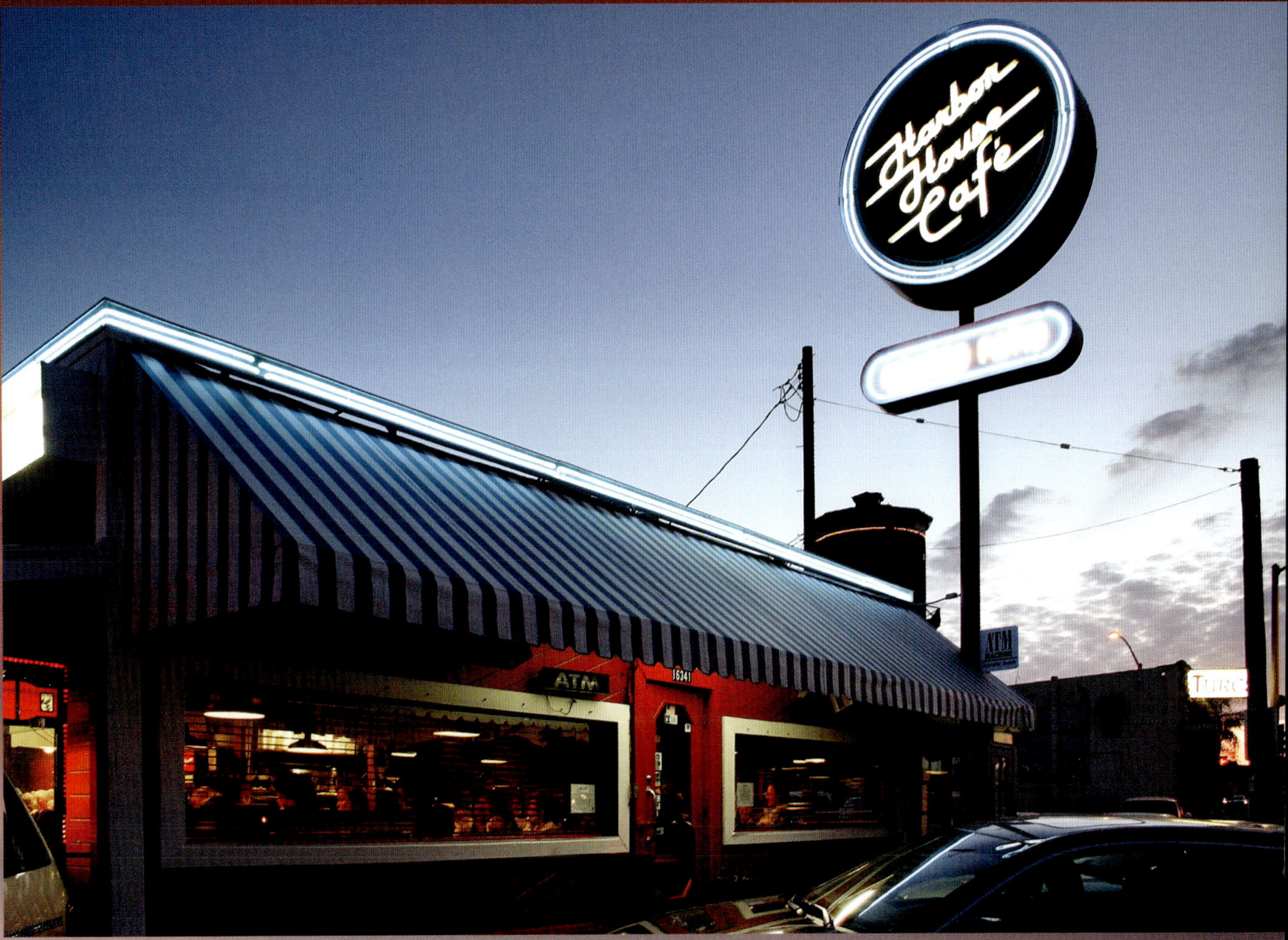
Harbor House Café
ATM
16341

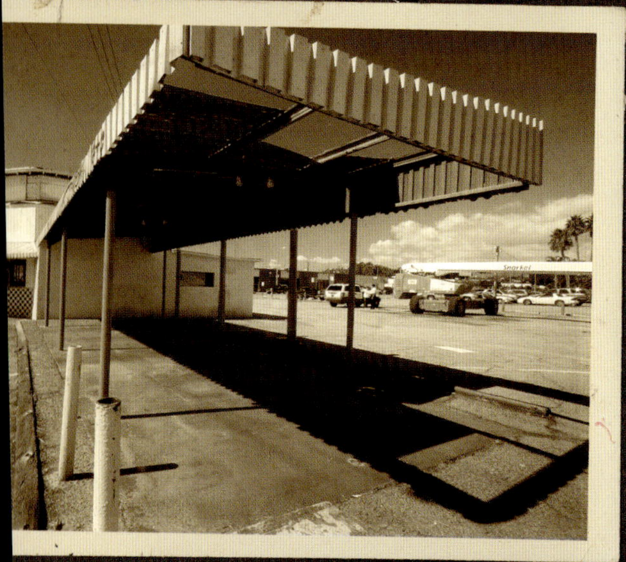

This abandoned Hat in the City of San Fernando does not seem to be long for this world...

The Hat

Multiple Locations

Celebrating over 50 years at this location, The Original Hat's distinctive checkerboard design adds to the charm and character of this intersection at Valley and Garfield in Alhambra. Originating in the San Gabriel Valley, The Hat has been operated by the Conzonire family since 1981, with additional locations serving So Cal's hungry pastrami-loving population. The Alhambra location has an old fashioned outdoor patio, so grab a seat and try their "World Famous Pastrami" dip sandwich served on a french roll. You won't be sorry.

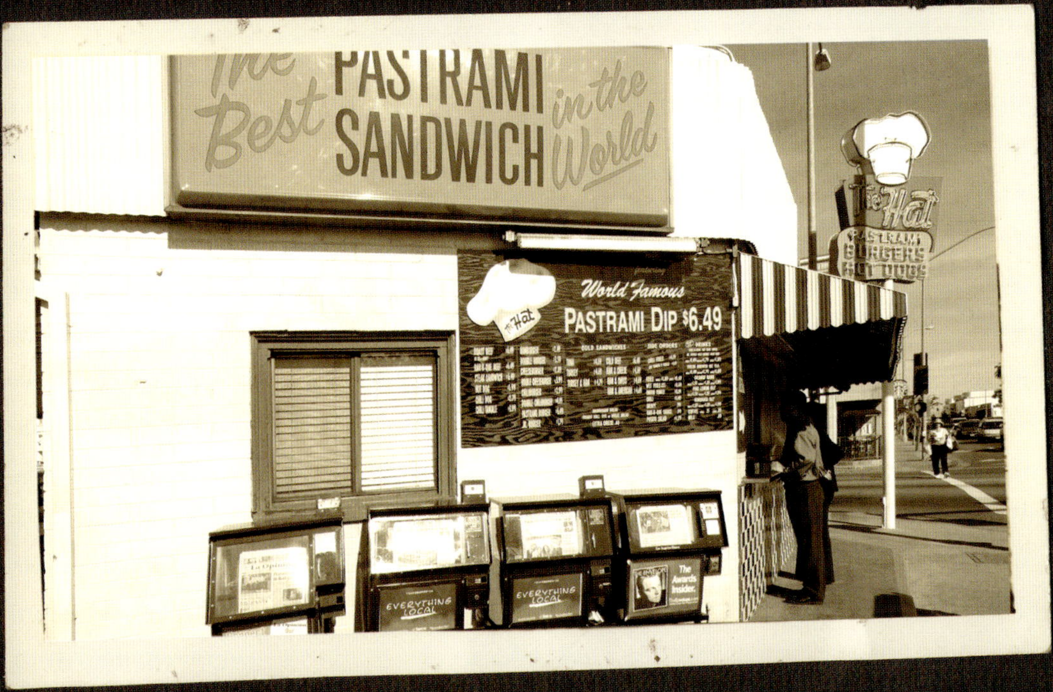

The Hat

Heart's Coffee Shop

16918 Saticoy Street, Van Nuys

Heart's is a classic diner style coffee shop that dates back to the '40s. It has lots of atmosphere and one of the longest counters we've seen. When we talked to manager Sue Wong, she told us that her parents moved here from China and were immediately put to work in their in-laws' coffee shop called Eleanor's. They put in 16 hour days for many years before scraping enough savings together to buy their own place in Van Nuys. John recalls going to Eleanor's in the early '80s when he worked at the old Desilu Studios around the corner. Heart's is one of the oldest coffee shops left in the San Fernando Valley, so it's often scouted as a filming location. Recently, we caught a glimpse of it in an episode of *My Name is Earl*.

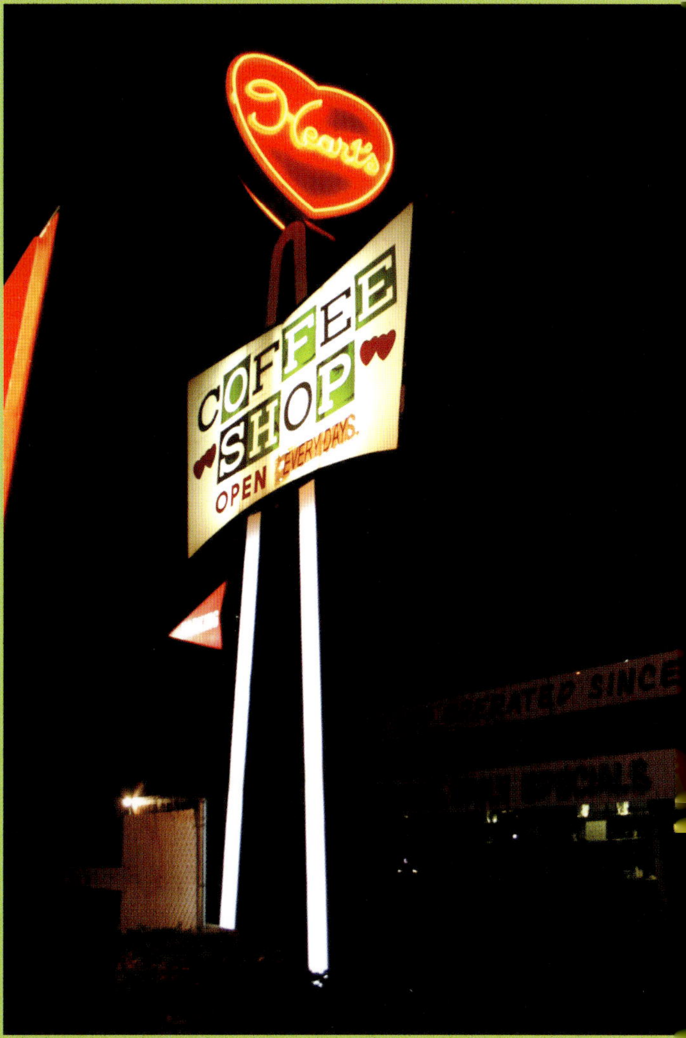

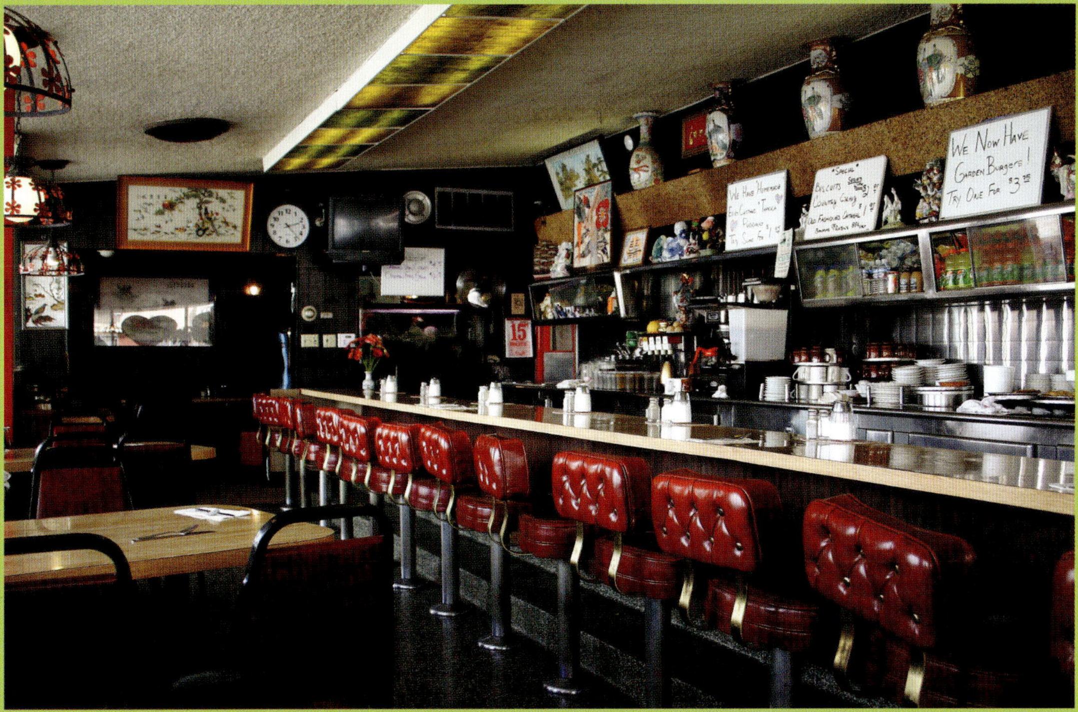

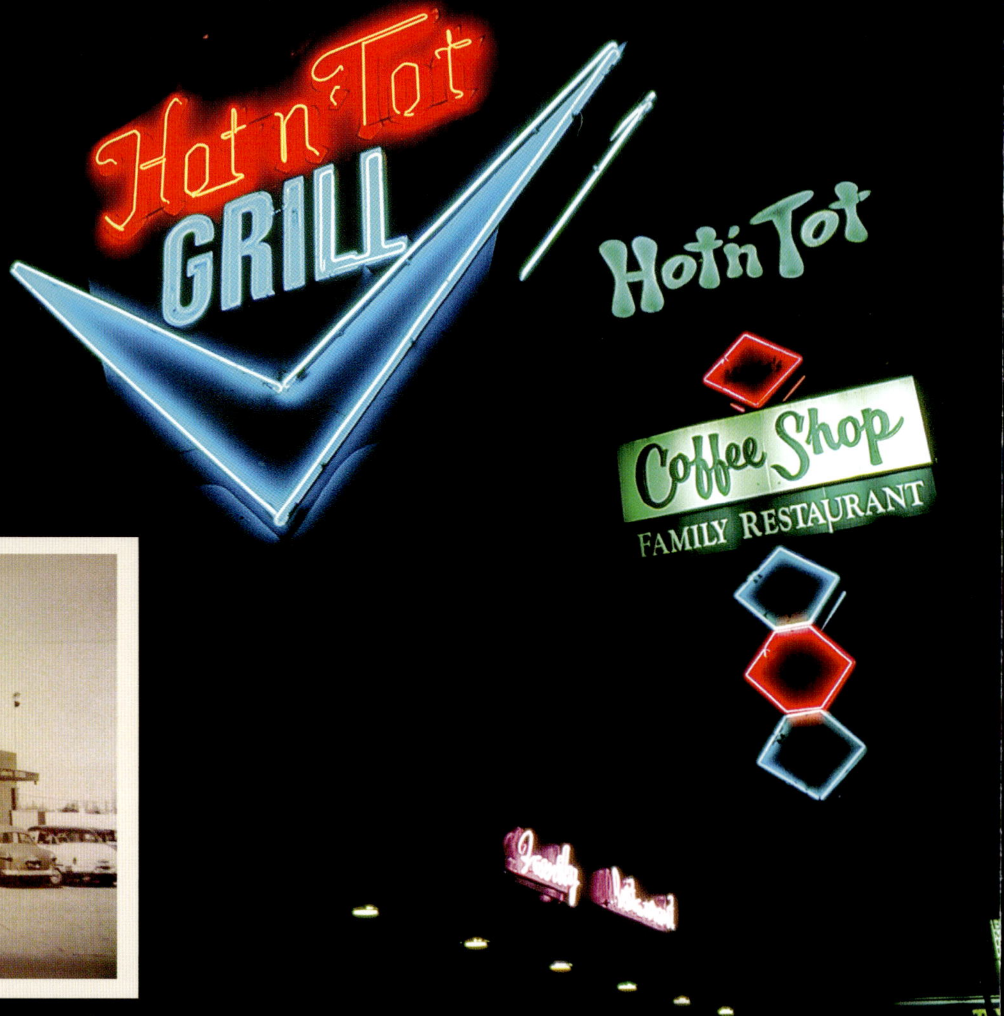

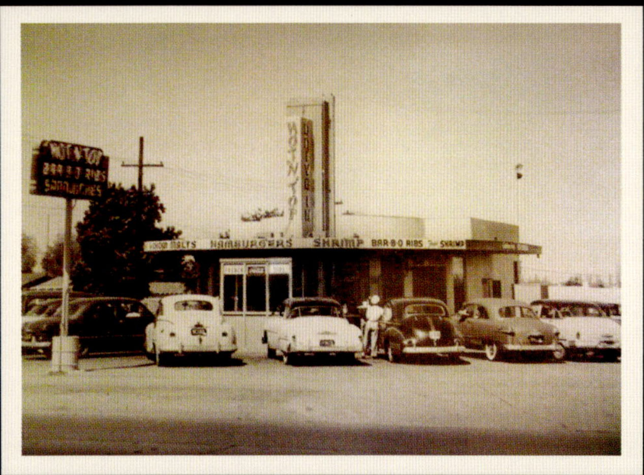

The original 1946 Hot n' Tot was a drive-in that served BBQ ribs, hamburgers, shrimp, and sandwiches. Courtesy of Hot n' Tot and Lomita Historical Society.

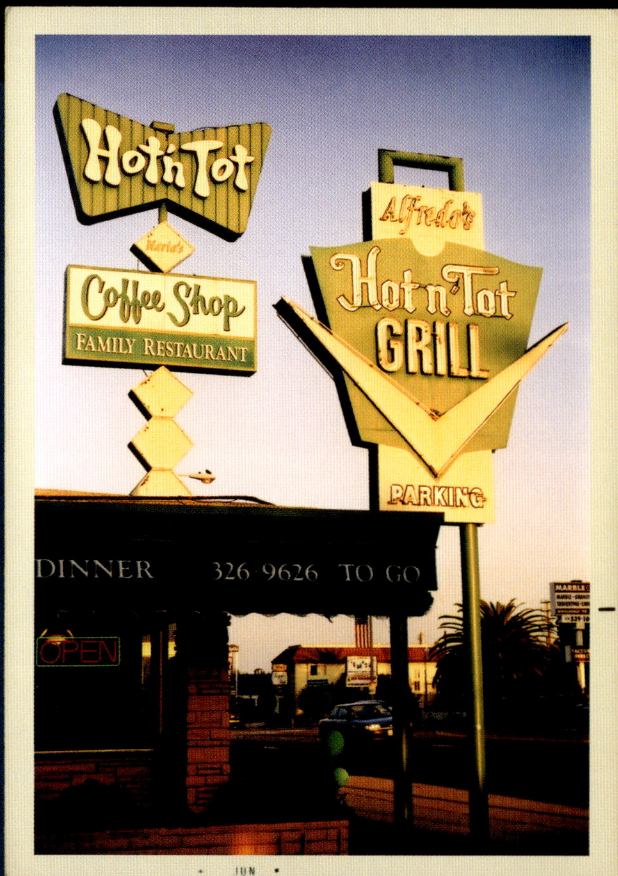

Hot n' Tot

2347 Pacific Coast Highway, Lomita

This restaurant was completely under the radar. We came upon it when we noticed two fabulous neon signs right off of Pacific Coast Highway. Flash forward two years, new owners, new paint job, new furniture, and the shorter neon sign is gone. Inside the entry, you'll find a terrific photo mural of the original Hot n' Tot back in the '40s and historic photos of early Lomita. Our pot roast dinner was delicious and the service was friendly.

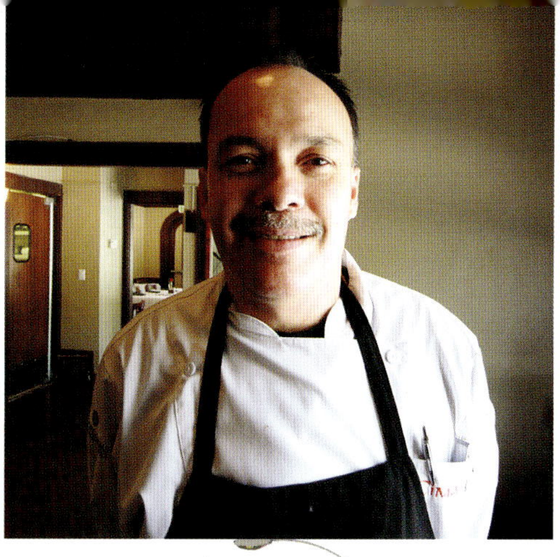

Mario Abrego is the proud owner of Hutch's.

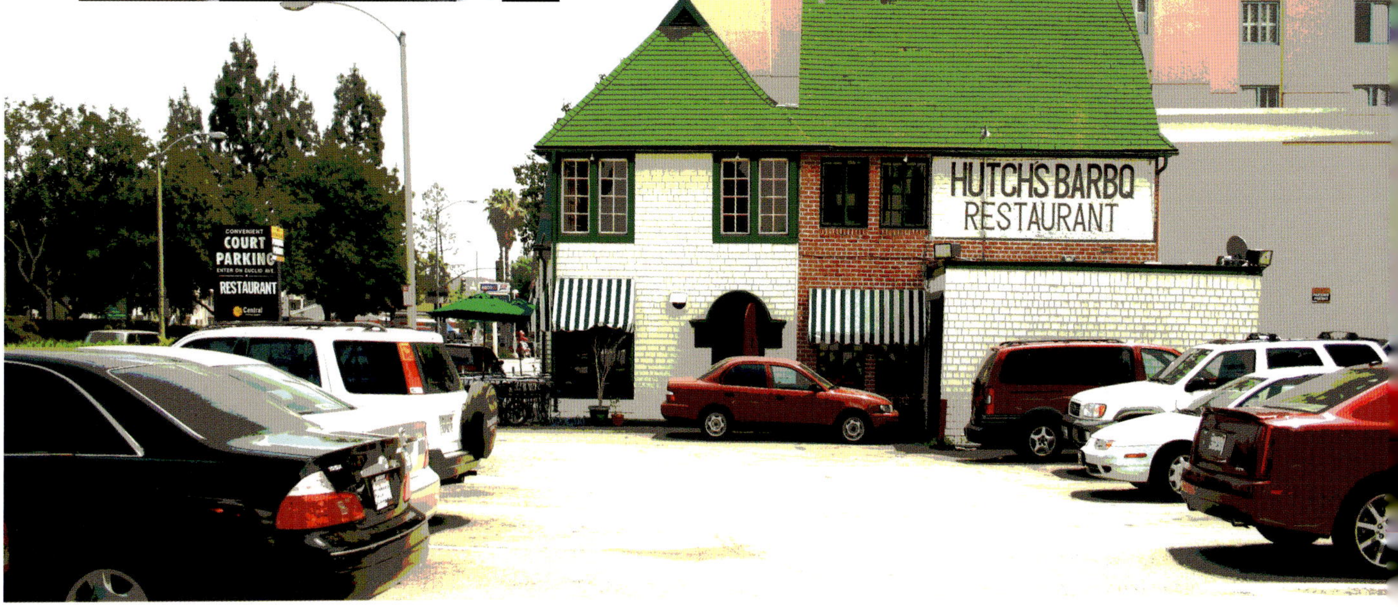

HUTCH'S BARBQ Restaurant

390 E. Walnut Street, Pasadena

Hutch's current owners are Mario Abrego and Hillford Phillips. Mario took us on a whirlwind tour despite the Mother's Day crowd arriving. The restaurant is centrally located in Pasadena, just around the block from Pasadena City Hall. The building is a 1947 English Country Tudor house that was converted into a restaurant some time ago. Their current menu includes a combination of Salvadorean and Caribbean food that is popular with locals, all served in a friendly cottage atmosphere.

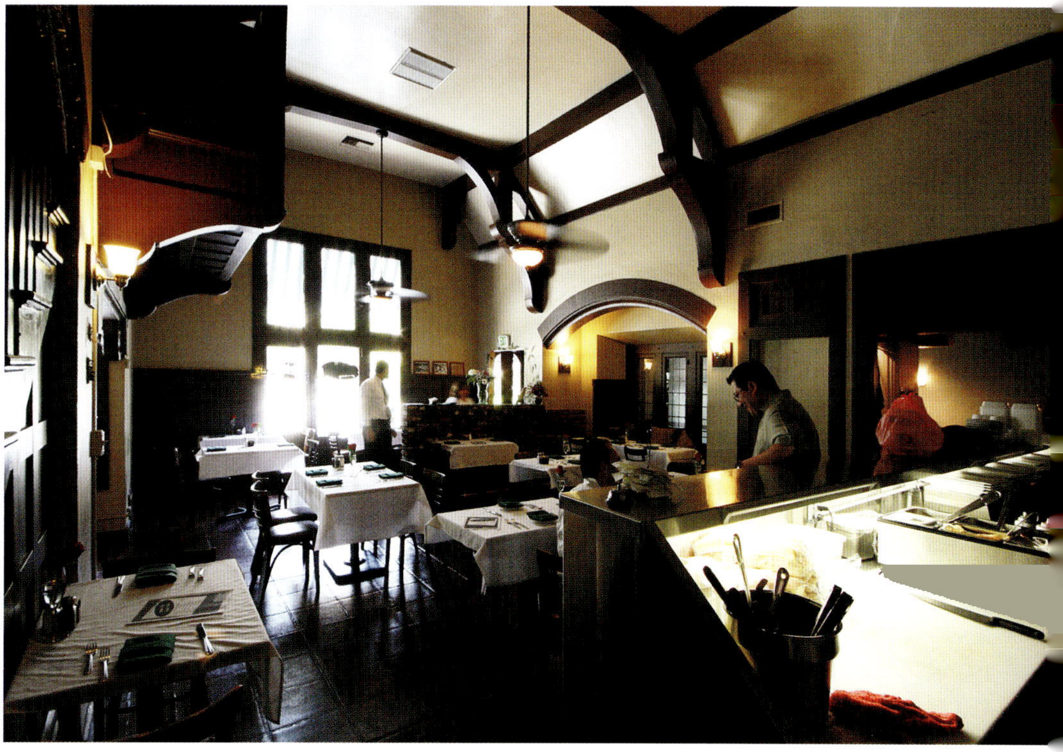

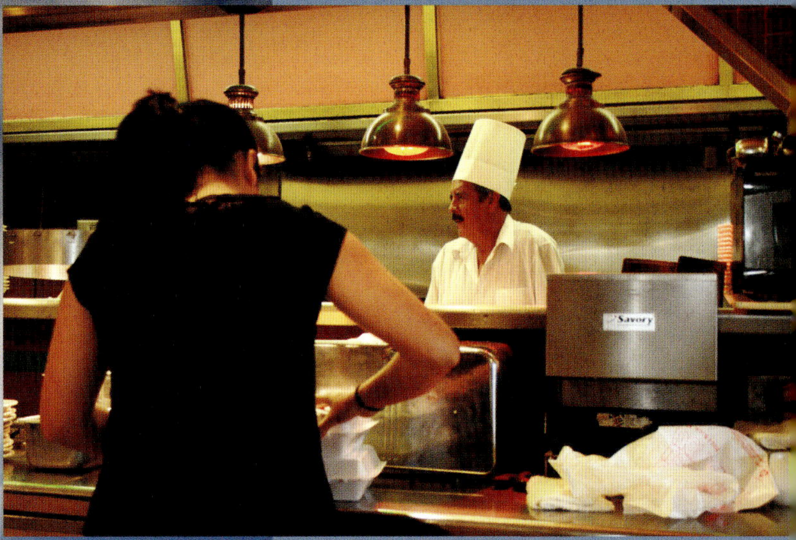

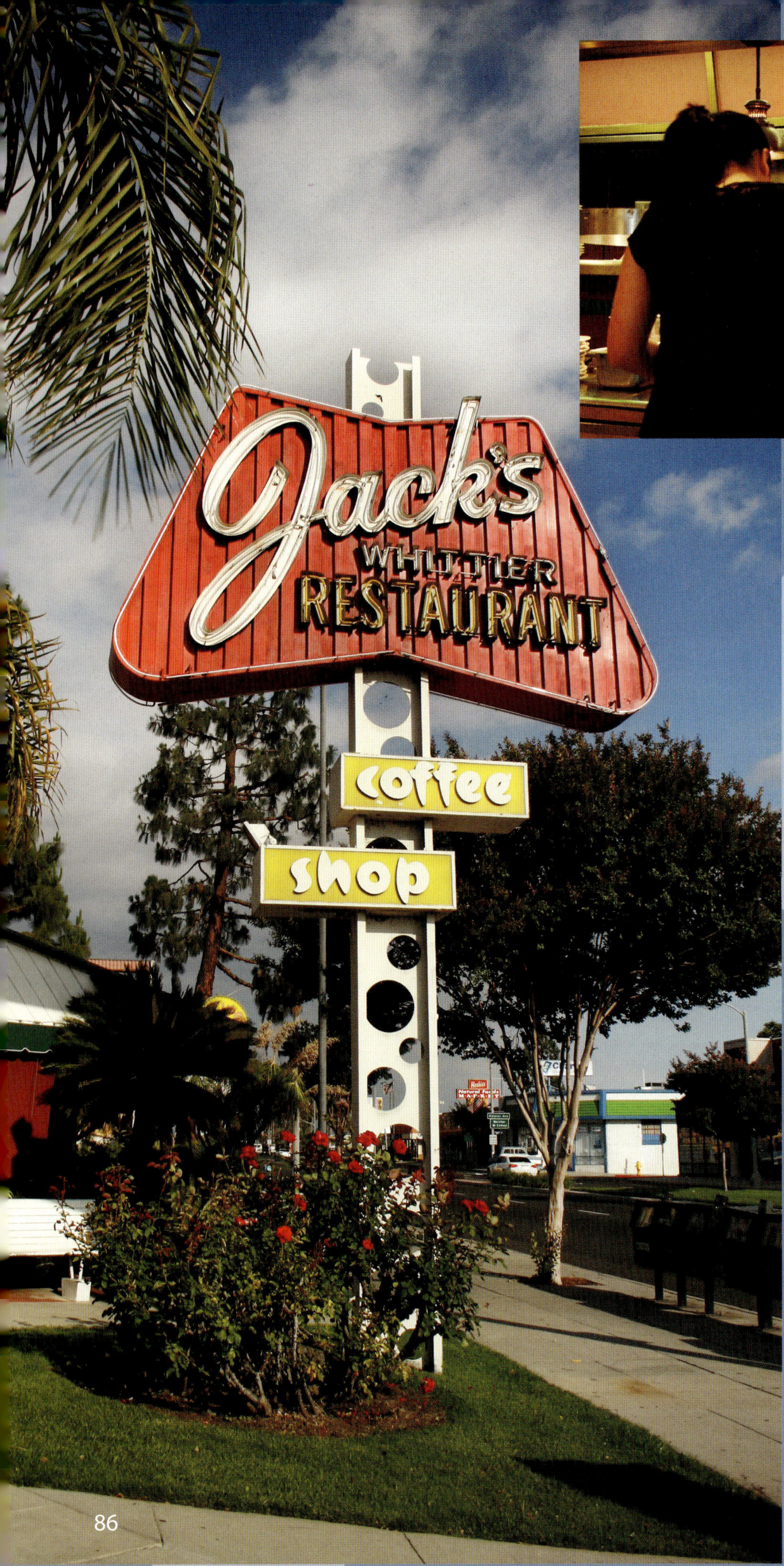
Jack's
WHITTIER
RESTAURANT
coffee
shop

Jack's WHITTIER RESTAURANT

13221 E. Whittier Boulevard, Whittier

A terrific 1957 coffee shop with a terrific sign, Jack's serves good old fashioned hamburgers, sandwiches, Mexican food, Italian dishes, seafood, salads, and breakfast anytime. Owner Greg Voudouris purchased this restaurant in 1975 when he was only 24 years old. Now Voudouris owns three other restaurants: Keno's in Anaheim, the Carriage Coffee Shop in La Mirada, and Lancer's in Burbank. For a time, he also owned Jack's Salad Bowl, but sold it in 2001.

Jack's distinctive neon sign is supported by a steel web lightener or what is also known as a "swiss cheese" I-beam. Considered quintessential '50s Googie design, there are only a handful of these signs left. This and its sister, Jack's Salad Bowl, just three miles west, were designed by Martin Stern, Jr., who was the architect for Ships on Westwood (demolished in 1983) and Ships on Overland (now a Starbucks). We enjoyed talking to manager John Droutsas who was very friendly and knowledgeable. The last time we visited, while waiting for our Greek gyros, John gave us a 10 minute condensed Greek history dating back to the Ottoman Empire.

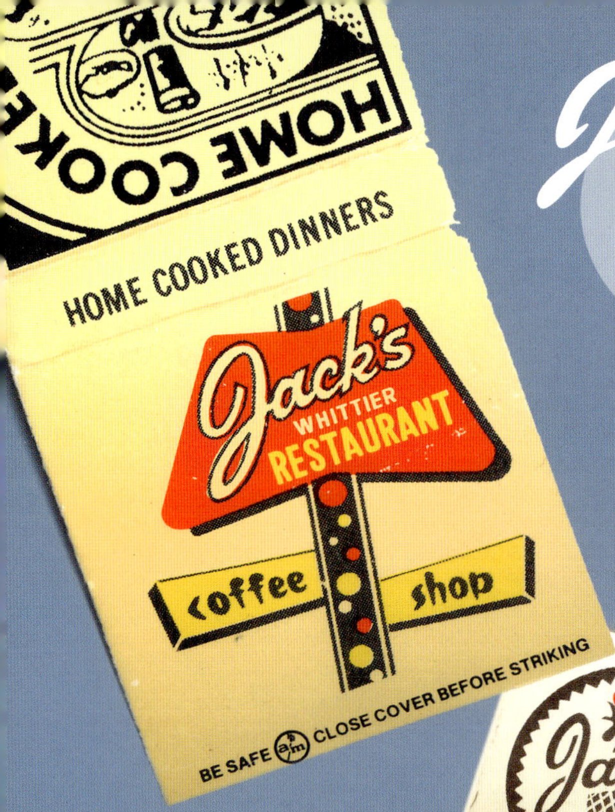

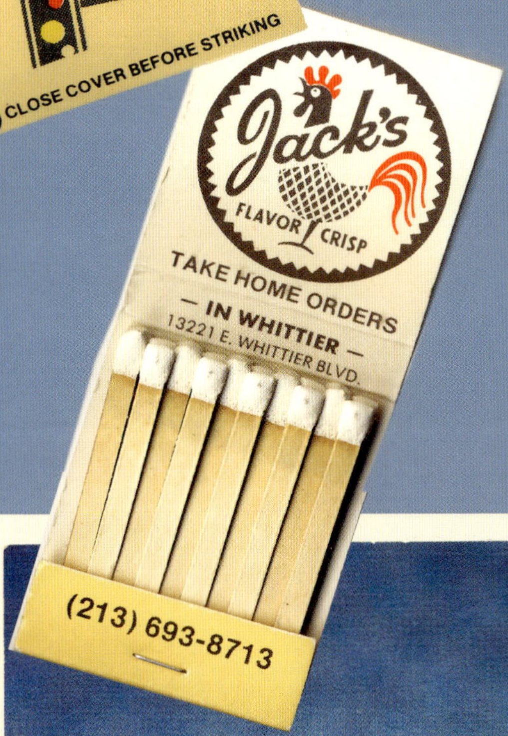

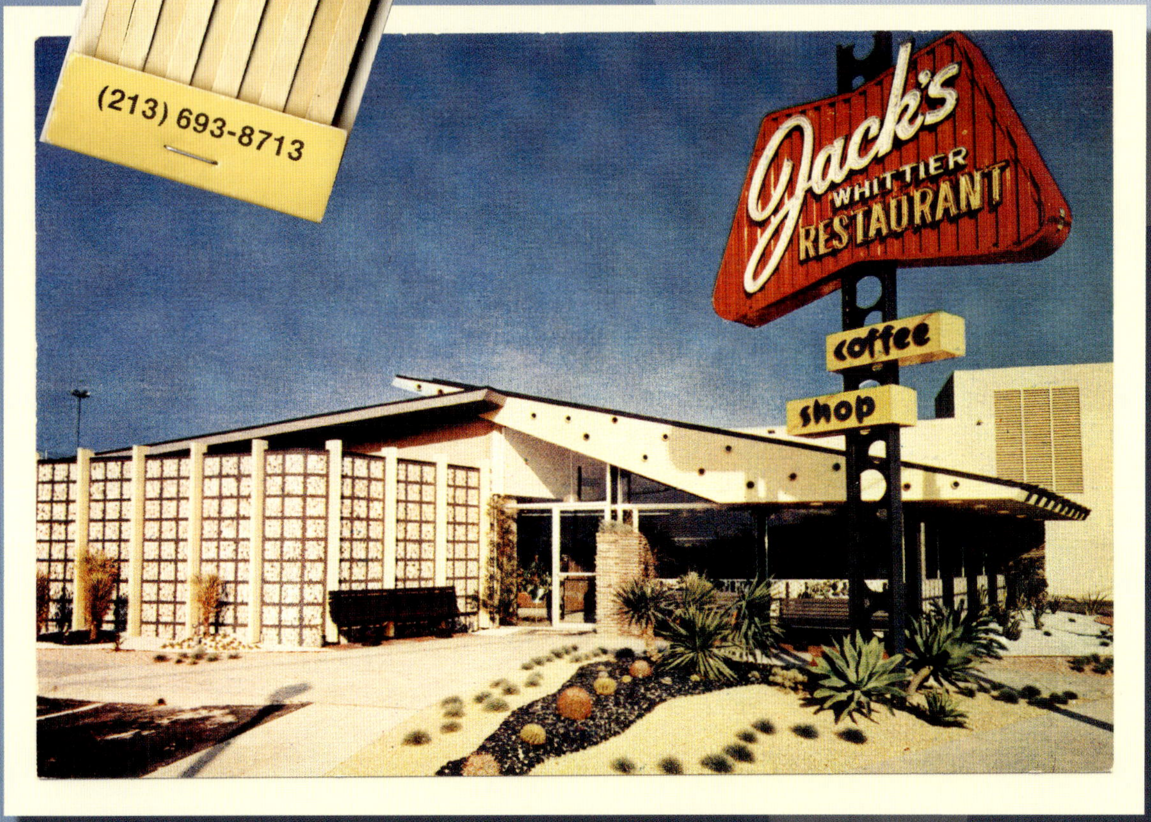

A vintage postcard of Jack's given to us by manager John Droutsas. Where have you ever seen a Googie coffee shop set in a desert landscape like this?

James

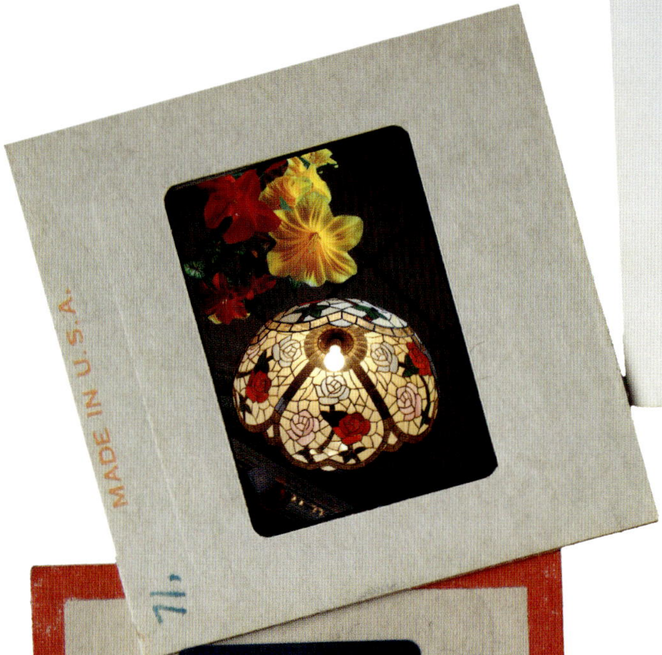

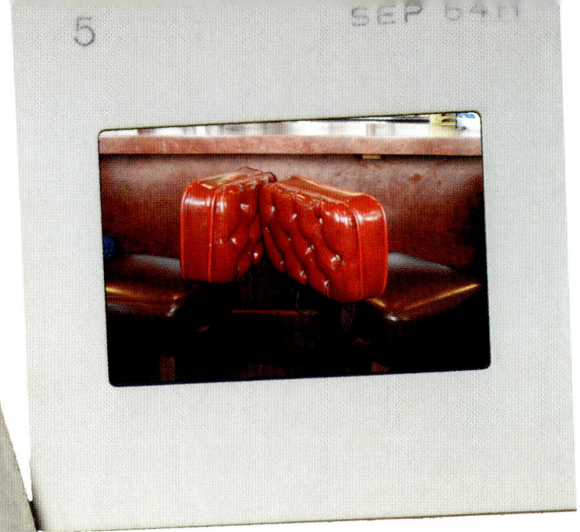

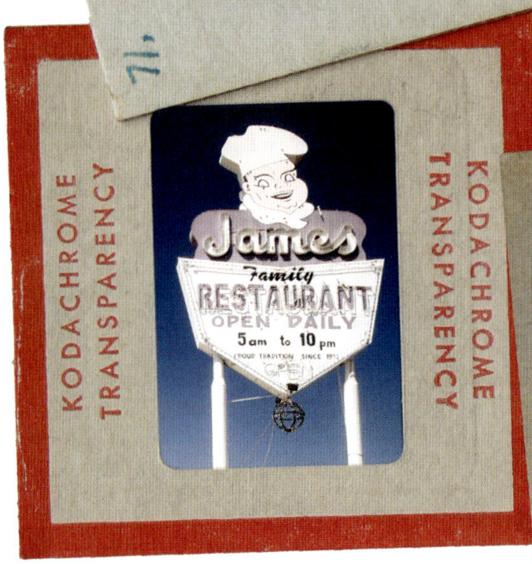

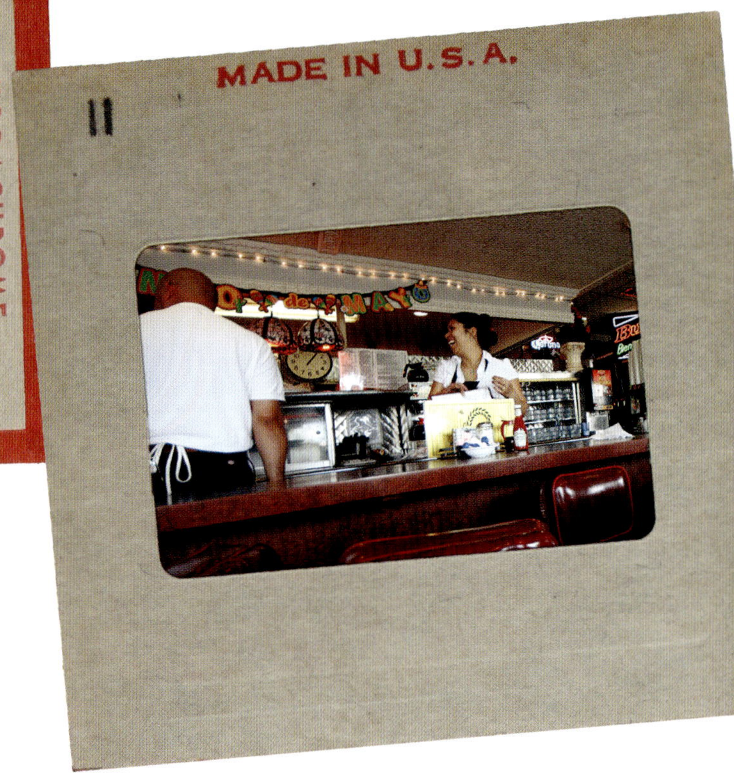

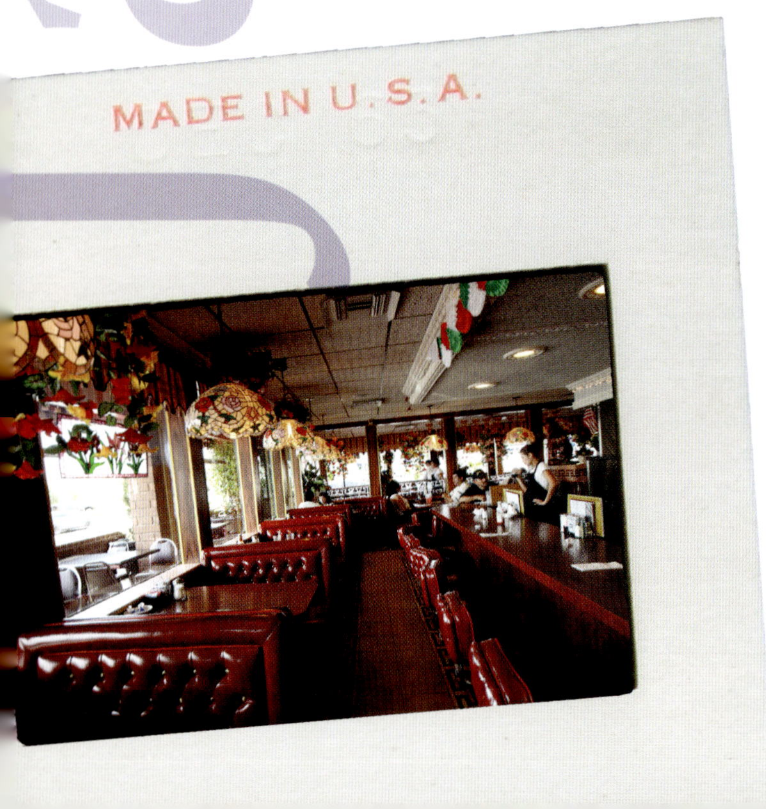

James Coffee Shop

739 Truman Street, San Fernando

Adriene's dad fondly recalls having coffee at the James at 4 A.M. back in 1957 while waiting for her brother John Jr. to be born. Back then James was a drive-in with carhop service. Though it's been renovated many times, the chef sign and the checkerboard aluminum door handles live on. The interior décor reminds us of a typical Greek diner on the East Coast. A San Fernando institution known for good food and service with a smile.

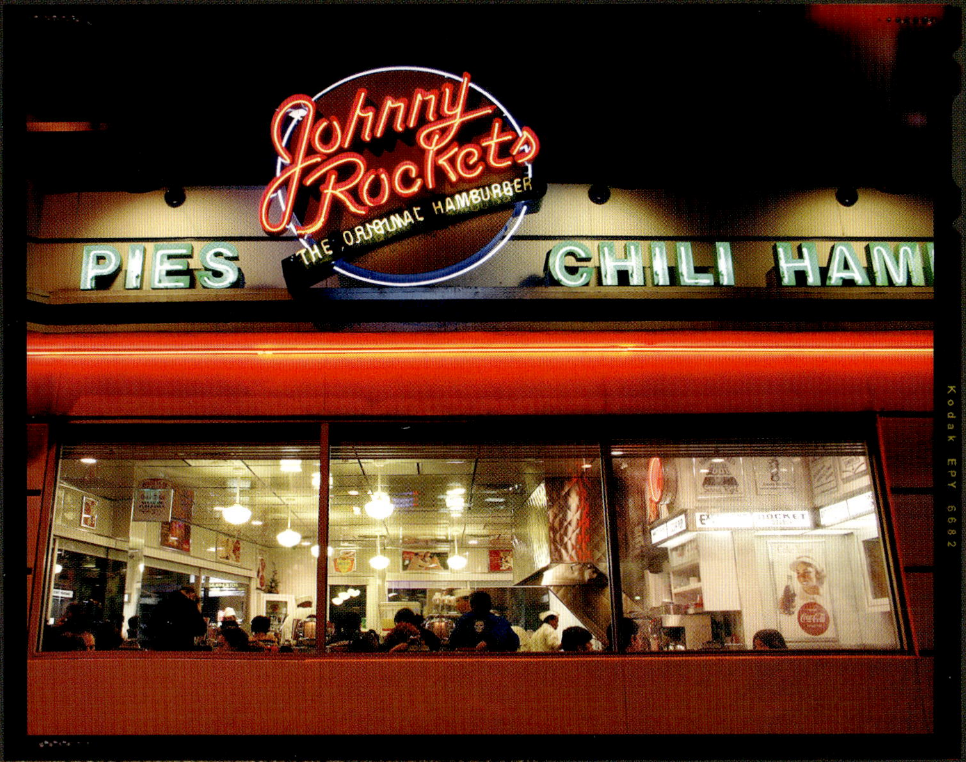

Johnny Rockets

Multiple locations around the world

This contemporary diner first opened on Melrose Avenue in Los Angeles on June 6, 1986. Today, the Johnny Rockets franchise has over 250 locations including Canada, Germany, Egypt, Saudi Arabia, Cyprus, Turkey, Taiwan, and the Philippines. With their classic American diner motif, they offer hamburgers, sandwiches, fries, salads, malts, and their very own Oreo Mint Shakes. You'll find a jukebox on every table. Their food and customer service is consistently good. After ordering burgers, our waitress demonstrated her artistic flair with her ketchup and mustard painting on a plate.

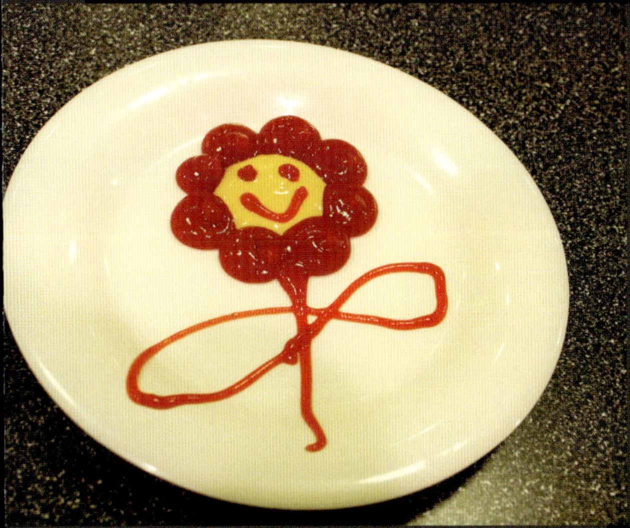

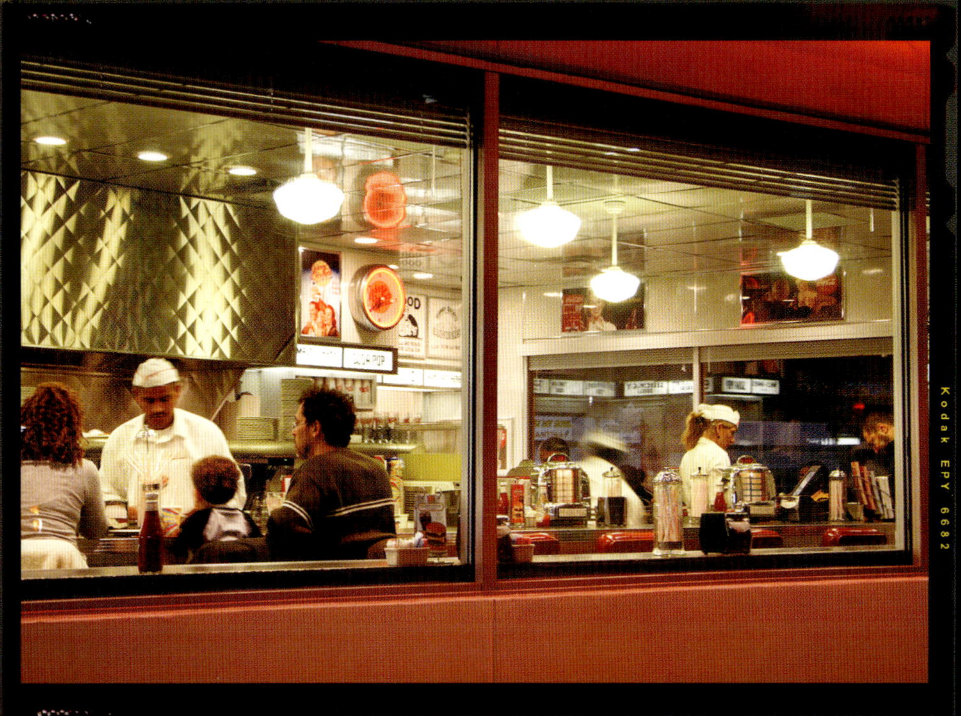

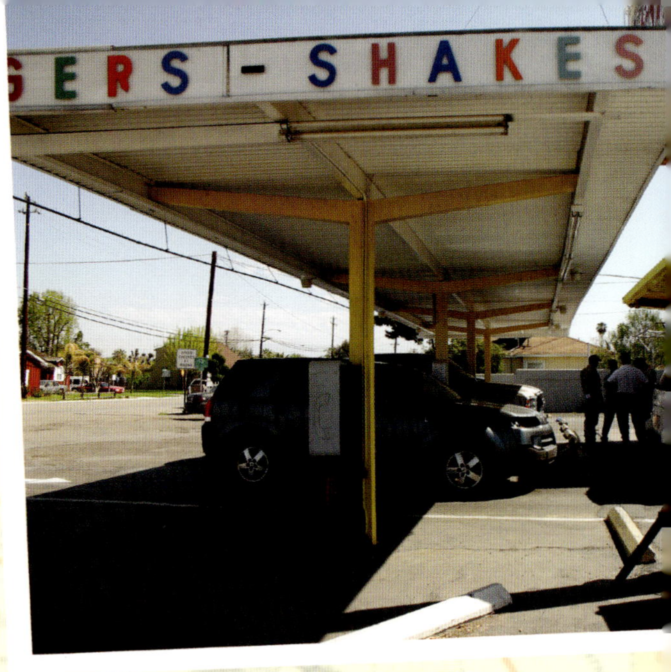

JOLLY KONE Drive-In

800 Wible Road, Bakersfield

Right next to Highway 99, off Brundage Lane, this drive-in with a quirky happy face ice cream sign hasn't changed at all since the '50s. Every time we come here there's always a wait. As we said, Bakersfield appears to be the ice cream capital of California. Metal "T"s support the awning for the cars, which is typical of drive-ins of this era. Perhaps the most unique element here are their trash cans. Painted bright red, their shapes remind us of the dancing mushrooms in Disney's classic film *Fantasia.*

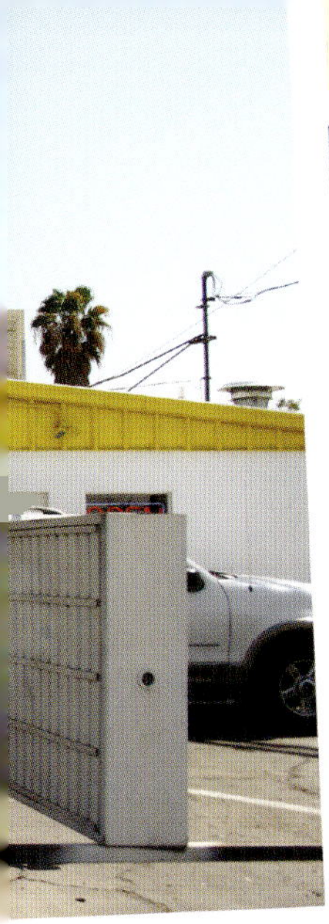

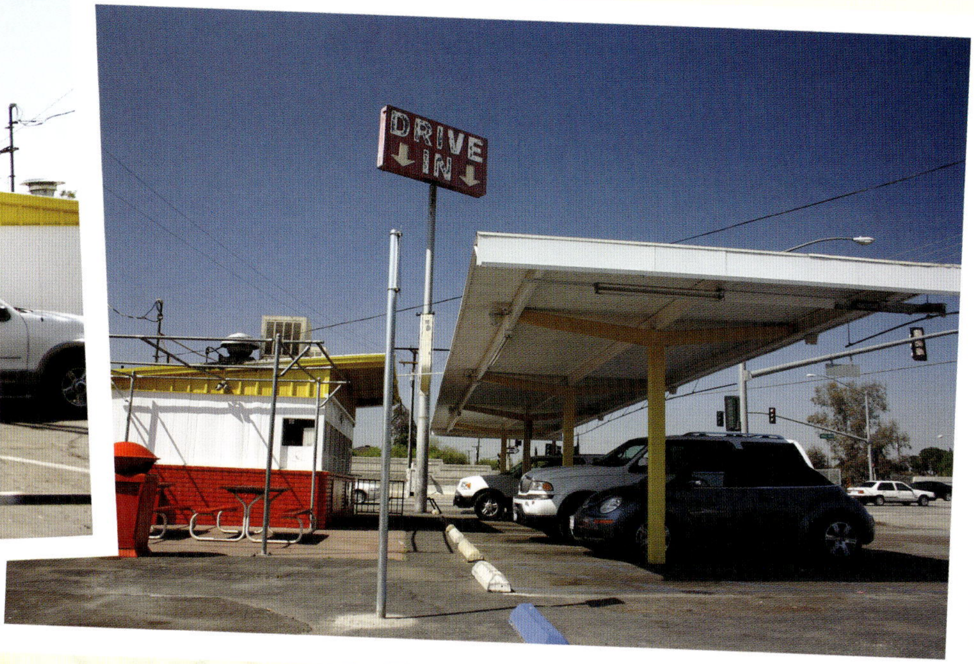
DRIVE
IN

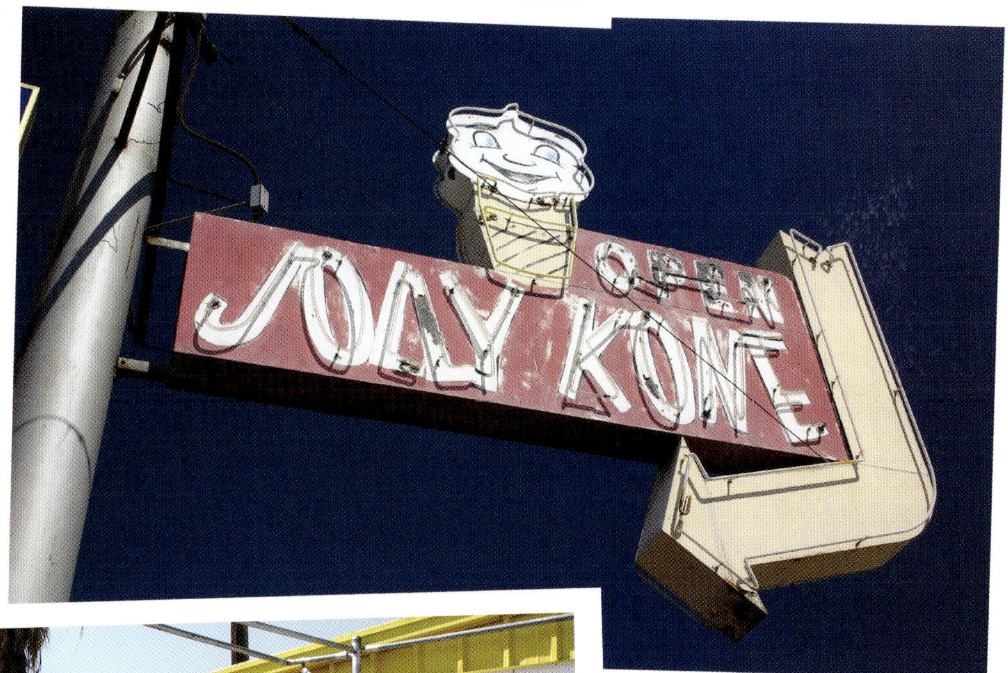
OPEN
JOLLY KONE

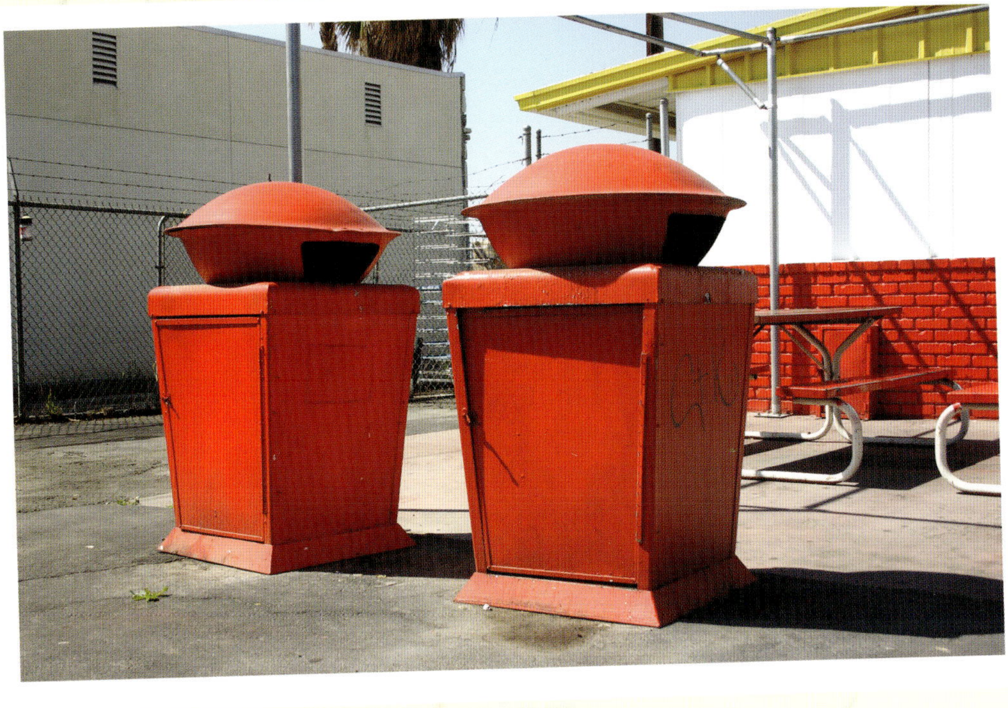

KENTUCK

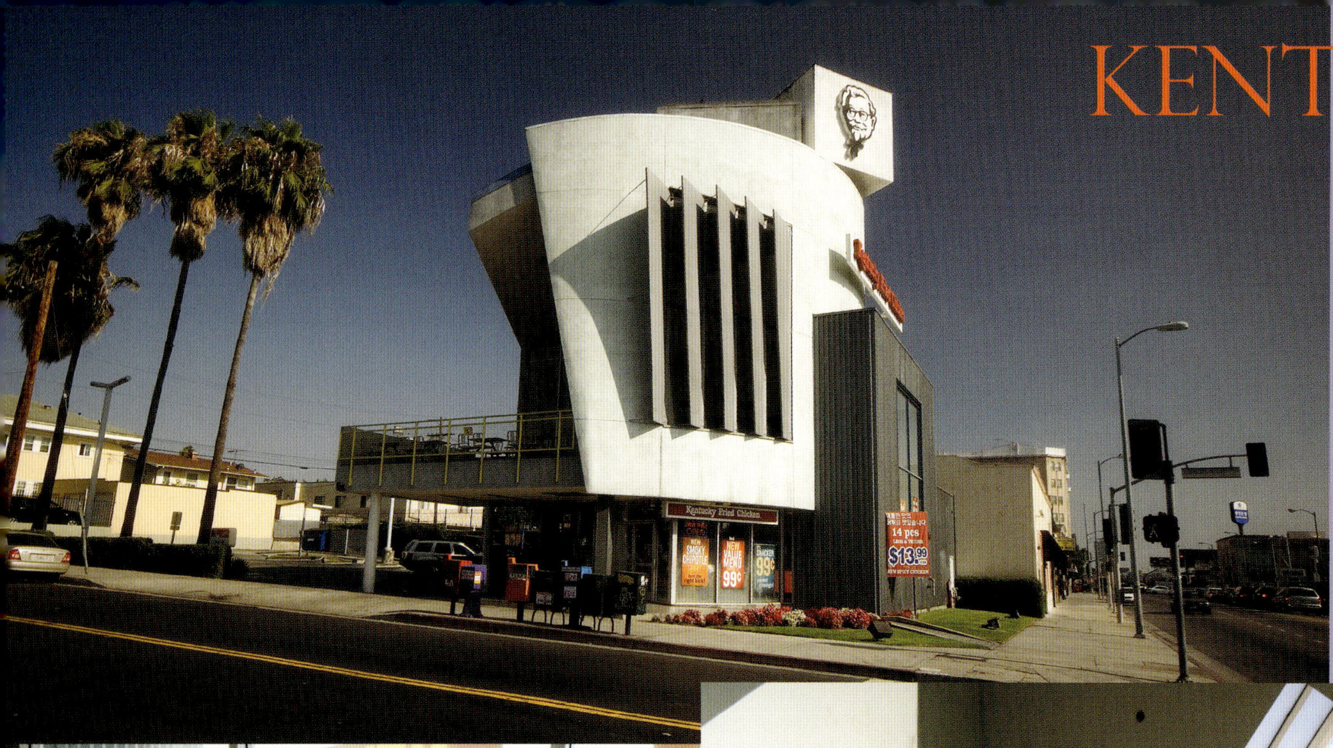

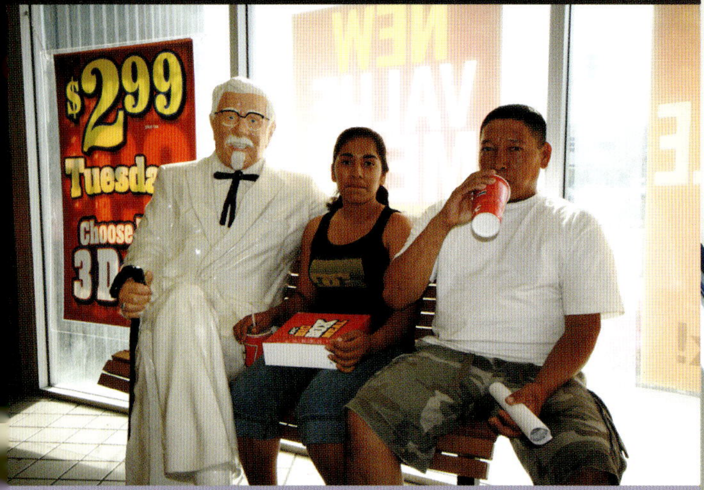

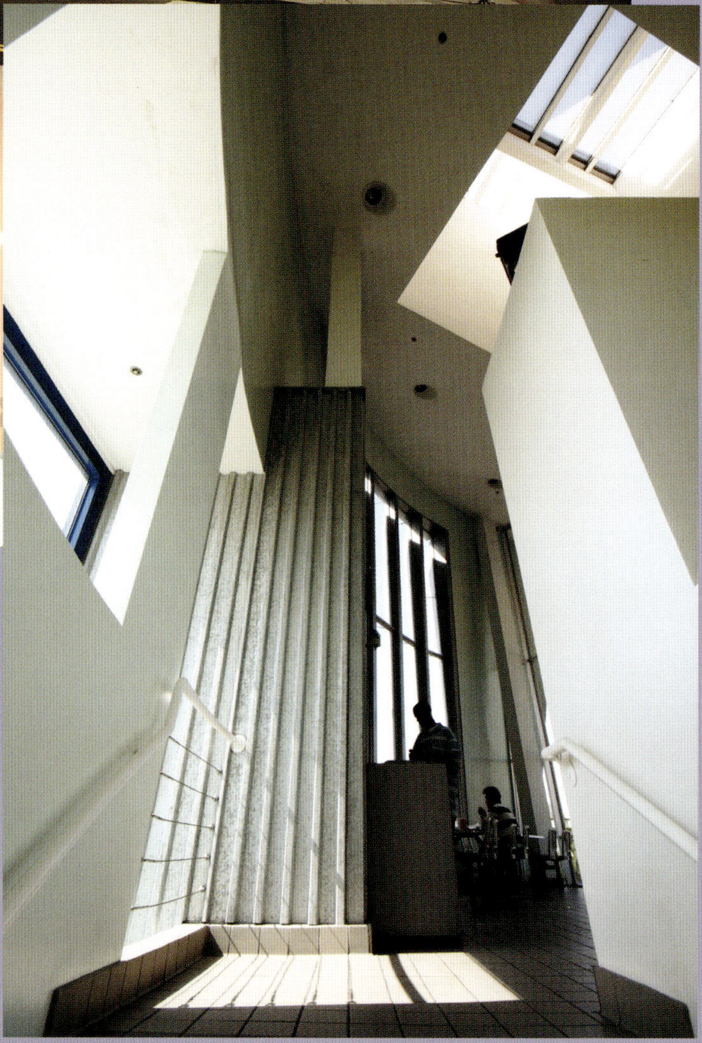

KFC Prototype

340 N. Western Avenue, Wilshire Center

A wildly imaginative take-off on the KFC bucket, this award-winning 1990 prototype was created in modern programmatic style by architect Jeffrey Daniels. A graduate of MIT, Daniels worked for the Taller de Arquitectura of Ricardo Bofill in Barcelona, Spain, as well as in Frank Gehry's offices from 1978-80. Daniels' projects include David Hockney's residence and Virgin Records' New York offices. A fiberglass figure of the Colonel sitting on a bench greets you on the first floor of this multi-story KFC. Place your order then head up to the second floor balcony and eat outdoors overlooking Hollywood, or just drive-thru if you're in a hurry.

RIED CHICKEN

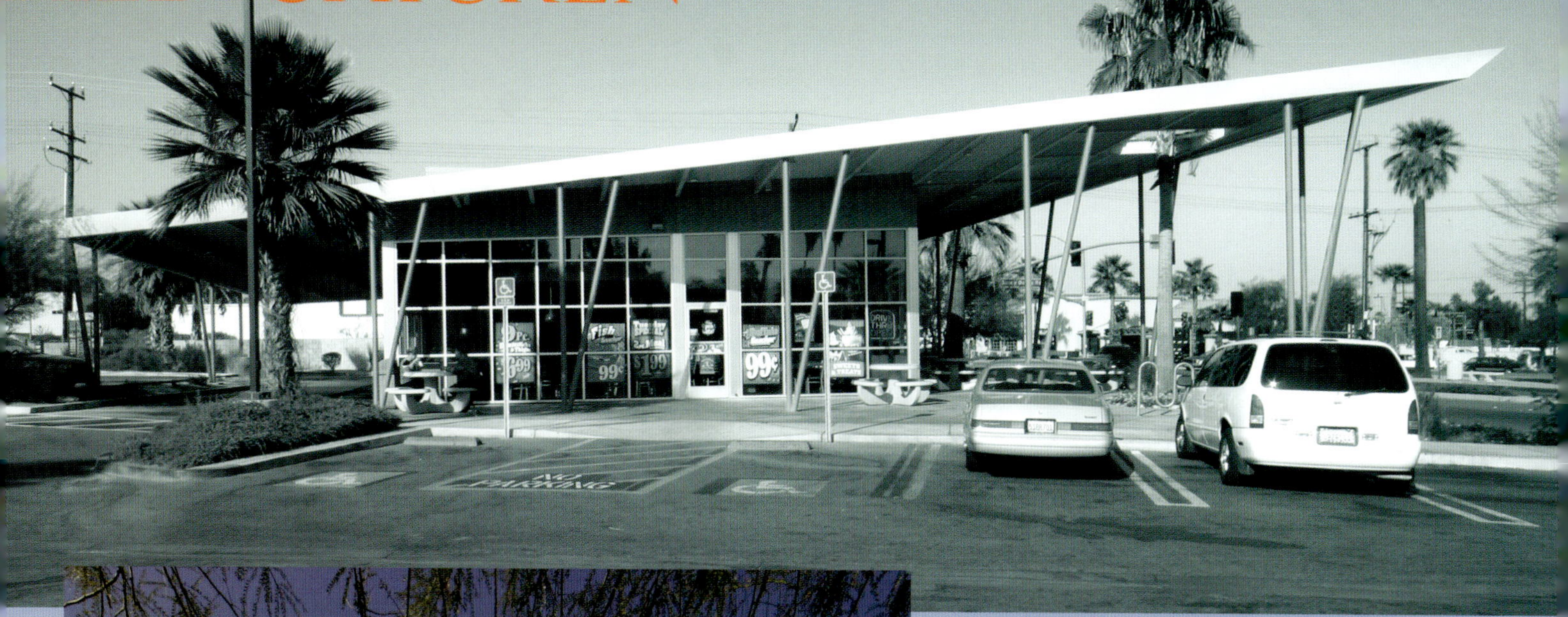

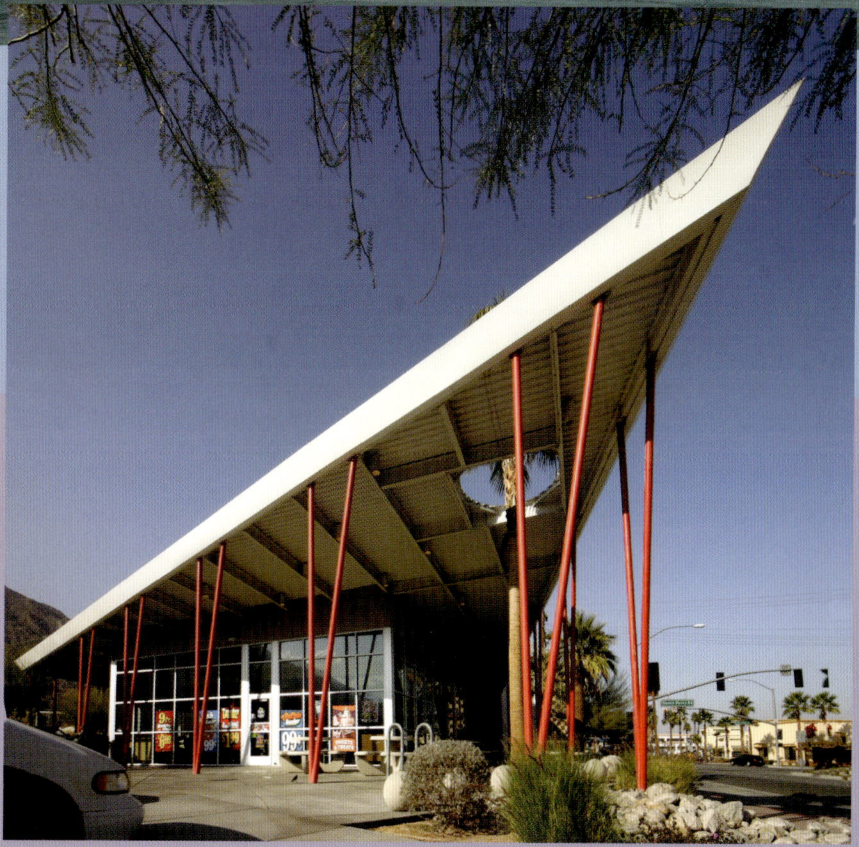

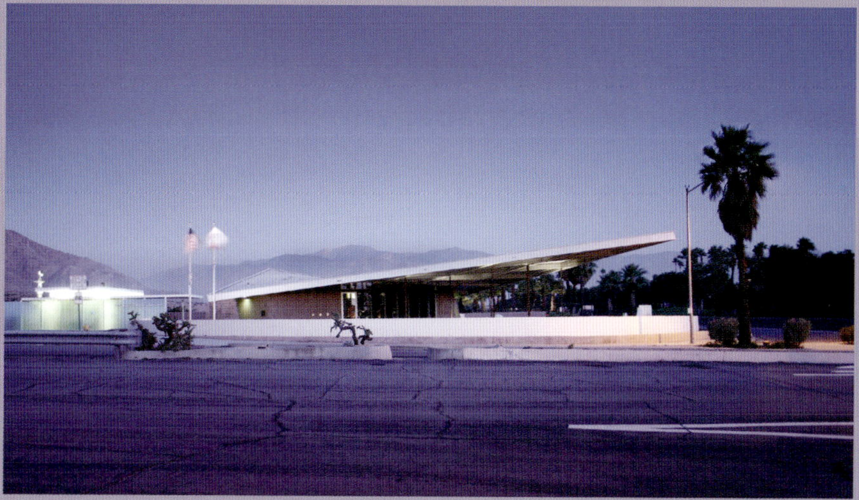

KFC + A&W Prototype

725 S. Palm Canyon Drive, Palm Springs

Have a root beer and order of fried chicken at this 2004 prototype located in the modern mecca of Palm Springs. It's great to see chain restaurants like these defying standardization. The architecture was heavily inspired by the famous Tramway Gas Station, a "hyperbolic paraboloid" design created by Palm Springs' modern guru Albert Frey, originally from Zurich, Switzerland. This fast food restaurant backs up to snow-capped Mt. San Jacinto, which is part of a spectacular, rugged wilderness that is reachable via the Palm Springs Aerial Tramway, once publicized as the 8th Wonder of the World.

The original inspiration for the KFC + A&W restaurant design is Albert Frey's Tramway Gas Station located on the northern end of Palm Springs.

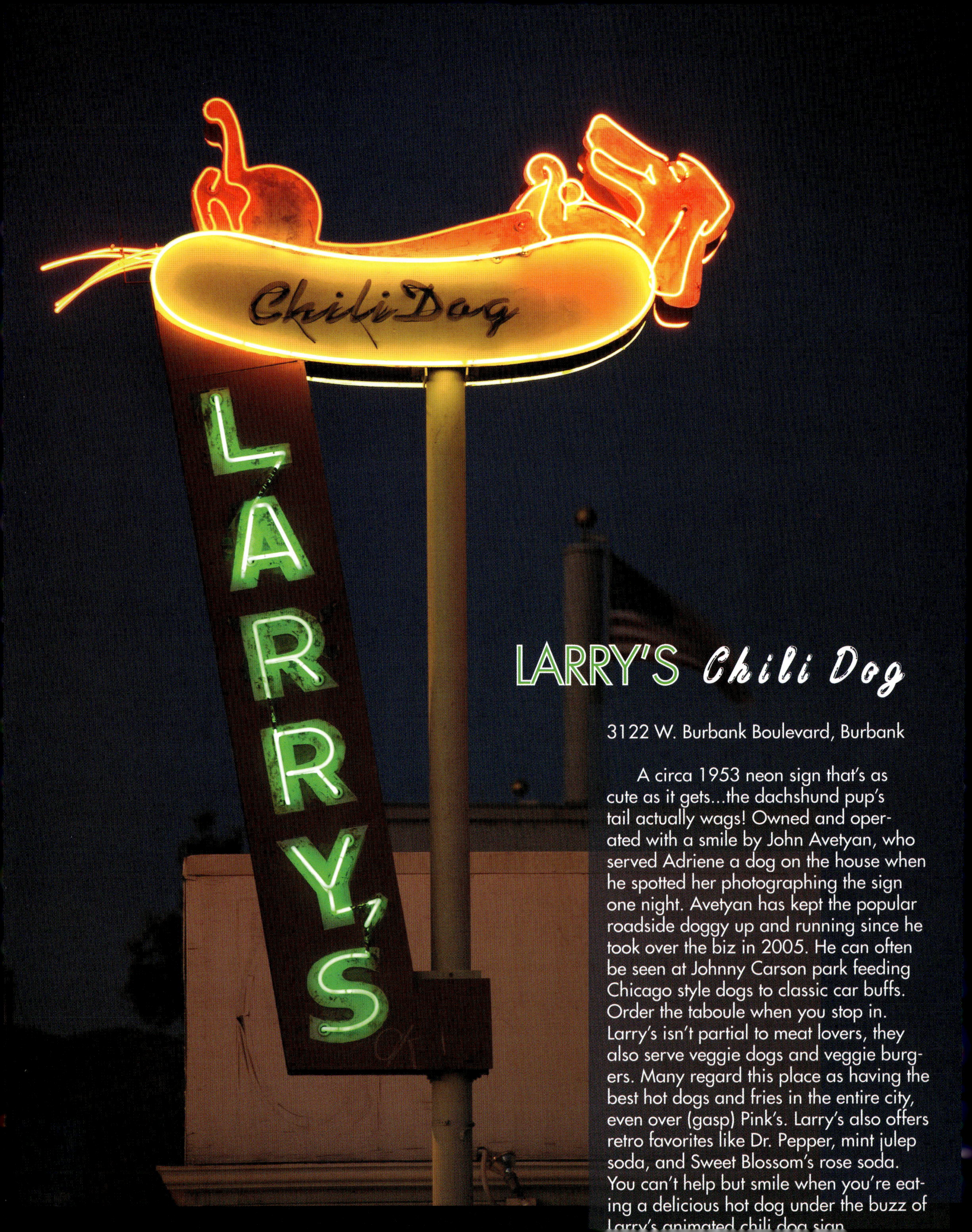

LARRY'S *Chili Dog*

3122 W. Burbank Boulevard, Burbank

A circa 1953 neon sign that's as cute as it gets...the dachshund pup's tail actually wags! Owned and operated with a smile by John Avetyan, who served Adriene a dog on the house when he spotted her photographing the sign one night. Avetyan has kept the popular roadside doggy up and running since he took over the biz in 2005. He can often be seen at Johnny Carson park feeding Chicago style dogs to classic car buffs. Order the taboule when you stop in. Larry's isn't partial to meat lovers, they also serve veggie dogs and veggie burgers. Many regard this place as having the best hot dogs and fries in the entire city, even over (gasp) Pink's. Larry's also offers retro favorites like Dr. Pepper, mint julep soda, and Sweet Blossom's rose soda. You can't help but smile when you're eating a delicious hot dog under the buzz of Larry's animated chili dog sign.

Lin's Chinese Food

Lin's Chinese Food

112 E. Harvard Boulevard, Santa Paula

In 1955, Santa Paula was a sleepy town just like the one in *The Last Picture Show*. Agriculture was the main industry and even today, more 10-gallon Stetsons roam the streets than bare heads. Chinese people are an industrial lot with capitalism in their blood so it's no surprise that Harry Ling Hom and his brother came all the way from China to make their fortune here. This Chinese-American restaurant has changed…nothing since that time, especially their recipes. The red sauce that came with the sweet and sour pork almost glowed. The chow mein was mostly bean sprouts, "and thus, very good for you." If anyone wants a real '50s experience, not the romanticized version, but the real deal, here it is.

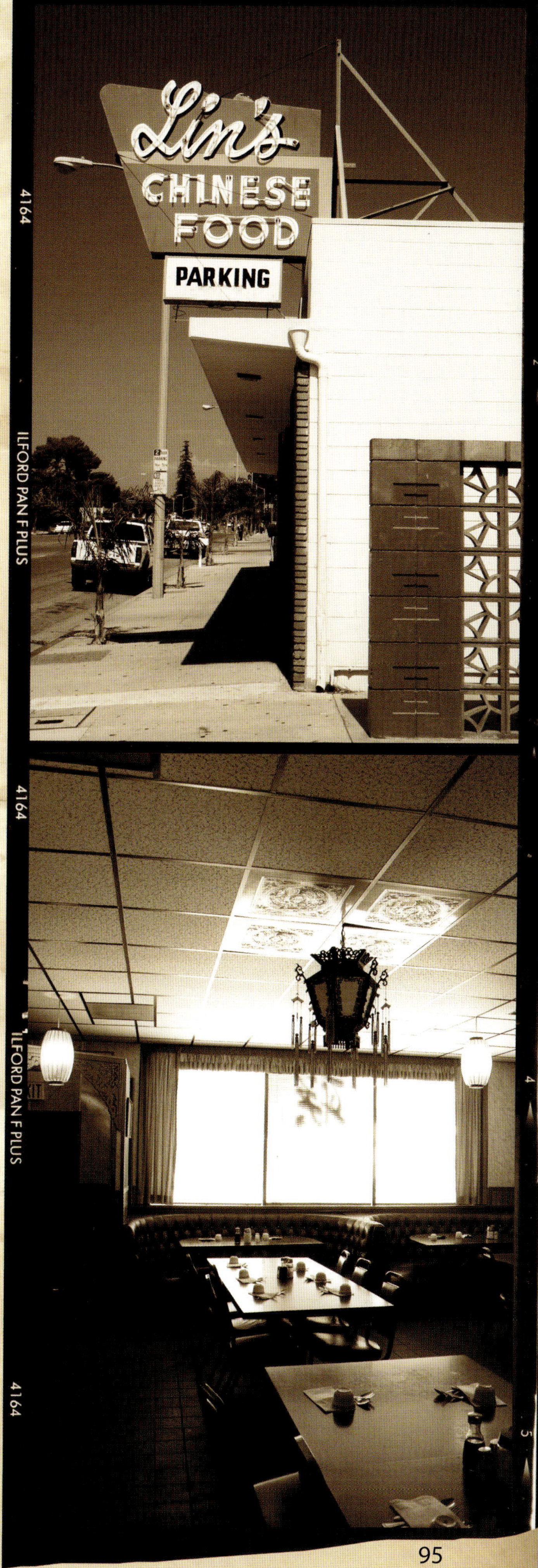

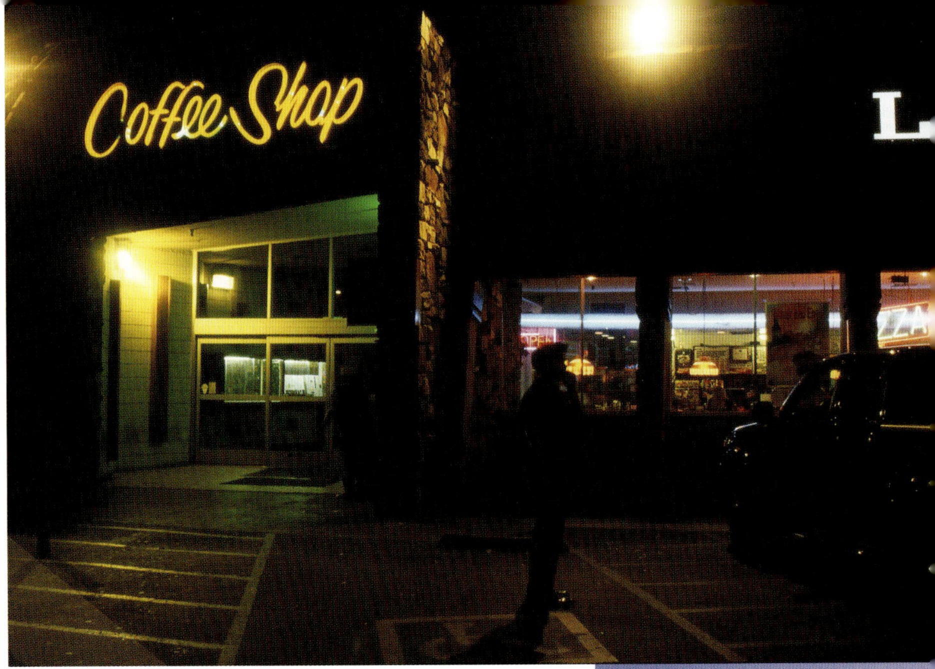

LINBROOK BOWL

Coffee Shop

201 S. Brookhurst Street, Anaheim

Called Linbrook because it's on the southwest corner of Lincoln Avenue and Brookhurst Street, Linbrook's magnificent rotating neon bowling pin is a vision to behold. Open 24 hours since 1958, it's 24-7 of Googie heaven in Orange County. Linbrook celebrated its 50th anniversary in 2008 with a parking lot BBQ, '50s style live band, karaoke contest, balloon art, raffle prizes, and, of course, bowling. The coffee shop is small but iconic, with cantilevered stools and booths that haven't changed much over the years. Enter Linbrook's amazing lobby at sunset and you'll instantly find yourself in a bygone era where rock and roll was king and space was the next frontier to be conquered. Check out the martini glass on the padded door to the cocktail lounge.

A half block north on Lincoln Avenue, is a pool hall from the '60s that should not be missed.

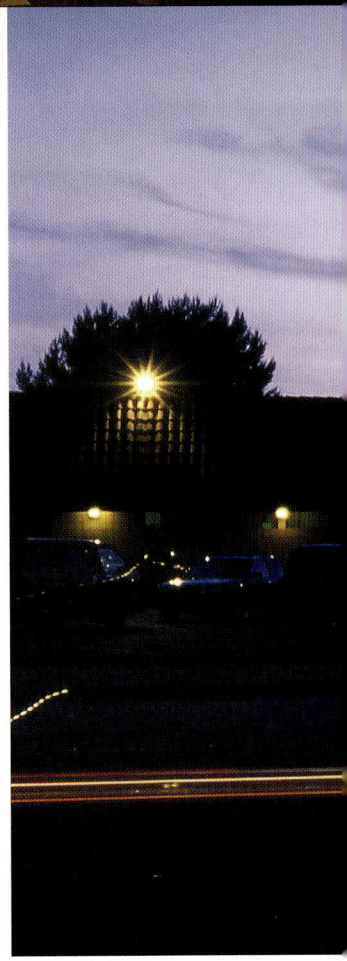

LINBROOK

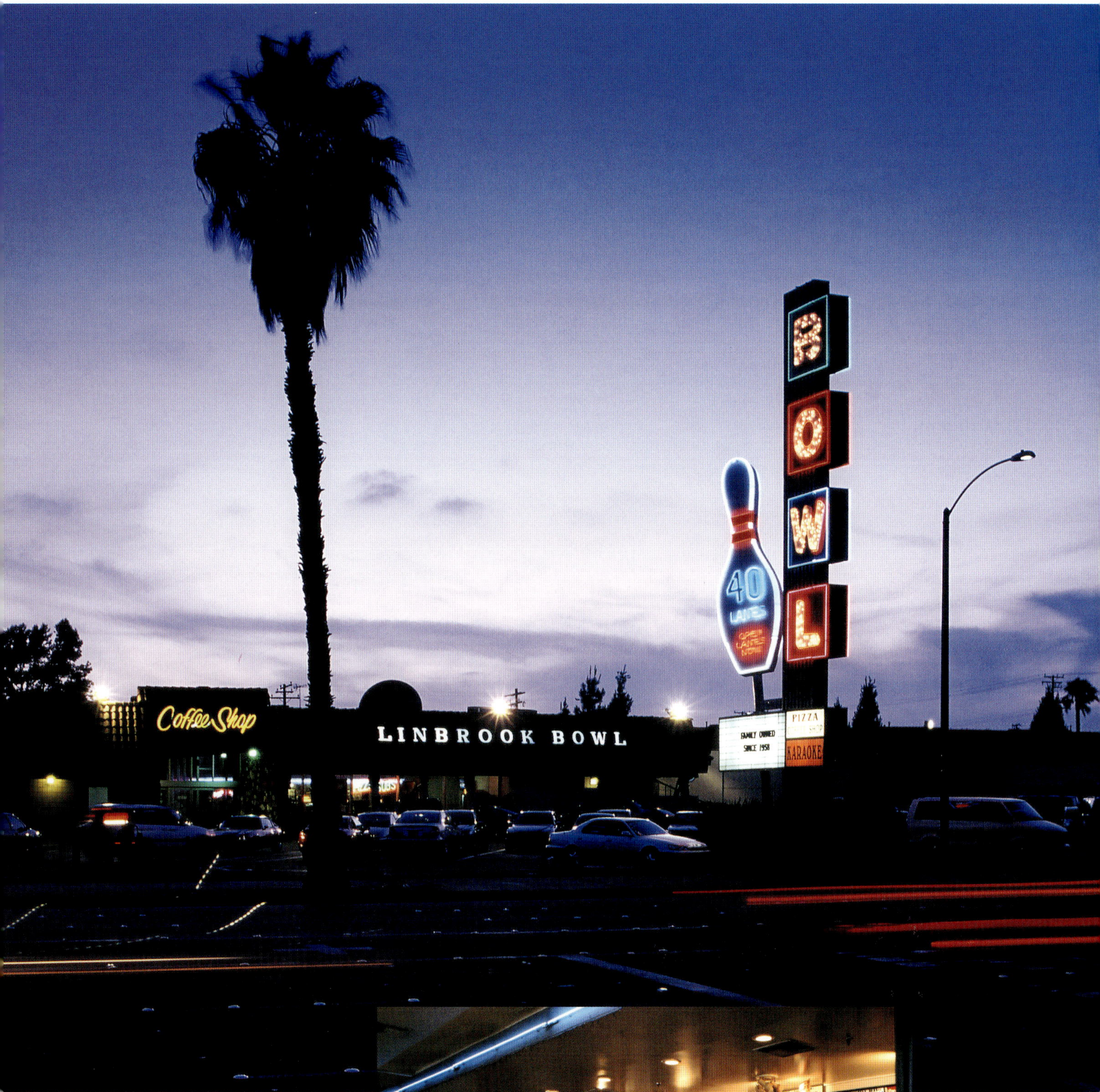
Coffee Shop
LINBROOK BOWL
BOWL
40 LANES
FAMILY OWNED SINCE 1951
PIZZA
KARAOKE

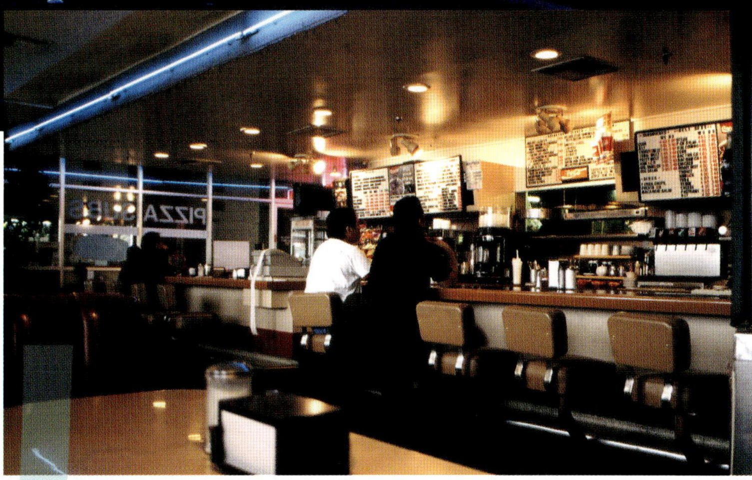

OWL

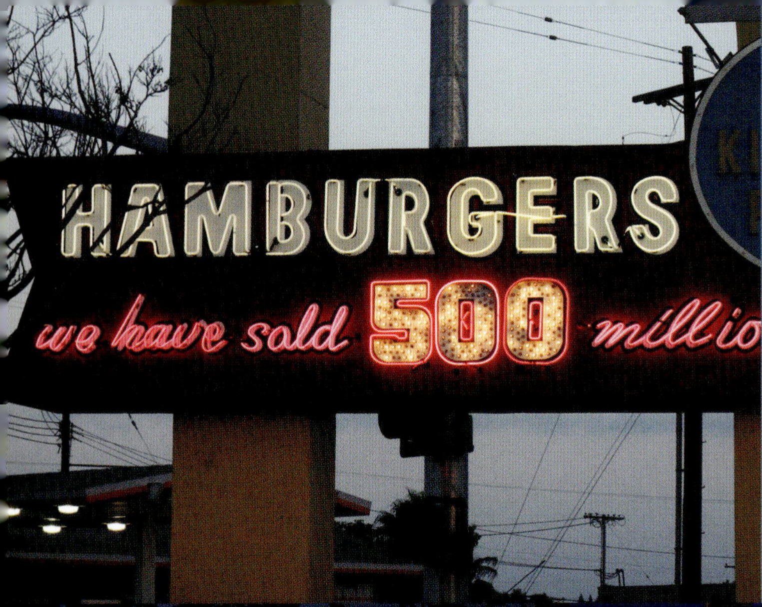
HAMBURGERS
we have sold 500 millio

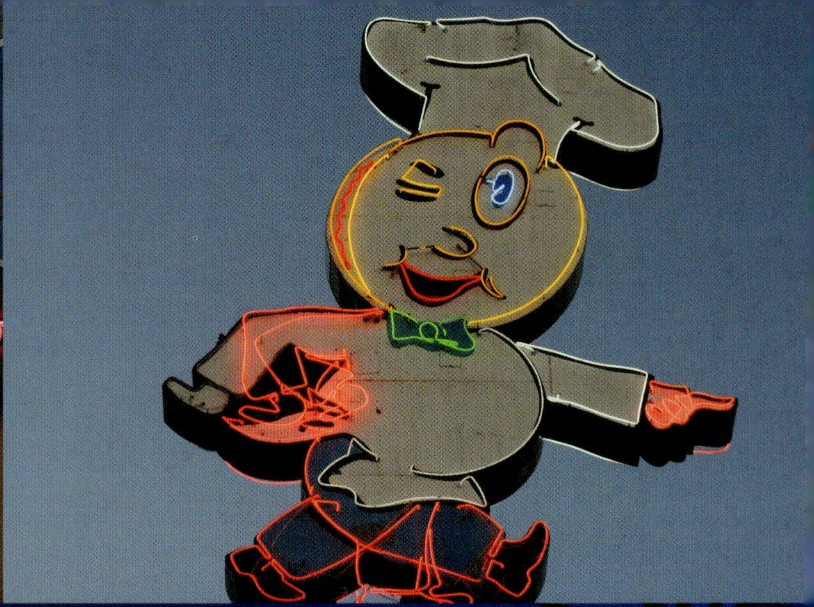

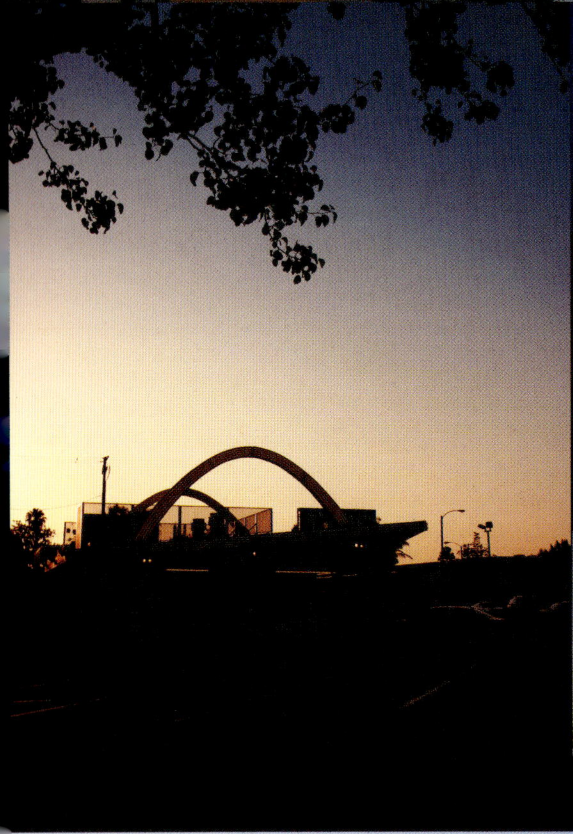

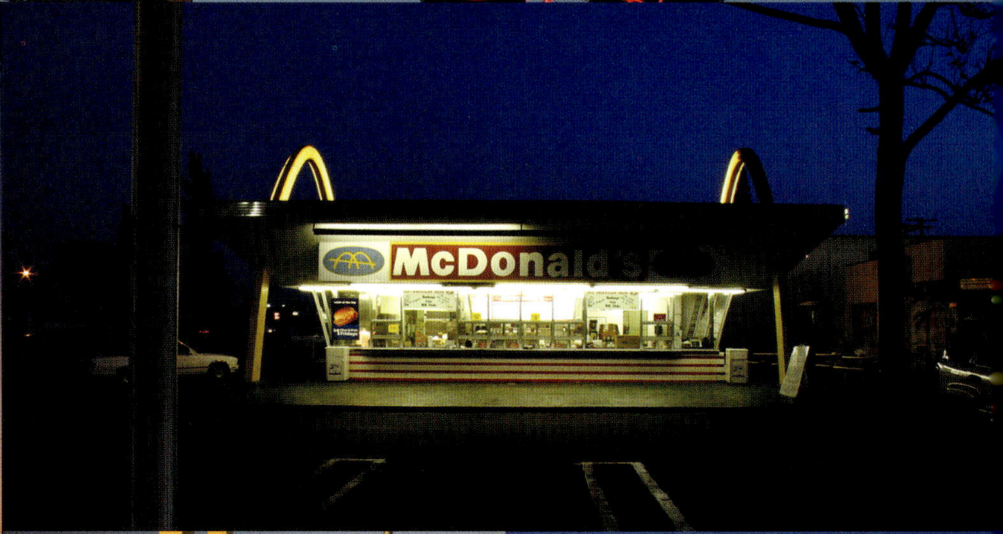
McDonald's

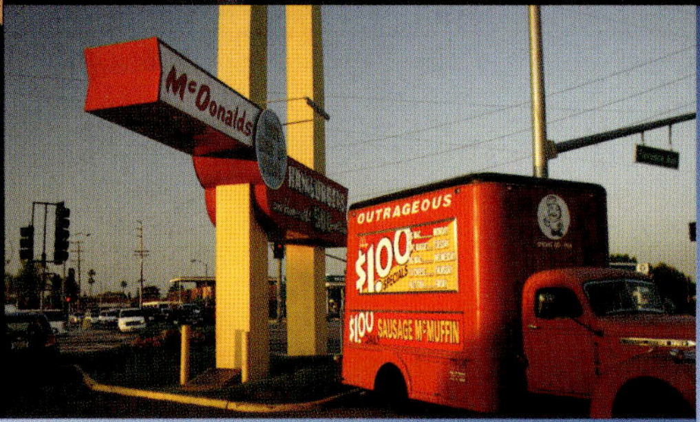
McDonalds
OUTRAGEOUS
$100
$100 SAUSAGE McMUFFIN

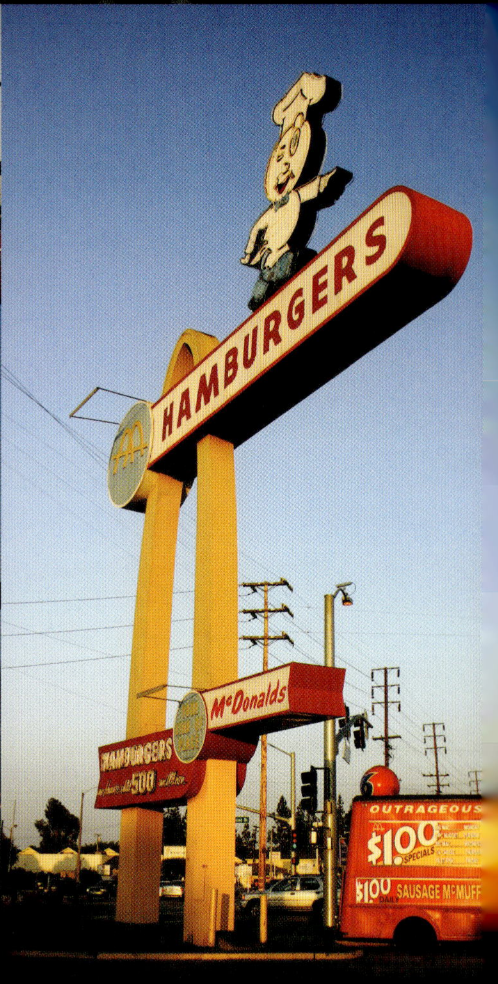
HAMBURGERS
McDonalds
OUTRAGEOUS
$100
SAUSAGE McMUFF

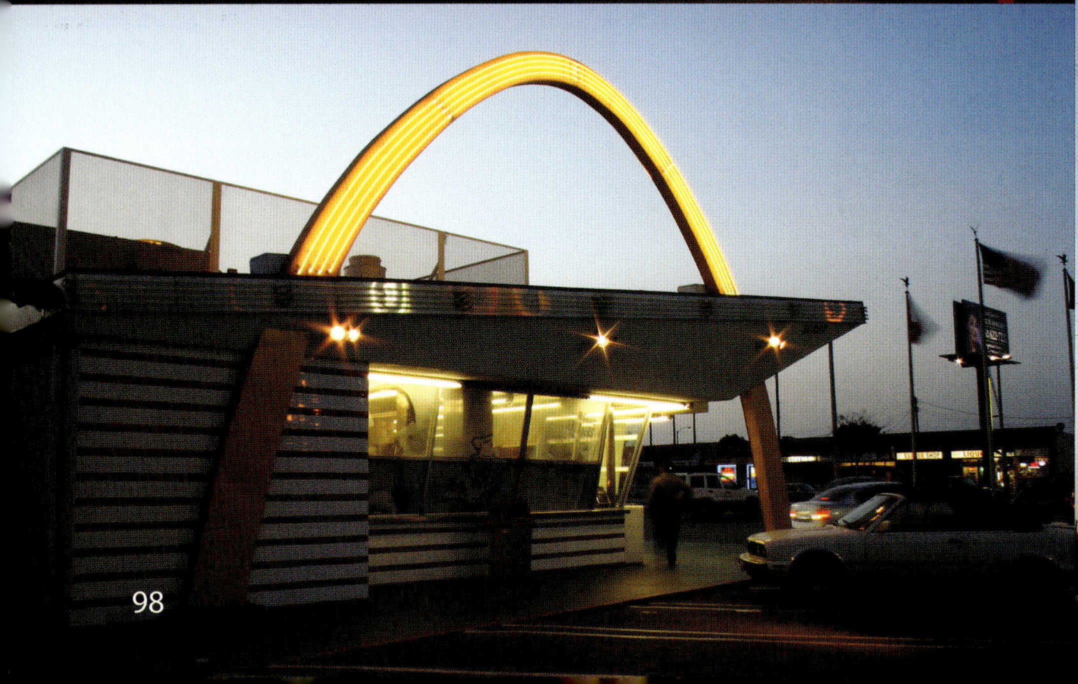

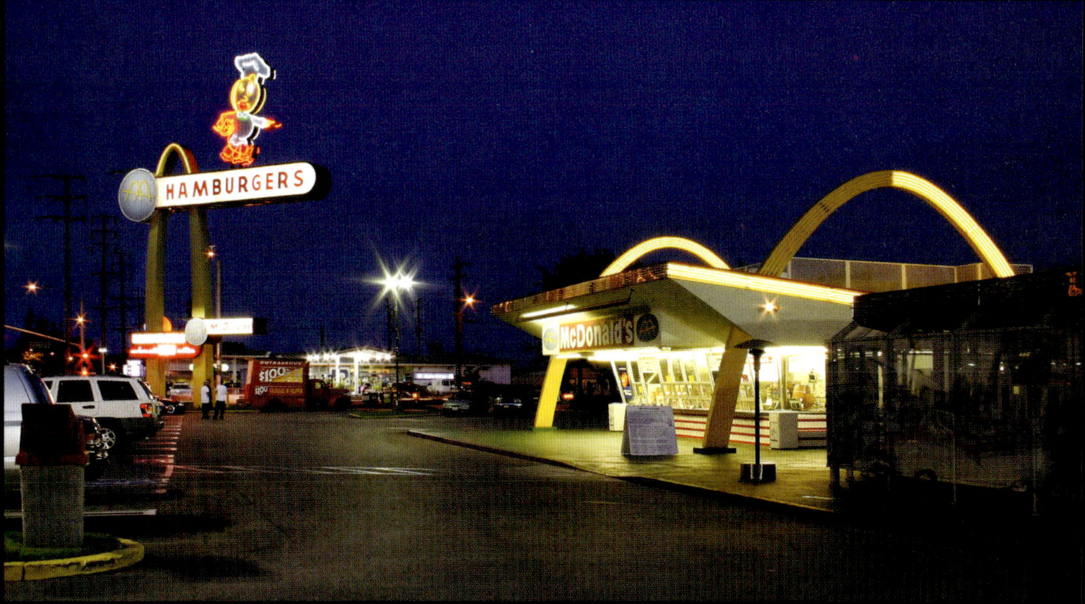

McDonald's - Downey

10207 Lakewood Boulevard, Downey

Opening its doors on August 18, 1953, this is the world's oldest operating McDonalds. It was also the third franchised McDonalds and was opened by Roger Williams and Burdette "Bud" Landon. Designed by architect Stanley C. Meston, this location remains the most intact example in Richard and Maurice McDonalds' revolutionary fast food enterprise. In 1984, architect/historian Alan Hess established its eligibility for the National Register of Historical Places. Traveling down Lakewood, you can't miss the 60-foot sign which was added in 1959 with "Speedee the Chef" running as fast as he can. Speedee was McDonalds' very first mascot and continues to draw travelers from all over the world.

Following the 1994 Northridge earthquake, this location was boarded up and threatened with demolition. The Los Angeles Conservancy's Modern Committee stepped in, taking emergency action to publicize Speedee's plight and gather support around the world. Ultimately, the McDonalds Corporation was persuaded to reopen the location. Speedee was renovated and on December 15, 1996, the restaurant returned with a brand new, on-site McDonald's museum. On their 50 year anniversary, a commemorative time capsule was buried, to be opened on their 100th anniversary.

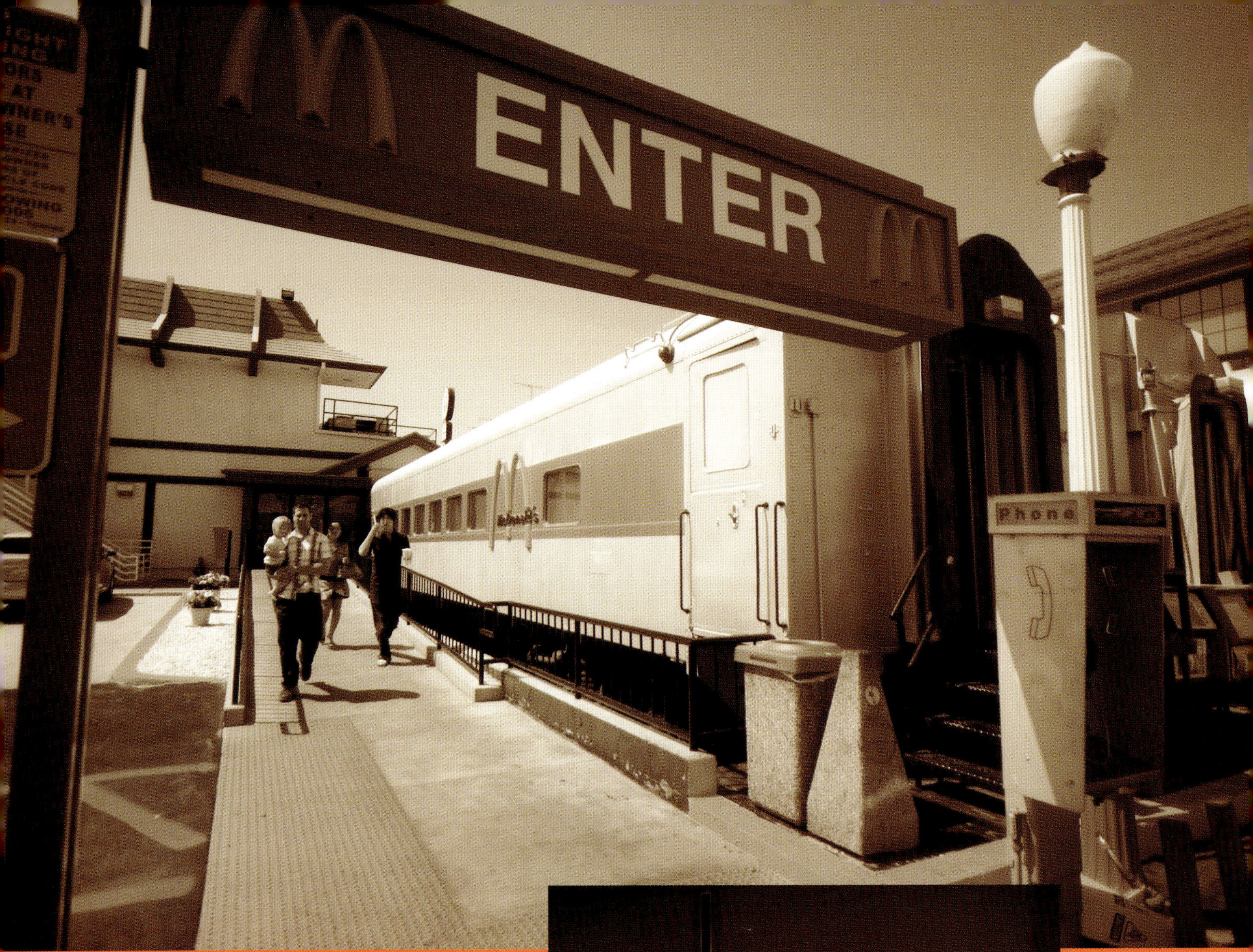

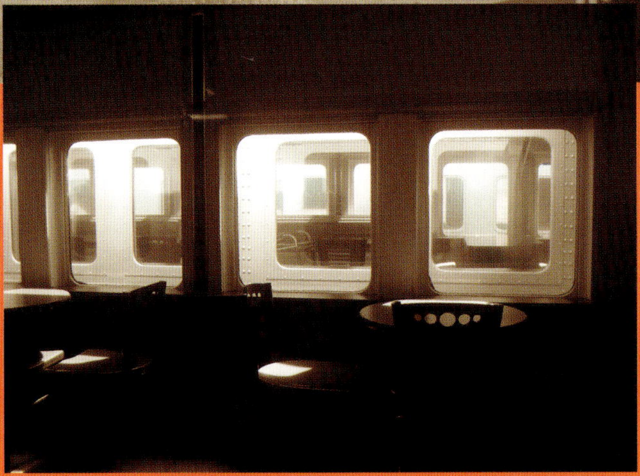

McDonald's - Barstow

E. Main Street, Route 66, Barstow

Just off Interstate 15 (the Old Mormon Trail) at the E. Main Street exit is a unique tourist/rest stop consisting of railroad cars connected by a central building. In this hub, there is a McDonald's, Panda Express, Quizno's, a fast food court with ice cream and candy shops, souvenir shops, and restroom facilities. This major stopover between L.A. and Las Vegas was teeming with people, RVs, and turnaround buses when we visited last summer. Lucky for us, we found a cool place to sit and have lunch in one of the air conditioned train cars.

Mearle's Drive-In

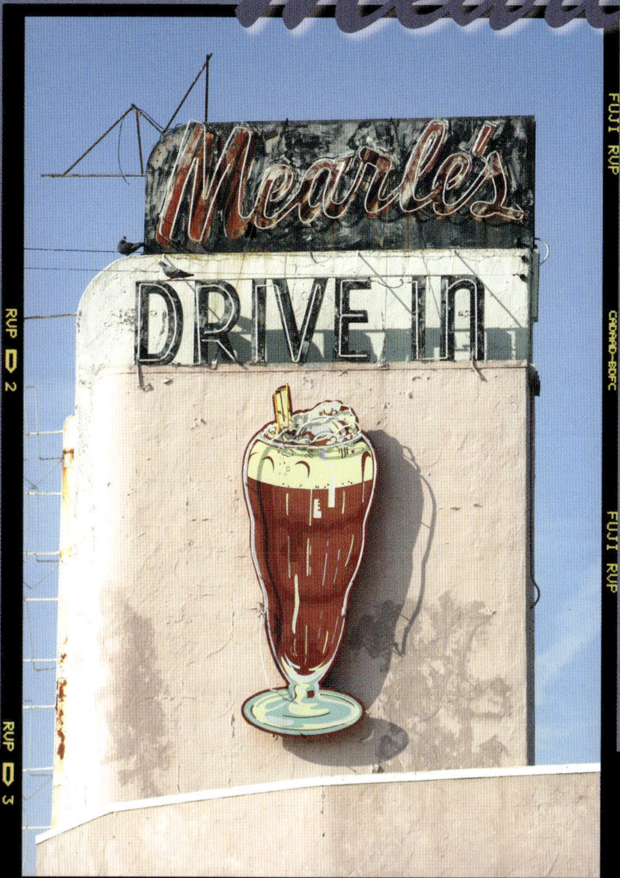

604 S. Mooney Boulevard, Visalia

A pre-war vision in streamline moderne design, this 1940 classic even spawned toy drive-ins for kids. Opening as Tad's Drive-In, the Breshwate brothers opened this restaurant across from the College of the Sequoias on September 27, 1940. Over the years Tad's went through a series of owners, becoming Nielson's at some point. Mearle Heitzman bought it in the 1950s and kept the legendary drive-in running for 50 years.

One of the last drive-ins to make it into the 21st century, we used to make a point of driving up to Mearle's and Mooney's Drive-In (recently demolished) every chance we could get. After a devastating fire in 2003, owner Melissa Ward reopened the restaurant and struggled with the business until August 2006, when Mearle's finally closed its doors. The building was added to the local historic register in November 2006. Still vacant after a public auction in 2008, Mearle's future remains uncertain.

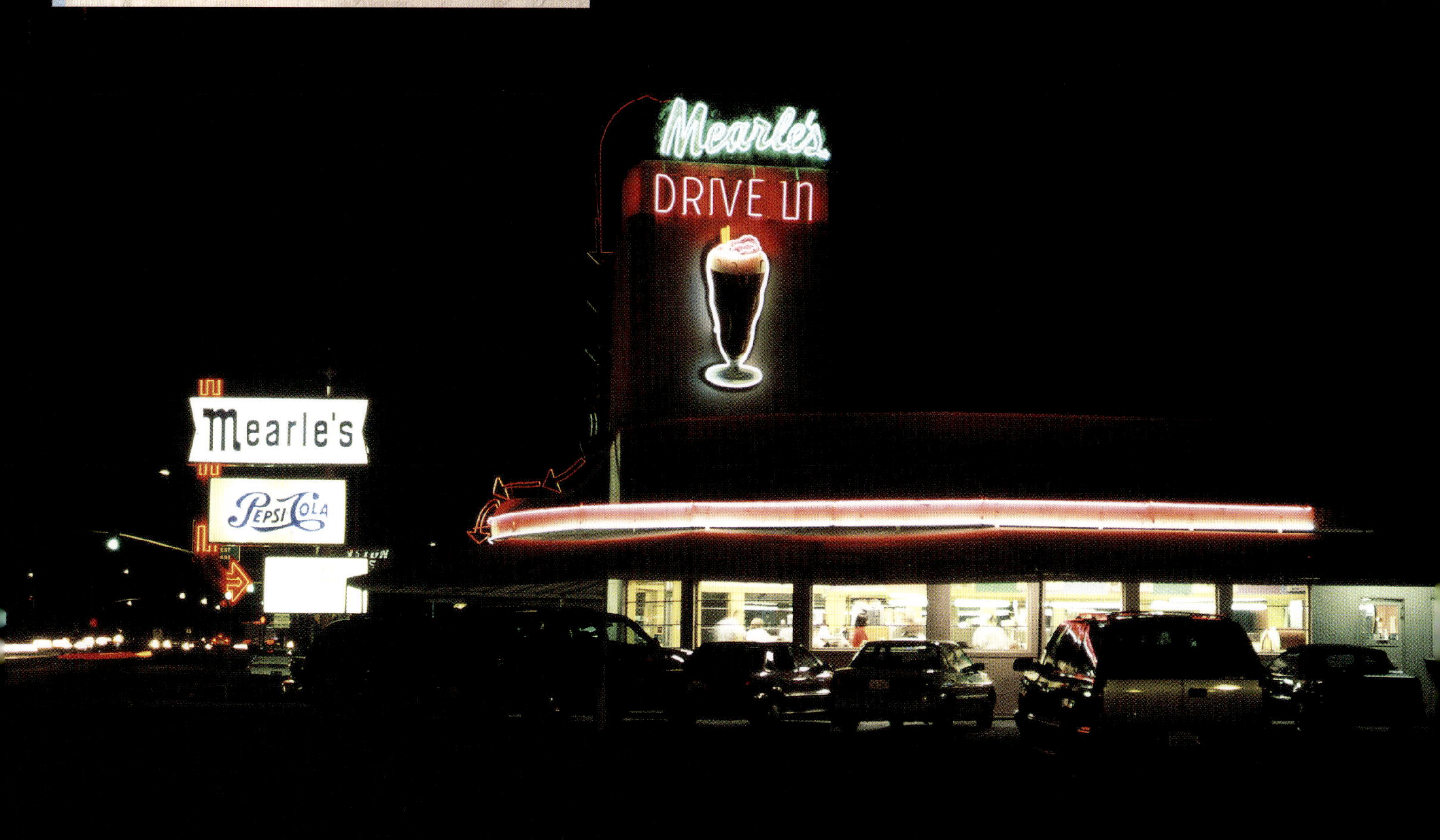

Mel's drive-in

Mel's drive-in

Multiple locations

Like an atomic bomb, the American automobile industry exploded across the US after World War II. In 1947, Mel Weiss and Harold Dobbs opened their first carhop drive-in. This soon expanded into 11 stores around the Bay area. These carhops were natural hangouts for teenagers looking for a place of their own away from their parents. Here they could listen to their own type of music and order what they wanted. Drive-ins gave them a place to show off their cars and meet girls. Weekend cruises reached their zenith during the late '50s and '60s, but their decline soon came when these unsupervised activities began to attract rowdy crowds, beer, and fights. The final nail in the coffin came with the proliferation of self-service fast food restaurants. By the early '70s, many drive-ins were already closed. So, when a young George Lucas wanted a location for

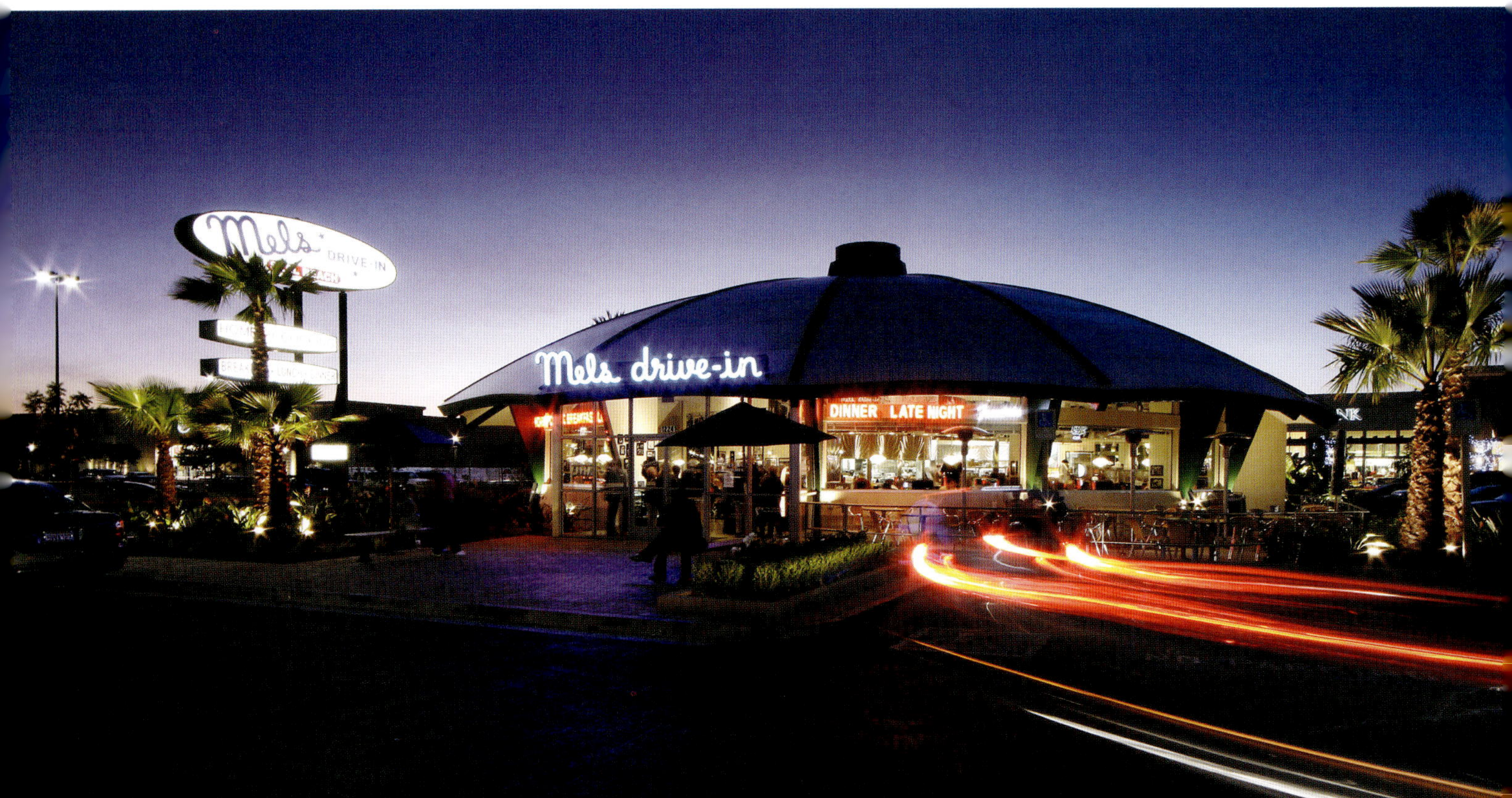

American Graffiti, a semi auto-biographical film about teenagers taking place in and around a drive-in, he used Mel's in San Francisco (just minutes before it was bulldozed).

Mel's son, Steven Weiss and partner Donald Wagstaff, opened their "Next Generation" Mel's drive-ins in 1985.

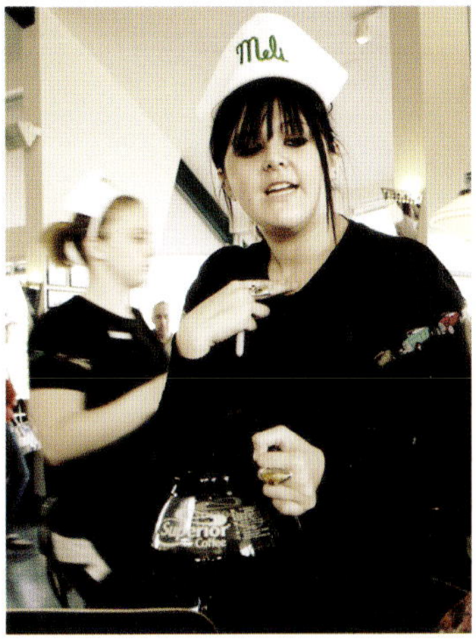

Now there are Mel's in various historic locations: on the Sunset Strip, in the Max Factor building in Hollywood, and in the former Kerry's in Sherman Oaks. Sadly, the Mel's Drive-In in Los Alamitos (formerly The Parasol) closed on October 19, 2009, the very day that Bob's Big Boy Broiler drive-in reopened in Downey.

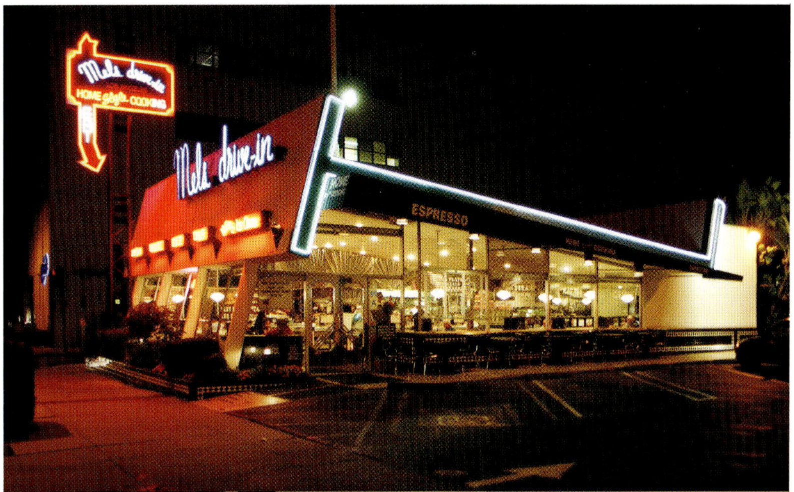

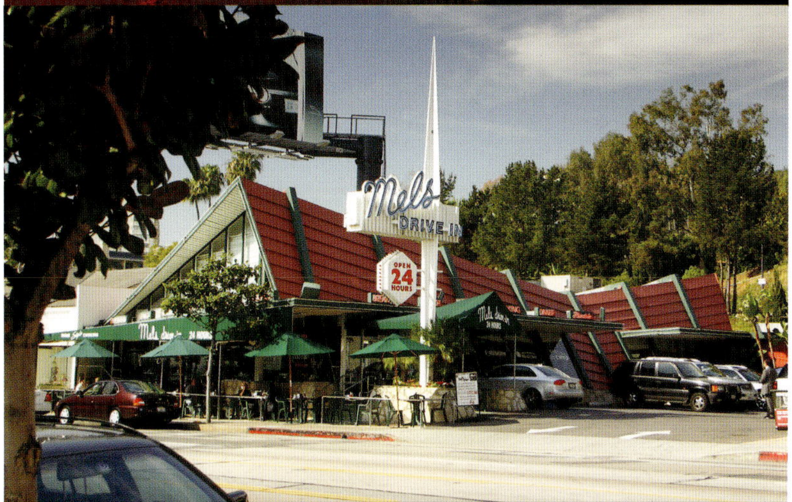

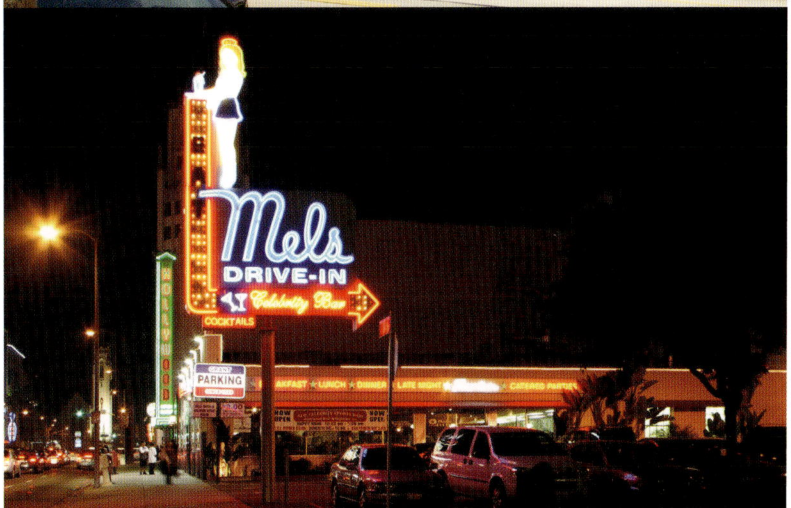

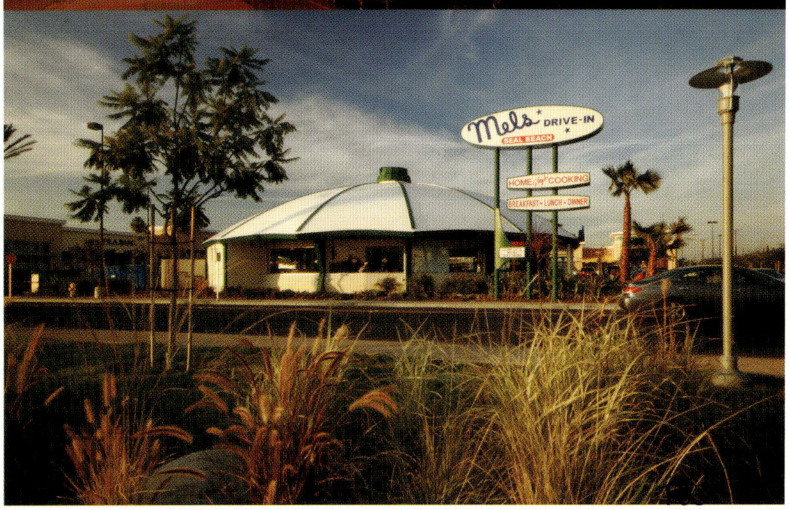

Top to bottom:
Originally Kerry's Coffee Shop, Sherman Oaks, 1953, designed by Armet + Davis.

Opened in 1962 as Ben Frank's, designed by Lane and Schlick. Googie galore on the Sunset Strip.

Housed in the Max Factor Building, Hollywood, 1931. S. Charles Lee turned a furniture warehouse and an automobile service garage into an elegant art deco classic for the Hollywood make-up pioneer.

Built as The Parasol, Los Alamitos, 1967, designed by Charles Kanner. Programmatic architecture with the building in the shape of an umbrella.

Me-N-Ed's Pizza Parlor

No. 1: 4735 N. Blackstone Avenue, Fresno, 1958
No. 2: 4289 N. Cedar Avenue, Fresno
So Cal: 4115 Paramount Boulevard, Lakewood

Partners Russ Johnson ("Me") and Ed Sandlin ("Ed") created the first Me-N-Ed's in Sacramento. Russ is the brother of Sherwood "Shakey" Johnson and cofounder of Shakey's Pizza. The franchise has grown to over 50 restaurants and is still owned and operated by family-owned Milano Restaurants International, headquartered in Fresno. In Nor Cal, No. 1 in Blackstone Village has a beautifully restored neon sign, though the interior was gutted during its mid-2000 renovation. The operator of No 2. estimates it was built a year or two later, but the original linoleum tile floor and copper refrigerators still shine like new.

The Me-N-Ed's here in So Cal's Lakewood sports the Ye Olde Beer Hall atmosphere popular in the early '60s. It's old school, down to the dark varnished wood bench seats and walk-in copper refrigerator. There's even the old-time Boraxo powdered soap in the restrooms! Not only does Me-N-Ed's serve a mean thin crust pizza (check out their rave reviews), but the Lakewood location offers live entertainment every Friday and Saturday evening with Big Al at the piano and bluegrass on Saturdays. A couple of doors to the north is a groovy '60s pool hall, and around the corner you'll find the very first Denny's (originally Danny's).

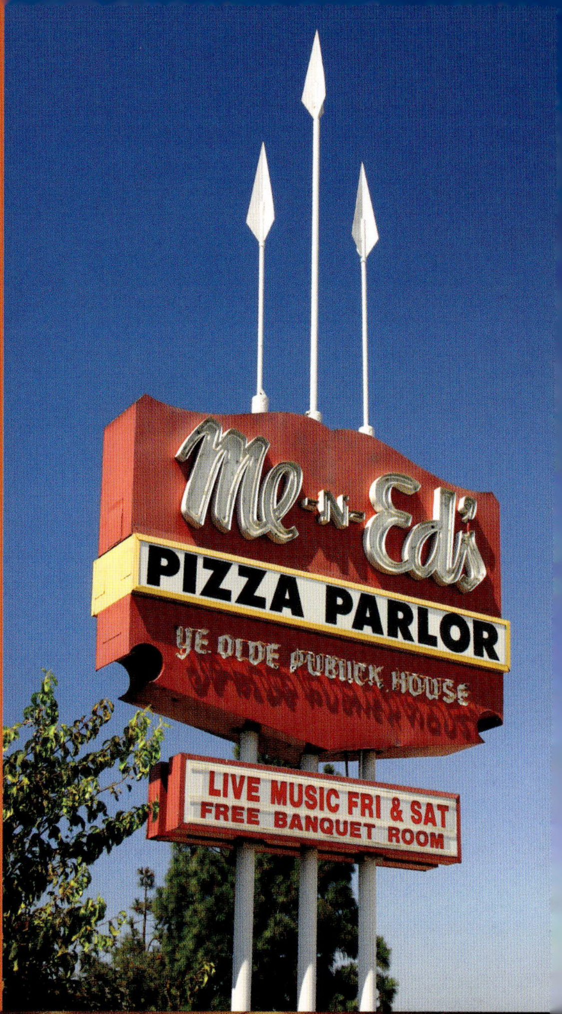

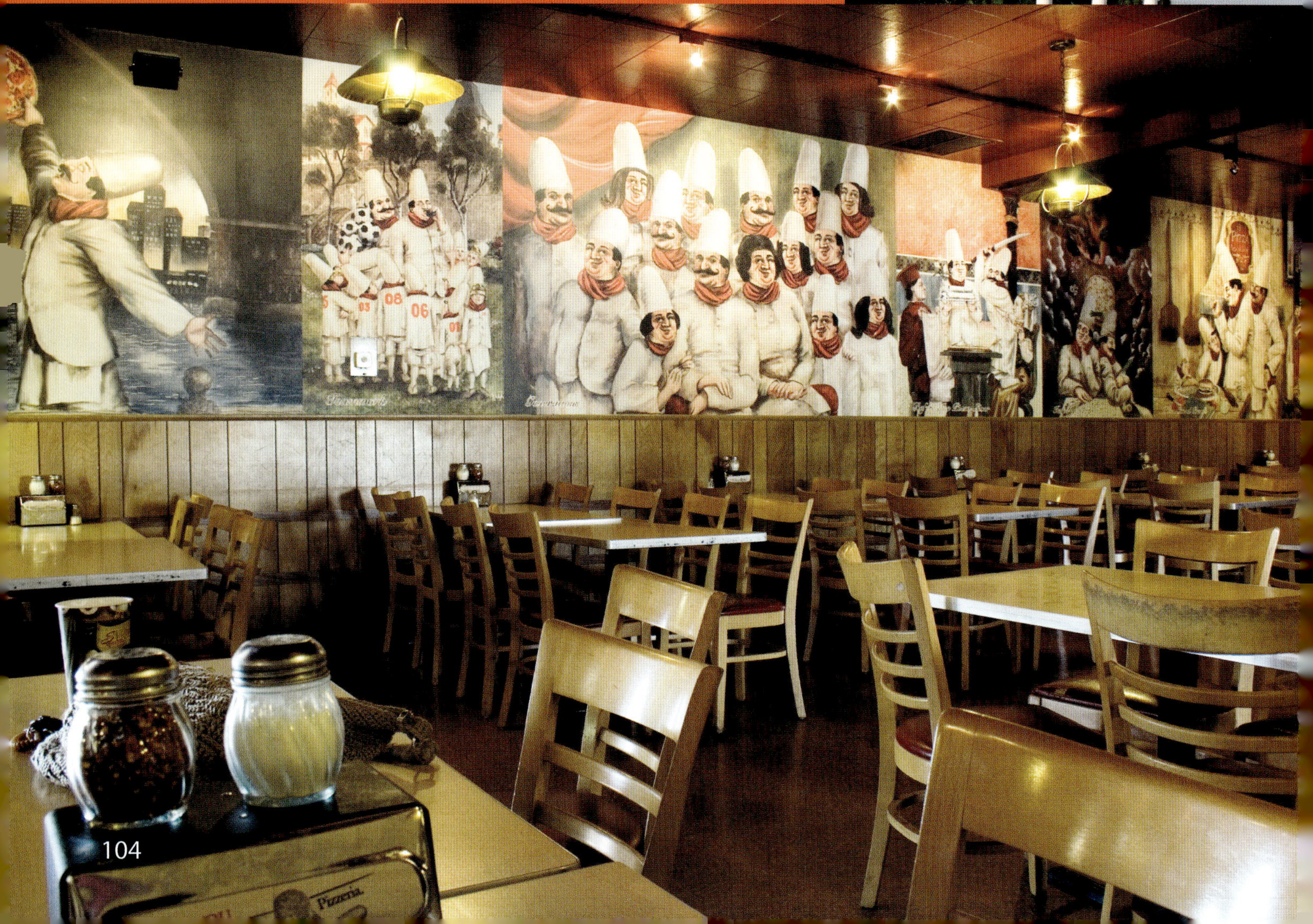

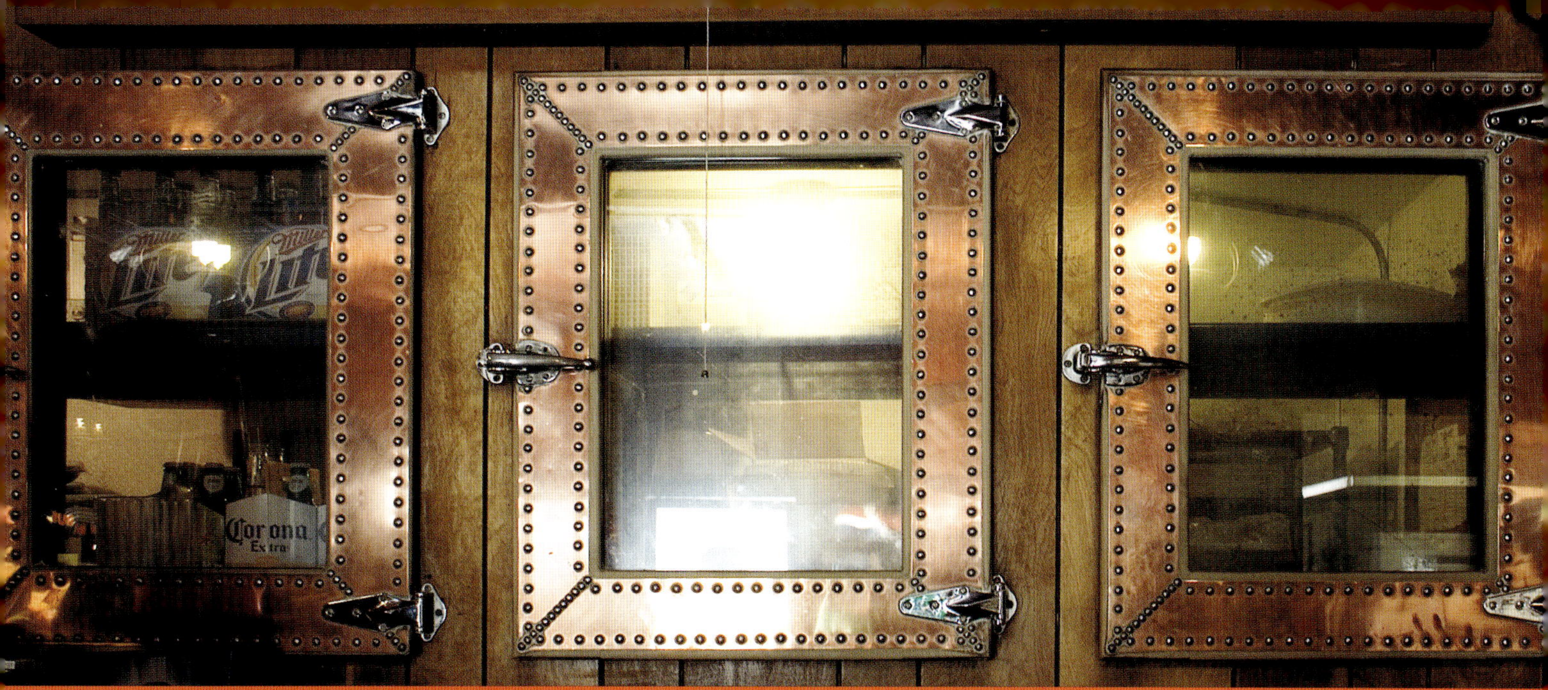
Corona
Extra

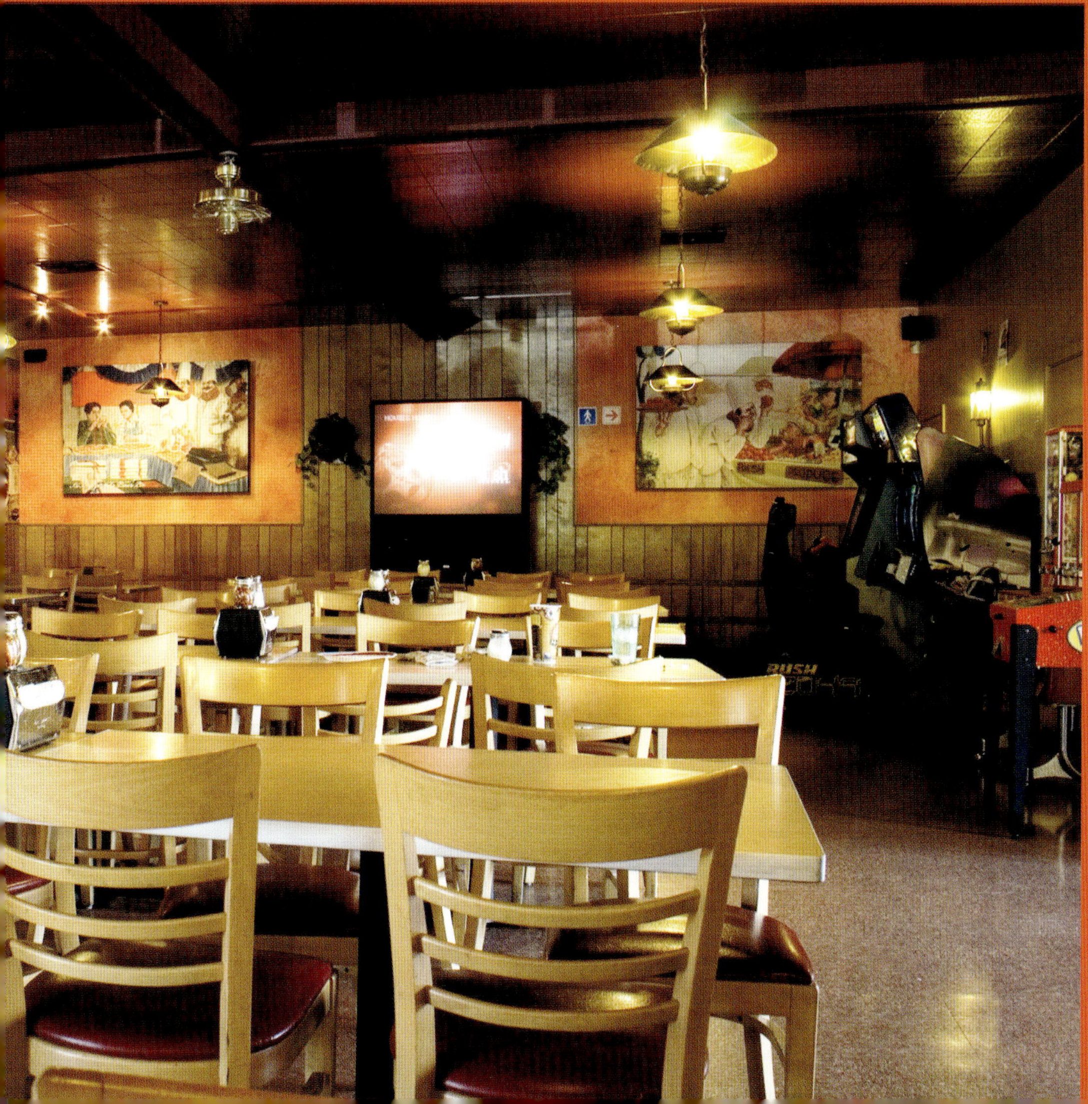
RUSH

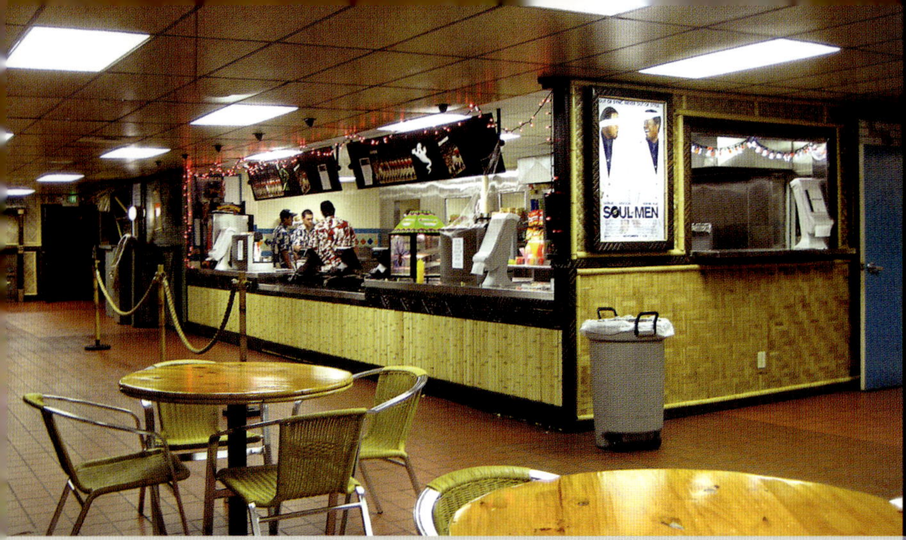

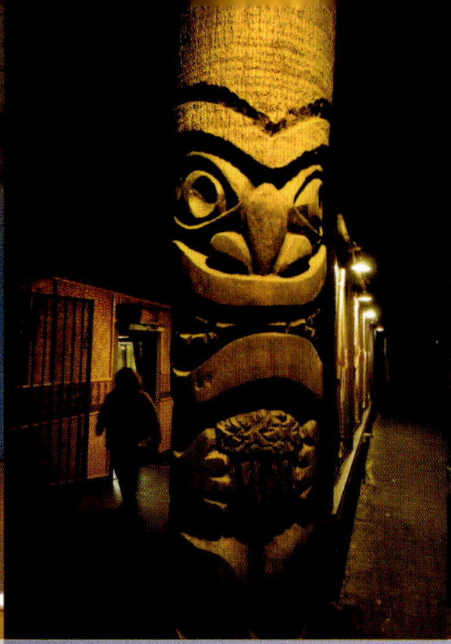

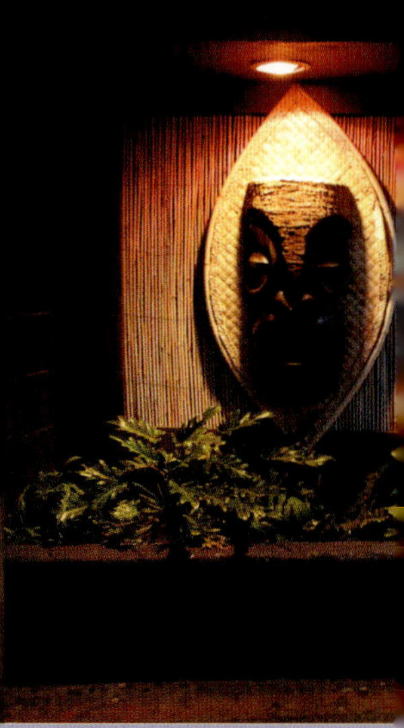

Mission Tiki Drive-In Snack Bar

10798 Ramona Avenue, Montclair

Opening in 1956 as the single screen Mission Drive-In Theater, three additional screens were added in 1975. In 2005, De Anza converted this conventional drive-in into a plush, tropical tiki paradise and reopened it as the Mission Tiki Drive-In. With first run features, original tiki sculptures by Tiki Diablo, tiki ticket huts, and a totally tiki-fied snack station, the Mission Tiki is putting the drive-in back on the map.

When we were here during the summer, the place was packed with people and cars. A group of us sat outside our cars in lawn chairs for deluxe viewing. While at the snack bar, John was treated to an impromptu tour of the projection room. He was stunned at the enormous reels spinning like the space station in *2001: A Space Odyssey*.

Later, as we watched *Ice Age*, a summer breeze washed over us and we looked at each other, communicating without a word, "Life doesn't get any better than this."

MISSION TIKI DR

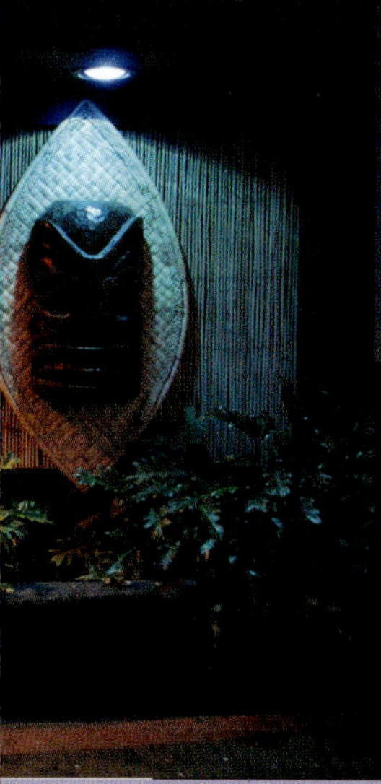
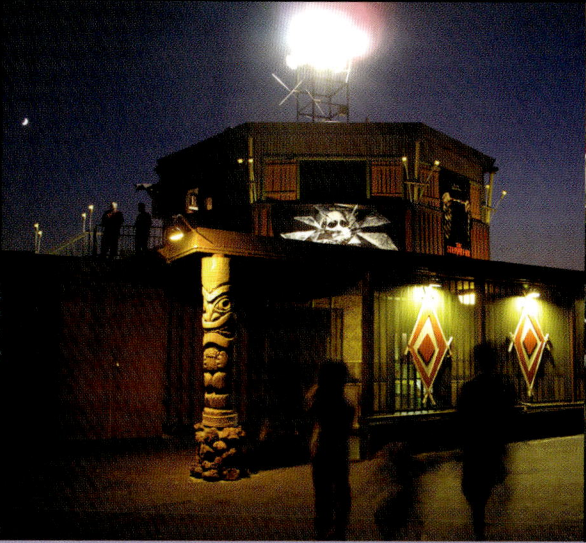
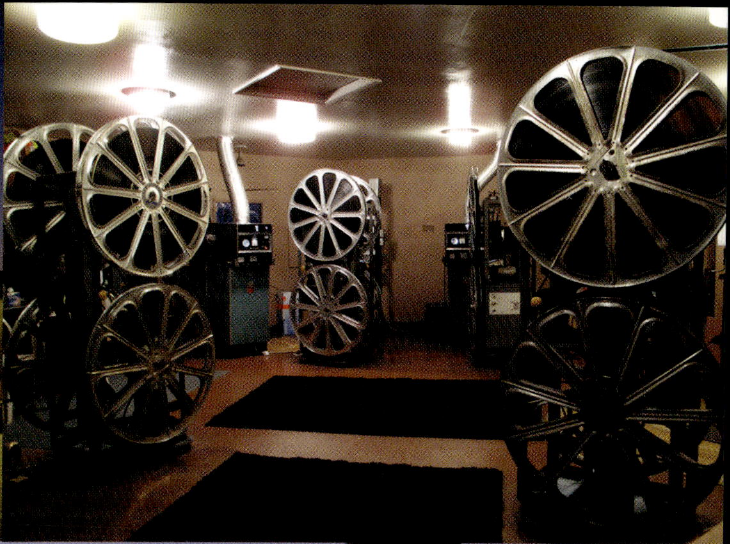
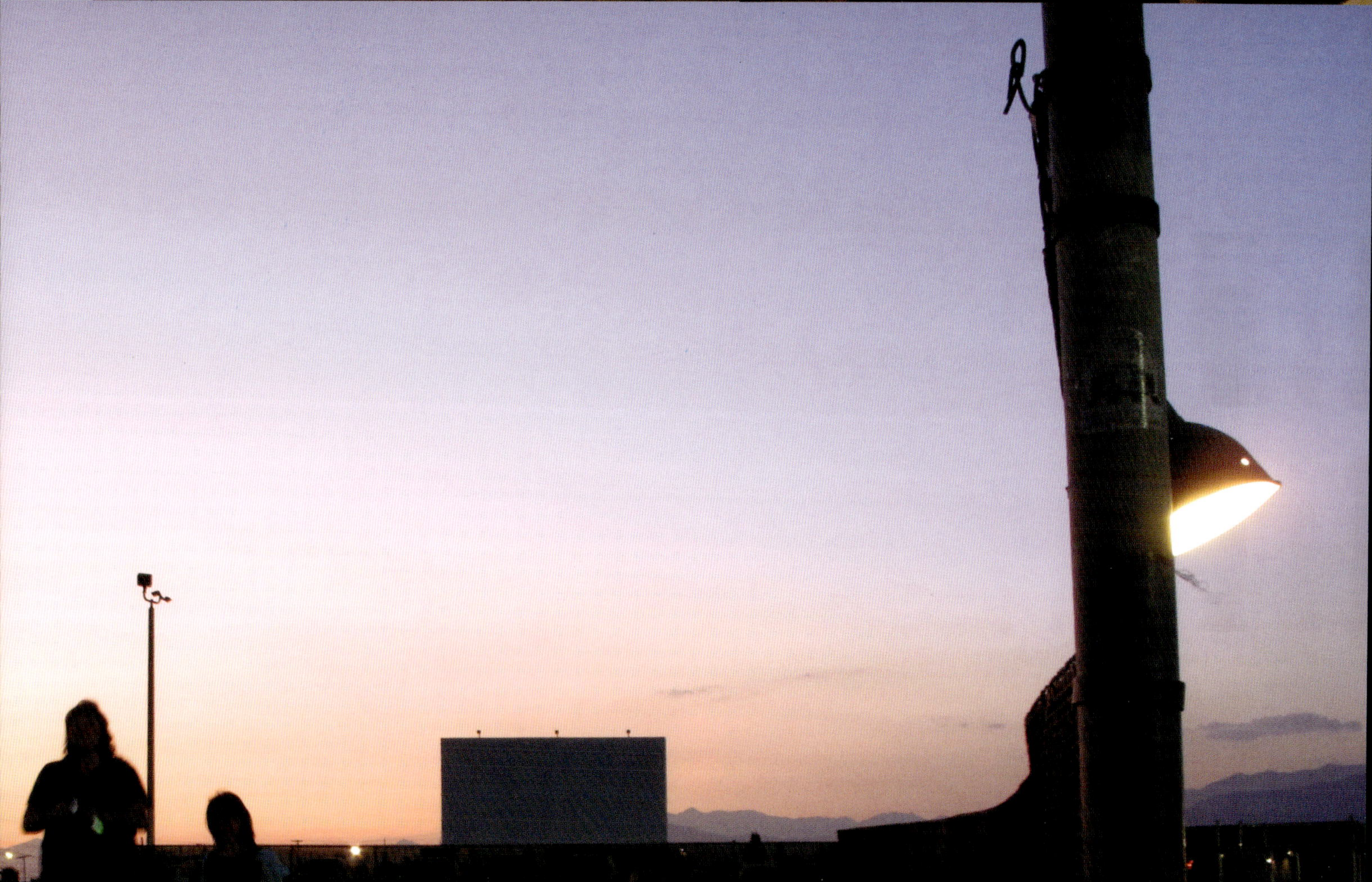

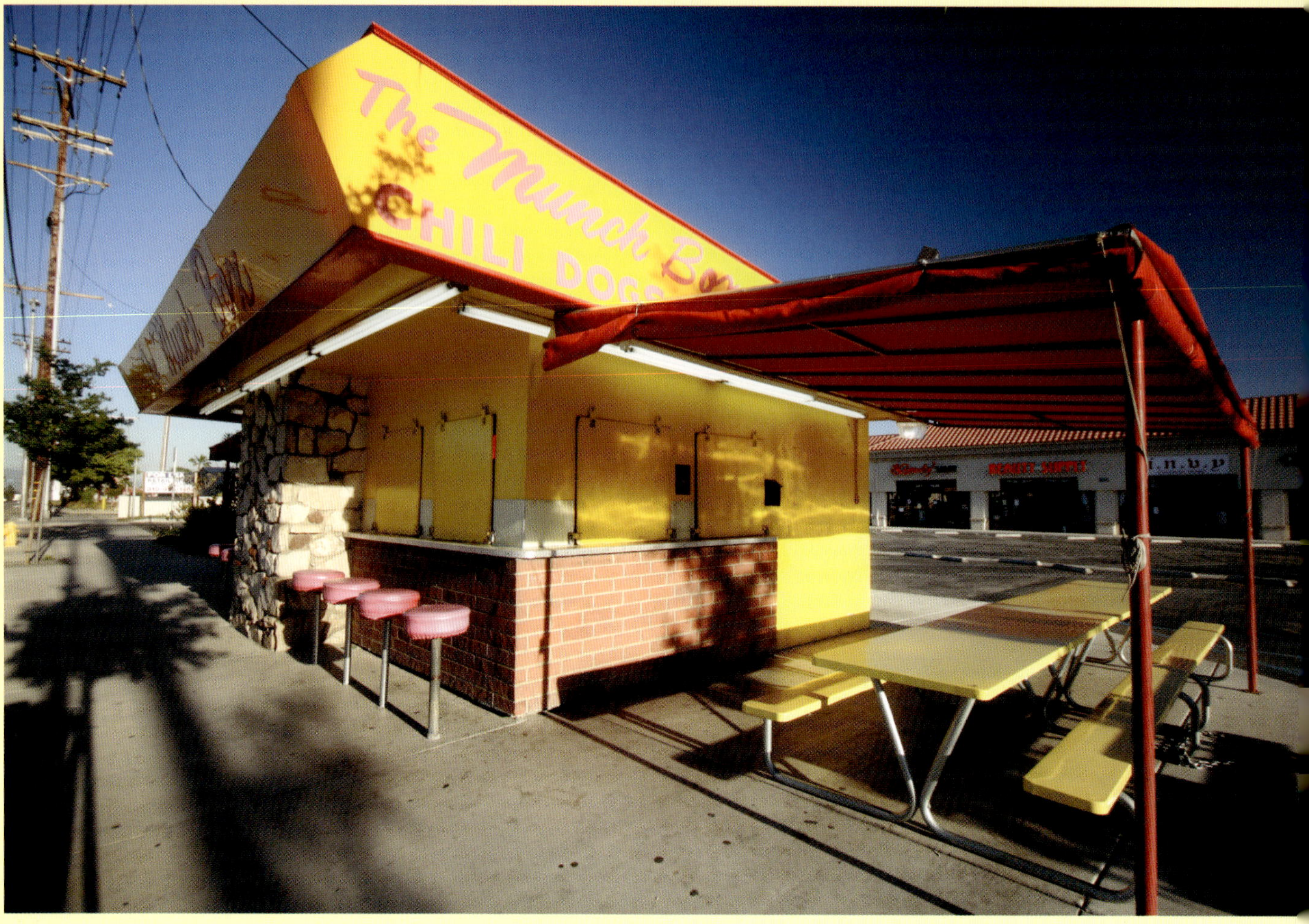

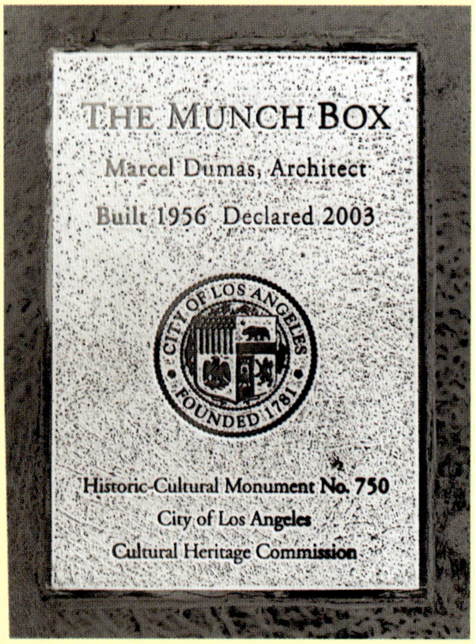

The Munch Box

21532 Devonshire Street, Chatsworth

There is something heartwarming about seeing this little survivor out by the railroad tracks on Devonshire. Fifty years ago, when the Munch Box was built, the San Fernando Valley was a movie star get-a-way dotted with citrus groves and celebrity-owned ranches. How lucky for us that we can still stop by for a smoky hickory burger and chili fries, and wash it down with one of their famous root beer floats. If you can't make it out to the valley, check out this little landmark on PBS. Huell Howser features it in one of his episodes 'cause it truly is a piece of "California's Gold."

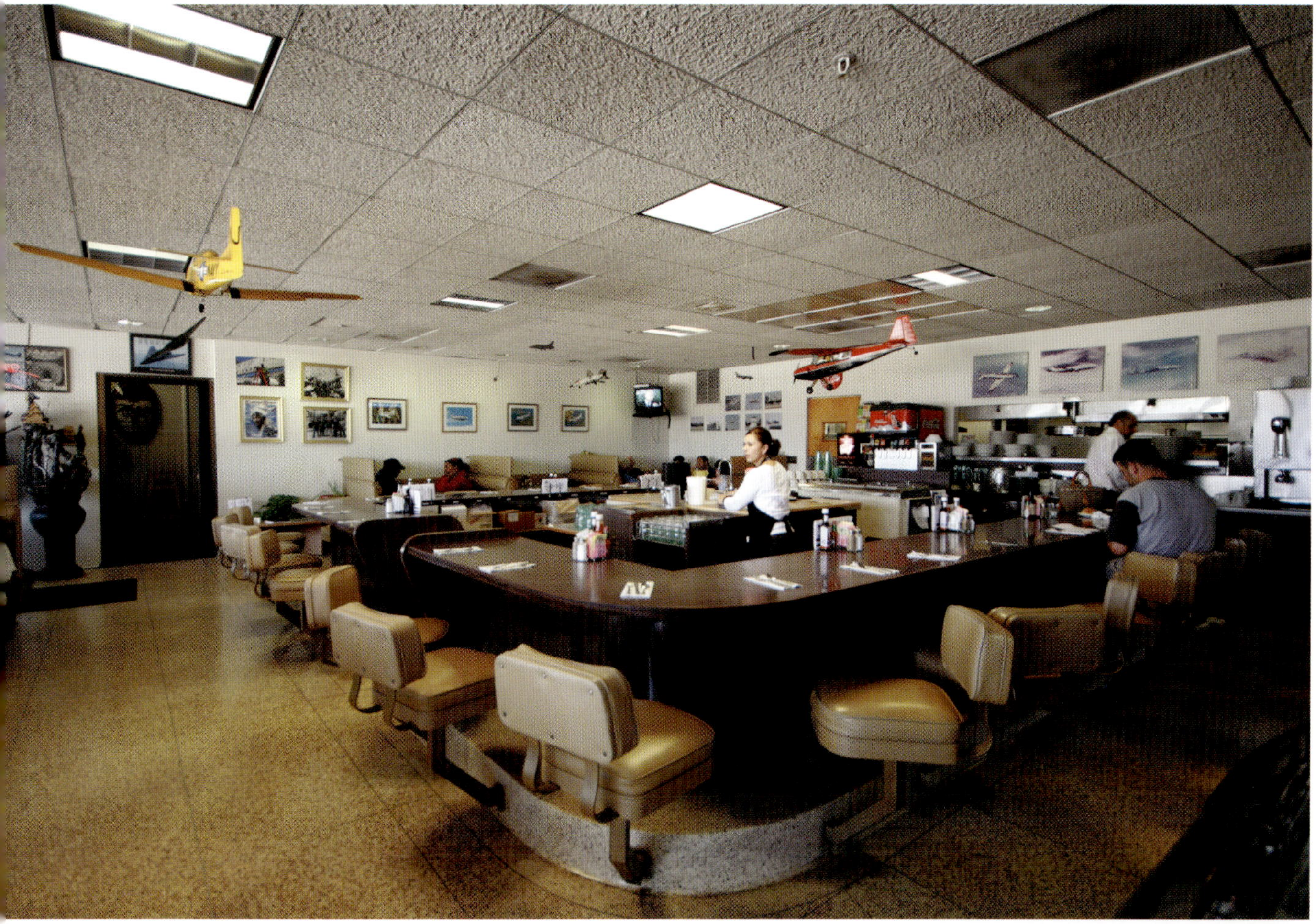

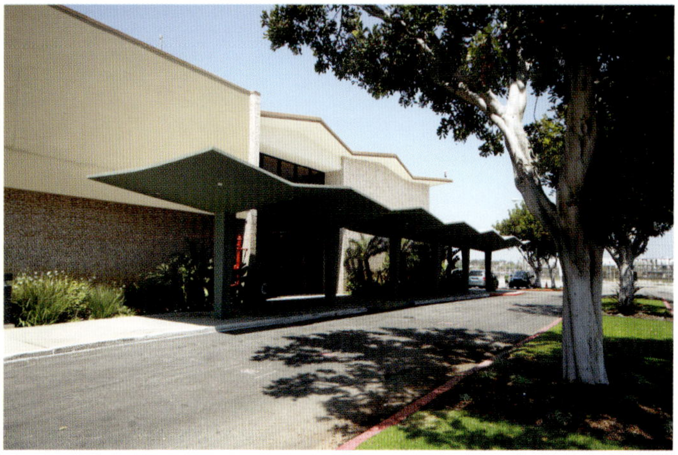

Nat's Airport Cafe

12101 S. Crenshaw Boulevard, Hawthorne

This not-so-little coffee shop is a surprise gem hidden within the mid-century modern Hawthorne Airport Terminal. The windows facing north open to the runway. On a recent visit, a 12-seater plane was leaving for a charter flight over the Grand Canyon.

This coffee shop has original cantilevered stools around a large U-shaped counter. Large scale model planes are suspended overhead from the ceiling. The outside entrance features a folded roof canopy and tropical plants unique to mid-century modern landscape design. A very fun place to visit when in the neighborhood.

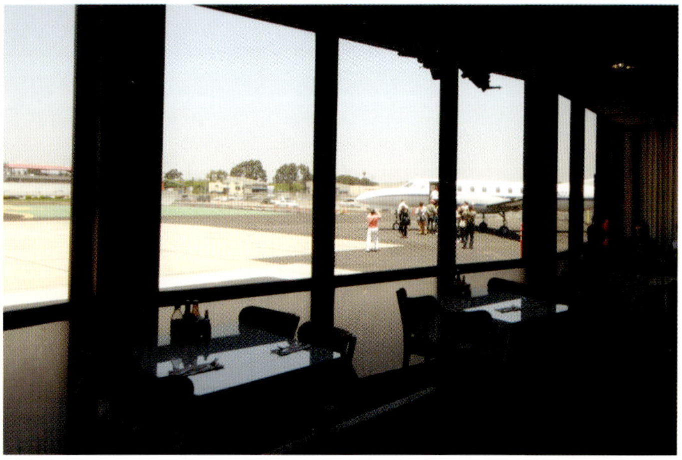

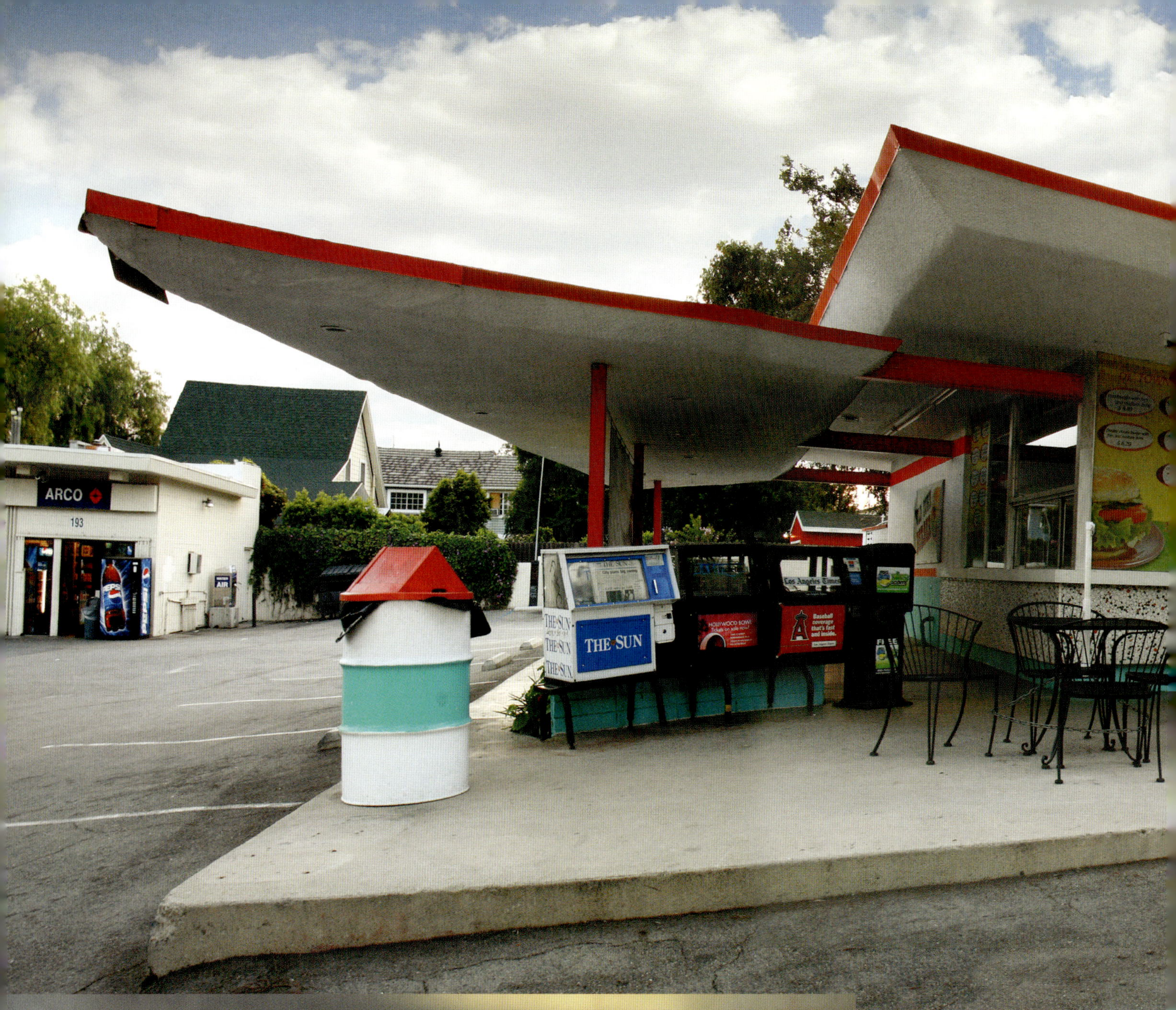
ARCO
193
THE SUN

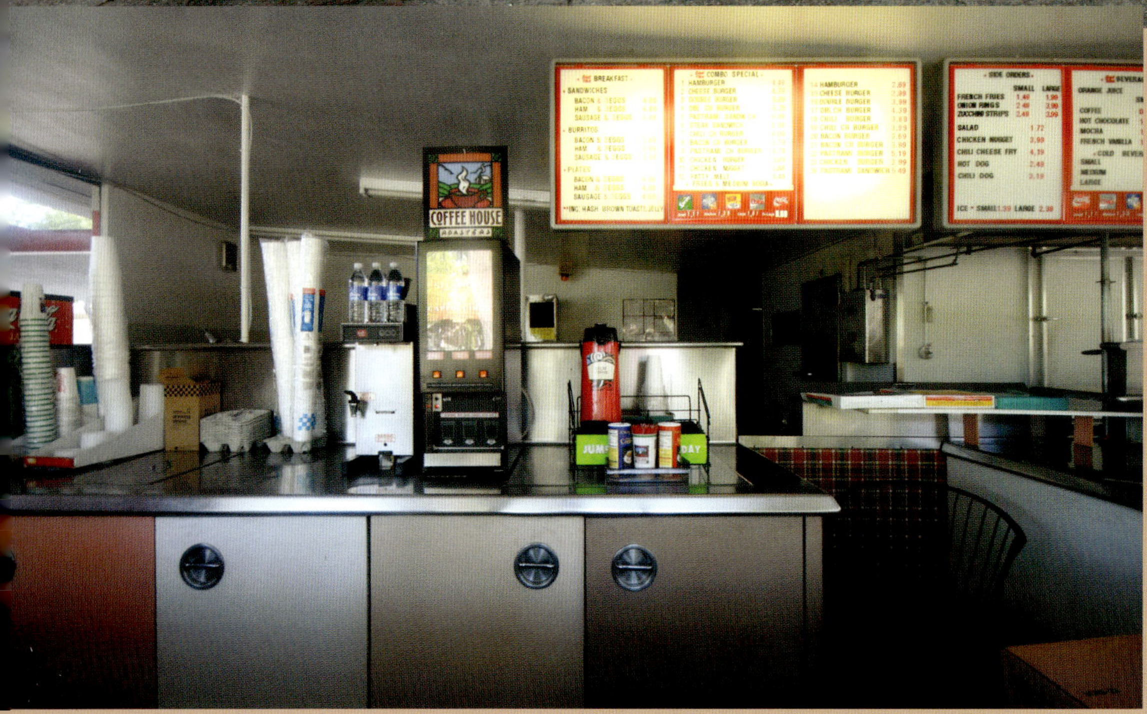
COFFEE HOUSE

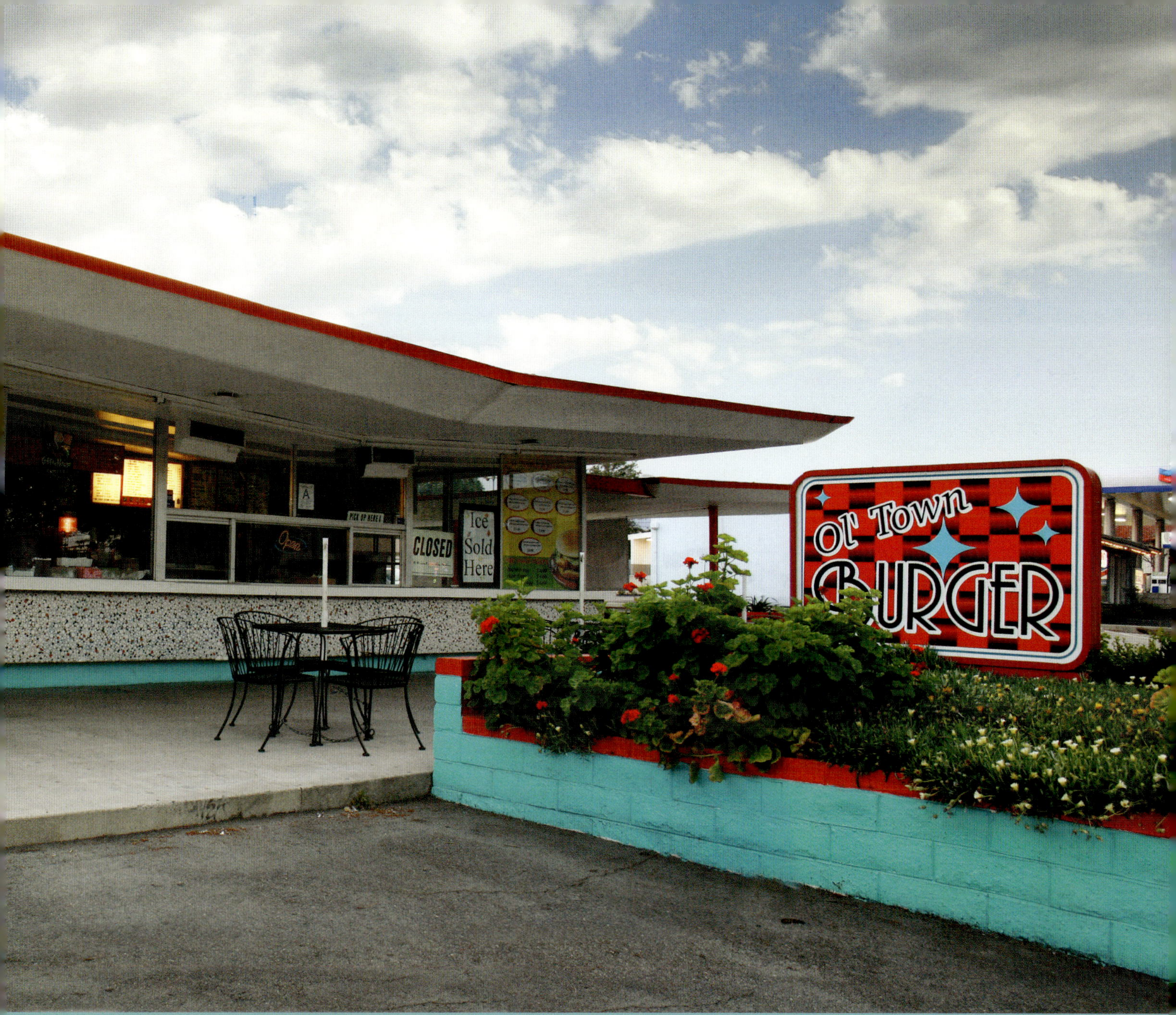

Ol' Town Burger

(AKA TACO AQUI AND GUS'S)

185 S. Euclid Avenue, Upland

The minute we discovered this place, we remembered the scent of Coppertone tanning lotion and flashed back to 1961. Suddenly, we were cruising in a Woody wagon in search of burgers after a hot summer day surfing at Zuma Beach. There is an unbeatable ambience at this drive-in. Details include a butterfly roof and drop wings over the patio eating areas, diamond shaped concrete screen at the rear, and circular tiles outlining the building. Colored Formica panels cover the kitchen cabinets a la Pann's. Previously Classic Burgers, it's a puzzle to us why this place isn't better known. How 'bout a classic car cruise starting here and driving out to the Grinder Haven and Vince's Spaghetti via Route 66, then out to Driftwood Dairy and over to Bob's Big Boy Broiler in Downey!

ORIGINAL PANCAKE HOUSE

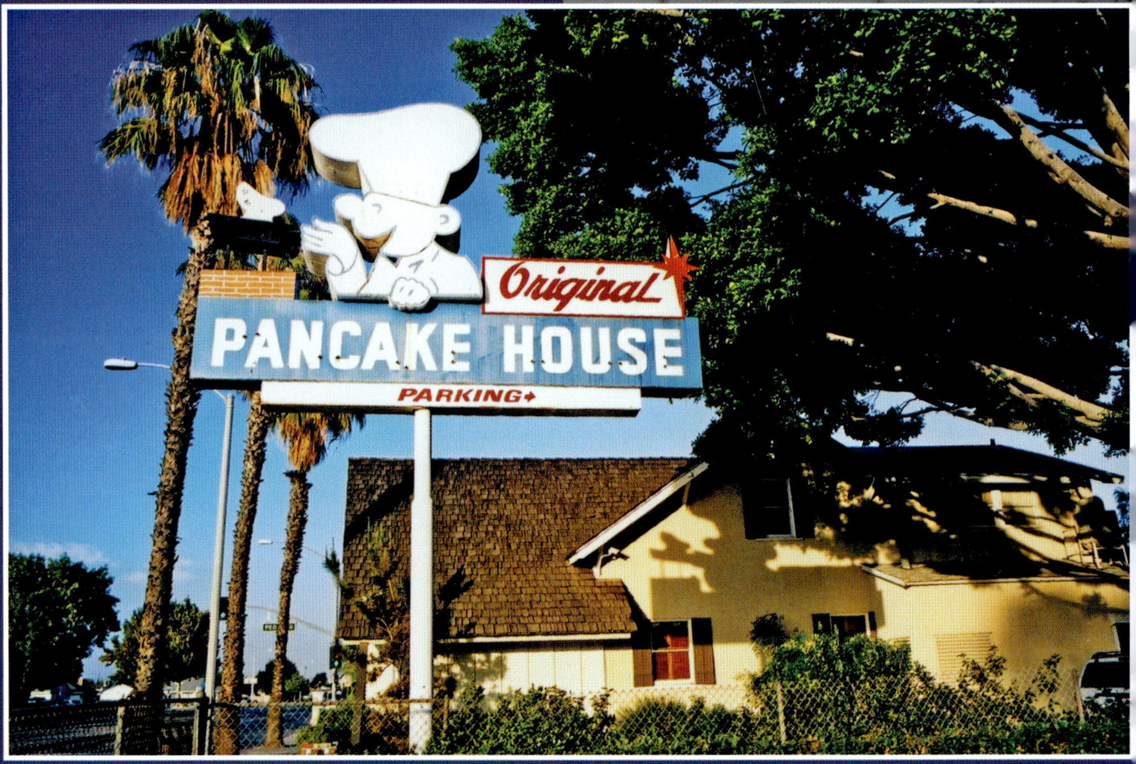

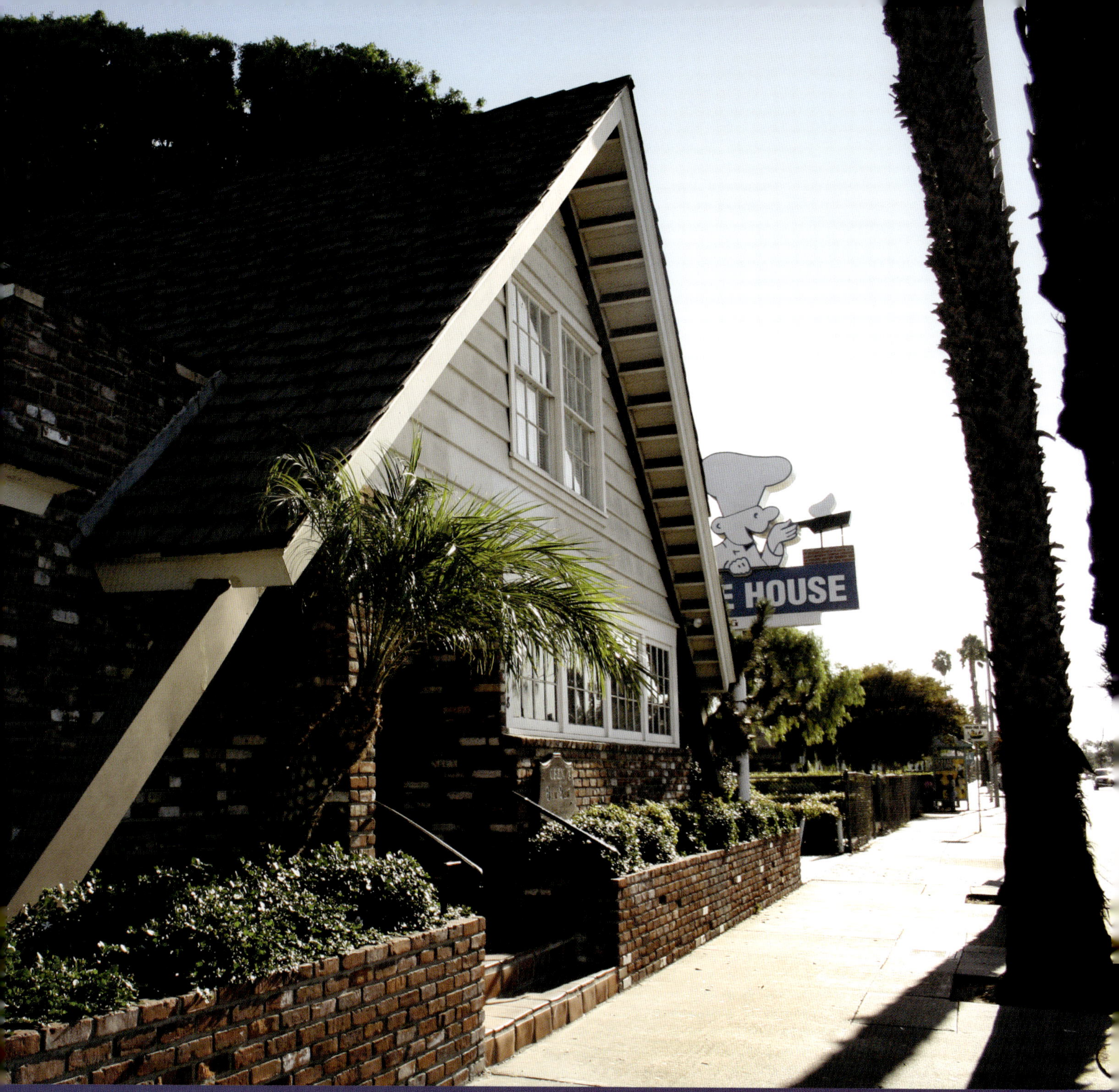

Original PANCAKE HOUSE

1418 E. Lincoln Avenue, Anaheim
Multiple Locations

Les Highet and Erma Hueneke started it all in Portland, Oregon, in 1953. Now, 50 years later, there are more than 100 franchises across most of the states in North America. Les and Erma spent years collecting recipes from all over the world. The food and comfy atmosphere is reminiscent of Old Europe.

The Original Pancake House's signature item is their mouth-watering apple pancake, a single pancake the size of a dinner plate covered with apples and cinnamon sugar. The menu includes a wide range of pancakes, fresh vegetarian omelettes, gourmet crepes, waffles, cereals, juices, and fruits. Remember, the food tastes incredible, but there's plenty of sugar and butter in everything, so don't come here if you want to get skinny. Or better yet, walk it off at nearby Disneyland.

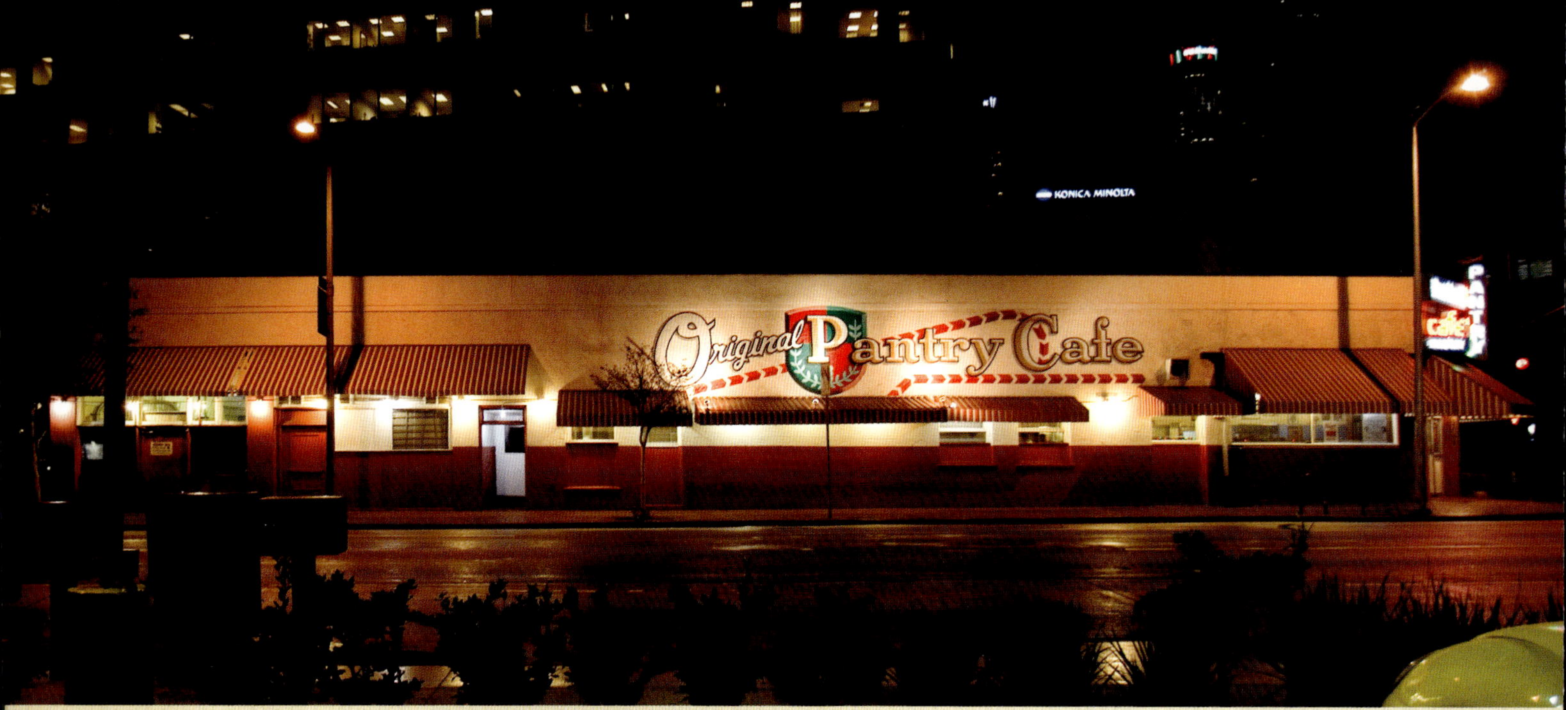

The Original PANTRY Café

877 South Figueroa Street, Los Angeles

The Original Pantry Café has been operating continuously since 1924. This historic eatery started out with only a grill, a hot plate, and a counter with fifteen stools. The rest is history. The Pantry is owned by former Los Angeles mayor Richard Riordan, who is fond of saying "We never close. We're never without a customer." A survivor of the Great Depression, the current Depression, several earthquakes, and World War II, The Pantry reestablished itself in 1950 after a move to its present location at Figueroa and 9th Street to make room for a freeway ramp. And even on that day, the restaurant served lunch at the old location and dinner in the new.

If you want a true taste of local LA culture, stop in for a unique dining experience. For decades one of our favorite waiters had the face of Humphrey Bogart. When you pay your bill at the cashier's cage, glance down at the well-worn layers of linoleum beneath your feet. Just as you can tell how old a tree is by the number of rings it has, you'll be reminded of the thousands of customers who stood here before you.

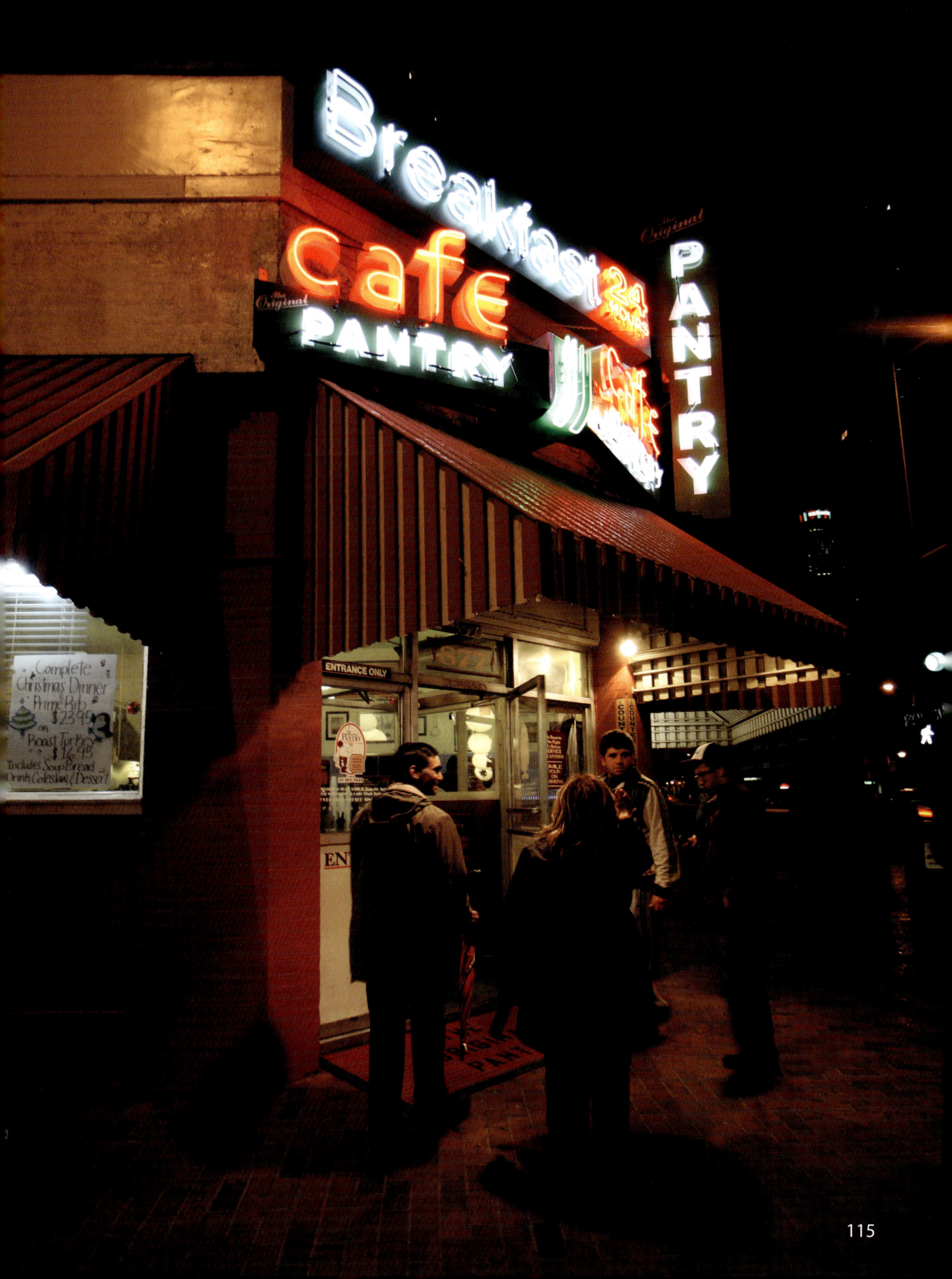
Breakfast
24 HOURS
cafe
The Original
PANTRY
The Original
PANTRY
ENTRANCE ONLY
Complete
Christmas Dinner
Prime Rib
$23.95
OR
Roast Turkey
$16.95
Includes Soup Bread
Drink Coleslaw & Dessert

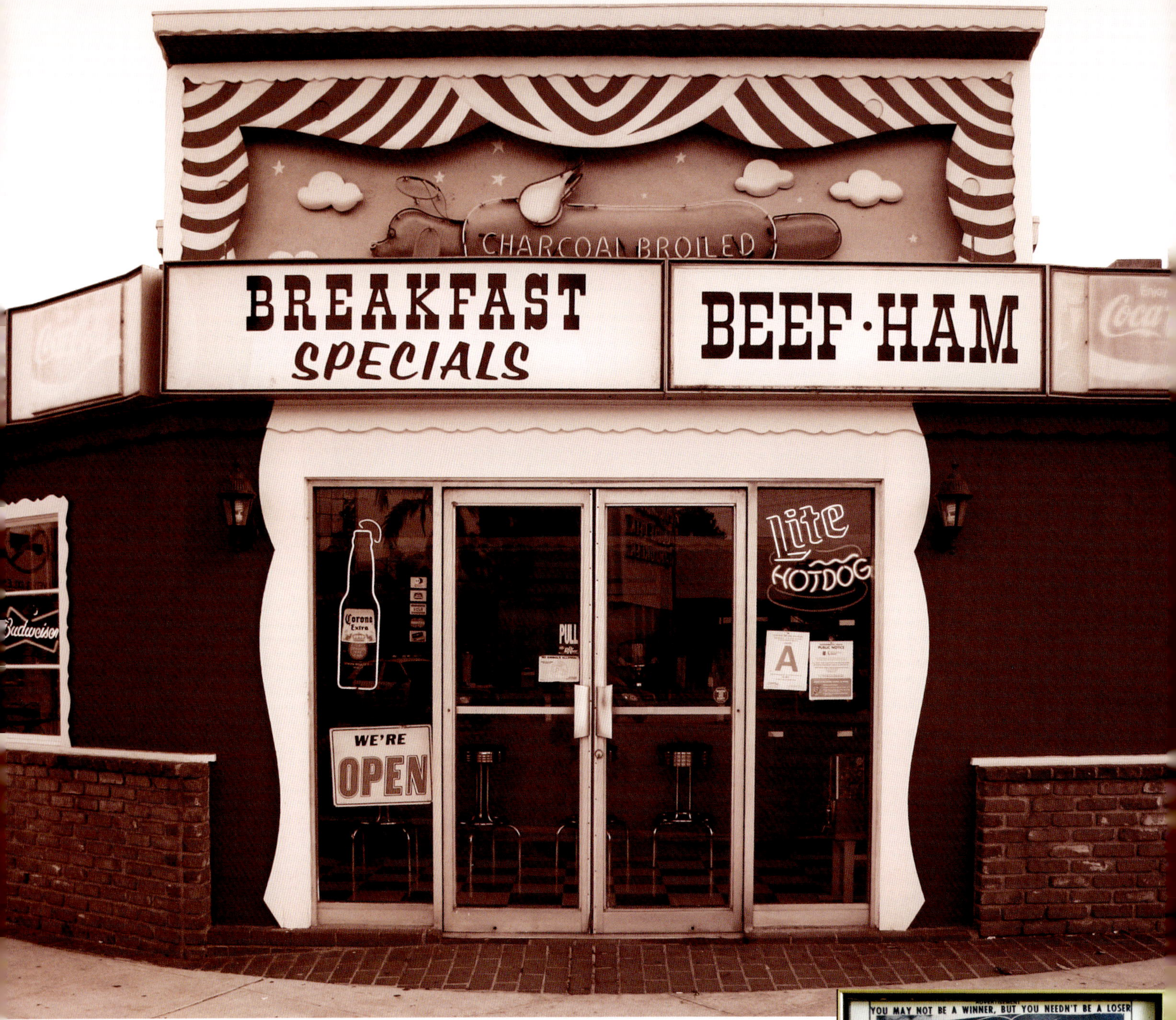

PAPOO'S HOT DOG SHOW

4300 W. Riverside Drive, Burbank

Kitty-corner from the famous Bob's Big Boy drive-in is this charming hot dog shop, also dating back to 1949. Papoo's insists they were here first! We were told that "Papoo's" means "Grandpa's" in Greek. The atmosphere is cozy and the food is good with generous portions. Back in the early days, Papoo's presented children's puppet shows on a miniature stage inside the building. Now it can still pack 'em in, especially on Friday nights when classic cars invade the area for Bob's cruise nights. And speaking of invasions, Papoo's sister store on Beachwood Avenue in the Hollywood Hills appeared in the '50s sci-fi thriller *Invasion of the Body Snatchers*. A timeless classic, all around.

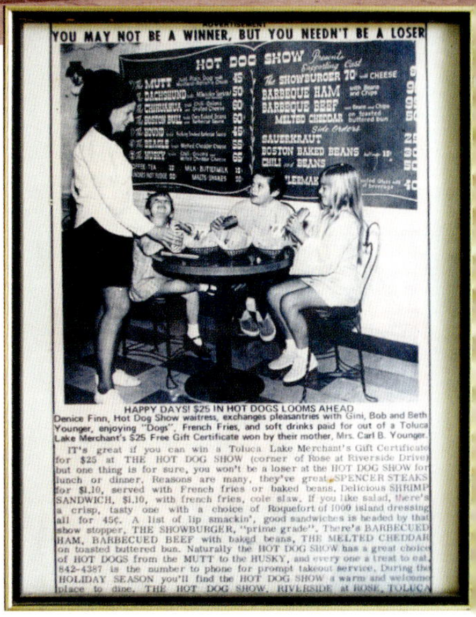

YOU MAY NOT BE A WINNER, BUT YOU NEEDN'T BE A LOSER

HAPPY DAYS! $25 IN HOT DOGS LOOMS AHEAD

Denice Finn, Hot Dog Show waitress, exchanges pleasantries with Gini, Bob and Beth Younger, enjoying "Dogs", French Fries, and soft drinks paid for out of a Toluca Lake Merchant's $25 Free Gift Certificate won by their mother, Mrs. Carl B. Younger.

IT's great if you can win a Toluca Lake Merchant's Gift Certificate for $25 at THE HOT DOG SHOW (corner of Rose at Riverside Drive) but one thing is for sure, you won't be a loser at the HOT DOG SHOW for lunch or dinner. Reasons are many, they've great SPENCER STEAKS for $1.10, served with French fries or baked beans. Delicious SHRIMP SANDWICH, $1.10, with french fries, cole slaw. If you like salad, there's a crisp, tasty one with a choice of Roquefort of 1000 island dressing all for 45¢. A list of lip smackin', good sandwiches is headed by that show stopper, THE SHOWBURGER, "prime grade". There's BARBECUED HAM, BARBECUED BEEF with baked beans, THE MELTED CHEDDAR on toasted buttered bun. Naturally the HOT DOG SHOW has a great choice of HOT DOGS from the MUTT to the HUSKY, and every one a treat to eat. 842-4387 is the number to phone for prompt takeout service. During the HOLIDAY SEASON you'll find the HOT DOG SHOW a warm and welcome place to dine. THE HOT DOG SHOW, RIVERSIDE at ROSE, TOLUCA

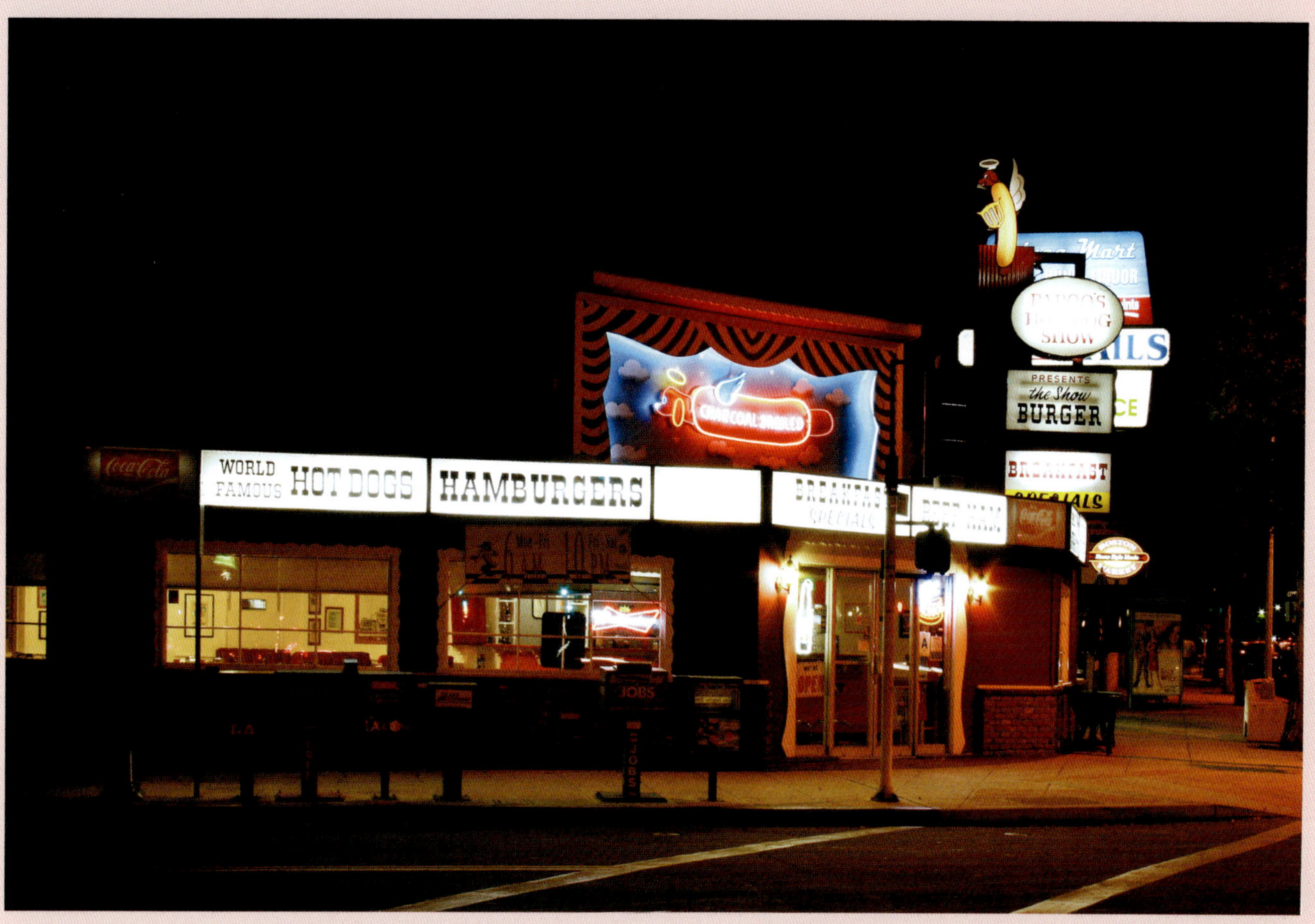
WORLD FAMOUS HOT DOGS
HAMBURGERS
PRESENTS the Show BURGER
JOBS

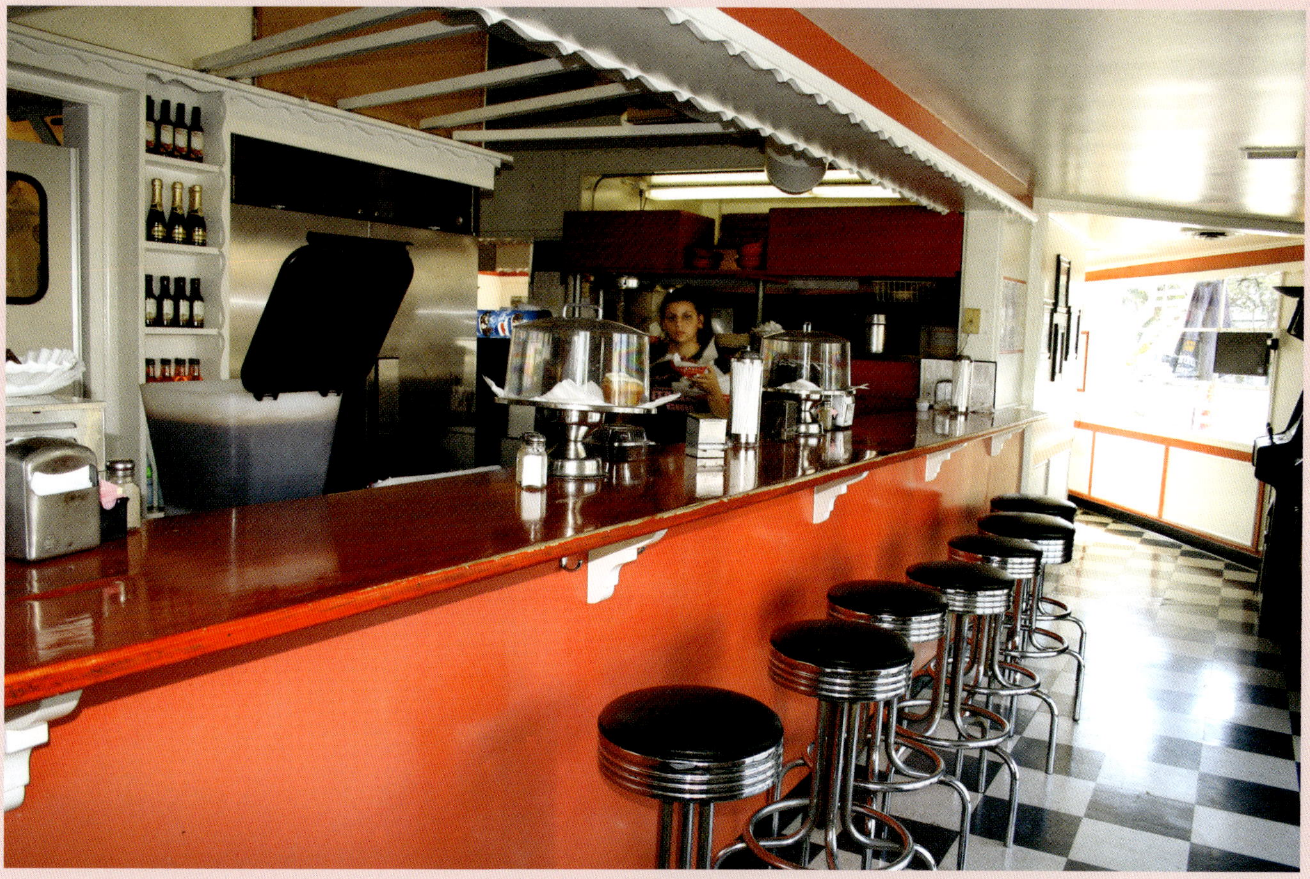

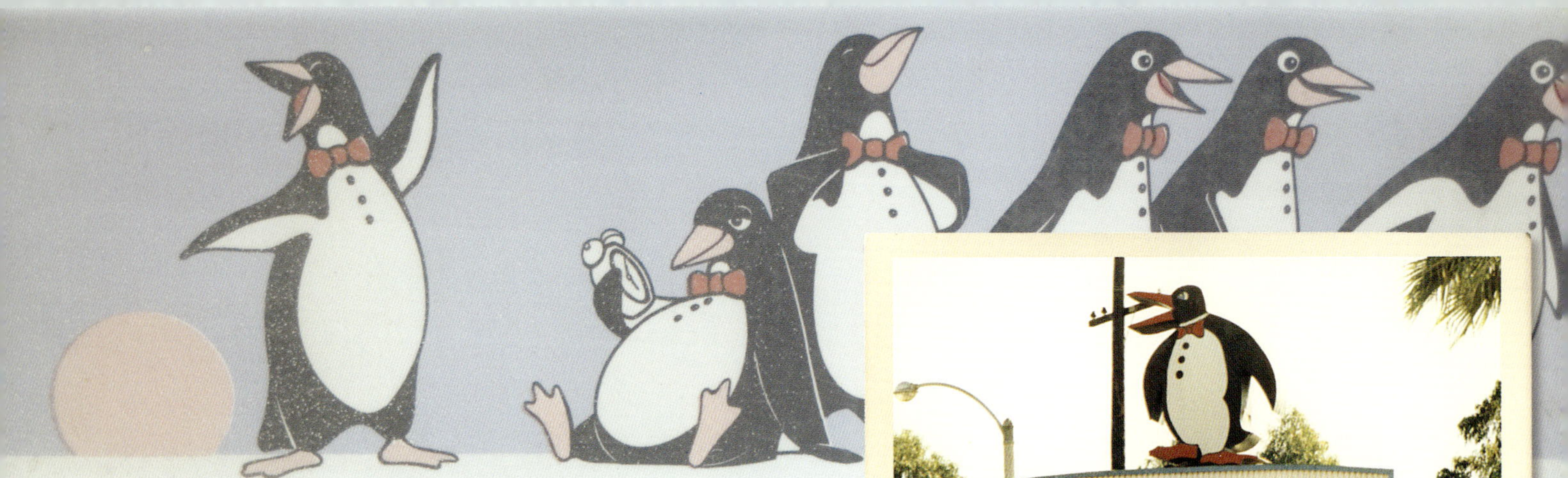

The Penguin Coffee Shop

1670 Lincoln Boulevard, Santa Monica

A 1959 Googie classic from award winning architects Armet + Davis, this ultra-modern structure incorporated an interior designed by Helen Fong, complete with rock walls, indoor planters, pleated banquettes, capiz shell globe chandeliers, brass heat lamps in the shape of trumpets, terrazzo floors, and acres of glass. A+D commissioned Hans Werner and Betsy Hancock to create original resin art that continued the restaurant's motif of frolicking penguins.

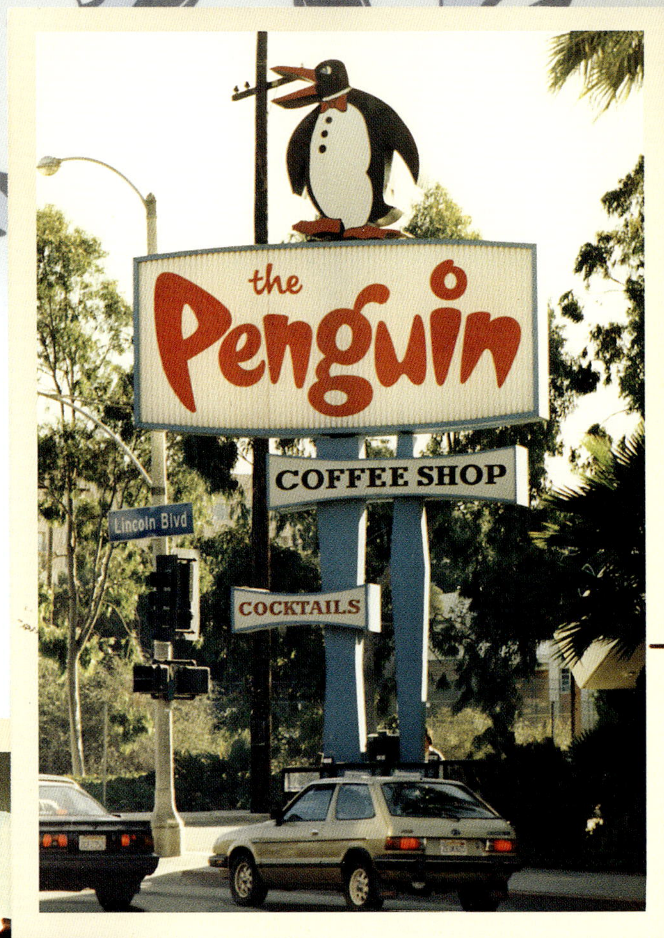

Now a historic sign advertising a dental office. The community will always have fond memories of this little coffee shop.

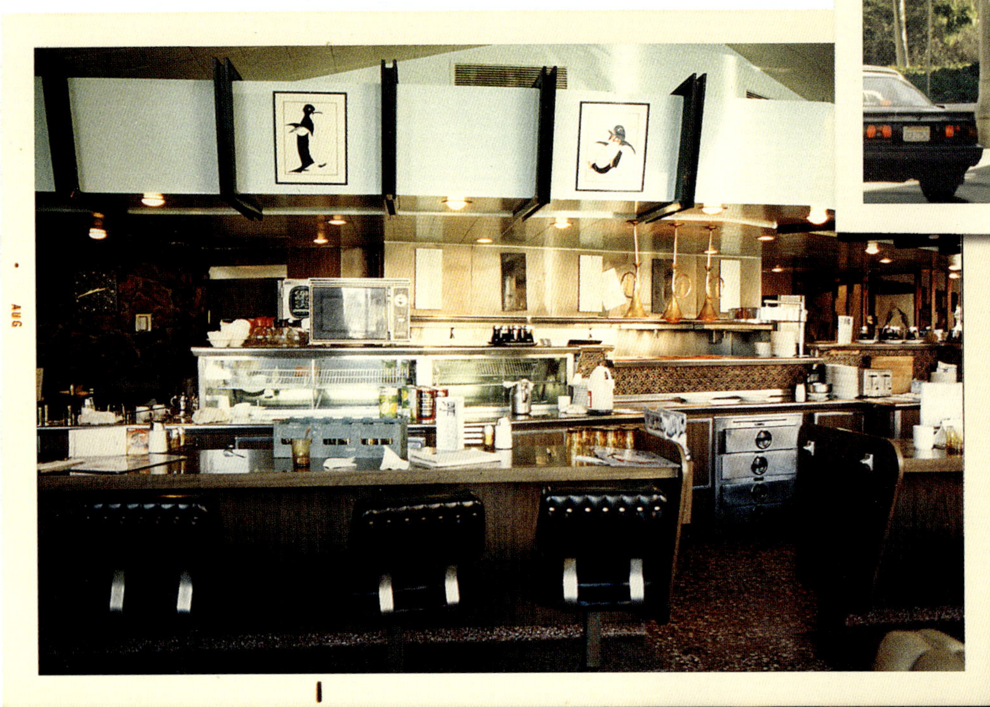

Note the trumpet-shaped heat lamps (right of center) and penguin artwork on the overhead soffit.

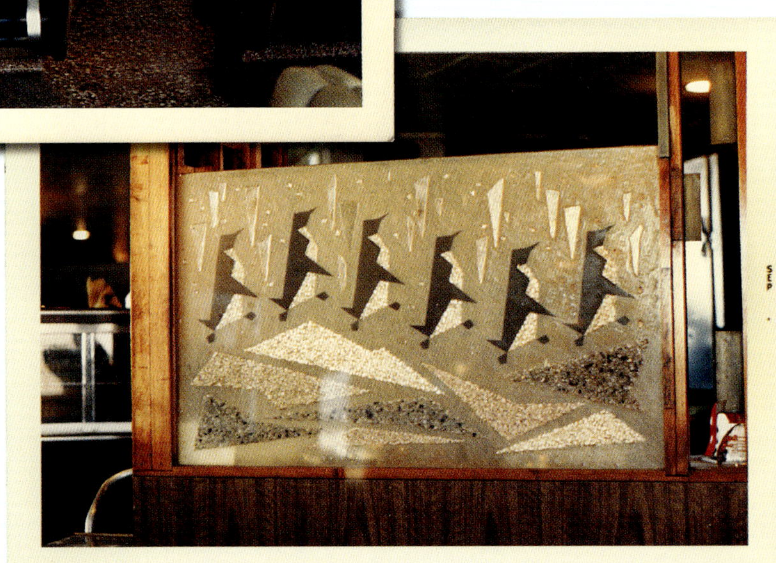

One of the most appealing examples of original resin art, this panel was custom made for The Penguin.

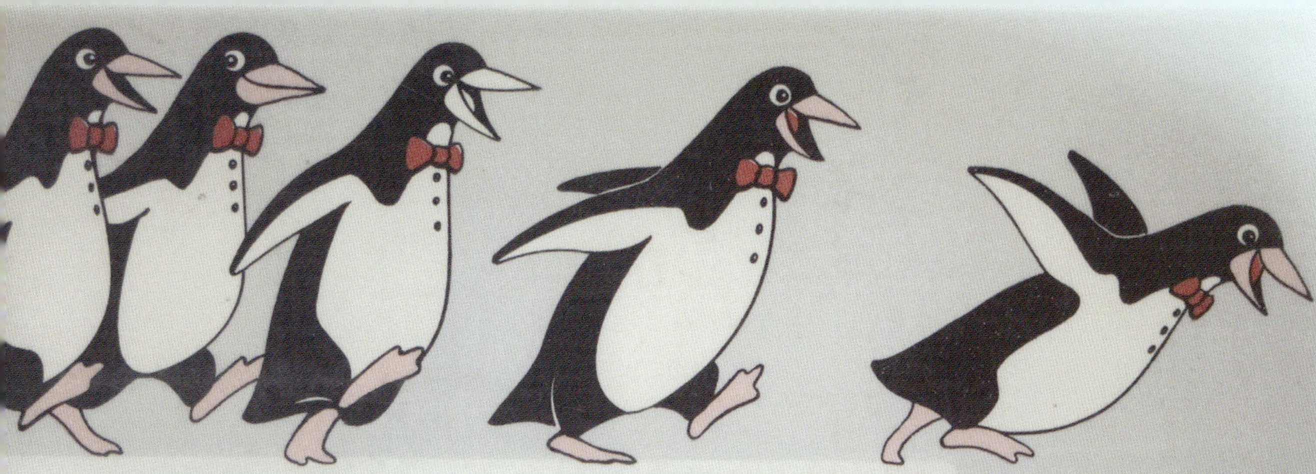

It was a sad, sad day when we took a drive down for their famous banana walnut pancakes only to find the coffee shop closed. These are the last photos taken through the windows in the winter of 1988. Soon after, it was renovated into Dr. Beauchamp's dental center, which it remains to this day. All dental work is monitored around the clock by the tuxedoed penguin sitting atop his meritorious signpost.

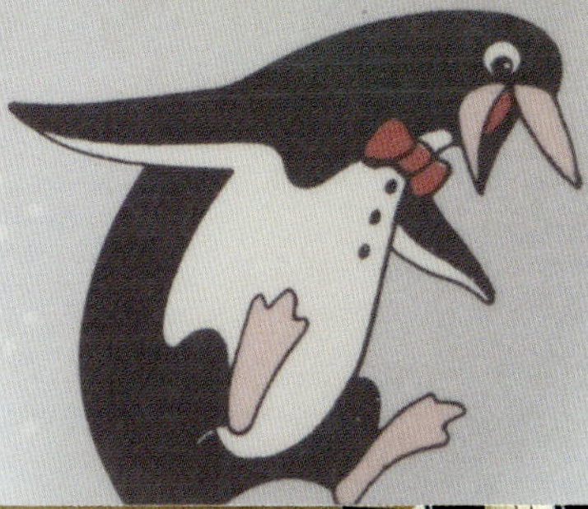

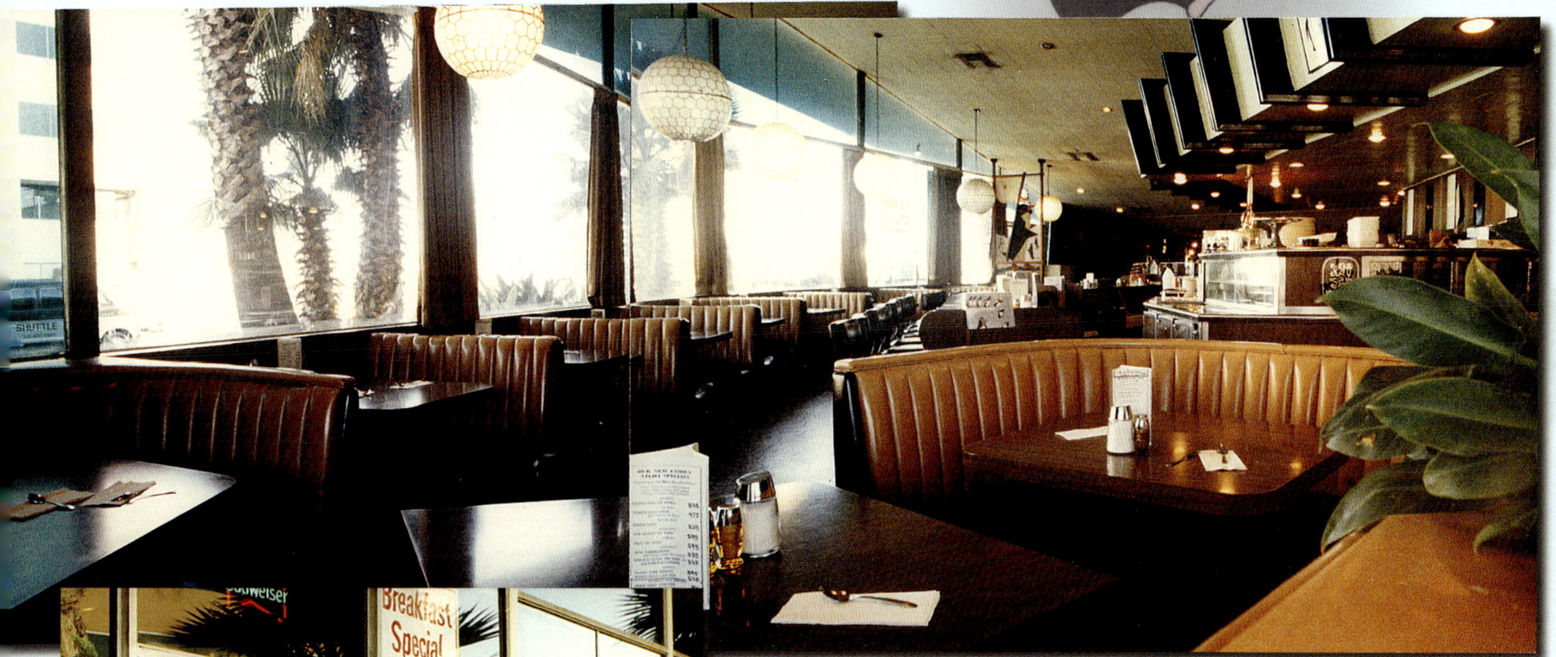

Looking southeast through their window just after they closed for good.

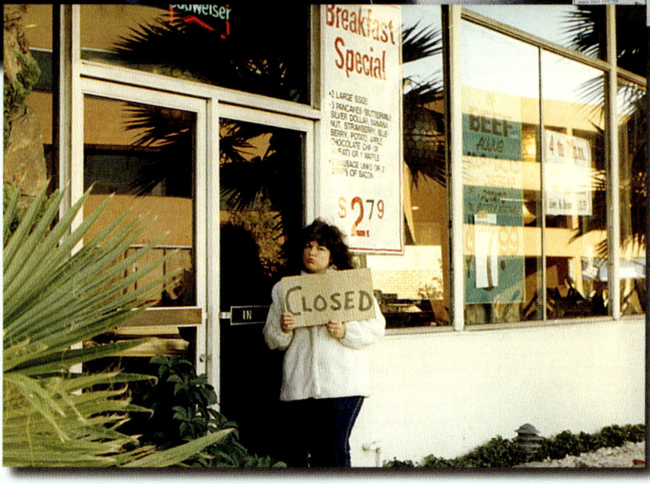

Adriene is saddened by their sudden closure in December 1988.

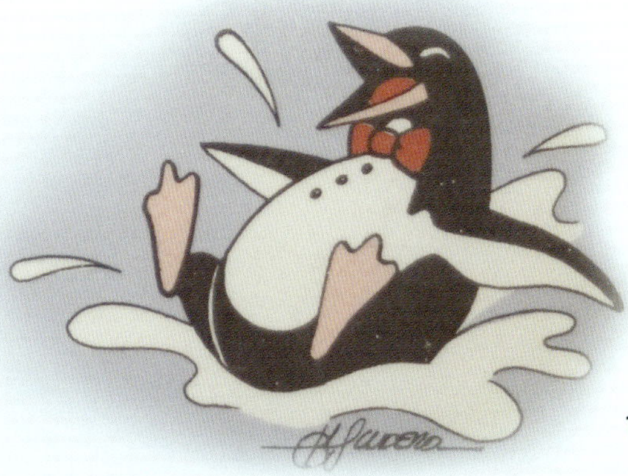

Pecos Bills

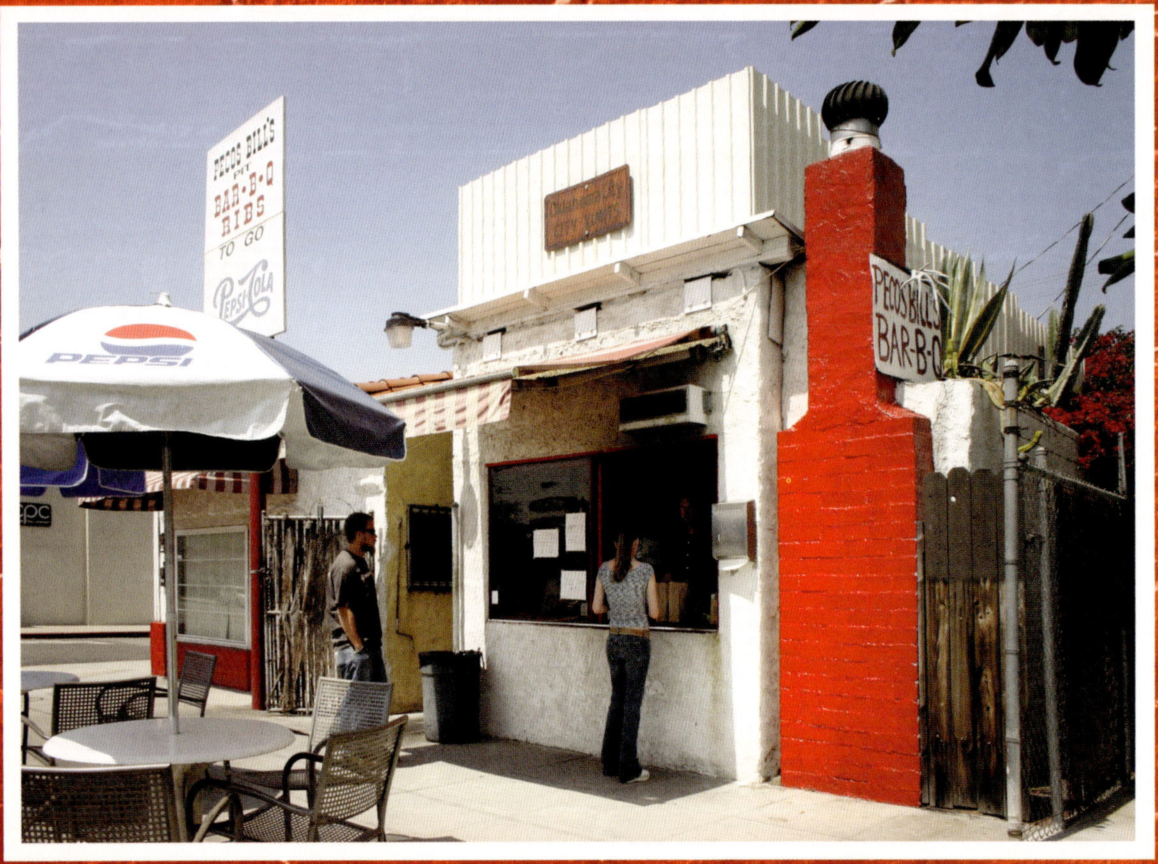

Pecos Bill's Pit Bar-B-Q

1551 Victory Boulevard, Glendale

This tiny hole-in-the-wall is a local legend. Owner Owen Stenzel told us it all began with his great grandfather who owned a saloon in Tennessee...."he would barbecue every Sunday for his 13 children. It got so popular they shut the saloon down and turned it into a restaurant." Through two generations and by way of Texas and Oklahoma, Owen's father, Bill, arrived in California in the '40s and bought the house next door. When Owen was just 16, he built the brick building that has housed Pecos Bill's ever since. Back then he operated part-time, only opening up when he was in the mood.

Most Angelenos don't even know about this BBQ joint and that's OK with Stenzel—he doesn't have room for them anyway. Up until just a few years ago, it was a strictly to-go business, then he added three patio tables with umbrellas right on the sidewalk. Some prefer to eat L.A. style, in their cars with the AC and music on. He and his wife Dale offer a basic menu of scrumptious ribs, beef, pork, ham, and turkey soaked in their famous sauce. And oh what a sauce, it's wet, sloppy, and just delicious. Get there early though, especially on the weekend 'cause it's "Open 'til 3pm or 'til the meat runs out!"

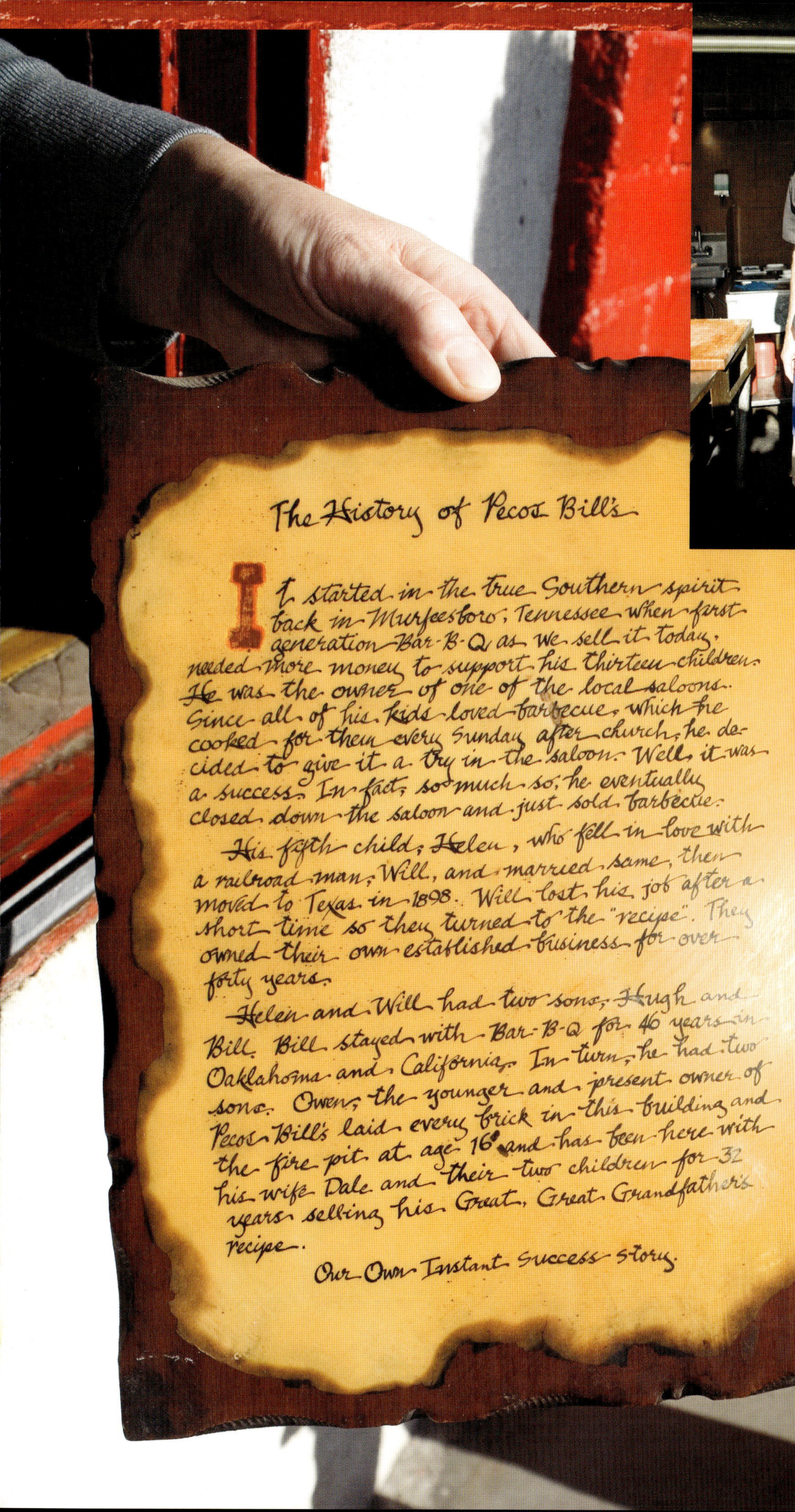

The History of Pecos Bill's

It started in the true Southern spirit back in Murfeesboro, Tennessee when first generation Bar-B-Q as we sell it today, needed more money to support his thirteen children. He was the owner of one of the local saloons. Since all of his kids loved barbecue, which he cooked for them every Sunday after church, he decided to give it a try in the saloon. Well, it was a success. In fact, so much so, he eventually closed down the saloon and just sold barbecue.

His fifth child, Helen, who fell in love with a railroad man, Will, and married same, then moved to Texas in 1898. Will lost his job after a short time so they turned to the "recipe". They owned their own established business for over forty years.

Helen and Will had two sons, Hugh and Bill. Bill stayed with Bar-B-Q for 46 years in Oaklahoma and California. In turn, he had two sons. Owen, the younger and present owner of Pecos Bill's laid every brick in this building and the fire pit at age 16 and has been here with his wife Dale and their two children for 32 years, selling his Great, Great Grandfather's recipe.

Our Own Instant Success Story

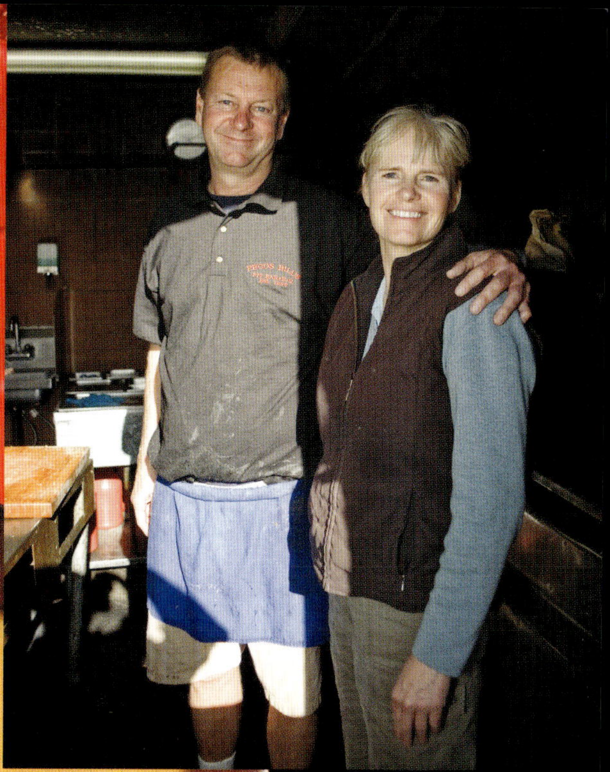

PINK'S

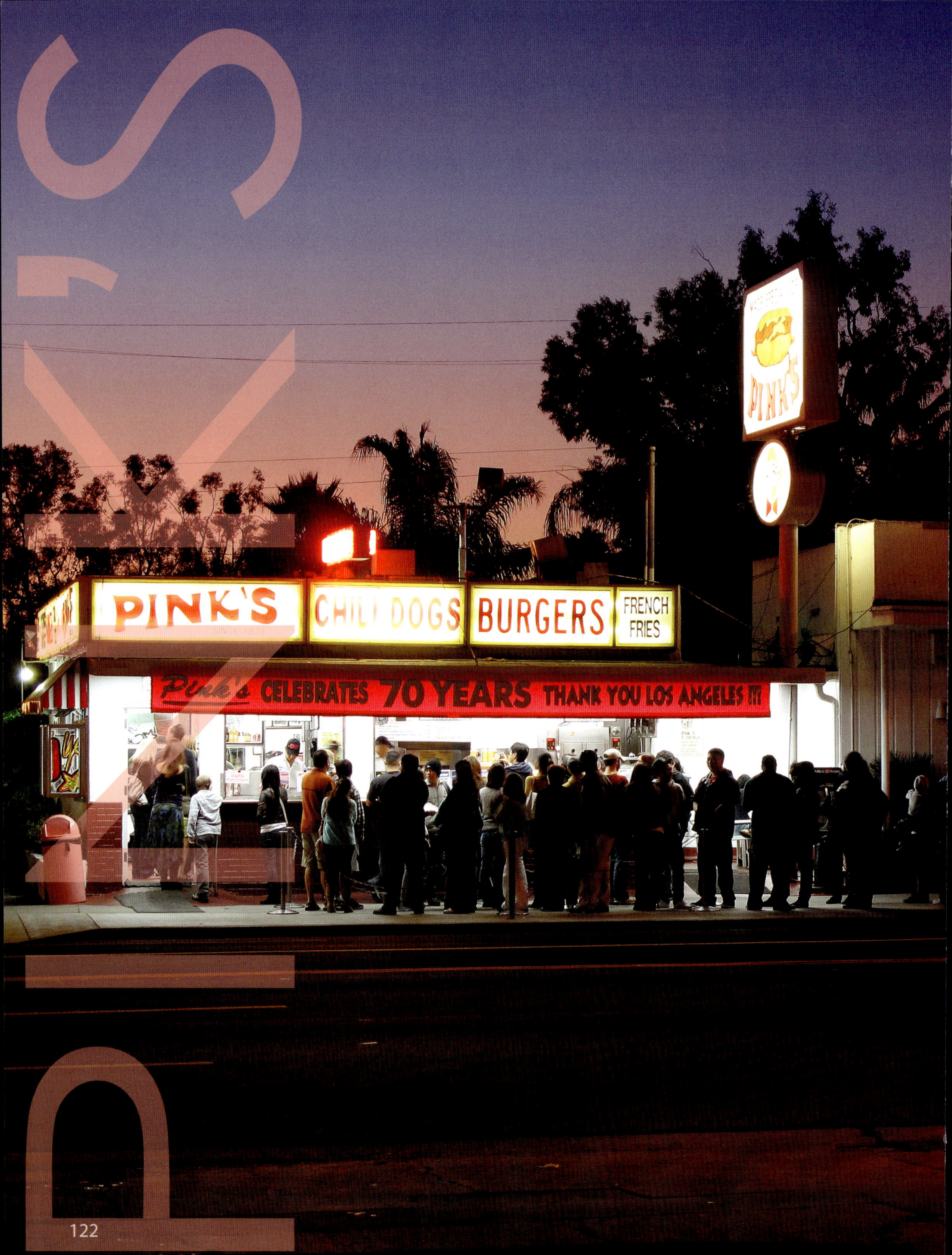

PINK'S
CHILI DOGS
BURGERS
FRENCH FRIES
Pink's CELEBRATES 70 YEARS THANK YOU LOS ANGELES!!!

Pink's Hot Dogs

709 N. La Brea Avenue, Los Angeles

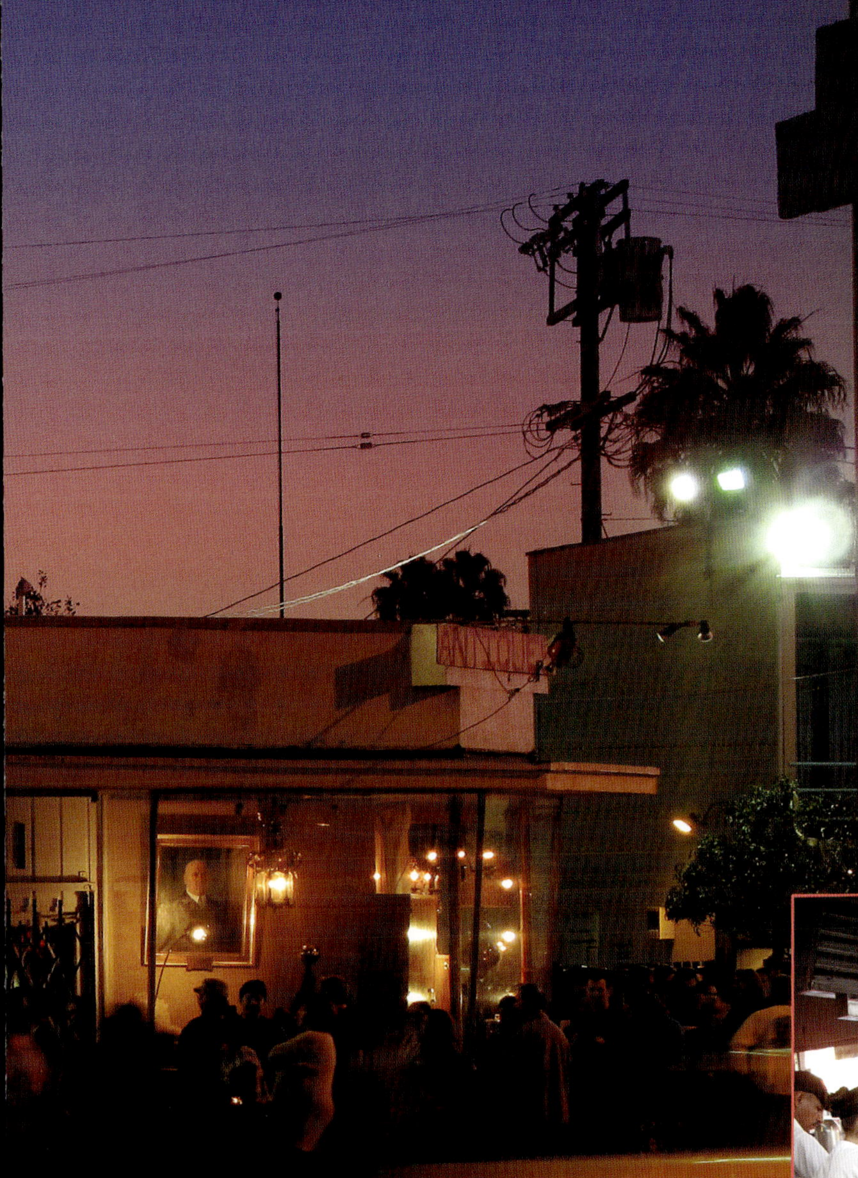

Pink's celebrated their 70th anniversary in 2009! Established in 1939, their website claims that Pink's is the most famous hot dog stand in America...well, certainly in Los Angeles. To think Paul Pink started this Hollywood institution with nothing more than a pushcart. The Great Depression was still on back when he charged 10 cents per hot dog (now it's an outrageous $2.85). Later, in 1946, at the same spot, he put up a small building that is still in use today. The crowd this place attracts is unbelievable, the line usually goes around the building. Very often, limos pull up and celebrity sightings are not uncommon. Tom Hanks, James Earl Jones, Bruce Willis, Aerosmith, Bill Cosby, Snoop Dog, Tyra Banks, and many, many more have eaten here. Since they don't take orders or deliver, these Pinkaholics gotta get their fix in person. The variety of hot dogs they serve is so extensive that it will make your head spin. Here's a few: the Huell (Howser) Dog, Three Dog Night, Martha Stewart Dog, and 'Lord of the Rings' Dog, along with nachos, guacamole, Yoo-Hoo, etc., etc. Pink's opens every day at 9:30 A.M. Sundays through Thursdays they close at 2 A.M., with late night Fridays and Saturdays, when they stay open 'til 3 A.M...so, get in line!

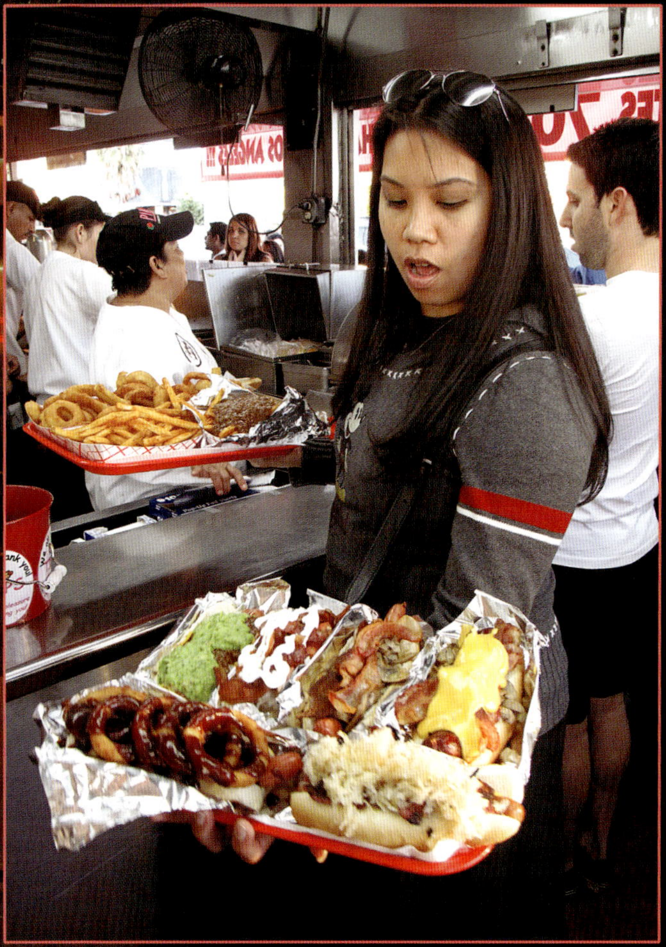

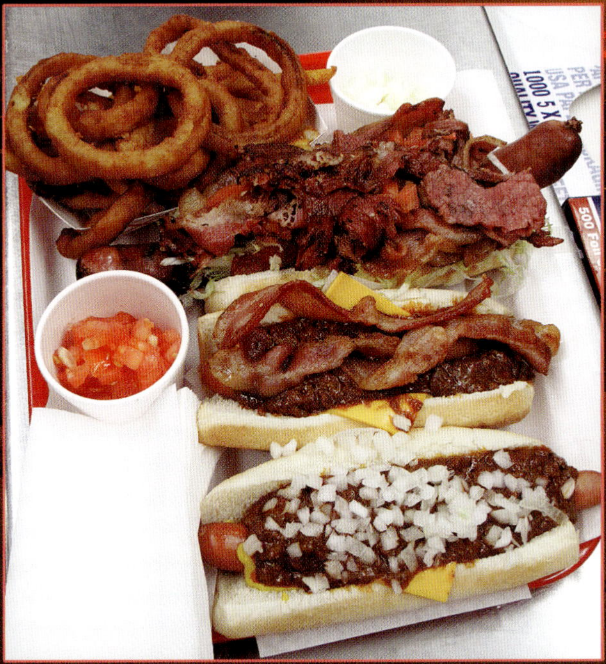

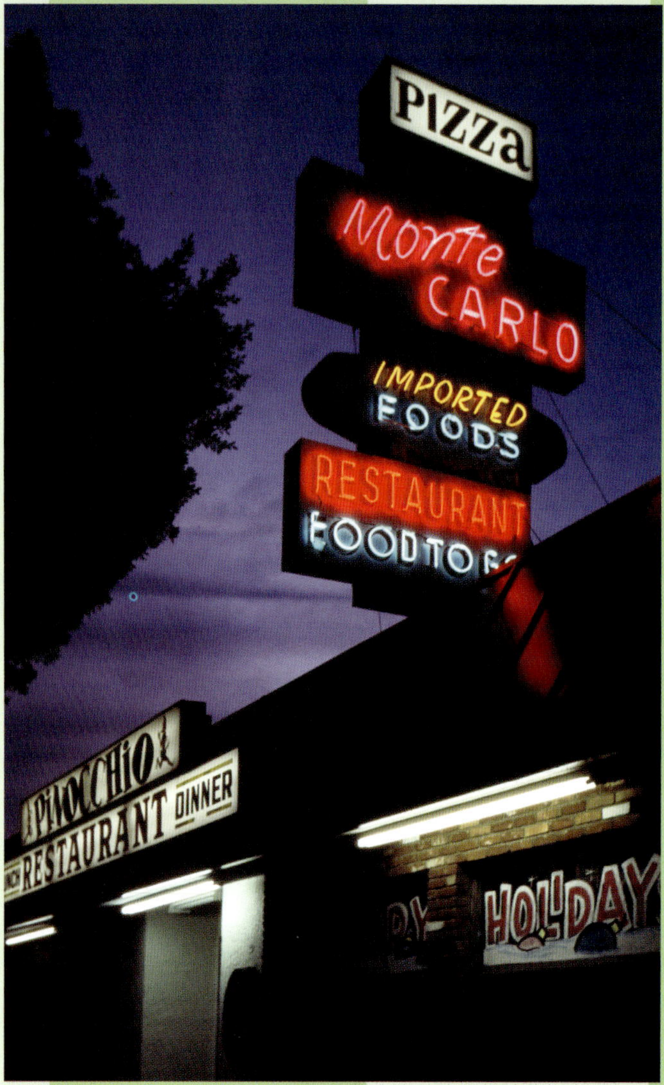

PINOCCHIO'S RESTAURANT AND MONTE CARLO DELICATESSEN

3103 W. Magnolia Boulevard, Burbank

Pinocchio's and the Monte Carlo Italian deli have been serving Burbank since the early '60s. Adriene's been coming here since the '70s, when they expanded and opened their restaurant. We love to sit in the room with all the wine corks embedded in the walls. It's so comfortable that the last time we were there we caught a worker napping in one of the booths. This quirky Italian restaurant is decorated with funky oil paintings of Pinocchio in a low-brow, thrift store style. In the room near the deli, framed pictures of various Lockheed projects are proudly displayed. Many of their customers worked at the Burbank aerospace company during the '60s and '70s. Unbelievably, the food hasn't changed a bit since the '70s and neither, it seems, have the prices. Pinocchio wouldn't lie about a thing like that!

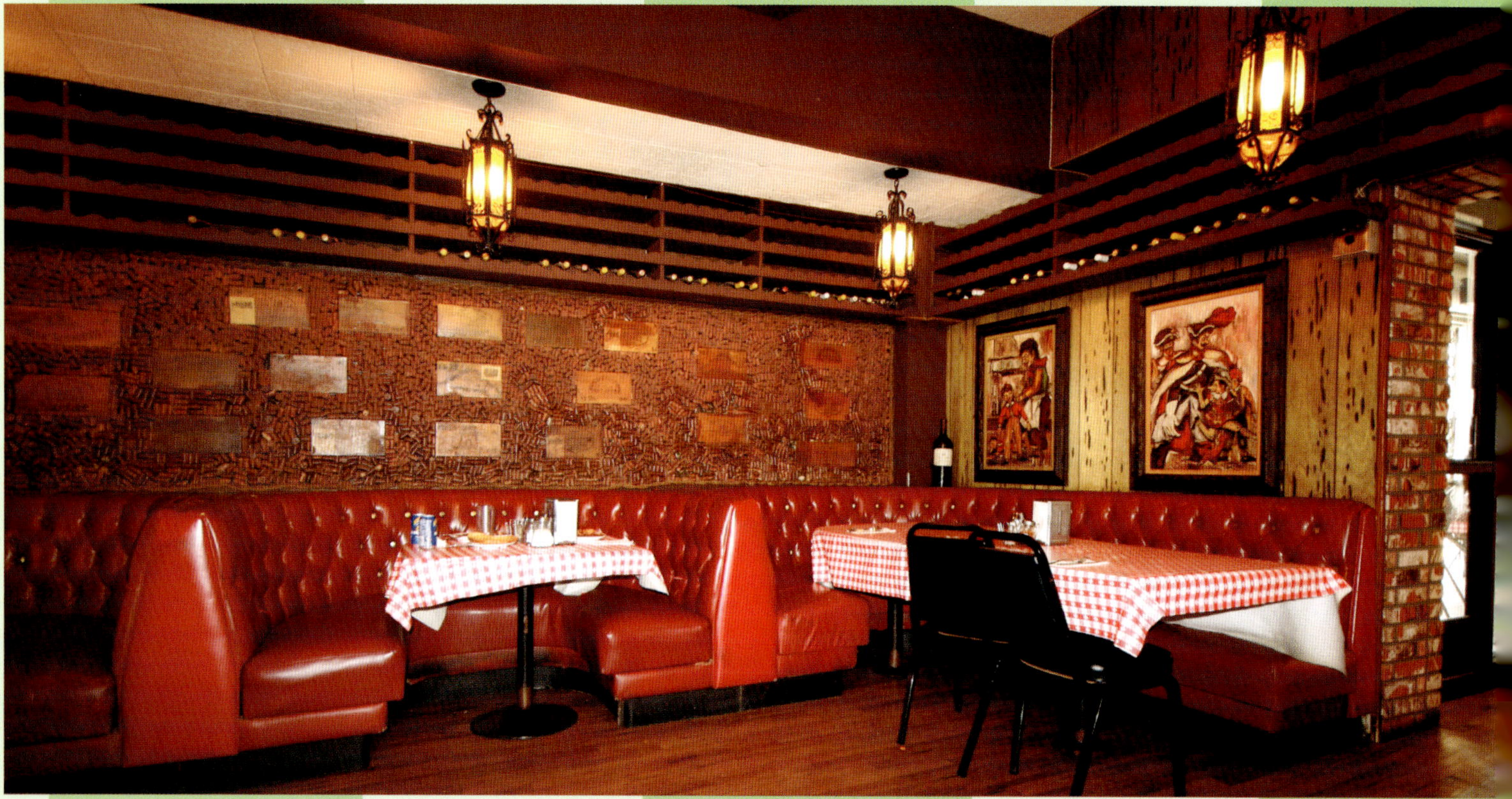

PIZZA SHOW

13344 Hawthorne Boulevard, Hawthorne

A family tradition since 1956, our waitress claimed the Beach Boys used to come here, and it's very possible since Hawthorne Boulevard was one of the main cruising routes in the '60s. The pizzas here are terrific. And they're delighted that their vintage ice machine still makes crushed ice. The Pizza Show received an "A" and we can confirm that this little known pizzeria is neat and clean with friendly service. On the day we had lunch there, their pizza chef Leo was looking for a partner for his patented pizza game for kids. Anyone interested?

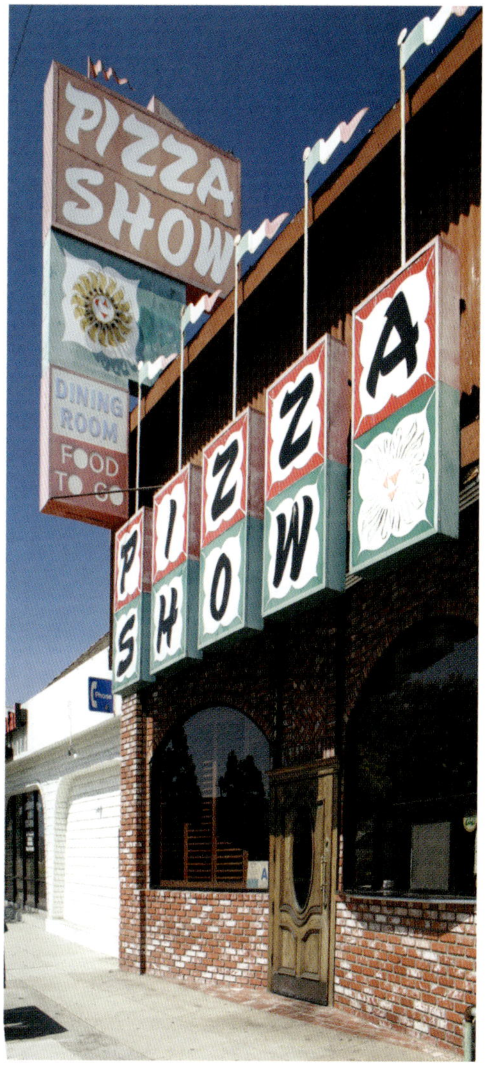

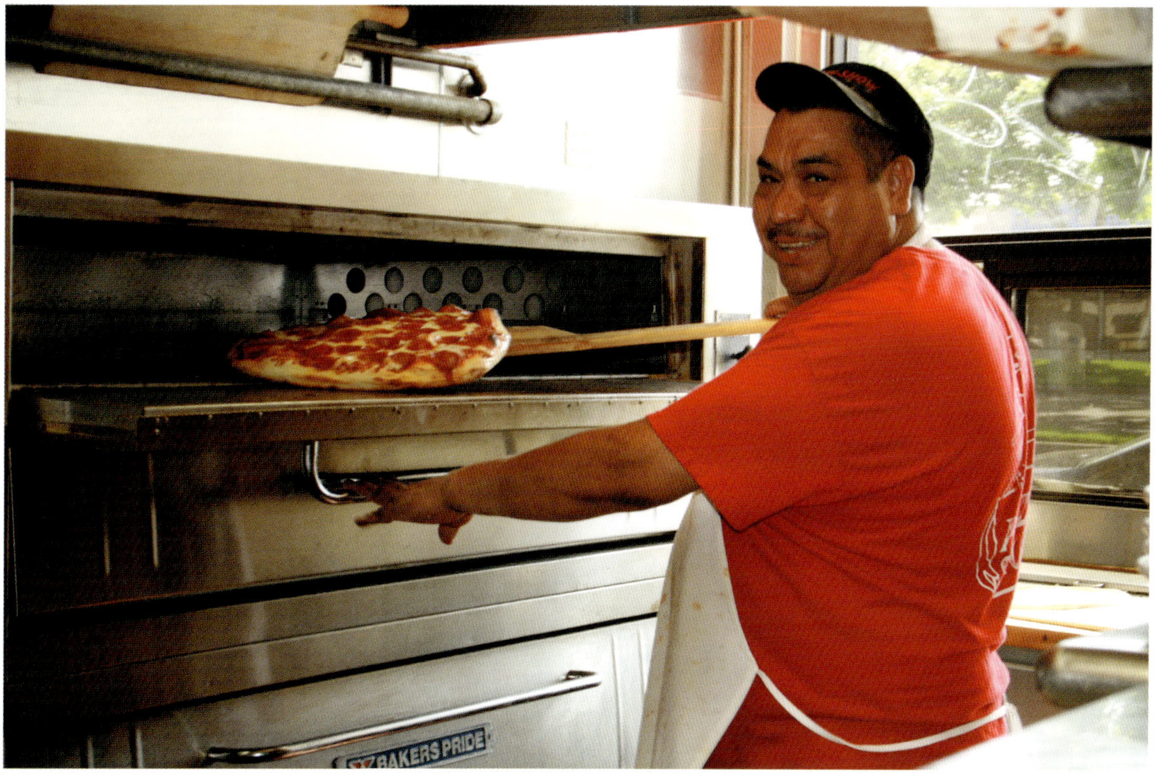

Leo looking at the camera *and* for a partner for his pizza game for kids, 2007.

Premiere Lanes

13210 Telegraph Road, Santa Fe Springs

Sadly, Premiere Lanes closed operations in May 2008, but its jet-age sign remains and is something to behold. Enormous stars orbit around boxes containing "B-O-W-L" like electrons within a magnetic field. Spectacular would not be an exaggeration; it was created by Wayne Heath of Heath Signs, the genius behind so many Los Angeles area signs, including Felix Chevrolet and Winchell's Donuts.

Designed by architect Dike Nagano, Premiere Lanes opened in 1960 with modern Brunswick equipment in salmon pink and gold and modern pinsetters. Built around a "premiere" show theme, after bowling, patrons would chill out with cocktails in the Encore Room. The red and white tiled coffee shop with cantilevered counter stools was virtually intact for almost half a decade. This nostalgic getaway filled a postwar craving that So Cal baby boomers will truly miss.

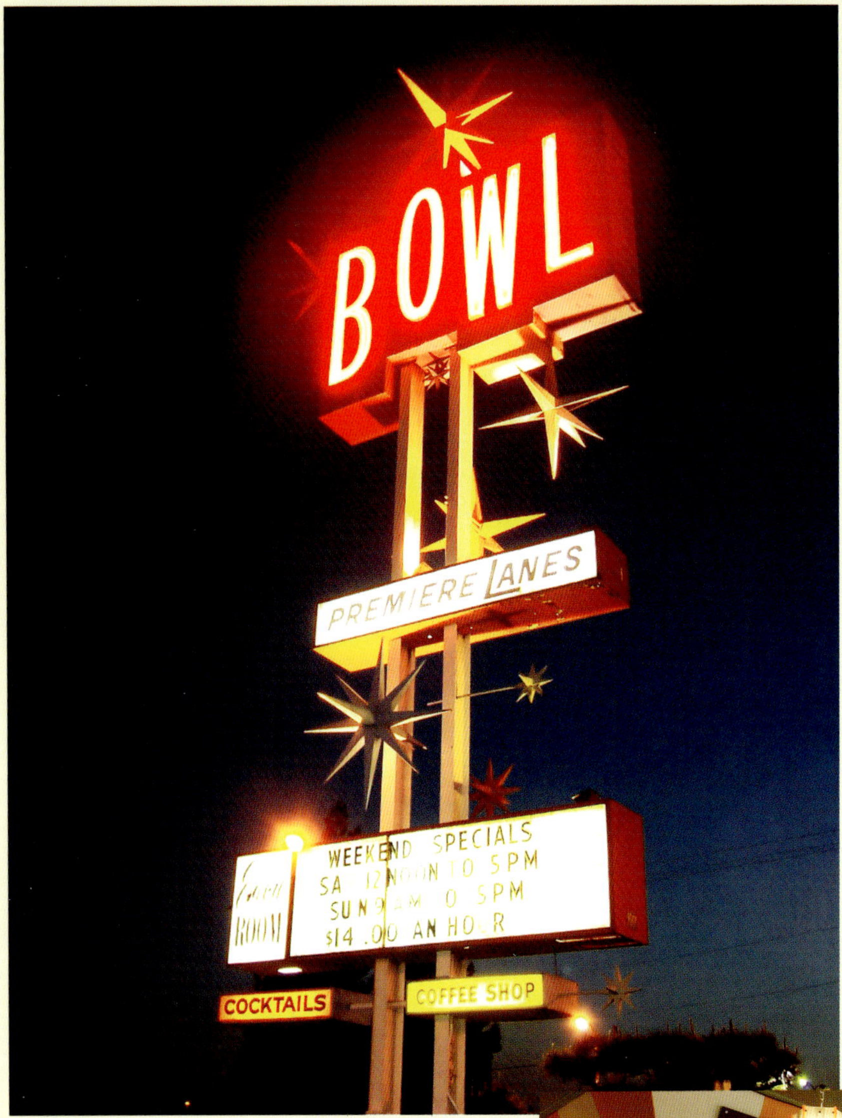

Seeing this, there was no question that the future was here. Premiere Lanes' incredible, atomic age sign is second to none. *Photo by Adriene Biondo*

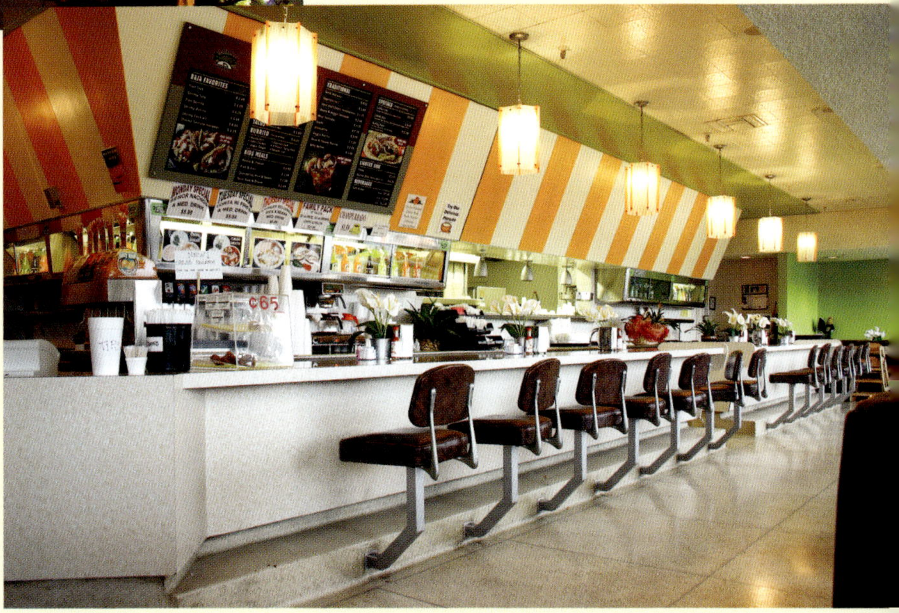

Up until 2009, this coffee shop/bowling alley saw very little change.

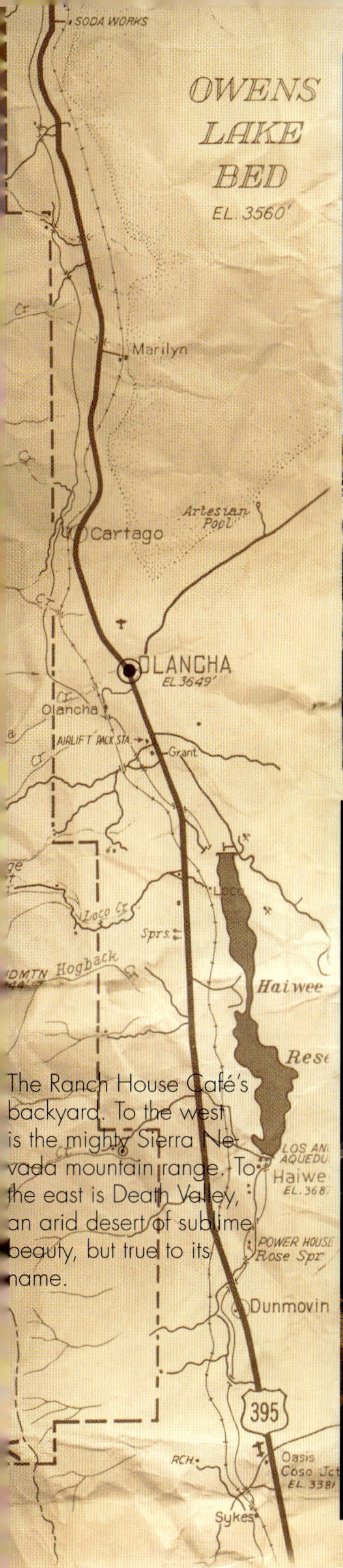

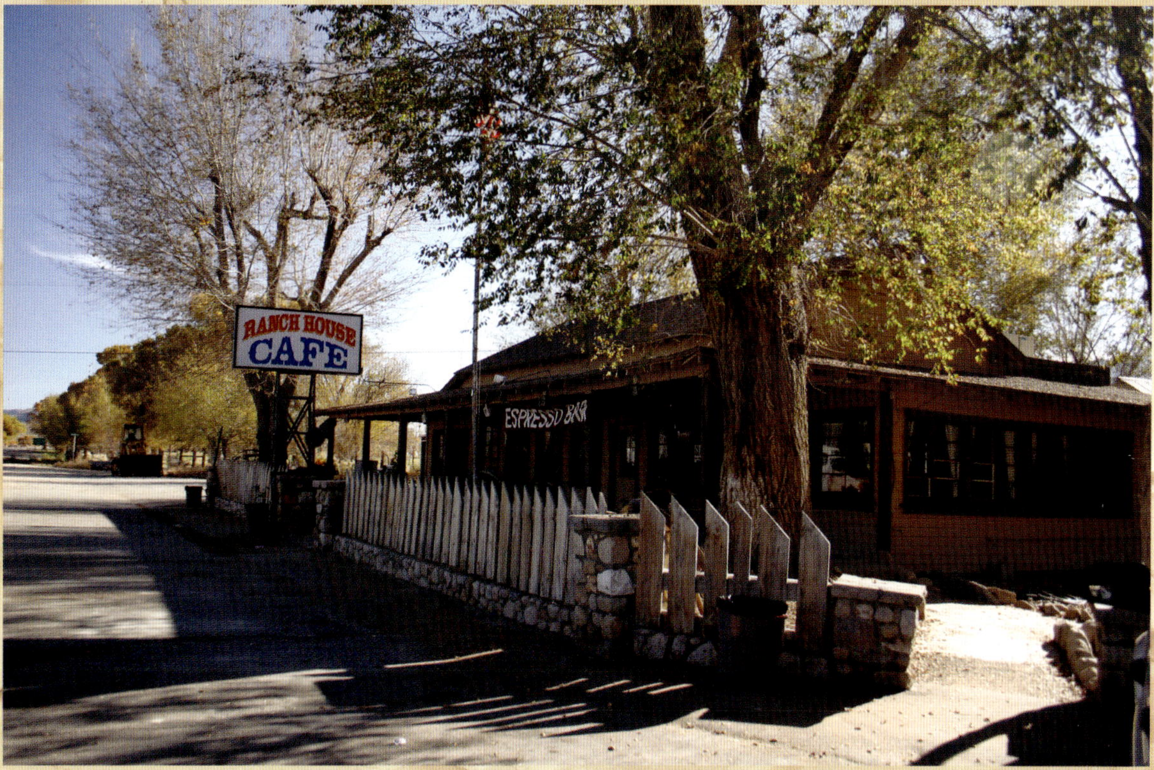

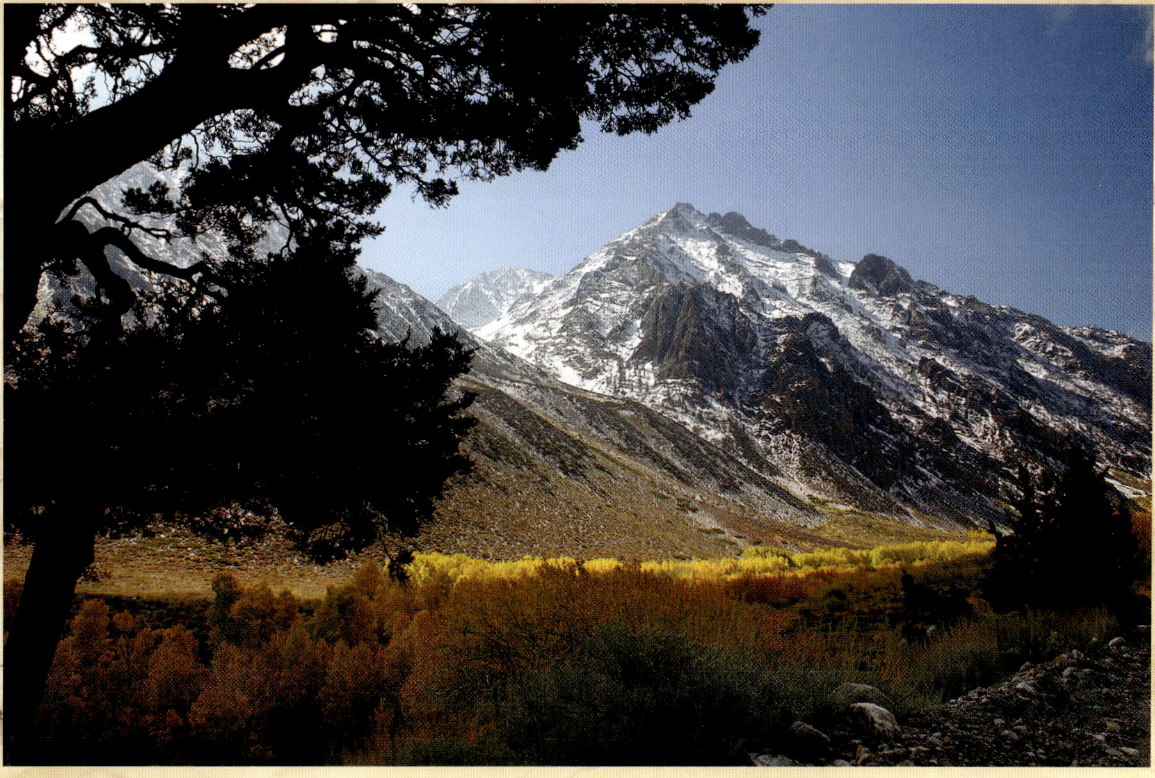

The Ranch House Café's backyard. To the west is the mighty Sierra Nevada mountain range. To the east is Death Valley, an arid desert of sublime beauty, but true to its name.

RANCH HOUSE CAFE

W. Highway 395, Olancha

This cafe is in a tiny town called Olancha, just off Highway 395. Huell Howser produced an entire show on this very scenic highway alone. The 395 travels through four states and doesn't stop 'til it collides with the US/Canadian border in Washington. In Southern California, not only does it parallel the Eastern Sierra (a sight to behold during any season), but it's also the western gateway to Death Valley National Monument. For Angelenos traveling north to the ski resorts of Mammoth, Olancha roughly marks the halfway point. The food at this Western stopover is American traditional, with steak and eggs, burgers, and sandwiches. They are known for their homemade biscuits with sausage gravy. A giant stuffed California brown bear keeps watch over the cash register.

RANDY'S DONUTS

805 W. Manchester Avenue,
Inglewood

No compilation of iconic L.A. eateries would be complete without this 1953 giant donut of a joint. While this is not the only giant donut shop around town, this is without a doubt, the most famous. Randy's seems to constantly pop up in magazines, commercials, music videos, and movies. It's been in so many movies that it deserves its own star on Hollywood Boulevard. Heck, it's taller than the Duke, for crying out loud. This 22 foot high, programmatic structure is visible from the adjacent 405 Freeway. John actually spotted Randy's from an airplane while coming in for a landing at LAX!

To make friends with perfect strangers, simply purchase one of Randy's custom t-shirts or hats along with your late-night bear claw or baker's dozen. Just the sight of this place will make you smile. It's futile to resist! Open 24 hours.

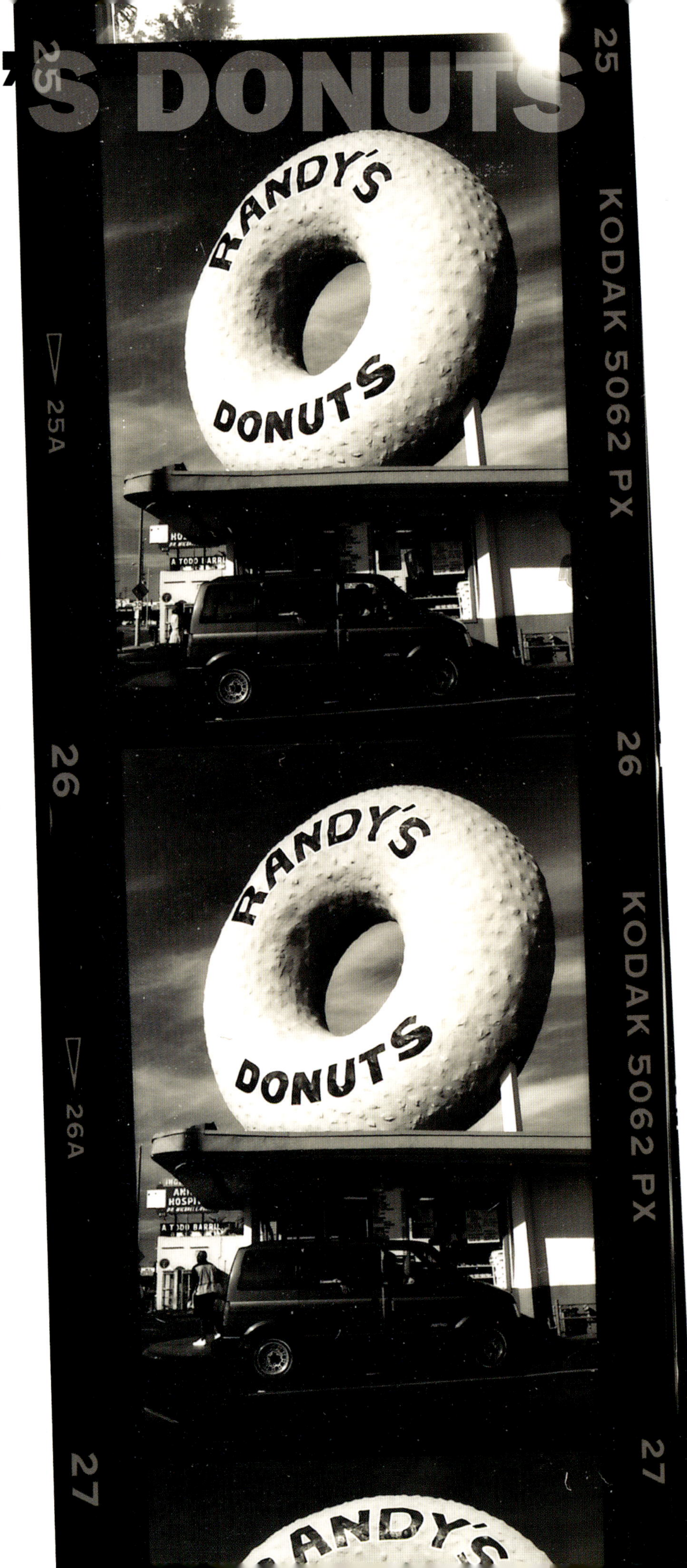

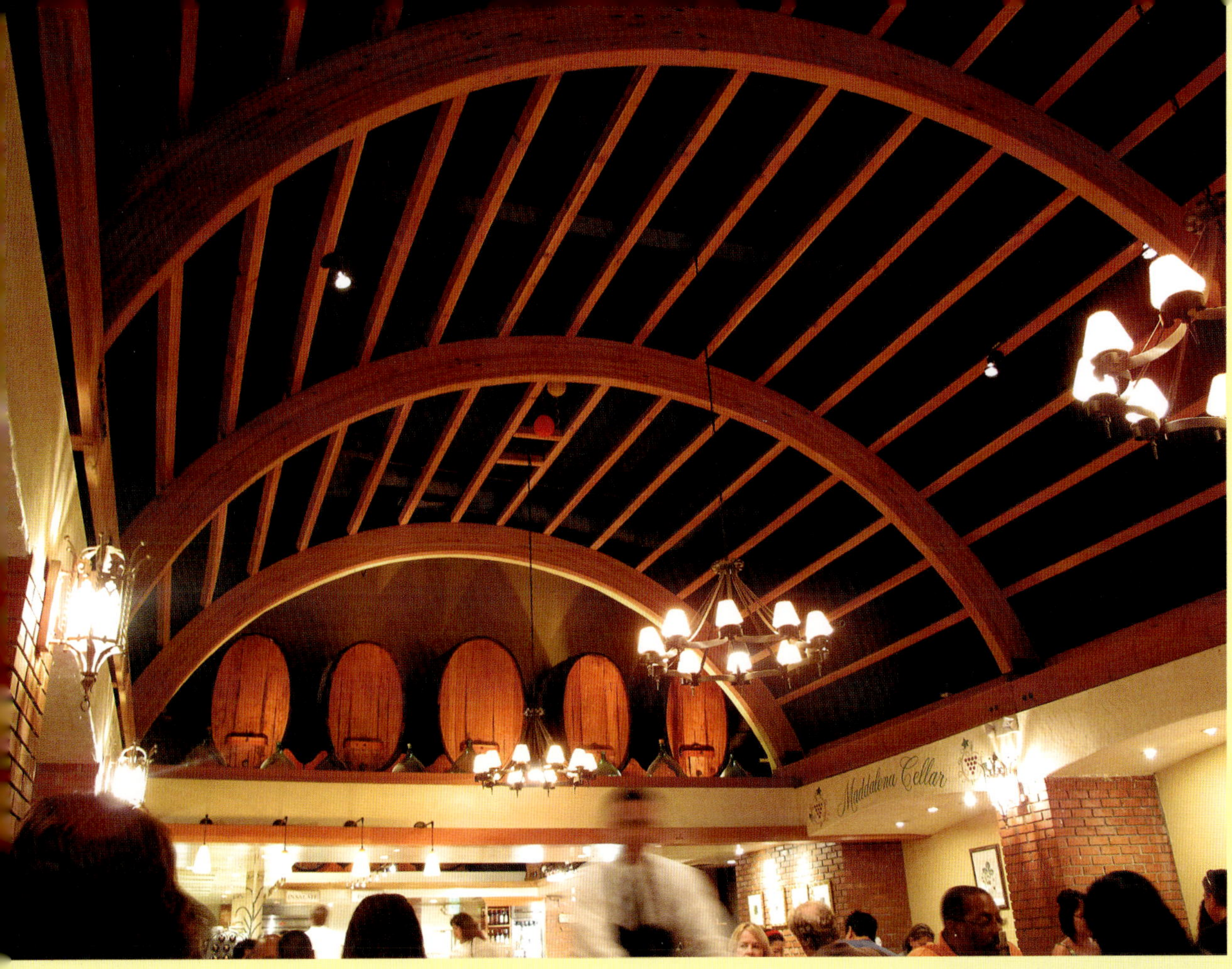

San Antonio Winery & Restaurant

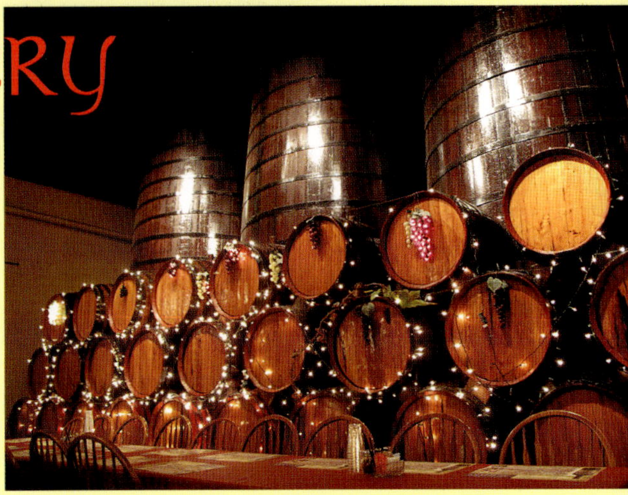

San Antonio Winery & Restaurant
737 Lamar Street, Los Angeles

This is one of those, "I passed that place a million times, but I never stopped in" places. After living in L.A. for almost 30 years and passing it on the 5 Freeway oodles of times, John was finally dragged in and was immediately delighted with the delicious cuisine, great atmosphere, and long history. This family-owned operation began in 1917 when Stefano Riboli's uncle, Santo Cambianica, founded the winery. At that time, over a hundred wineries dotted this region but in the 90+ years since, San Antonio Winery became the only winery left standing in the City of Los Angeles. Now, through four generations of Ribolis, the family continues the art of fine winemaking. They have their own vineyards throughout California, including Napa Valley.

In September 1966, the San Antonio Winery became Historic Cultural Monument No. 42. The winery compound includes the Maddalena Restaurant (where you can dine amongst the giant redwood casks), wine tasting, winery tours, banquet rooms, and their own international wine shop. It's located just east of Chinatown and west of the 5 Freeway. Remember to go early, they close at 7 P.M. every night.

key's Pizza Parlor

Shakey's Pizza Parlor
10340 Reseda Boulevard, Northridge
Multiple locations

Adriene was only 16 when she accepted her first job playing honky tonk piano at Shakey's. In those days, Shakey's was in full swing and she had to play loud in order to compete with the loudspeaker's interruptions as they'd call out, "Number 7! Large pepperoni pizza with MoJo's!" Back then, Shakey's proudly featured live bluegrass and Flatt & Scruggs style banjo and guitar.

In 1954, Sherwood "Shakey" Johnson, realizing how much he enjoyed people, food, beer, and Dixieland music, opened the first Shakey's Pizza Parlor and Ye Olde Public House in Sacramento, California. The story on Sherwood Johnson is that he picked up the nickname "Shakey" after contracting malaria during World War II. He was popular and known to stop in and personally entertain restaurant guests by playing ragtime piano for them.

This Shakey's in Northridge still has the original plastic chef rubbing his belly as part of their sign. People love Shakey's all-you-can-eat "Bunch of Lunch" buffet, especially their fried chicken, gourmet pizzas, and, of course, MoJo's Potatoes!

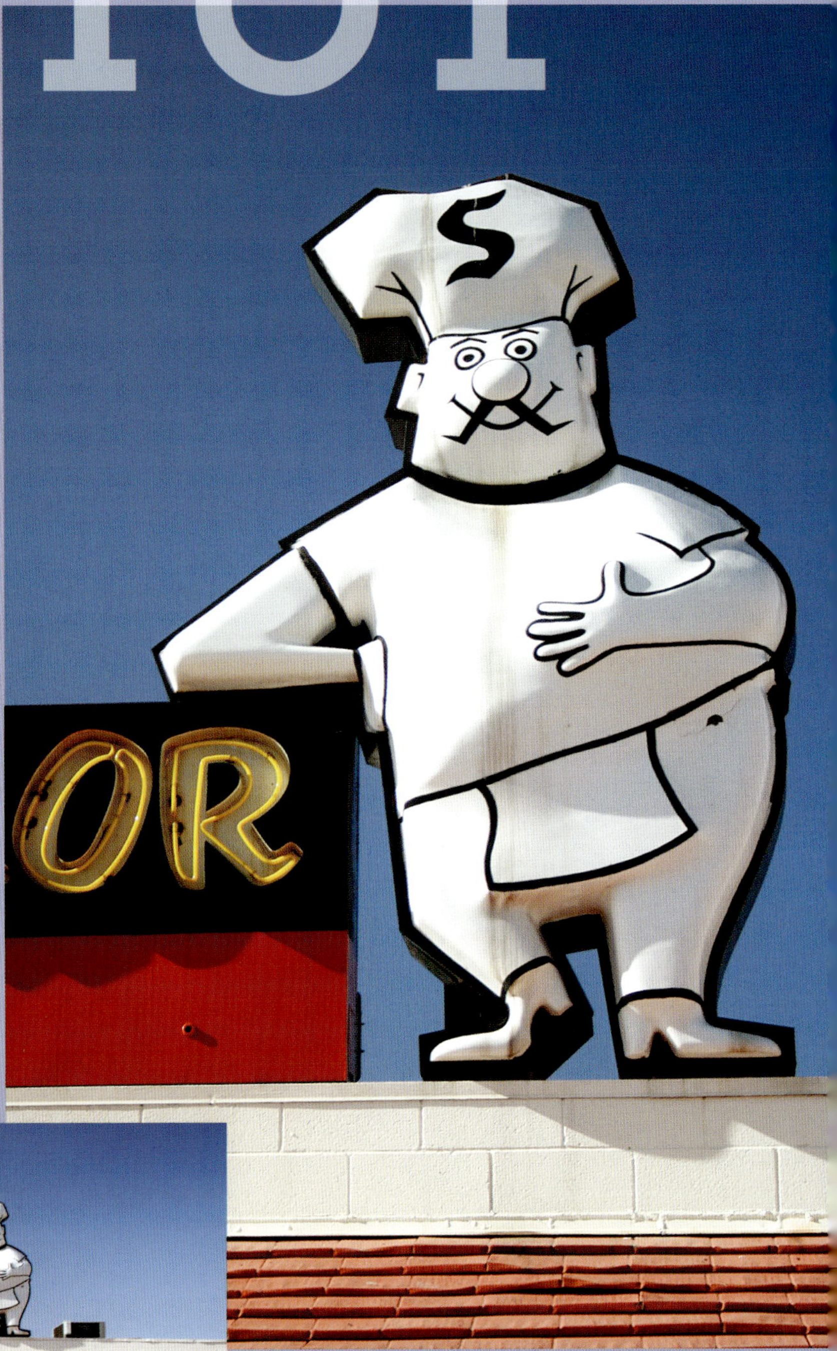

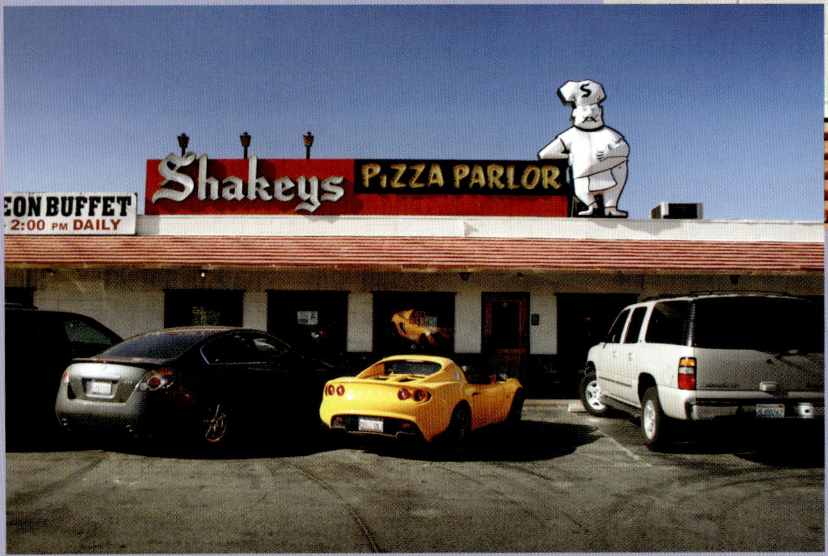

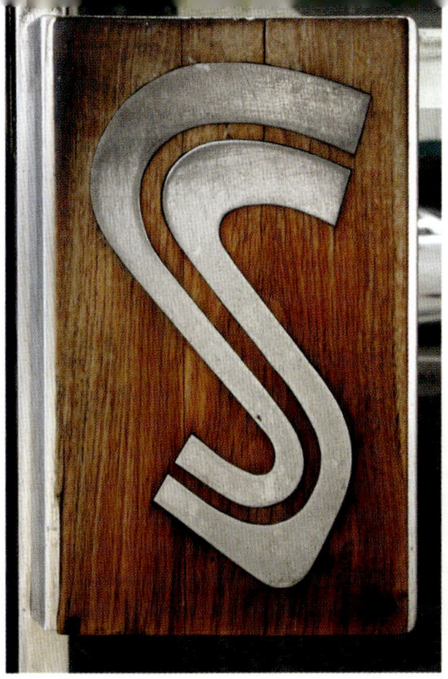

The original custom inlay handles still bear the letter "S" for Sheri's.

heri's

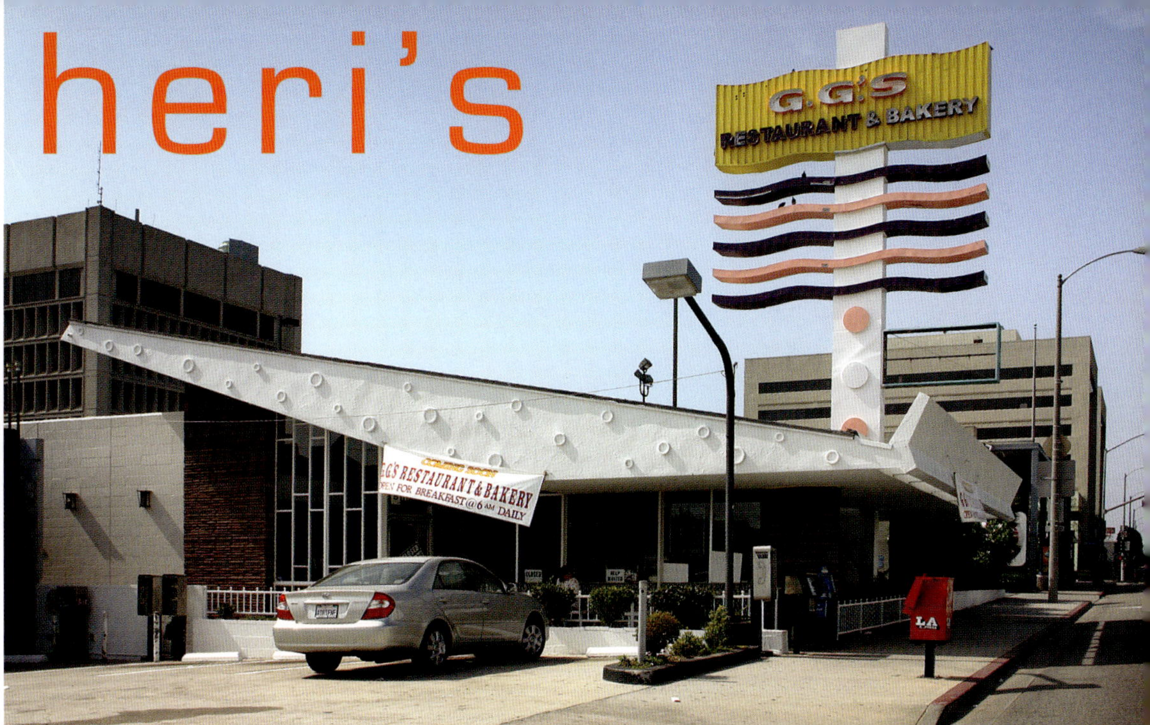

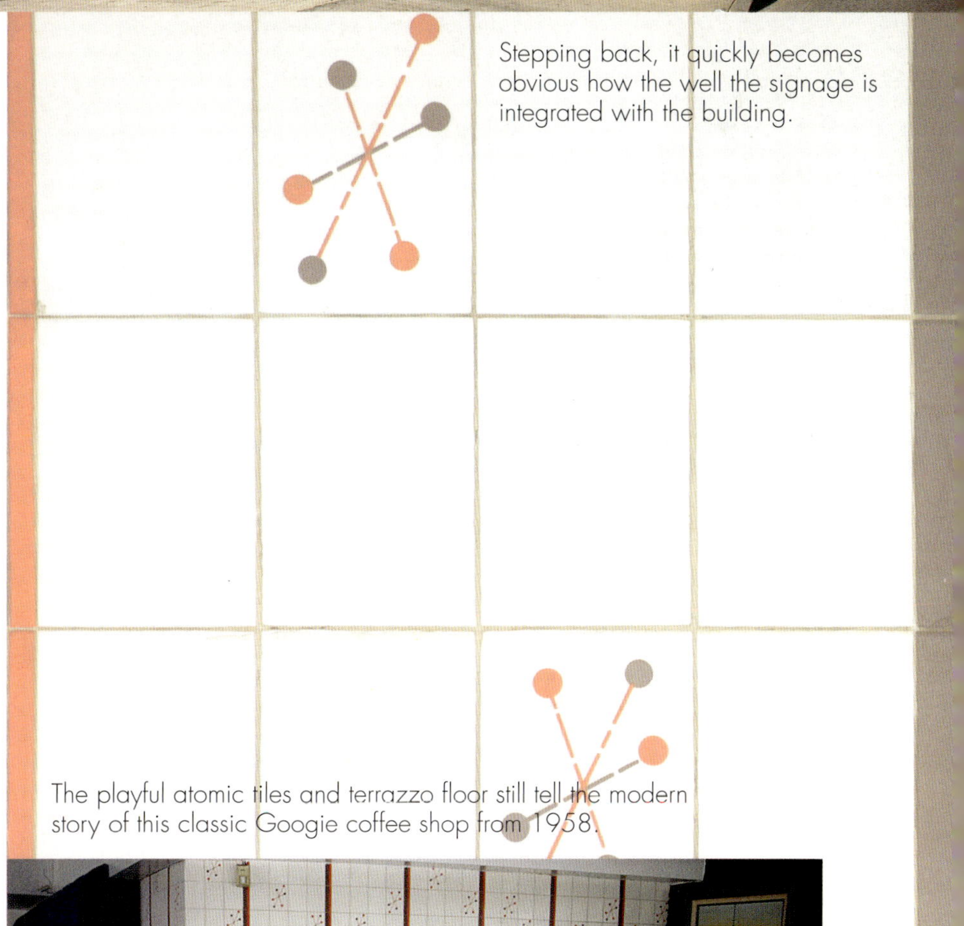

Stepping back, it quickly becomes obvious how the well the signage is integrated with the building.

Sheri's (aka Farmer's and GG's)

115 S. La Brea Avenue, Inglewood

From the versatile architect Martin Stern, Jr., this Googie coffee shop dates back to 1958 and represents only one of many commercial and residential design projects during his career. Along with coffee shops, Stern designed bowling alleys, shopping centers, apartments, and during the '60s, he pioneered casino architecture. Of the coffee shops, he also designed the famous Ships in Westwood, the first Ships in Culver City, Freyer's (later Lyon's) in Venice, and two Jack's in Whittier.

Sheri's was built the same year as Ships Westwood (demolished in 1984). At a glance, the two coffee shops exhibit many similarities: a triangular-boomerang roof with circular patterns, the same black and white terrazzo floor, cantilevered counter stools, stainless steel kitchen fixtures, Formica countertops, custom tile, flagcrete, and custom door handles with an aluminum letter "S" inlaid in wood . But taking a closer look, there are many elements unique to Sheri's: the tile design at Sheri's is atomic and there is a bank of windows with a vertical pattern reminiscent of a chapel. Equipment designer Stan Abrams credits founder Matt Shipman for his many years of experience in the restaurant business and his *time and motion studies*. Structurally, this coffee shop is fairly unaltered and most of its Googie elements are still intact.

The playful atomic tiles and terrazzo floor still tell the modern story of this classic Googie coffee shop from 1958.

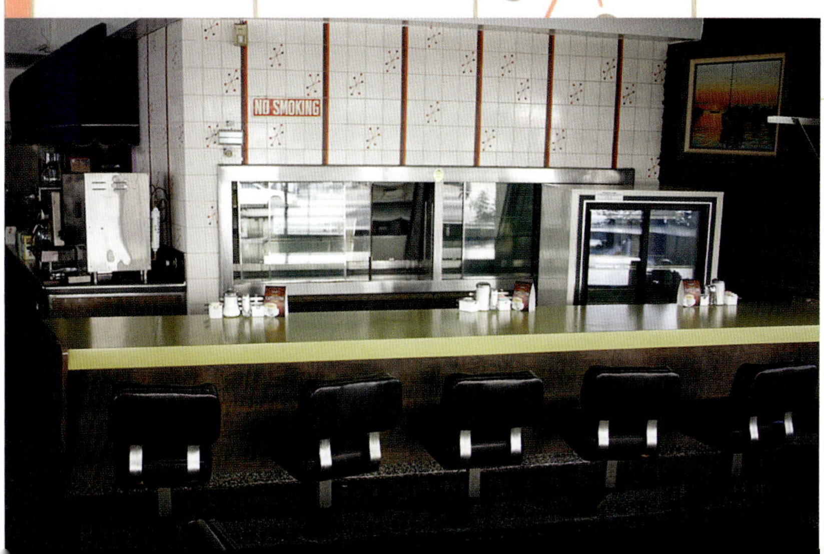

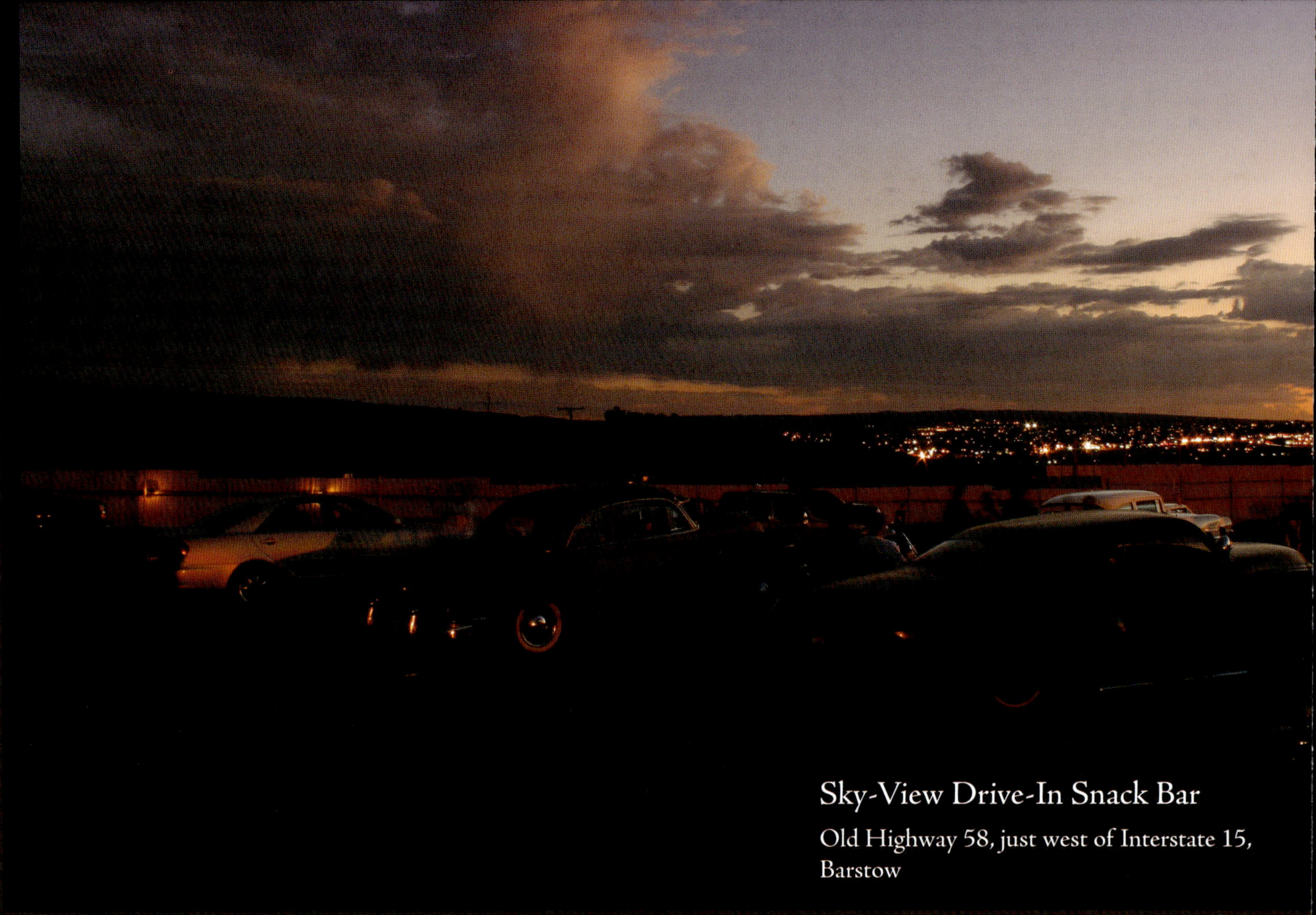

Sky-View Drive-In Snack Bar

Old Highway 58, just west of Interstate 15, Barstow

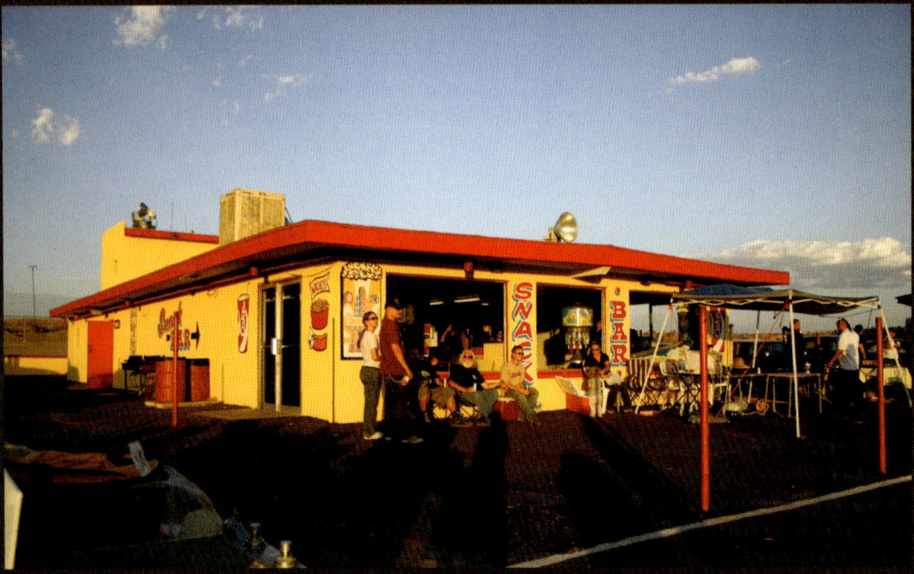

This two-screen drive-in is out on the northern outskirts of Barstow, a Route 66 town in the kidneys of the Mojave Desert. We drove out to this drive-in on a special day when there was a car show sponsored by Dr. Frankenstein Body Shop along with a screening of *American Graffiti*. A live rockabilly band played directly below the giant screen throughout the day. We were intrigued by a game people were playing where they tossed a heavy mag wheel like a shot put. At sunset, the screen flickered on and Lucas' film was preceded by a series of nostalgic snack bar commercials from the '60s. We cheered for our all-time favorite "Let's all go to the lobby!" For us, it wasn't just an intermission ad, it was the main attraction.

The very first drive-in theatre appeared in 1933 with the drive-in heyday starting to wane in the '70s. By the '80s, numbers had dropped drastically. Now, there's a mere handful per state. The Sky-View Drive-In opened in 1966. Even in this modern age of video games, cell phones, and YouTube, we noticed that kids are still excited when they experience going to a drive-in.

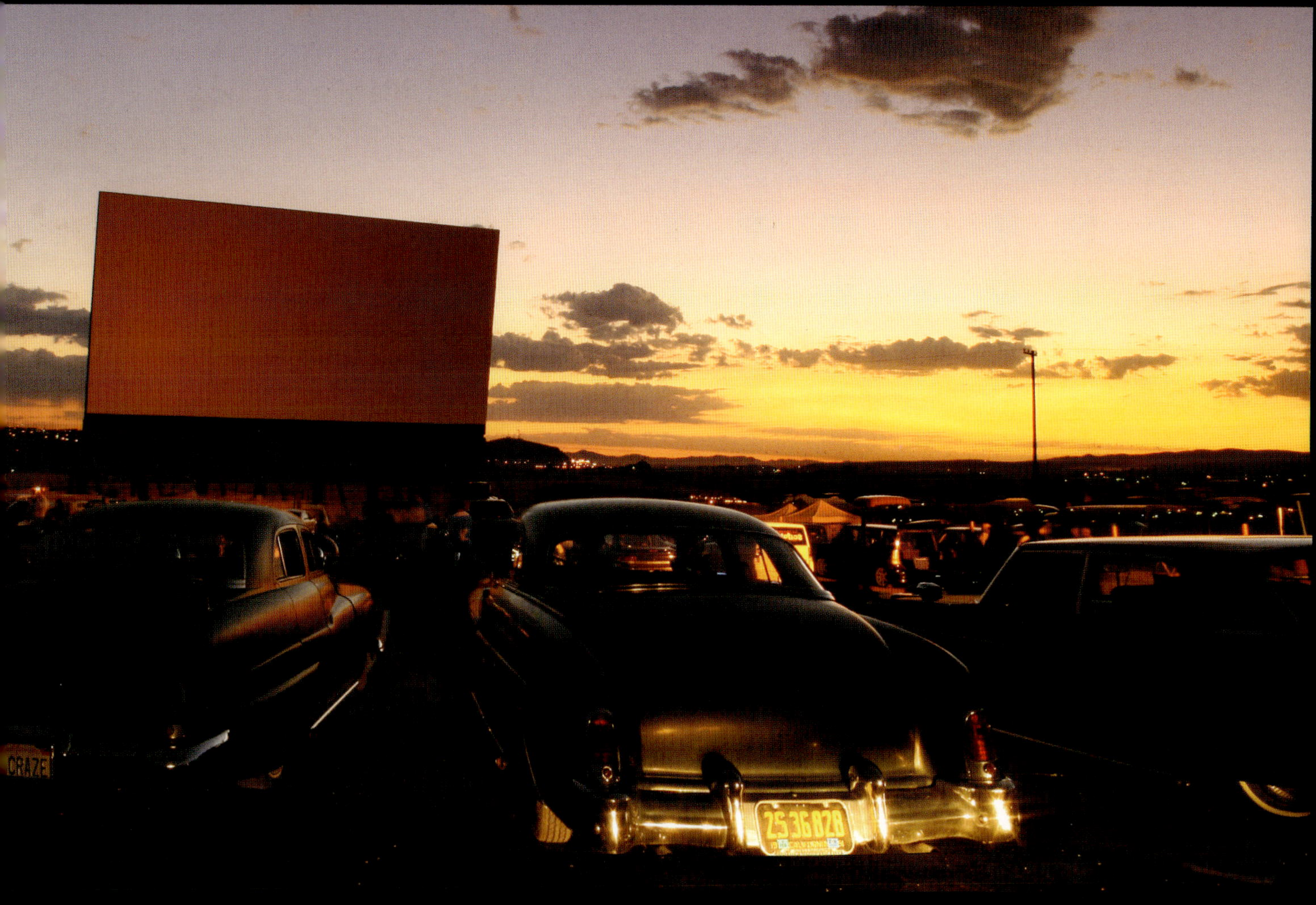

SKY-VIEW DRIVE-IN

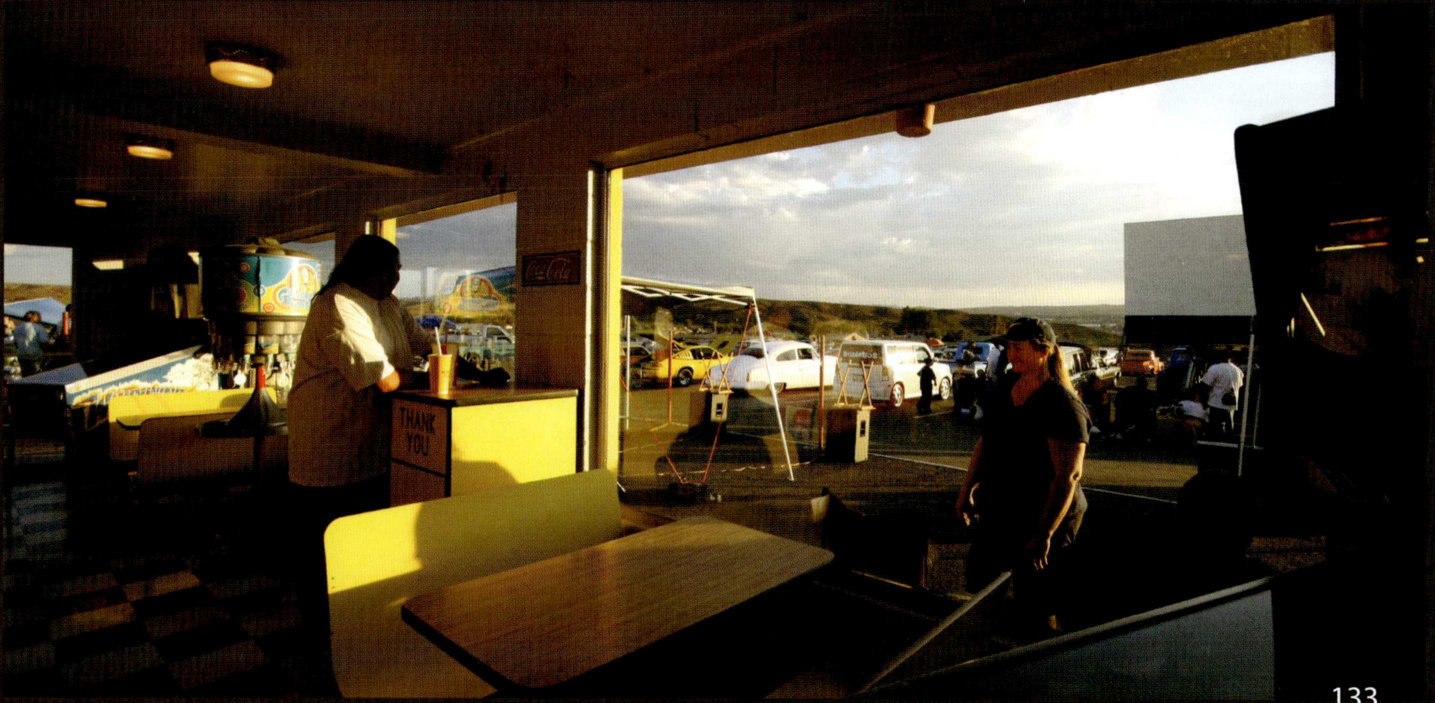

SMOKEHOUSE

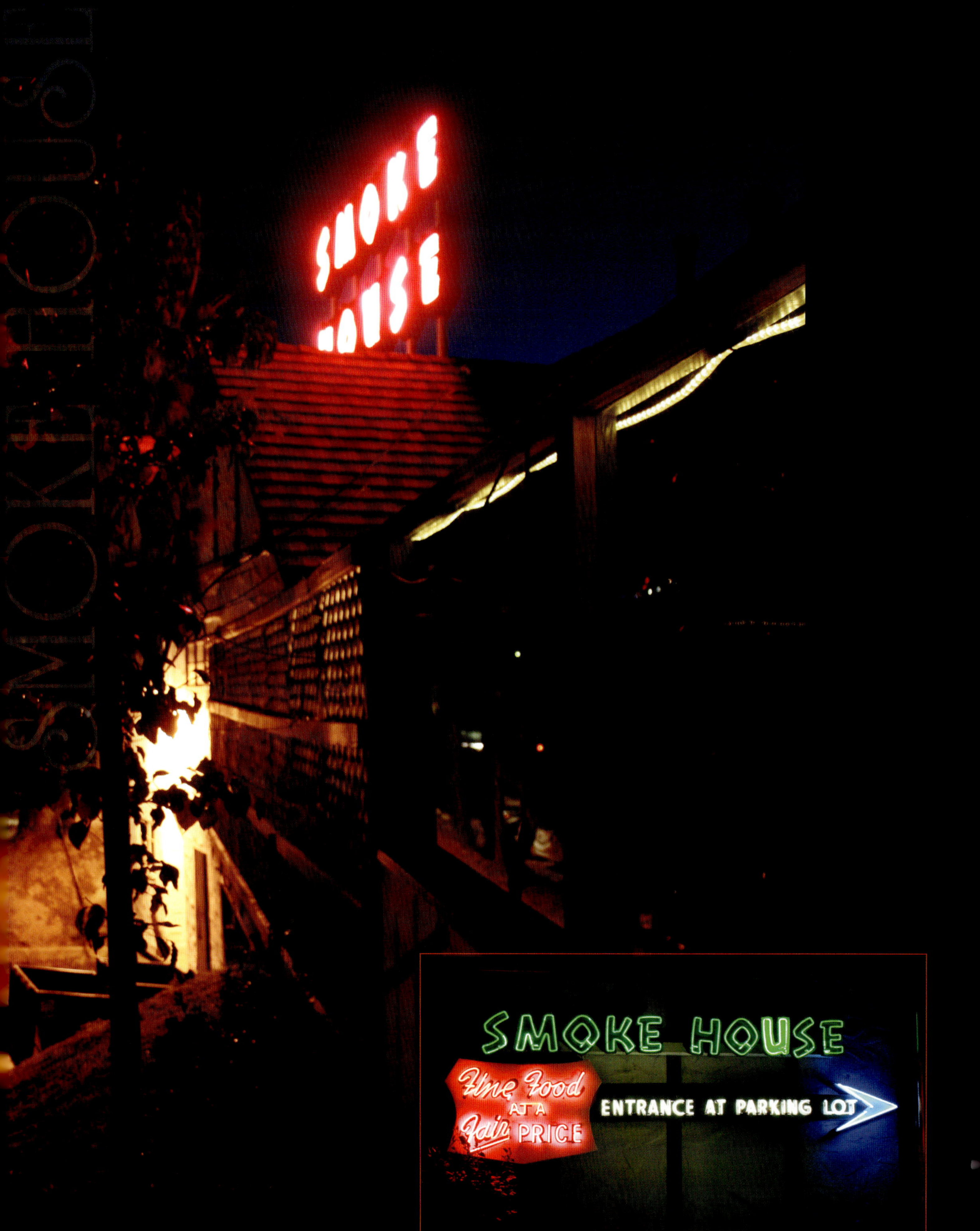
SMOKE
HOUSE
SMOKE HOUSE
Fine Food
AT A
Fair PRICE
ENTRANCE AT PARKING LOT

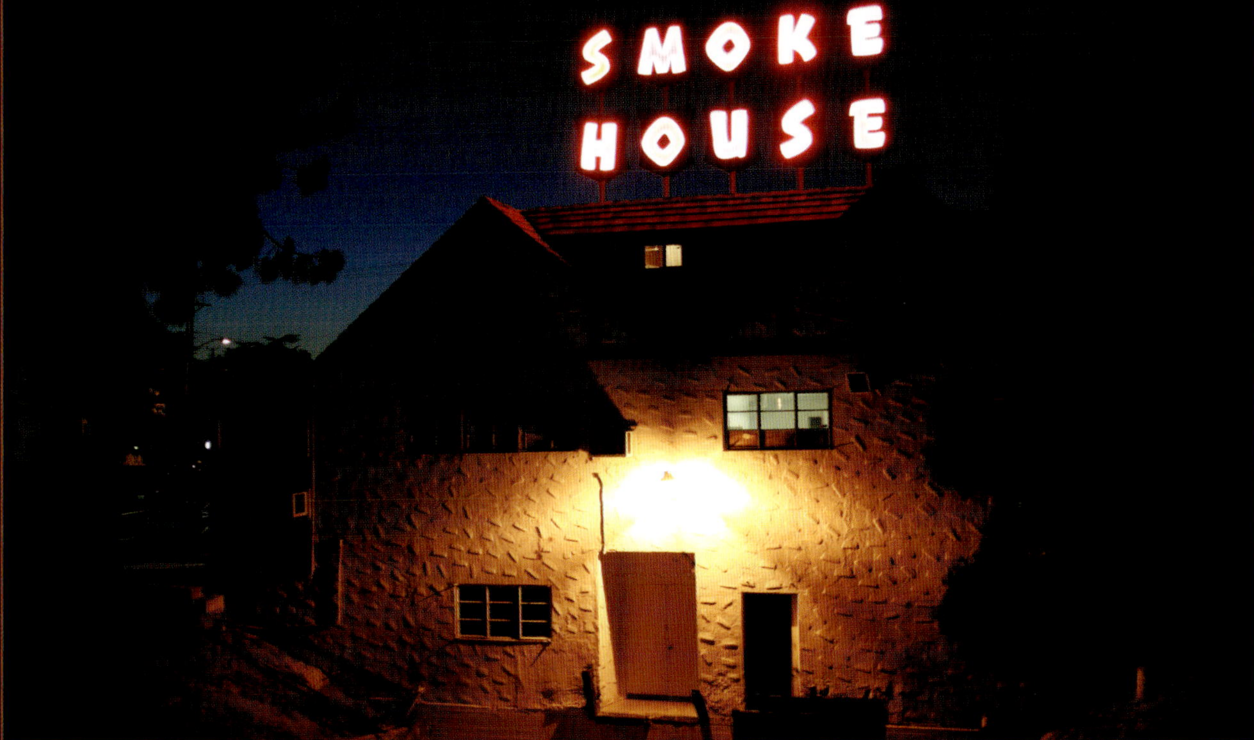

THE SMOKE HOUSE

4420 W. Lakeside Drive, Burbank

Directly across the street from Warner Brothers Studios, the Smoke House is in close proximity to Universal Studios, NBC Studios, and Disney Studios. The original Smoke House opened in 1946 on the corner of Pass and Riverside, but within two years they moved to this larger location. Hollywood stars such as Bob Hope, Bing Crosby, Errol Flynn, Judy Garland, Milton Berle, and Robert Redford frequented the restaurant. Feature entertainers, including the Ink Spots, The Drifters, and Captain & Tennille played here throughout the '70s and '80s. Its present owners, Lee and Martha Spencer, also own the Warehouse Restaurant in Marina Del Rey and Billy Reed's in Palm Springs. Smoke House specializes in steak and seafood. Another rare time capsule, the interior and exterior of this English Tudor has changed very little since the '40s. Out front, their motto "Fine Food at a Fair Price" glows in pink neon.

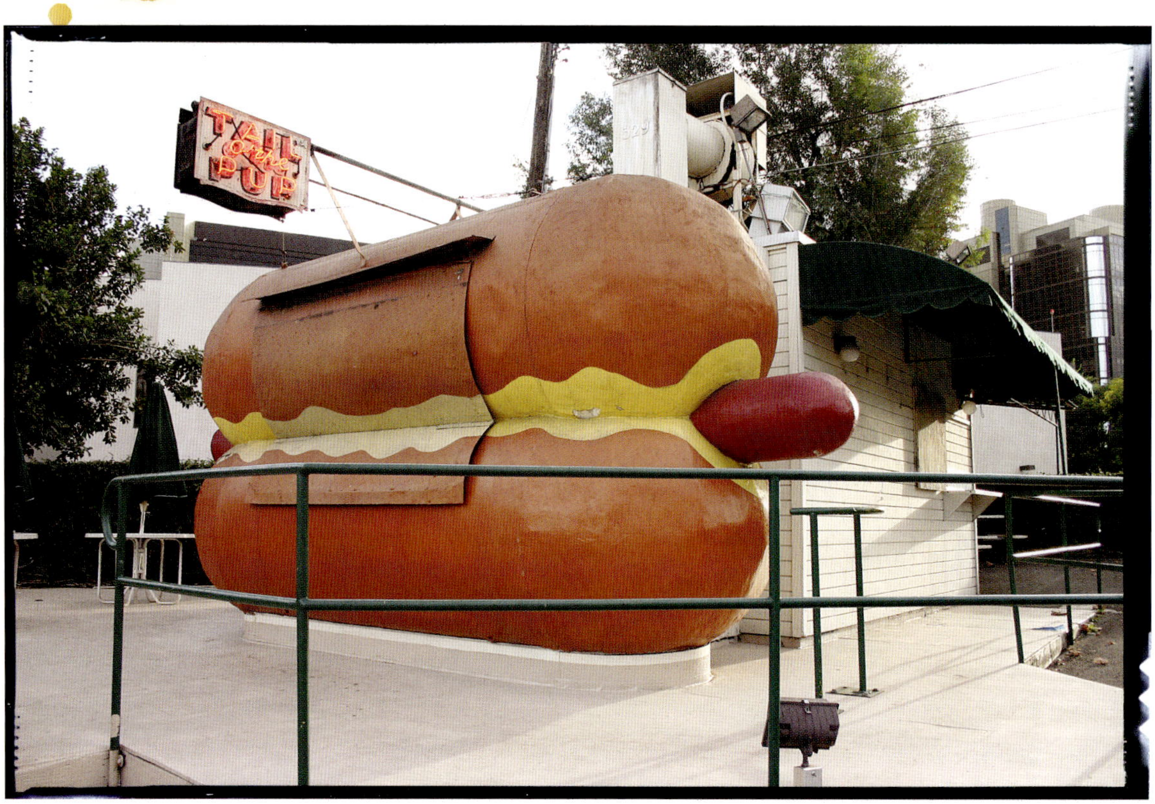

Tam O'Shanter

2980 Los Feliz Boulevard, Los Angeles

A part of Lawry's Prime Rib, Five Crowns, and Lawry's Carvery, the Tam's claim to fame is that they are "the oldest restaurant in Los Angeles owned and operated by the same family in the same location." In 1922, Lawrence Frank and Walter Van de Kamp opened this eatery on a dusty country road on the outskirts of a potential city. Since they were near the Mack Sennett Studios and Disney Studios, some of their regulars were Fatty Arbuckle, Mary Pickford, Tom Mix, Walt Disney, and most of his animators.

The Tam is renowned for prime rib and Old World specialties like Scotch rarebit, toad in the hole, and bangers and mash. Vintage photos of this historic Tudor icon are displayed in the lobby, showing its evolution over the years. To experience early 20th century L.A. dining is as simple as making a reservation and showing up.

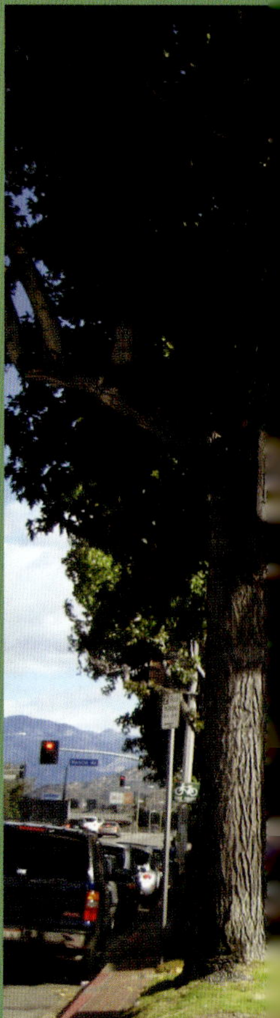

TAIL O' THE PUP

Location unknown, last seen on San Vicente Boulevard, Beverly Hills

Much documented and missed, since 1941, patrons were delighted to order dogs from this early programmatic fast food stand. Things were great 'til land in this prime area started getting scarce and expansion plans for Cedars-Sinai medical facilities were announced, threatening to encroach on the famous doggy's home. Then, suddenly one night he went missing. Someone forgot to tie his leash. Now stashed away in an undisclosed location, we hope he'll reappear again soon to take his rightful place in the L.A. landscape.

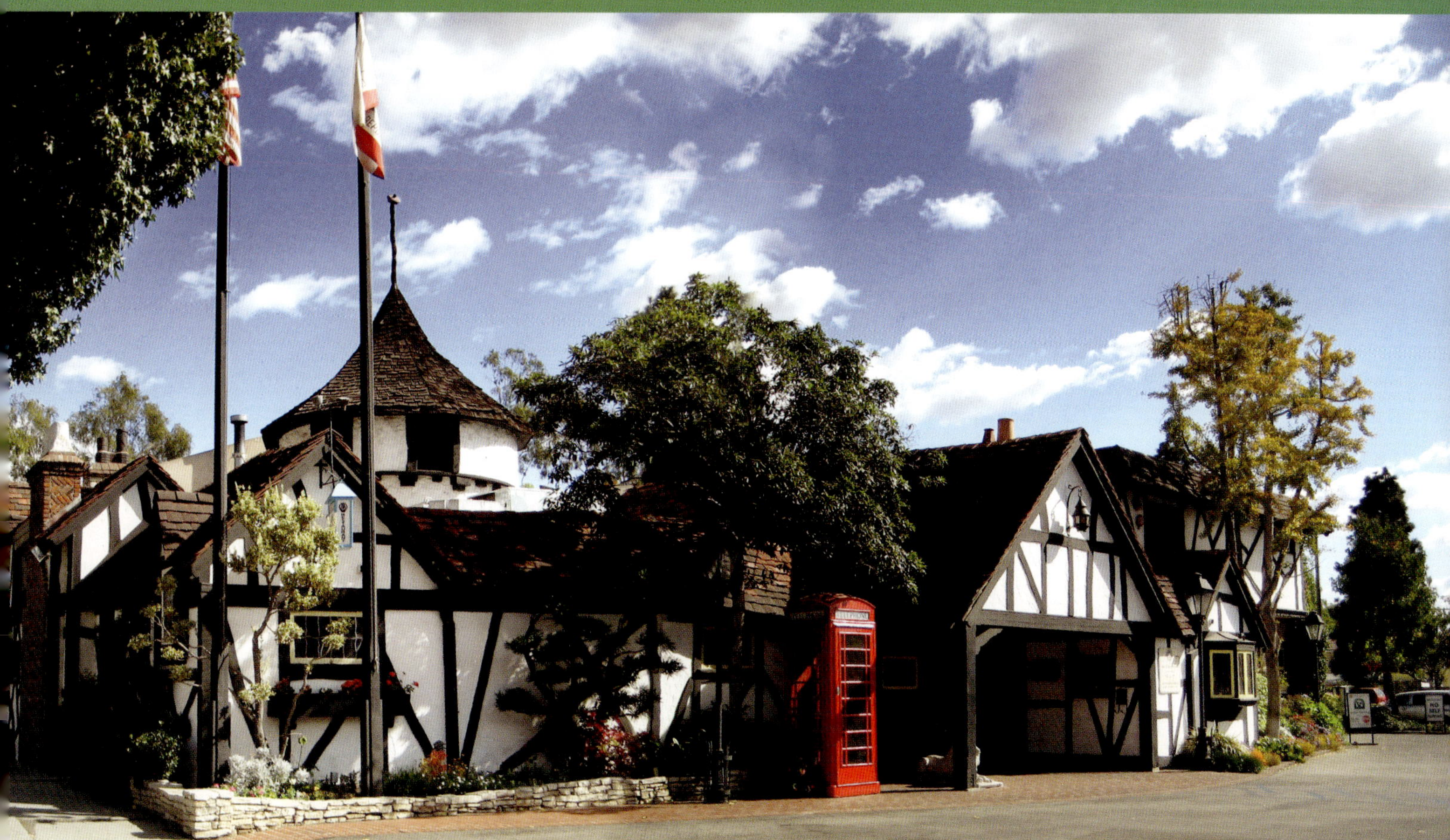

Tastee-Freez

Multiple locations

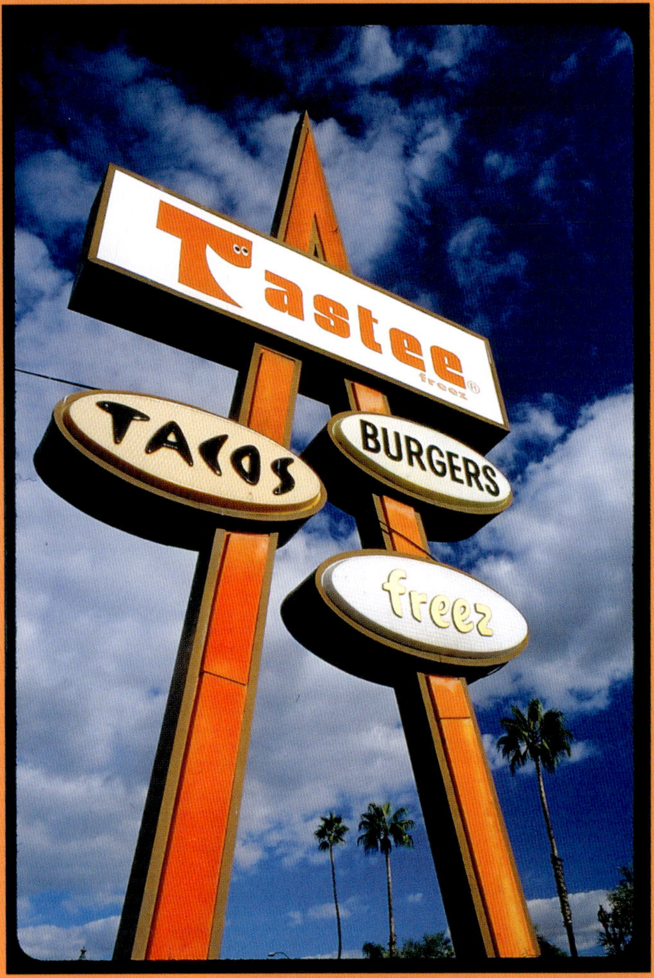

Vying with Fosters for the original soft serve, Tastee's roots go back to 1950, when inventor Leo Moranz and entrepreneur Harry Axene partnered up. Soon they began marketing a more efficient soft-serve pump and freezer to the industry. It wasn't long before walk-up stands began to sprout up as the franchise grew, eventually offering a full menu of fast food items, including burgers and tacos. Tastee's distinctive orange and white A-frames can be recognized a mile away. Tastee-Freez remains one of the most enduring franchise operations in the US.

Tastee in Perris, near the Orange Empire Railway Museum.

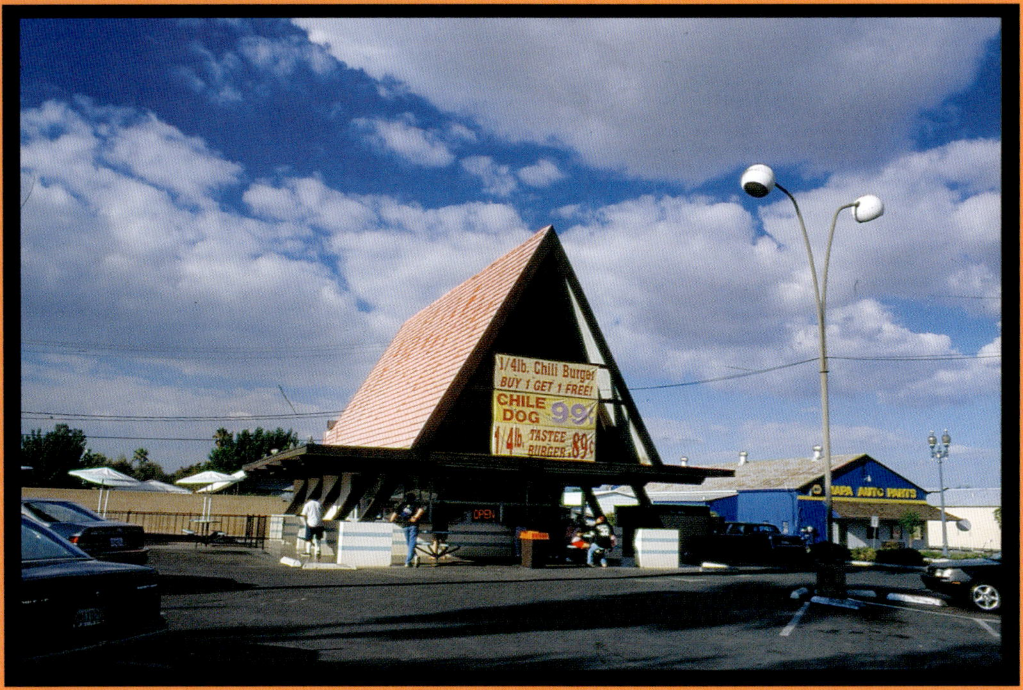

A rare survivor of the 1930s White Log Coffee Shops that once spread throughout the Pacific Coast.

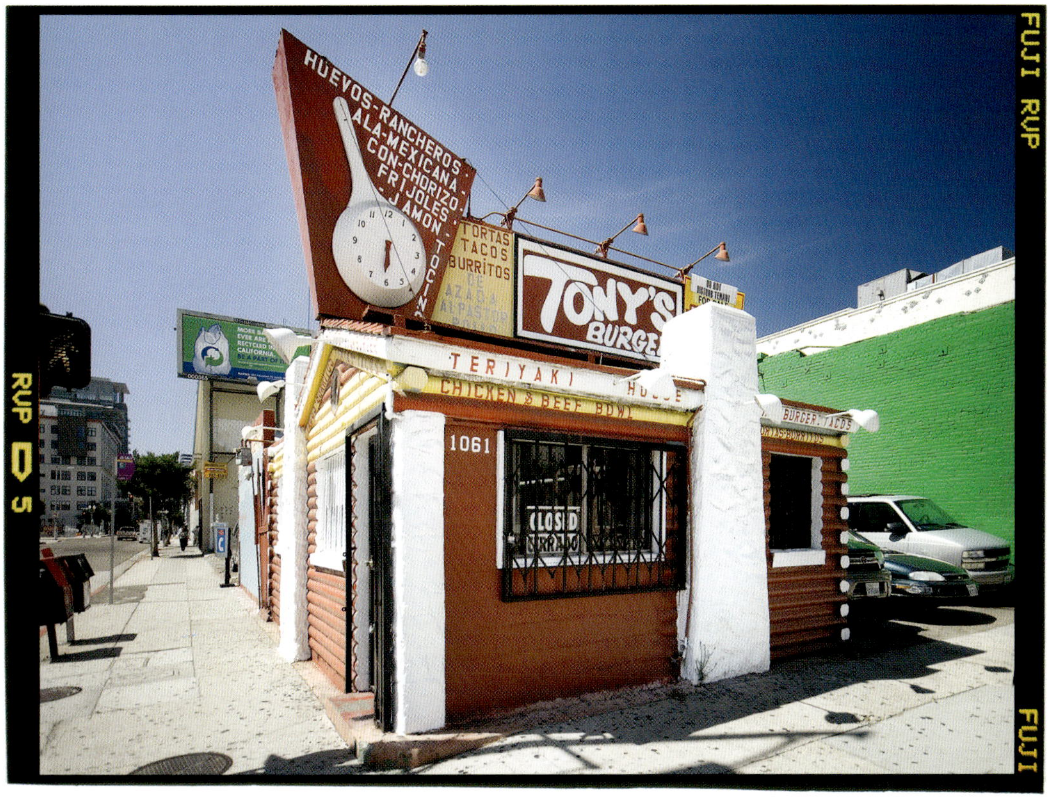

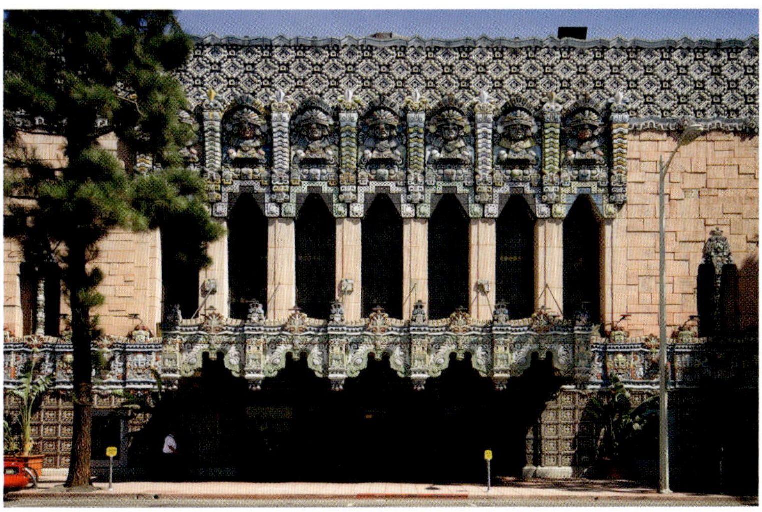

The landmark Mayan Theater sits just across the street from Tony's Burger.

Tony's Burger

(aka White Log Coffee Shop and Dave's Charbroiler)

1061 S. Hill Street at 11th Street, Los Angeles

Smack in the southern end of downtown L.A., you can find this 1932 log cabin burger joint with an oversized skillet clock over the front entrance. Kenneth Bemis was responsible for building over 60 log cabins along the Pacific Coast during the '30s. Everyone looks for Tony's ever-popular working class breakfast and lunch stand. As they say, "keeping in real." The new owner, Gladys, is very friendly and open to film shoots.

It's impossible to talk about Tony's without mentioning the landmark Mayan Theatre, which is directly across the street—Historic Cultural Monument #460. This theater was designed in 1927 by Morgan, Walls & Clements with Francisco Cornejo responsible for the Mayan decorations throughout the building. Originally built for live musical comedies (it opened with George Gershwin's musical *Oh, Kay!*), the Mayan now serves as a salsa club on Friday and Saturday nights, as well as a concert hall and Lucha Va Voom, a unique mixture of retro-burlesque and masked, midget Mexican style wrestling.

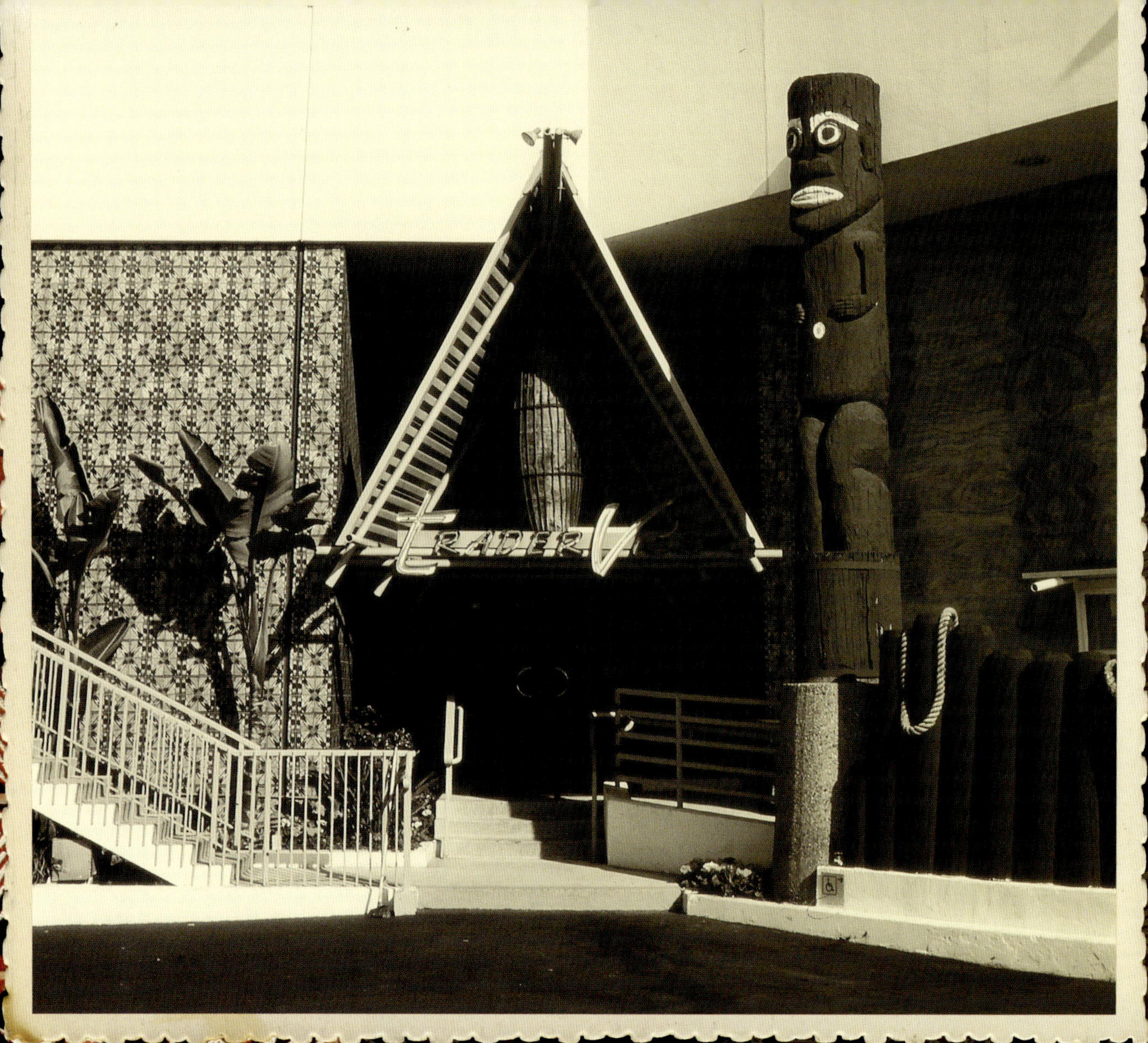

TRADER VIC'S

The Beverly Hilton
9876 Wilshire Boulevard, Beverly Hills

In 1934, Victor Bergeron, Jr. started a Polynesian styled bar and restaurant called Hinky Dink's in Oakland. Renowned columnist, Herb Caen gave the place good reviews. Then after a visit to the South Seas restaurant and Don the Beachcomber in Hollywood, Bergeron decided to revamp his restaurant into Trader Vic's. Instantly, he became Trader Vic himself, entertaining guests by "accidentally" sticking his wooden leg with an ice pick. He lost one leg as a child due to tuberculosis, but as Trader Vic, he let it be known that he lost his leg in a shark attack! Bergeron was a natural promoter. He wrote a series of cocktail and recipe books and created the mother of all Tiki drinks, the Mai Tai. When the Polynesian fad was quite the rage in the '50s, Bergeron had restaurants in Seattle, San Francisco, Denver, Chicago, New York, Portland, Boston, Houston, Dallas, Hawaii, London, Munich, Osaka, Abu Dhabi, Cairo, Beirut, Oman, and even Havana. It is generally accepted that he was responsible for introducing the Polynesian pop culture to Hawaii in response to tourist expectations.

For many years, the world famous Beverly Hills Trader Vic's was a familiar site at the southeast corner of the Beverly Hilton, a grand hotel designed by Welton Becket and Associates for Conrad Hilton in 1955. Becket's credits include some of the most iconic buildings in L.A., such as the moderne landmark Pan-Pacific Auditorium, Bullock's Pasadena, the Capitol Records Tower, Santa Monica Civic Auditorium, Cinerama Dome, Music Center, etc. Becket pioneered the concept of "Total Design," where his firm not only designed the building, but also the custom furniture, lighting fixtures, carpeting, signage, restaurant china, menus, promotional brochures, and all visual contents. Each element was created under a single concept specific to the client.

St

Pirates, Buccaneers and
with their drinking. For th

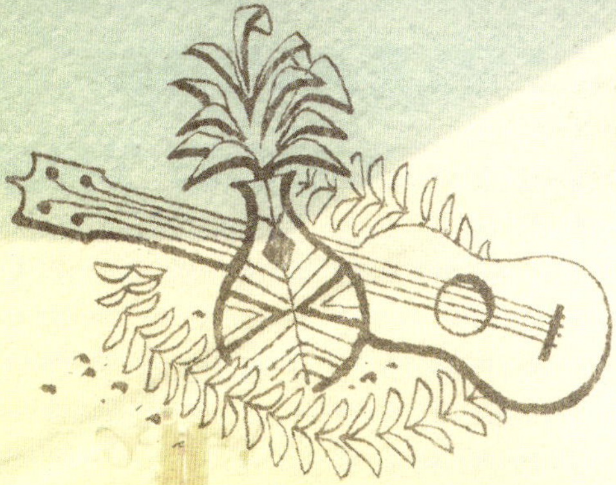

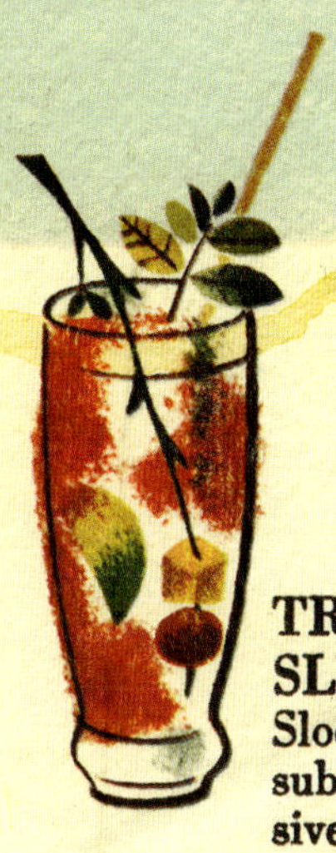

TRADER VIC'S SLING 1.75
Sloe gin, dry gin, lime with subtle flavorings . . . persuasive ammunition for toppling giants

DR. FUNK'S SON 1.95
A chip off the old block

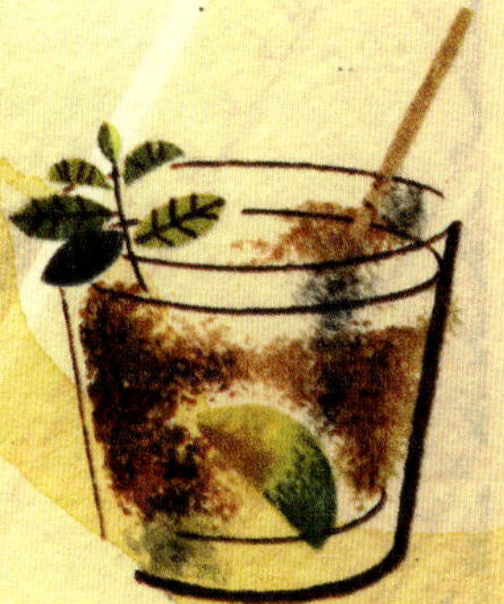

NAVY GROG . 1.95
A truly great drink . . . a blend of fine Rums and Tropical Fruits with an accent of Pimento Dram

Medium *And now we come to those drinks of medium strength and larger volume than a cocktail, which to me are delightful.*

BARBADOS PUNCH 1.50
A simple punch — Barbados rum makes the difference

BAHIA 1.75
A snowy concoction of white rum with coconut and pineapple. Innocent looking but watch it

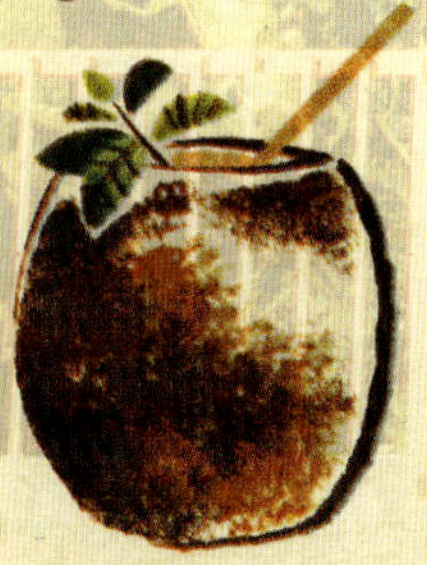

KAMAAINA . 1.80
"Old Timer" to you . . . served in a ceramic coconut which is yours to take home

KONA NIGHTINGALE 1.50
Named after the little braying jackasses of Honolulu . . . it has a kick like one!

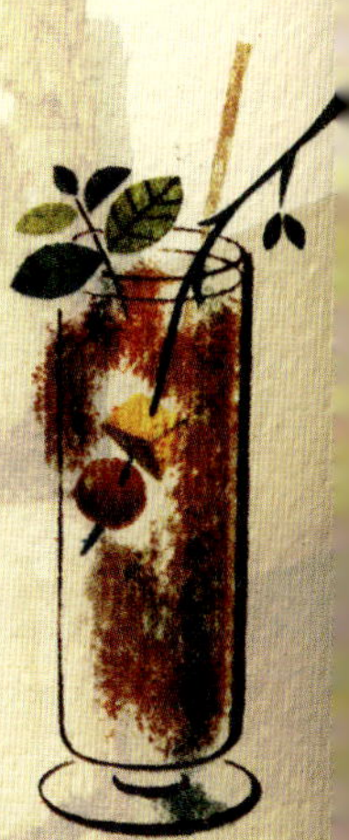

DOCTOR FUNK OF TAHITI . . 1.75
A truly Tropical Drink, originating in Papeete and redolent of French Rums and Herbsaint

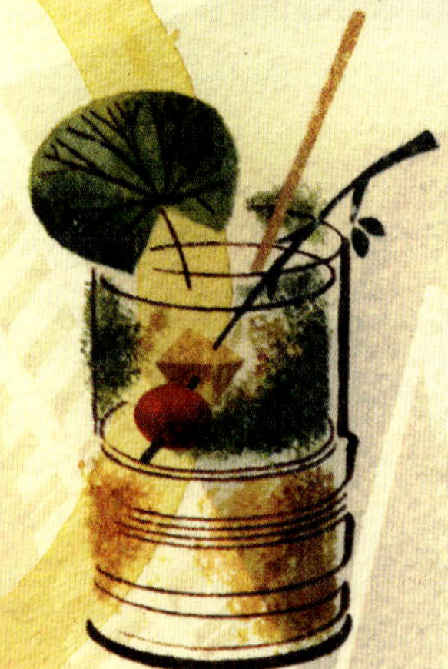

GUN CLUB PUNCH . . 1.75
Duck Hunters' Special . . . a blend of dark and light Rums with Fruit Juices

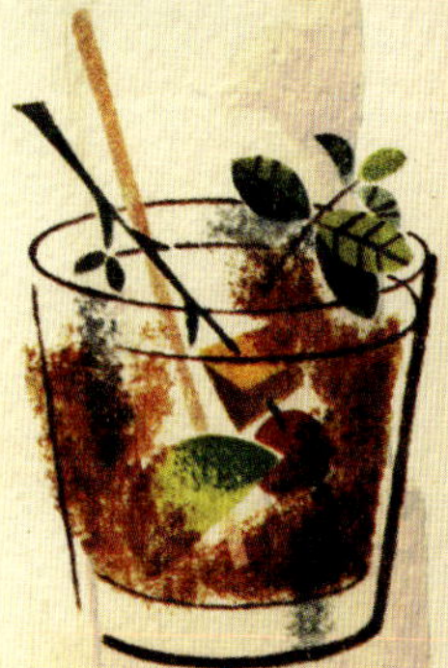

MAI TAI . 1.75
This means "the best" in Tahitian . . . and it is. 15-year-old Jamaica Rum makes this so

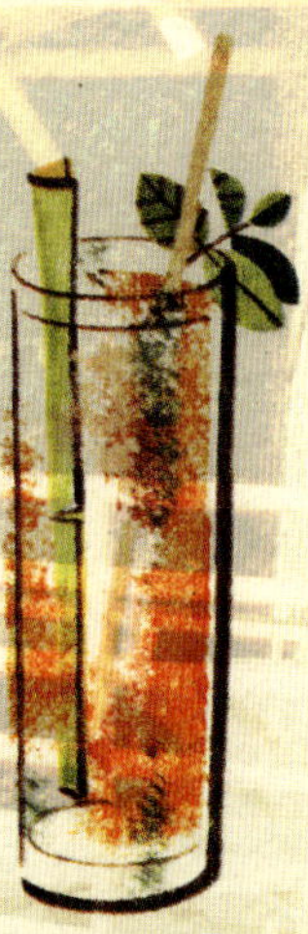

TONGA PUNCH . . 1.70
A famous happy mixture that is always a favorite

TRADER VIC'S GROG 1.80
A potent blend of tropical fruits and Jamaica Rum in a man's size goblet

BARBADOS RED RUM SWIZZLE 1.50
A Real "Guzzler"

THE COLONEL'S BIG OPU . . 2.25
Champagne pleasantly spiked with Gin, Liqueurs and Lime

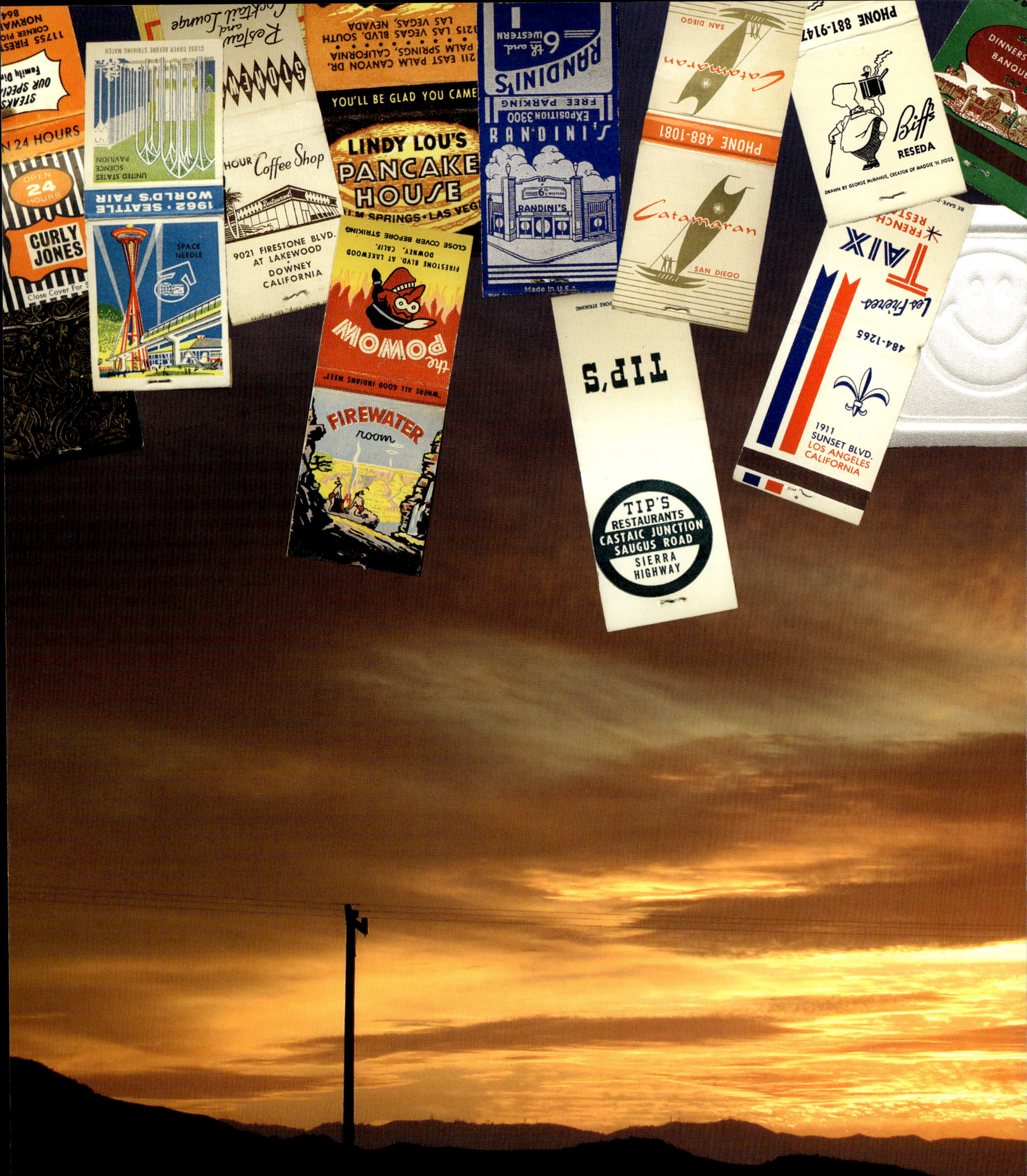

24 HOURS
OPEN 24 HOURS
CURLY JONES
1962 · SEATTLE WORLD'S FAIR
UNITED STATES SCIENCE PAVILION
SPACE NEEDLE
Coffee Shop
9021 FIRESTONE BLVD. AT LAKEWOOD DOWNEY CALIFORNIA
YOU'LL BE GLAD YOU CAME
LINDY LOU'S PANCAKE HOUSE
211 EAST PALM CANYON DR. PALM SPRINGS, CALIFORNIA
3215 LAS VEGAS BLVD. SOUTH LAS VEGAS, NEVADA
CLOSE COVER BEFORE STRIKING
FIRESTONE BLVD. AT LAKEWOOD DOWNEY, CALIF.
the POWOW
WHERE ALL GOOD INDIANS MEET
FIREWATER room
RANDINI'S
EXPOSITION 3300
FREE PARKING
6th and WESTERN
Made in U.S.A.
Catamaran
SAN DIEGO
PHONE 488-1081
PHONE 881-9147
Biff's
RESEDA
DRAWN BY GEORGE McMANUS, CREATOR OF MAGGIE 'N JIGGS
TIP'S
TIP'S RESTAURANTS CASTAIC JUNCTION SAUGUS ROAD SIERRA HIGHWAY
TAIX
FRENCH RESTAURANT
Les Frères
484-1265
1911 SUNSET BLVD. LOS ANGELES CALIFORNIA

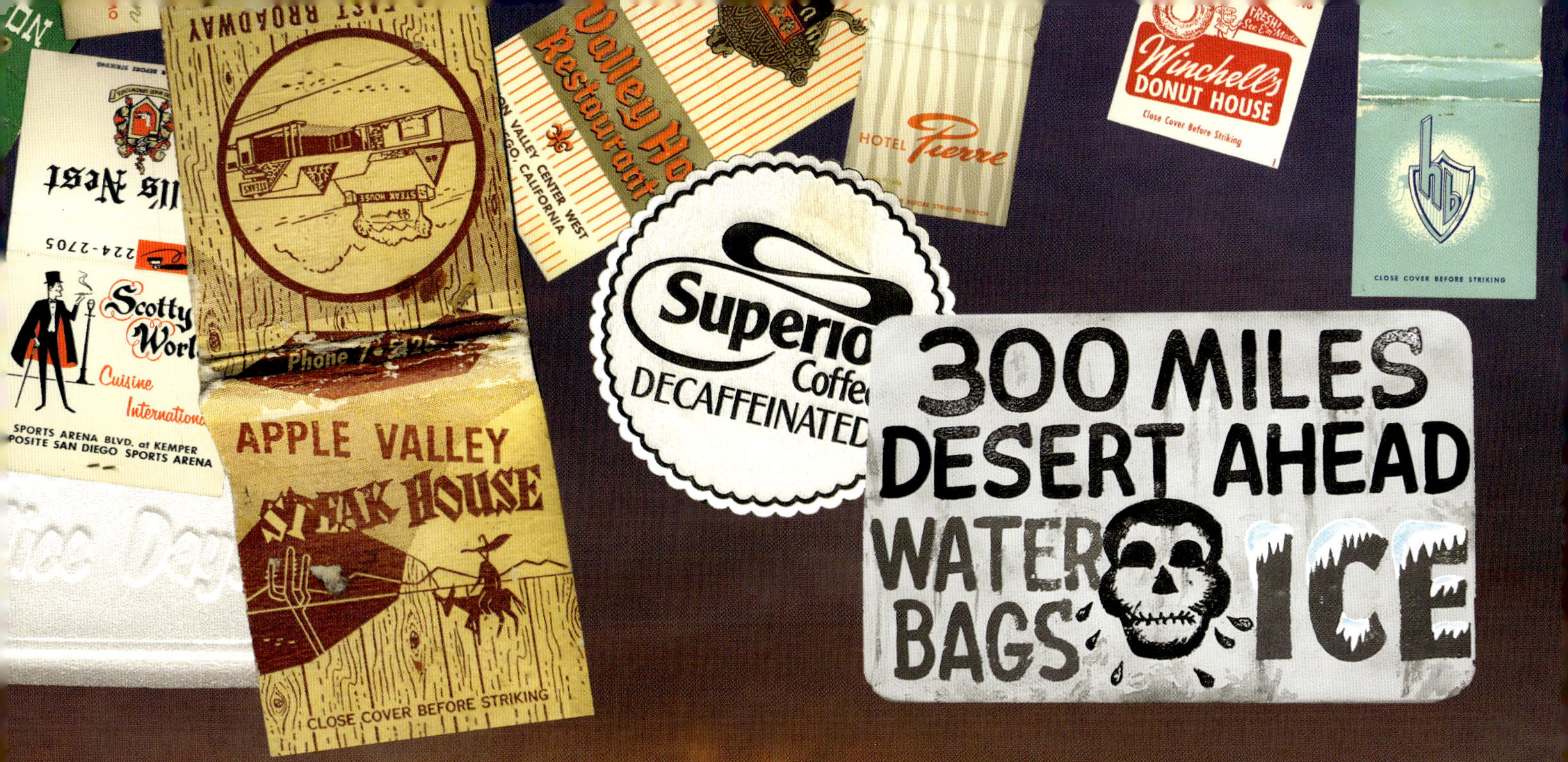

REFERENCES

Garn, Andrew, Paola Antonelli, Udo Kultermann, and Stephen Van Dyk. *Exit to Tomorrow: History of the Future, World's Fair Architecture, Design, Fashion 1933-2005.* (New York: Universe Publishing, 2007).

Gebhard, David, and Robert Winter. *Los Angeles, An Architectural Guide.* (Salt Lake City: Gibbs, Smith, 1994).

Hess, Alan. *Googie Redux, Ultramodern Roadside Architecture.* (San Francisco: Chronicle Books, 2004).

Langdon, Philip. *Orange Roofs, Golden Arches: The Architecture of American Chain Restaurants.* (New York: Alfred A. Knopf, 1986).

Liebs, Chester H. *Main Street to Miracle Mile: American Roadside Architecture.* (Boston: Little, Brown and Company, 1986).

Marsak, Nathan, and Nigel Cox. *Los Angeles Neon.* (Atglen: Schiffer Publishing, 2002).

Sunset Books. *Los Angeles, Portrait of an Extraordinary City.* (Menlo Park: Lane Magazine & Book Company, 1968).

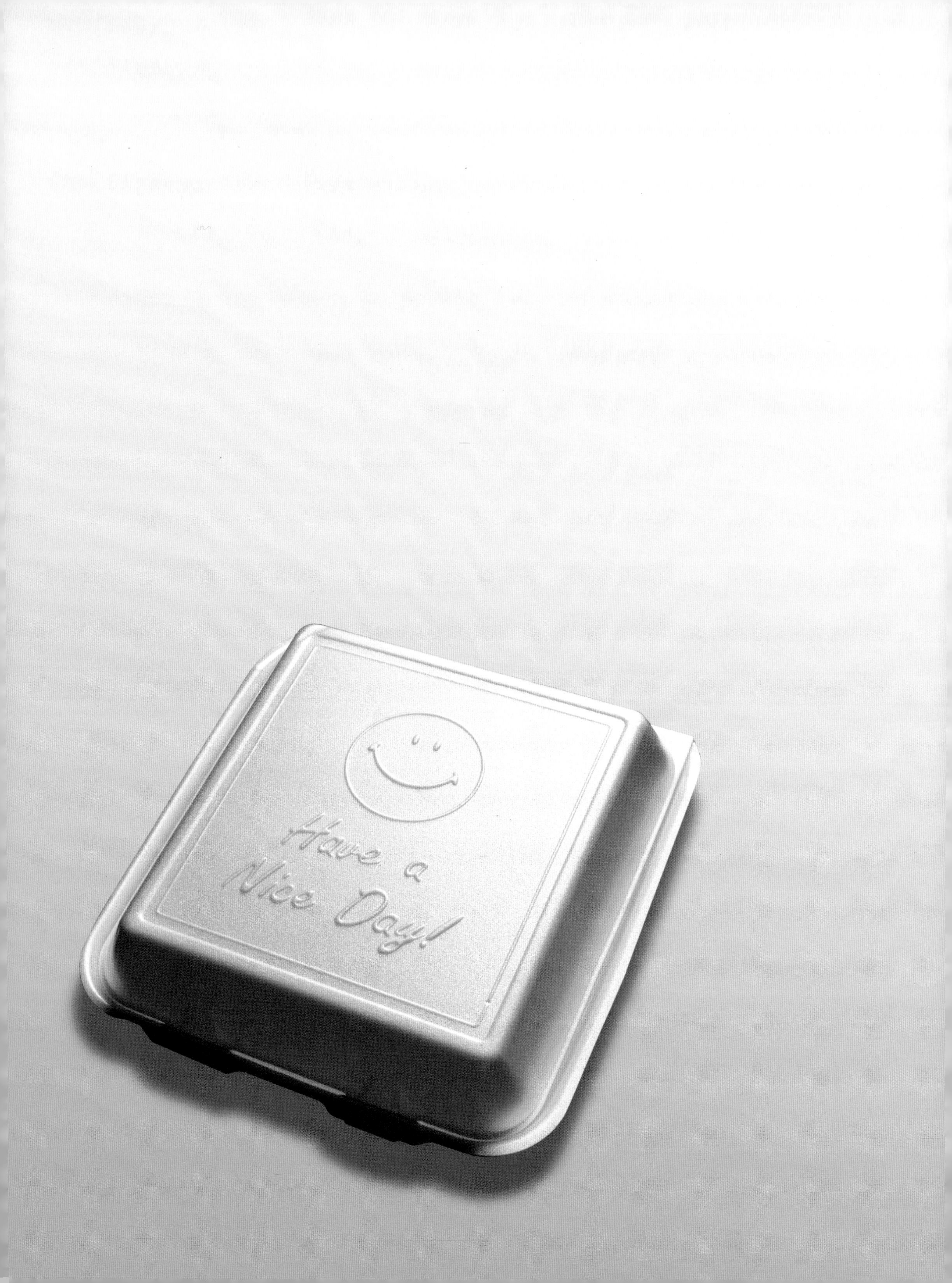
Have a
Nice Day!